What the Critics [Say about] the Works of America's Most Provocative Author Priest

"His fiction, like his own personal search, is the story of man's search—his search—our search—for reunion with the infinite. In doing so, Father Greeley explains, with clarity and grace and wit, our times and ourselves to ourselves."

—David D. Anderson
in *"The Greeley Phenomenon, or some Parish! Some Priest!"*

"As an evangelical Baptist, my own theological tradition is considerably removed from that of Greeley. . . . In the discovery of Greeley's fiction I found stories of the God I was coming to know—a Lover pursuing us with unrelenting tenderness, graciously offering to us a love that can never be earned, a God who, according to Father Blackie, breaks all Her own rules in order to lure us to Herself."

—Kirby Wilcoxson
in *"The Sociologist as Storyteller: Science and Fiction in the Novels of Andrew Greeley"*

"In a Greeley novel, we consistently feel a divine presence, a continual reminder of God as irrepressible. . . . In *Angels of September*, Fr. Blackie Ryan defines hell, for example, as 'a place where God puts people until She figures out a way to give them a second chance.'"

—Philip H. Kelly
in *"Greeley's Fiction and Reader Response Criticism"*

"Greeley has a massive hearing among Catholics—and now a growing audience of other Americans as well. . . . The reason they read Greeley is very simple, so I think: in his imagination they find, and understand, their own reality."

—Jacob Neusner
in *"No Prophet in His Own Village: Chicago and Its Bard"*

INGRID SHAFER

ANDREW GREELEY'S WORLD

An Anthology of Critical Essays

1986-1988

WARNER BOOKS

A Warner Communications Company

Warner Books, Inc., 666 Fifth Avenue, New York, NY 10103
w A Warner Communications Company

Printed in the United States of America
First Printing: May 1989
10 9 8 7 6 5 4 3 2 1

Library of Congress Cataloging-in-Publication Data

Andrew Greeley's World: an anthology of critical
  essays, 1986–1988.

  Includes bibliographies and index.
  1. Greeley, Andrew M., 1928– —Fictional works.
I. Shafer, Ingrid H.
PS3557.R358Z94   1989   813'.54   88-27776
ISBN 0-446-38988-9 (pbk.) (U.S.A.)
ISBN 0-446-38989-7 (pbk.) (Can.)

Designed by Giorgetta Bell McRee

The alternative is not an escape into the transient pleasures of irony or a flight into despair and cynicism. The alternative is not a new kind of innocence or a passivity masking apathy. Whoever fights for hope, fights on behalf of all of us. Whoever acts on that hope, acts in a manner worthy of a human being. And whoever so acts, I believe, acts in a manner faintly suggestive of the reality and power of that God in whose image human beings were formed to resist, to think, and to act. The rest is prayer, observance, discipline, conversation, and actions of solidarity-in-hope. Or the rest is silence.

DAVID TRACY
in *Plurality and Ambiguity: Hermeneutics, Religion, Hope*

CONTENTS

Preface: The Greeley Phenomenon, or Some Parish! Some Priest!
DAVID D. ANDERSON   ***xi***

Introduction   INGRID SHAFER   ***xv***

I/*Thistles or Roses: Peeking into Andrew Greeley's Secret Garden* 1

1. *Catholic Priests on Andrew Greeley*   INGRID SHAFER   ***3***
2. *The Sacramental Body: Andrew Greeley's Autobiography*
   ROGER J. BRESNAHAN   ***11***
3. *Andrew M. Greeley: Ethnic Historian or Social Reformer?*
   PATRICIA W. JULIUS   ***17***
4. *No Prophet In His Own Village: Chicago and Its Bard*
   JACOB NEUSNER   ***23***

II/Soil, Seed, Sun, and Rain: Folktales, Scripture, and Symbolic Imagination 29

5. Chin Music: Popular Storytelling as the New Oral Tradition
    MICHAEL T. MARSDEN *33*
6. The Symbolism of the Song of Songs ROLAND E. MURPHY,
    O. CARM. *39*
7. Theology and the Symbolic Imagination: A Tribute to Andrew
    Greeley DAVID TRACY *47*
8. The Virgin and the Grail: Archetypes in Andrew Greeley's Fiction
    INGRID SHAFER *63*

III/Opening the Gate: Critical Parameters 77

9. Andrew Greeley and the Author = Narrator Fallacy: Confessions
    of an English Professor MIRIAM ESPINOSA *79*
10. John Updike and Andrew Greeley: Two Visions of God and
    Humanity INGRID SHAFER *95*
11. The Sociologist as Storyteller: Science and Fiction in the Novels
    of Andrew Greeley KIRBY WILCOXSON *111*
12. The Reader as Hero: Reader-Response Criticism and Greeley's
    Fiction PHILIP H. KELLY *119*
13. A Reader Responds: Andrew Greeley and the Magic Flaw
    JAMES M. HARKIN *129*

IV/In the Garden: Novels 139

14. The Catholic Imaginative Universe in the Novels of
    Andrew Greeley INGRID SHAFER *141*
15. Sin, Guilt, and Forgiveness in Greeley's Passover Trilogy
    PHILIP H. KELLY *159*
16. Renew Your People, O Lord: Andrew Greeley's Passover Trilogy
    KATHLEEN ROUT *169*
17. The Feminine Divine: A Search for Unity in Andrew Greeley's
    Passover Trilogy MICHAEL T. MARSDEN *175*
18. *Virgin and Martyr*: A Story of God? ALLIENNE R. BECKER *185*
19. *Lord of the Dance*: A Parable for Modern Catholics
    BERNARD J. GALLAGHER *193*

20. *Parables of Love: The Fiction of Andrew M. Greeley*
MARY ANN LOWRY *211*

21. *Andrew Greeley's Time Between the Stars Series and the Religious Imagination* MICHAEL T. MARSDEN *221*

22. *The Legenda Aurea Lives Again: Andrew Greeley's Use of the Saints' Lives in His Novels* ANNE K. KALER *231*

23. *The Dance of Creation and Incarnation: God, Woman, and Sex in the Novels of Andrew Greeley* INGRID SHAFER *253*

V/Exploring the Labyrinth: Mysteries and Speculative Fiction *267*

24. *Expanding Parameters of Crime Fiction: George C. Chesbro and Andrew Greeley* RAY B. BROWNE *269*

25. *Father Brown, Father Blackie: The Priest as Detective* JUDITH J. KOLLMANN *283*

26. *Death Under a Beatitudinal Umbrella: The Mysteries of Andrew Greeley* MARY ANN LOWRY *295*

27. *Seraph Fire and Science Fiction: Andrew Greeley's Use of Angels in His Novels* ANNE K. KALER *303*

28. *God, Greeley, and the Computer: Andrew Greeley's New Narrative Trinity in God Game* ANNE K. KALER *317*

29. *Once Upon a Time* NICK ROSSI *333*

VI/A Few Words from the Landlord *339*

30. *Imagination as a Ragpicker* ANDREW GREELEY *341*

CONTRIBUTORS *351*

DAVID D. ANDERSON

Preface:
The Greeley Phenomenon, or Some Parish! Some Priest!

*W*hen H. L. Mencken wrote in an essay entitled "The Literary Capital of the United States," published in the English *Nation* on April 17, 1920, that "With two exceptions, there is not a single American novelist, a novelist deserving a civilized reader's notice—who has not sprung from the Middle Empire that has Chicago for its capital ...," that "Chicago, however short the time it has him, leads him inevocably through a decisive trail of his talents ...," he had in mind Sherwood Anderson, Theodore Dreiser, Frank Norris, Henry Black Fuller, and Robert Herrick. Still on the horizon were Ernest Hemingway, James T. Farrell, and Richard Wright; still more remote were Saul Bellow and Harry Mark Petrakis, any of whom Mencken might have foreseen.

What, one wonders, might Mencken have said or thought of Andrew Moran Greeley? A sociologist, novelist, Professor of Sociology at the University of Arizona, and priest of the Roman Catholic archdiocese of Chicago, a man whose "parish is his mailbox," Greeley is a success at each, most recently as a best-selling novelist. Unlike the other Chicago novelists, he gives credit for his successes to

> Celibacy and hard work.
> And maybe a little talent, too.

Reprinted, with minor revisions, from *Midwestern Miscellany* 15 (1987): 7–10.

Born in Oak Park, Illinois, on February 5, 1928, Father Greeley is of County Mayo ancestry and middle-class Irish Catholic Chicago origins, a product of the Great Depression and of New Deal Democratic politics, of Saint Angela Grammar School on Chicago's West Side, where, in Sister Alma Frances' second-grade classroom in the late autumn of 1935, he knew who he was and knew, too, that he would be a priest. He was a product, too, of Chicago Cubs baseball and 1930s radio—Tom Mix, Orphan Annie, Jack Armstrong, Don Winslow—and of the books he devoured to the detriment of his social life and his classroom behavior. "I'm afraid I was a trial to my teachers," he remembers. "Alas, I was too naive to realize that the best thing a bright little boy with encyclopedic knowledge can do is keep his big Irish mouth shut."

Greeley is a product, too, of Quigley Minor Preparatory Seminary (now in the shadow of the Hancock Building, where he sometimes lives), a high school for boys who would be priests, to which each day he rode a Chicago Avenue streetcar across the city and back again. At Quigley, Greeley remembers, he experienced the "famed openness, tolerance and liberalism which had been a historical characteristic of the Chicago clergy..."; he discovered the world of ideas and the "incredible heritage of American Catholicism"; he learned to write "sentences and paragraphs," and he learned "to appreciate good literature. Newman, Chesterton, Dickens, Scott, Joseph Conrad, Francis Thompson, Gerard Manley Hopkins, Willa Cather, Sinclair Lewis, Thackeray, Wilkie Collins, Churchill, Hawthorne, Melville, Belloc, Dawson: such writers occupied most of my time when I was not at school, or not sleeping, or not playing basketball."

"Slowly," he recalls, "it dawned on me that the Church once was the matrix for all the arts. What ever happened? I began to wonder."

Of more importance, Greeley learned—I suspect at least as much from his reading as from anyone at Quigley—to understand the nature of faith and the substance of his own:

> I came to Quigley with a religious faith as unexamined as it was intense. I learned during those years to examine it candidly and objectively without losing either the faith or its intensity. The pilgrimage from Paradise Lost...to Paradise Found is a going forth and a coming back, an exploration of new colored lands (Chesterton) and a return to the place from which he began only to know it once more for the first time (Chesterton first, then Eliot).

When Greeley graduated from Quigley in June 1947, he still knew who he was and where he was going. The solid foundations of his intellect, his faith, his art were laid; he was beginning to understand himself and his faith and the richness of his heritage, and he had begun to acquire a mature understanding of a symbolism that too often remains not symbol but reality. I suspect that in the eighteen-year-old seminarian who that fall entered Saint Mary of the Lake Seminary at Mundelein, Illinois, we should recognize the professor-novelist-sociologist-parish priest of forty years later.

Whether we would have recognized him during those years at Mundelein— or whether Greeley found himself closer to his own personal Grail through his studies there—is, however, questionable. There he found an institution and men unable to deal with human sexuality, their own or that of half the human race, except by denying it; he found intellectual and personal regimentation, and institutionalized dullness of the mind and spirit, a system that was tired and afraid of its tiredness, observing a rote ritual four hundred years old and steeped in stagnation.

And yet Greeley not only did not leave Mundelein, as many of his contemporaries did, nor did he leave the priesthood, as many of his teachers were to do, but he used the system to his own ends and continued his intellectual and spiritual growth. At Mundelein, on his own, he escaped boredom by reading sociology, labor history, philosophy, the newer European theologians never mentioned in class— Congar, de Lubac, and others; their forerunners Rousselot, Gardeil, Blondel; and, curiously, Greeley comments, John Henry Newman. He learned that history—the history of the Church—is not static but dynamic, as is reality, that faith is an act of love, that the defensive posture of the Church has remained unchanged since the Reformation, that there must be reform. More than a decade before his American contemporaries and elders he was seeking Vatican II. On May 5, 1954, he was ordained to the priesthood, at ease with his identity and with human sexuality, a confirmed celibate, intellectually ready not only for change in the Church but for a ministry he could not imagine.

From this point Greeley's story belongs as much to myth as it does to Church history or sociology or literary history—myth compounded of news items and clerical gossip and theological controversies and defiances of hierarchal authority and denunciations by those who disagree with his sociological conclusions without having read them and references to his novels as steamy by those who haven't read them, by the constant public references to him as "controversial" by those journalists striving ineffectually for objectivity.

All this is the public Father Greeley, the Father Greeley who has become a paradox as his life has become a myth by which those who resent Vatican II—or the Church—explain it to themselves, or, perhaps, as they explain themselves to themselves.

Like all myths, the complex myth of Andrew Greeley has in it something of the truth, but beyond it all is a dimension of his ministry—of his post-office-box ministry—that gives him the utmost satisfaction: it is the constantly increasing numbers of those who report having returned to the Church after reading one of his novels. His fiction, like his own personal search, is the story of man's search—his search—our search— for reunion with the infinite. In so doing, Father Greeley explains with clarity and grace and wit our times and ourselves to ourselves.

He is committed to his Church, his people, the written word, and the life of the mind and the imagination; he deals honestly and compassionately and courageously with the human problems of our age in all their complexity and confusion. And somehow, he suggests an ultimate human if not ecclesiastical triumph.

And what might Mencken think of Father Greeley as novelist, as reflective of the times and the city out of which he comes and of which he writes? Mencken had championed other, earlier Midwestern Irish Catholic novelists—Jim Tully (1891–1942) of Saint Mary's, Ohio, and Hollywood, who had been driven from his Church by the brutality that provides the substance of much of his fiction, and James T. Farrell (1904–79) of Chicago and New York, an intellectual and political refugee—or, to paraphrase Greeley, a tragedy of grace refused—and I'm sure that Mencken would recognize the wit, the faith, the determination of Andrew Greeley. And whether Mencken would approve is irrelevant: he would understand.

INGRID SHAFER

Introduction

$\mathcal{F}$or years Andrew Greeley has insisted that he tells stories to help his readers recognize purpose and meaning in their lives; to open their minds to the power of grace in the everyday; to kindle their hearts to the fire of God by allowing them to sense divine passion in their loving sexual relationships. His theology is as old as the Church and as new as tomorrow—a theology of a God who both transcends all finite categories and is a real person who fervently cares for each and every one of us; an incarnate God who with Jesus has come to live incognito among us, in our spouses, children, parents, friends—our human community, our neighborhood.

True to his vocation as "catholic" poet/priest, Greeley writes not for the chosen few, but for the broadest possible audience. Given this agenda, it is hardly surprising that the perennially popular romantic mode, with its presupposition of order beyond chaos and (in its Christian adaptation) divine love as central ordering principle of the universe, should pervade Greeley's fiction. The gospel story itself, examined in terms of theme and structure, is an archetypal romance. Following the career of a romantic hero, Jesus was born miraculously, showed exceptional powers in childhood, considered himself on the supernatural mission/quest to reconcile God and humanity, appeared vanquished by his enemies, died a disgraceful death, but rose from the tomb and emerged victorious over the powers of convention and evil. Love stronger than Death.

Thus it is not surprising that Christians came to understand heroism in terms of the triumph of the weak and suffering, a victory paradoxically won precisely by submitting to suffering. In practical life, this transvaluation of heroism combined with the survival skills of a persecuted underground minority to emphasize such stereotypically "feminine" virtues as obedience and humility (with their "shadows" of guile and deception). According to Northrop Frye, this uniquely Christian perspective largely accounts for the prominence of the female figure in the romance, where she even assumed "a redemptive role...like her divine counterpart in the Christian story" (*Secular Scripture* 87).

Since Frye interprets Christianity from the official Protestant perspective, he is blind to the alternate *feminine and Christian* God concept ensconced within the popular feminine savior image beneath the elite patriarchal doctrinal surface. He also fails to associate the redemptive female of the romance with the essential position assigned to Mary in the Catholic tradition and celebrated in the literary climax of the Middle Ages, Dante's romance *par excellence*, the *Divine Comedy*. Dante not only focuses on the redemptive Virgin but allows the image of Beatrice, his human, flesh-and-blood, *married* (and hence nonvirginal) sweetheart, to fuse with that of Mary and even Christ. In Canto 30 of *Purgatorio*, Beatrice's arrival is announced with the passage from the Song of Songs 4:8, "Come, my spouse, from Lebanon" (98), a verse ordinarily applied *only* to the Church and the Virgin. In the final Canto of *Purgatorio* Beatrice applies to herself the words of Christ, "*Modicum et non videbitis me, et iterum, ... modicum et videbitis me*" (110): "Within a short time you will lose sight of me, but soon after that you shall see me again" (John 16:16). According to Mircea Eliade, "one knows of no more striking example of the divinization of a woman. Evidently, Beatrice represented... the mystery of salvation" (102). Obviously, Eliade sees no conflict between Dante's Christian faith and his apotheosis of a flesh-and-blood woman. He continues: "Dante had written the *Divine Comedy* in order to save mankind, bringing about this transformation not by the aid of theories but by terrifying and fascinating the reader.... Dante illustrates in an exemplary manner the traditional conception according to which art, and especially poetry, is a privileged means not only for communicating a metaphysic or theology, but for awakening and *saving* mankind" (102).

Frye, on the other hand, argues that the pervasive presence of the "Eternal Feminine" in the romance "means that the myth of romance, though closely related to the myth of Christianity, and for centuries contemporary to it, should not be thought of as derived from it. As soon as we think of redemptive female descents to a lower world we think of Euripides' Alcestis, who is pre-Christian" (*Secular Scripture* 87). Would he also insist that the redemptive male should be thought of as originating not with Christ, but with the ancient Mesopotamian god Tammuz (shepherd son of Ianna, the queen of heaven, his mother/bride), who descended into hell after he had been tortured and killed? Certainly not. Frye wants to keep the two traditions separate, and never goes further than admitting that there are close parallels between the imaginative universes of the romance and Christianity. He writes that while "the myth of Christianity is also a divine comedy which contains a tragedy as an episode within the larger comic structure, . . . they are not the same thing, and should not be confused" (87). Greeley, on the other hand, as a Catholic Incarnationalist convinced of the sacramentality of the world can confidently combine the two traditions.

In keeping with its premier story and in contrast to the Greek sense of inexorable, calamitous, tragic fate, the Christian religious imagination, particularly in its popular Catholic forms, most typically weaves comic romances. Thus, Greeley's "comedies of grace" are heir to a rich tradition, albeit a tradition out of favor with the twentieth-century literary establishment, which feels called to demonstrate that the Warm Opium of Meaning must be sacrificed to the Cold Reality of Truth; that the Grand Lie of Cosmic Order and Love must be exposed and annihilated by holding it up to ridicule; that in our post-Einstein, post-Auschwitz, post-Hiroshima world no literature can be considered "serious" except the ironic.

This attitude is clearly expressed by Christopher Lasch[1] in *The Culture of Narcissism* when he writes, " . . . much popular art remains romantic and escapist. . . . Advertising and popular romance . . . promise . . . a part in the drama instead of cynical spectatorship. Emma Bovary, prototypical consumer of mass culture, still dreams" (95). Lasch has managed to pack this passage with buzzwords such as "advertising," "popular," "romantic," "escapist," "promise," "consumer," "mass culture," "dreams," all of which are contrasted with "cynical spectatorship," obviously the *only* mature stance open to contemporary humanity according to Lasch. In fact, at this critical moment in history, Lasch's "cynical spectatorship" with its implied Freudian pessimism concerning human nature, its acceptance of the presumed impossibility of human intimacy, and its nostalgic respect for patriarchal authoritarianism seems less a solution to the modern dilemma than at best a form of surrender and at worst part of the very problem it seeks to combat. Proponents of "cynical spectatorship" tend to forget that after legitimately exposing the inauthenticity of modern attempts to recapture the primal innocence of Ricoeur's first naiveté (*Symbolism of Evil* 351), their stance has outlived its purpose, and the time has come for them to yield to the forces of growth and change lest they become the escapists.

In many ways, the contemporary contempt for romantic modes is no more than an extreme variant of a tradition begun with Plato's expulsion of the poets from his ideal state. "Popular literature," notes Northrop Frye, referring primarily to the romance, with its structuring elements of violence and sexuality, "has been the object of a constant bombardment of social anxieties for over two thousand years, and nearly the whole of the critical tradition has stood out against it. The greater part of the reading and listening public has ignored the critics and censors for exactly the same length of time" (23).

Consequently, his use of romance has brought both renown and notoriety to Greeley. On the one hand, by adopting what J. Bard McNulty calls "the basic...narrative form of literature" (15), his stories resonate with the pervasive natural human tendency to identify with a perilous quest, have faith in the power of love, and hope for a happy ending. Hence they end up on best-seller lists. On the other hand, both their popularity and their comedic romanticism have made them suspect in contemporary critical eyes which view their specimens through spectacles of elitist irony or despairing cynical realism. According to McNulty, prior to the late nineteenth century, irony, the parody of romance, existed alongside other accepted narrative patterns. Since that time, however, "irony has so dominated the literary scene that few works are given serious critical attention unless the element of irony is strong in them" (149).[2] This contemporary apotheosis of irony as the *only* acceptable form for "serious" literature is so pervasive that even authors seeking to escape its tentacles find it difficult to do so. McNulty quotes Saul Bellow's complaint that "the contemporary artist has been 'forced to watch the sewage flowing in the Thames'" (149), and notes that while Bellow considered his *Adventures of Augie March* and *Herzog* examples of breaking away from the ruling tendency toward absurdism, the novels are in fact "essentially ironic in pattern" (149).

Parenthetically, much of what Greeley considers anti-Catholicism may instead reflect the reactions of an academic elite brought up at the sterile, synthetic nipple of irony instead of the moist, natural mother breast of genuine *literary* romance. Catholics whose vision is dark, such as Graham Greene and Flannery O'Connor, are readily accepted by the literary establishment. It is only when the Catholic vision appears in its *popular*, romantic, hopeful form that it becomes suspect. This interpretation would also explain Greeley's ongoing battle with *Commonweal*, a journal dedicated to ridding Catholicism of its "irrational" elements.

McNulty, however, sees the present age as harbinger of a postironic mode. While he does not make the association, his analysis follows the pattern of Hegelian dialectic in which each stage of organic development is superseded in the next stage of growth. He senses an essential shift from a cosmology of chaos and alienation toward a cosmology of order and renewed emphasis on the worth of individuals as members of the human community. As the following survey of selected major theorists in disparate disciplines shows, McNulty is correct when his intellectual seismograph picks up strange, subterranean tremors rippling through the very foundations of the Universal Ironic Temple to the Absurd.

Clifford Geertz challenges sociology's pretensions at objectivity while providing us with a contemporary definition of religion as a symbol system which mediates our encounter with the ambiguities of life. Though he reports the death of the great master-narratives (first and foremost the Christian "myth"), Jean-François Lyotard affirms narrative as a "central instance of the human mind and a mode of thinking fully as legitimate as that of abstract logic" (11). Fredric Jameson (in his introduction to Lyotard's book) resolves the tension by relegating the prematurely buried master-narratives to the cultural unconscious, whence they continue to affect ways of thinking (xi–xii). This may give them great power, if we accept Michael Polanyi's argument for the dependence of the "scientific method" on its preconscious, "tacit" matrix. In an attempt to elucidate the quantum-mechanical superimposition of states, Douglas Hofstadter suggests that we might think of the universal wave function "as the mind—or brain, if you prefer—of the great novelist in the sky, God, in which all possible branches are being simultaneously entertained" (472). Paul Ricoeur (despite his "hermeneutic of suspicion"—which is itself grounded in an acceptance of the narrative structure of consciousness) challenges theologians to find the way toward the second naiveté (*inter alia, Symbolism of Evil* 352–57) and (like C. G. Jung, Teilhard de Chardin, and Bernard Lonergan) elaborates on the Platonic roots of the Freudian concept of desire, envisioning it as thrusting toward ever higher (or more profound) levels of consciousness; E. G. D'Aquili and others consider myths bridges which provide us the means for left-right brain hemispheric homeostasis. Stephen Clark argues that we are driven by myths and archetypes which, while they are rooted in neuroendocrine patterns of instinctual response, are also present as highly abstracted symbol systems, thus constituting the linking mechanisms between emotion and rationality.

Finally, to return to one of McNulty's sources, Northrop Frye sees the present as the dawning of a new age, characterized by "return" to a form of metaphorical language of primitive communities (analogous to Ricoeur's second naiveté), adding that "God may have lost his function as the subject and object of a predicate, but may be not so much dead as entombed in a dead language" (*Great Code* 16).

This suggests an intriguing agenda for contemporary poets and theologians: the destruction of God's linguistic cenotaph by allowing ancient symbols to speak again through a return to romantic modes of thought and expression. A return to the popular. Frye (like McNulty), convinced of the intuitive wisdom of the people, insists that the much-maligned romance represents the vital core of the literary tradition in its entirety, providing something like an eternally fruitful womb for ever-new variations of literary forms. Due to its close association with the primary processes of mythic imagination, he considers it particularly active during transitional periods of instability when the possibilities of the elite conventions have been exhausted and new forms are about to be born. "This happens with Greek literature, when Greek romance emerged; it happened at the end of the eighteenth century in Britain, when the Gothic romances emerged, and it is happening now after the decline of realistic fiction. . . ." (*Secular Scripture* 29).

As Carl Gustav Jung, Joseph Campbell, and Mircea Eliade, among others, have noted, myth and symbols, precisely because they flow from the prerational strata of our psyche, have the power to bring us nearer the simple truths which have been buried under countless strata of philosophical, theological, and scientific speculation. They provide us with the immanent patterns, the archetypes and preconscious paradigms which shape our civilizations. They help us give meaning to the primordial struggles we intuit within ourselves. They allow us to organize the preconscious and chaotic desires, the amorphous needs and wants which invariably come into conflict with the demands of communal life. They integrate the individual into the larger patterns of society by uniting past, present, and future into a coherent whole.

Symbols give birth to new meanings when confronted by the social and individual conditions of a new age. They go through countless incarnations, speaking in new modes to human beings as distant in time and space as the first-century scribe at Corinth and the twentieth-century executive assistant at her Compaq 386 Deskpro. We cannot afford, Greeley insists, to tear down the bridges connecting us with the past. Temporarily silent symbols will come to speak again in a new mode; they will shed unexpected light on the ambiguities of the present; they will disclose new meaning important for contemporary life. Sensitive to the new experience in the Church, it is the task of the Christian not to repudiate the symbols of the past but to reinterpret them, to discern their meaning in and for a new age, to make them the key for understanding the present. This is precisely what Greeley does in his stories, as the authors who have contributed to this volume will show.

As long ago as 1961, Greeley, then curate at Christ the King Church and a graduate student at the Univeristy of Chicago, wrote in *Strangers in the House: Catholic Youth in America*, "Our young people have retreated into a world of fantasy and noninvolvement because they, like the rest of Western civilization, have lost faith in the world and in themselves" (15). He attributed this spiritual malaise largely to the failure of Christians and most particularly the clergy to provide effective alternatives to a prevalent sense of despair and alienation. Yet, he argued, there was cause for hope. "The human spirit is not defeated. The longing for meaning and significance is still very much with us" (22). The contemporary loss of self rooted in what he called the collapse of community was a passing disorder which could be healed once its cause was understood. "If man is not related to God," he argued, "then he cannot be related to nature and his fellow man; but on the other hand, by using natural signs, physical symbols to relate to nature and his fellow man, he can relate to God" (61). After deploring the lack of meaningful symbols in modern society, he diagnosed the illness and suggested a course of therapy for the ailing human spirit:

> To harmonize the city and nature, the technical and the numinous, the profane and the religious is never easy; in the world of

Einstein and Planck it is terrifyingly difficult.... A new cosmos must be built, a cosmos in which nature and technology are seen as restored in Christ. Technology will not be abandoned, the big city will not be deserted, but *both must be sanctified*. How this is to be done, where we must begin, I do not know. To suggest answers to these problems is the work of the poet, the metaphysician, and the theologian (64).

In many ways, the future of humankind depends on the moral and intellectual courage of those who affect the minds of the young (and not so young) at home, in the classroom, from the pulpit, through books, films, and television. The term "self-fulfilling prophecy" applies not only to individuals but to humanity as a whole. If we abandon hope, we shall indeed find ourselves in Dante's icy pit of nuclear winter and frozen hearts. If we dare hope, on the other hand, if we don't allow ourselves to be paralyzed by cynical pessimism, there is no reason why the world of the future cannot be inhabited by people who use technology for the good of the earth and humanity; men and women who have made what Sean Desmond of Greeley's *Angel Fire* calls the "small [evolutionary] leap toward more cooperation between peoples and nations," adding, "Otherwise we won't be around for the next really big leap" (6). Sean is an intriguing blend of Stephen Gould and Pierre Teilhard de Chardin, uniting in his fictional evolutionary theories the "punctuated equilibrium" of the former with the latter's quantum jumps of consciousness fueled by love, according to both Teilhard and Greeley, the primal, universal psychic energy.

Exploring ways for furthering intergroup cooperation is hardly a new theme for Greeley. In 1971, when he was the director of the Center for the Study of Ethnic Pluralism, he noted: "The critical problem then for those who wish to expand the area of trust and love in human relationships is not to eliminate diversity but to understand how diversity can be integrated in some form of unity.... The critical question is how to use these tensions and diversities to create a richer, fuller human society instead of a narrow, frightened and suspicious society" (*Why Can't They Be Like Us?* 16).

Thus, the Greeley troika of priest, sociologist, and storyteller is perfectly in step with an ever-increasing number of scholars in the humanities and social/natural sciences who have realized that this kind of open, multifocal world cannot be created unless its citizens live in peace with nature, respect others, and address their differences through conversation rather than war. The future of humanity literally depends on learning to have faith in the possibility of cosmic order; on overcoming our dread of intimacy; on abandoning our suspicious fear of the "other"; on going beyond the level of intellectual critique; on daring to take Paul Tillich's "leap of faith" into or at least toward Ricoeur's second naiveté. These are the kinds of insights which Greeley translates into popularly accessible symbolic language in his stories. His literary work clearly fits McNulty's projections:

Now, if creative artists come to believe that the scientists, philosophers, and critics are right, that the universe manifests more order than chaos, then the art forms of the future will probably reflect in many as yet dimly suggested ways the changed conceptions held by human beings about their universe and their place in it. And if there is any substance in the observation of critics that there is a current tendency to return to myth and romance, then it should be possible to suggest not the specific forms of literature that will appear in the years ahead, but what to look for as signs of the new mode. Early signs would include an increased interest in the marvelous (as in science fiction), in the naive and primitive (as in Westerns), in fantasies (including sex fantasies); a shift toward a lesser concern for ironic detachment, and a greater willingness to accept emotional, even sentimental involvement with characters in stories; an increased confidence in the worth of the individual human being both because of the extension of their powers through technology and because of a new view of humanity's place in a rational and orderly universe (178).

To illustrate his argument, McNulty gives the example of John Gardner's *Nickel Mountain*, the tender pastoral tale of middle-aged, grossly obese Henry Soames, who is "reborn" through the love of sixteen-year-old Callie. "The explicit theme of rebirth is the reverse of ironic; it points, instead, toward the archetypes of conquest over death in myth and romance. *Nickel Mountain* . . . may be the product of an emerging nonironic mode developed out of the ironic tradition" (180).

McNulty's book came out in 1977, one year before Lasch's *The Culture of Narcissism* and the same year Greeley published *The Mary Myth: On the Femininity of God*, his first extended and deliberate engagement with romantic themes, and his response to a world without hope, a universal sellout to cosmic futility. In the first chapter, by way of introduction, Greeley takes issue with the kind of cultural pessimism represented by scholars such as Robert Heilbroner and proposes to counter Heilbroner's masculine symbol of nobly stoic resignation, the Greek mythological Atlas,[3] "resolutely bearing his burden" (7), with Henry Aolam's smiling Virgin of Chartres, which he considers an analogue of the feminine aspect of God. A scholarly book, *The Mary Myth* nevertheless diverges from academic convention by Greeley's refusal to hide behind third-person objectivity and his decision to include original poetry to introduce several chapters. The poems are largely romantic in language as well as subject matter, written with an ear for the *sound* of words, and a sense of the divine, uncanny, demonic, preconscious. Central are the power of woman to reveal the love of God and a vision of the Church as warmly accepting flexible family rather than harshly censorial rigid dictatorship. Consider verses like the following from "Our Lady's Day in Harvest Time" and "The Black-Eyed Wife."

The blue mantle hangs useless from the peg
Dust and darkness dim the window
Stale air presses heavy on the land
Summertime—and yet we are cold.

. . . .

The generous belly, the breast soft and warm,
The merry eye, the tender hand—all long, long gone.
Now the icy ideologue, the ivory ikon,
The sickly cult, the papal text,
The dry debate, the dismal "no."

. . . .

The wind shifts,
The mantle lifts,
White fingers on blue cloth,
Flashing brown eyes in the sudden sunlight,
A smile explodes against the gloom.
Laetare. Alleluia! *(3)*

A great man lies dying
Gray, haggard, hollow
But there is worse than death in this room
With its thick rugs and rich drapery
Energies and forces fill the air
Fearsome, primal, ancient
Spirits, good and evil
And something terrible in between.
I like it not
This roar of heaven's wars.

. . . .

I do not deal with demons and seraphim
With psychic principalities and powers
I only minister the Final Rites.

. . . .

The black-eyed wife straightens the sheet,
Smoothes the spread
Gently wipes his brow
Calmly takes his hand
Softly repeats the prayers
Her sensuous warmth routs the haunting chill
The angels begin to hum
And mother church quietly goes to work.
The two mothers, church and wife,
Will not give up on their son
Save to the One Who Is to Come (184).

Greeley's *Mary Myth* is a celebration of the healing power of human intimacy, the nurturing role of the human community, the sacramental potential of maternal and sexual love. Almost every novel which Greeley was to write during the subsequent decade is already anticipated in this book and especially its poems with their embryonic stories which would develop into his versions of romance, science fiction, fantasy, and mystery, all swirling round the hub of a passionately loving God and a tender nonjudgmental mother church. Did the one who insisted, "I like it not/This roar of heaven's wars/ . . . /I do not deal with demons and seraphim/With psychic principalities and powers," intuit, ever so dimly, that soon he would write *Angels of September, War in Heaven, Rite of Spring*, and *Angel Fire*, all tales of cosmic confrontation? As though he had deliberately followed McNulty's projections, Greeley developed the very genres which McNulty called the early signs of the paradigm shift.

Significantly, the *Mary Myth* ends with poetic references to the two symbols which were to become the central structuring elements in Greeley's future works: fire and water. "The whole idea is that God wants to turn us on. He (She, It, They) wants to remake us. If the Mary symbol has any meaning at all, then it tells us that God prays in a fashion not unlike these words from Roethke's poem, 'Meditation of an Old Woman'" (219), which concludes, "May they be taken by the true burning;/May they flame into being" (219). But fire is incomplete without its complement, water. A few lines below, as the final paragraph of the *Mary Myth*, Greeley cites a stanza from T. S. Eliot's "Ash Wednesday," ending the book with "Sister, mother/ And spirit of the river, spirit of the sea,/Suffer me not to be separated/And let my cry come unto Thee."

What about the people who read Father Greeley's fiction, what about his public, his "congregation in the mailbox"? Do they deserve to be dismissed as tabloid-devouring cultural illiterates? Do they see a theological message? Fortunately, hundreds of them have written letters to Greeley, describing their reactions to the stories. The following passage is typical:

> What do I enjoy in your books? First of all, of course, the diversion provided. But . . . there must be something more than that. And I don't think it's just what you call the homily, though I certainly recognize its value. Possibly, in part, it's a certain shock of recognition, a feeling of being back on familiar ground. [There is] . . . a sense, reflected in the books, that something more than meaningless stars, galaxies, quasars, pulsars, black holes, etc. is going on Out There. It seems to me that since George Eliot, and aside from some science fiction and fantasy, fiction has largely lost this sense. Not altogether, of course—there's always a Graham Greene or a Brian Moore—but most writers aren't even despairing existentialists, telling us there is *nothing* out there. I am saying this very badly, but they seem to be totally unaware that there is even a question, anything to despair of or to take heart in. . . . (John R. H.)

Andrew Greeley, the contributors to this volume believe, is indeed a major storyteller, a contemporary descendant of the priest/bards of old, one who speaks to and for the people in a time when they feel abandoned by much of the literary establishment. "The magnetic core of the Greeley novels," notes Wendy Doniger O'Flaherty, a mythologist close to the oral tradition, "is a mythology in which the fire of sexual passion, diffused into all aspects of human emotional experience, lights the way to the grail of an upbeat grace" (Shafer xiii). Greeley does not write to uplift and indoctrinate; he writes to fascinate and illuminate. He lures, beguiles, seduces his readers, challenging them to take a new look at themselves, their relationships to others, and their unexamined religious presuppositions in the process of imaginatively joining his fictional world with their personal experiences.

Again, Greeley is at the leading edge of postmodernity. In *Time and Narrative* Paul Ricoeur points to the meaning-constituting event of the intersection of the "world projected by the text" and the "life world of the reader" and insists that this new focus will demand the "radical reformulation of the problem of truth" to include "the capacity of the work of art to indicate and to transform human action" (160). Ricoeur sees this new focus as a possible center of approachment and interweaving of the truth claims of fictional and historical narrative. This concept of "interactivity" (also explored by Hans Robert Jauss) opens up as yet unforeseeable opportunities for entirely new models of communicating and expressing. The paradigms will both depend on and develop the human imagination, and may demand that we redefine the notion of "conceptual act" (completed) as "conceptual event" (open-ended) and broaden it to include the process of "imaging" as epistemological category. In addition, like lovemaking and other authentic forms of communication, interactivity is reciprocal: not only do the author's ideas fuse with the life world of the reader, but the reader's response can in turn (if communicated to the author) affect the author's private symbolic cosmos, turning the entire creative act into an ongoing dialogical process. Greeley has taken advantage of this horizon by "listening" to an official panel of readers while his manuscripts are still being written and revised.[4]

As many of the letters from his worldwide readership (and "parish") demonstrate,[5] in the minds of his public, Greeley's stories take on a life of their own, becoming occasions for imagination leaping to imagination, reminding his readers that every Good Friday is followed by an Easter Sunday, allowing them to believe once again what their deepest intuition has told them all along: that human life is, after all, *not* a "tale written by an idiot," or worse still, a random assortment of isolated events pointing nowhere; to believe once again that good has the edge, however slight, over evil; to believe once again that homecoming and renewal are possible; to believe once again in the power of love.

NOTES

1. I am indebted to Bernard Gallagher, a contributor to this volume, for sending me his paper "Stephen King, Christopher Lasch, and Psychic Fragmentation" while I was working on this introduction. This fortuitous coincidence provided my scavenger imagination (see Greeley's contribution to this volume) with all sorts of threads to weave into the piece-in-progress.

2. In 1986, to test my hypothesis that many of Greeley's detractors were motivated by preexisting bias, I conducted a two-part survey of four hundred randomly selected PCA/ACA members whom I asked to rank identified or anonymous erotic passages from the work of Greeley and a number of other writers of varying reputations.

In part one of the survey 34 percent of respondents to anonymous passages ranked Greeley either first or second compared with 6 percent for Irving Wallace or John Updike. When the authors were known, Greeley dropped to 20 percent while Wallace received 23 percent and Updike 61 percent of the vote. In part two, Greeley passages received 37 percent of the anonymous top rankings, compared with 23 percent for Joyce Carol Oates and 11 percent for Saul Bellow. When the authors were known, Oates' and Bellow's scores went up to 41 percent and 34 percent respectively, while Greeley's score dropped to 16 percent. Quality judgment emerged indeed as a function of the author's positive or negative reputation. And that reputation, in turn, appears largely the result of the author's willingness to submit to the "Tyranny of Irony."

A forty-seven-year-old (agnostic) English professor from Minnesota may well have spoken for many of his colleagues: "The clinical descriptions seldom offend me, and I have marked the section accordingly. But the bullshit romanticizing . . . *does* offend me a great deal."

3. In many ways our age is similar to Roman Hellenism where the elite responded to the uncertainties of the times by desperate Stoic fulfillment of duty (Heilbroner), Cynical withdrawal of the social atom (Lasch), and Gnostic rejection of the material world (an assortment of right- and left-wing fundamentalist movements).

4. I asked one of those prepublication readers, Jim Harkin of Tucson, Arizona, to write a paper for this collection. Precisely because he is not a professional critic or professor of literature, his understanding of Greeley's work shows exceptional insight. The time may have come for a new and democratic approach to literary criticism in general (to supplement, not to displace existing models): the response of "lay" readers to works.

5. In the summer of 1986 I read hundreds of letters sent to Andrew Greeley between 1981 and 1986, and was surprised to discover letters from Africa, Austria, Australia, England, Ireland, Japan, and South America.

WORKS CITED

Alighieri, Dante. *The Divine Comedy*. Translated and edited by Thomas G. Bergin. New York: Appleton-Century-Crofts, 1955.

Eliade, Mircea. *A History of Religious Ideas. Vol. 3, From Muhammad to the Age of Reforms*. Translated by Alf Hiltebeitel and Diane Apostolos-Cappadona. Chicago: University of Chicago Press, 1985.

Greeley, Andrew M. *Angel Fire*. New York: Warner, 1988.

————. *The Mary Myth: On the Femininity of God*. New York: Seabury, 1977.

————. *Strangers in the House: Catholic Youth in America*. New York: Sheed & Ward, 1961.

————. *Why Can't They Be Like Us? America's White Ethnic Groups*. New York: E. P. Dutton, 1971.

H. John R. Letter to Andrew Greeley. 21 Sept. 1984.

Frye, Northrop. *The Great Code: The Bible and Literature*. New York: Harcourt Brace Jovanovich, 1981.

————. *The Secular Scripture: A Study of the Structure of Romance*. Cambridge: Harvard University Press, 1976.

Hofstadter, Douglas R. *Metamagical Themas: Questing for the Essence of Mind and Pattern*. New York: Bantam, 1986.

Lasch, Christopher. *The Culture of Narcissism: American Life in an Age of Diminishing Expectations*. New York: W. W. Norton, 1978.

Lyotard, Jean-François. *The Postmodern Condition: A Report on Knowledge*. Translated by Geoff Bennington and Brian Massumi. Foreword by Fredric Jameson. Vol. 10 of *Theory and History of Literature*. Minneapolis: University of Minnesota Press, 1984.

McNulty, J. Bard. *Modes of Literature*. Boston: Houghton Mifflin, 1977.

Ricoeur, Paul. *The Symbolism of Evil*. Translated by Emerson Buchanan. New York: Harper & Row, 1967.

————. *Time and Narrative*. Vol. 2. Translated by Kathleen McLaughlin and David Pellauer. Chicago: University of Chicago Press, 1985.

Shafer, Ingrid H. *Eros and the Womanliness of God: Andrew Greeley's Romances of Renewal*. Chicago: Loyola University Press, 1986.

I

Thistles or Roses: Peeking into Andrew Greeley's Secret Garden

1

INGRID SHAFER

Catholic Priests on Andrew Greeley

In the fall of 1984 I conducted a small-scale national survey concerning clerical reactions to Andrew Greeley's novels. One of the most intriguing patterns which emerged in that initial survey was the finding that three-fourths of those most hostile toward Greeley and most critical of his fiction had read none of the novels. An irate monsignor wrote, "I do not read anything by Greely [sic]. I consider him a desgrace [sic] to the Church." Another extremely hostile respondent put it bluntly, "His novels have been reviewed and read by people whose opinions I respect, and he has been judged by them a waste of their time and therefore mine."

In contrast, over one-third of those who had read two or more of the novels reported that they had actually recommended the books to their congregations, and almost two-thirds said they might recommend them. Thus it appeared not only that clerical opinions concerning Greeley and his work were extremely polarized but that a great deal of hostility supposedly engendered by the novels themselves was in fact the result of entirely unconnected and possibly prior factors which may themselves be responsible for both the decision to read the works and attitudes toward them and their author. What other explanation is there for such antithetical reactions as Father William Smith's published estimation of Greeley as a priest with the "dirtiest mind ever ordained" (*National Catholic Register*, 4 Sept. 1983)

Reprinted, with minor revisions, from *Chicago Studies* 25 (Aug. 1986): 189–97.

and one of my survey respondent's insistence that "without Andrew Greeley, the American Church would be even more dishonest, boring and irrelevant than it is. He loves his ecclesial family so deeply that he is willing to serve her with courageous independence and fierce love"?

In this context it is interesting to note that a gracious or graceful ("grace-full") God-image appears to be becoming the rule among diocesan priests. Among respondents to the preliminary "Clergy on Greeley" survey, slightly more than half of those ordained before 1955 opted for a maternally tender God-image. This proportion rose to two-thirds of those ordained after 1970. The shift is most pronounced for the categories of Mother/ Father and Spouse/Master. While still slightly less than one-half of the younger priests thought of God primarily in terms of Mother, this is proportionately more than twice the number of those ordained prior to 1955. In the category of Spouse/Master the break occurs later. Those ordained before 1955 and between 1955 and 1969 scored 63 percent and 65 percent respectively in favor of a Spouse-oriented God-image. This proportion rose to 89 percent among those ordained after 1969.

Four-fifths of the respondents ordained after 1960 (a little over half the total) with a graceful God-image did not consider Greeley's novels a threat to the faith of young people and would not discourage their congregations from reading them, while only about two-thirds of those with low scores on the Grace scale were opposed to repressing the books. Among the older priests no such correlation emerged.

Thus it appears not only that priests are envisioning God more and more in traditionally feminine terms but also that this graceful God-image is increasingly being internalized, leading to a more positive view of human nature and greater tolerance in general.

A number of supportive respondents specifically asked to remain anonymous. "I am afraid that several bishops would no longer invite me to speak to their clergy," wrote one, "if they knew I had *great respect* for Father Greeley!"

Those findings were sufficiently intriguing (though admittedly only preliminary) to suggest to me that a more thorough study might be worthwhile. In the original survey favorable reactions to Greeley's work correlated strongly with the fact that respondents were among readers rather than nonreaders, were younger than their critical colleagues, and had a graceful God-image. In order to arrive at more conclusive findings, I decided to concentrate on Chicago, both because it is Greeley's home diocese and because the Illinois response rate had been exceptionally high (and polarized) in my original study.

In the spring of 1985 I mailed three hundred additional surveys to Chicago archdiocesan priests, leaving out retired men and members of the hierarchy identified as such, thus contacting close to one-third of the target population.

As in the national mailing, each of the surveys contained four parts. Part one (items 1 to 4) dealt with general background information. Part two (items 5 to 30) was designed to elicit attitudinal value judgments concerning Greeley's novels. It consisted of a total of twenty-six statements (equally balanced to allow for thirteen positive and thirteen negative reactions), each of which could be answered as "agree," "disagree," or "not sure." Several of the statements were identical or very similar to statements included in Greeley's reader survey of *Ascent into Hell* and *Lord of the Dance* to allow for possible comparison. Part three asked respondents to locate themselves on five scales (each with seven points) between images of God as Mother/ Father, Master/Spouse, Judge/Lover, Friend/King, Creator/ Healer, Redeemer/ Liberator. Part four allowed respondents to voice additional comments.

The response rate was unusually high, 135 responses (45 percent), of which 131 (44 percent) could be tabulated. (Of the remaining four, two were totally blank, one contained only comments, and one was limited to reactions to the God-images.)

The proportions favorable and unfavorable in both Chicago and the nation were roughly the same. Even though Chicago priests were more likely to have read the books, this did not change their response pattern. Apparently reading the books does not appreciably affect reaction to them, a phenomenon which will be explored in more detail in the course of this report. Overall, clerical respondents in general and Chicago priests most specifically differed substantially in their estimation of Greeley's fiction from nonclerical readers who returned research questionnaires included in the paperback edition of *Ascent into Hell* and the Literary Guild subscription readers of *Lord of the Dance*. These responses Greeley summarized in his articles "Who Reads *Those* Books?" (*America*, 16 May 1984) and "Fiction and the Religious Imagination" (*America*, 6 Apr. 1985).

Over three-fifths of Greeley's nonclerical readers indicated that the novel *increased* their respect for the priesthood, and roughly the same percentage said it helped them understand the Church better. Only 6 percent considered the book a disgrace to the Church, and the same number charged that it made them feel contemptuous of the priesthood. Twelve percent reported a loss of respect for the Church. Contrast this with the Chicago clergy of whom almost 25 percent would discourage members of their congregations from reading Greeley's fiction, another 16 percent might do so, and 19 percent either thought Greeley should be officially silenced or were not sure whether such drastic action would be appropriate. Exactly two-thirds considered his portrayal of the Church negatively biased, and almost one-quarter insisted that it is distorted and slanderous.

Of the lay readers, 70 percent said the book caused them to think seriously about religious issues, 60 percent considered it a book with a deep spiritual message, 45 percent found it helpful in coming to understand the meaning of divine love, 38 percent reported that it had increased their sensitivity to the relationship between religion and sexuality, and a little over 25 percent said it had deepened their religious faith.

On the other hand, 80 percent of the Chicago clergy did not consider the novels parables of grace or theology in story form, and while only 9 percent considered them pornographic and 5 percent blasphemous, fewer than 20 percent thought they were conducive to reaffirmation of faith.

Eight percent of the readers said Greeley should be ashamed of writing such trash, and ten percent said he writes merely to make money. Among the clergy, almost one-third considered the novels sleazy exploitations of the mass market, and 27 percent said the books were motivated by love of money and notoriety.

At least as interesting as the survey itself are the comments added by respondents. "In my opinion Father Greeley is one of the greatest thinkers of the Catholic Church in Modern times," wrote one respondent, ordained in 1938. "He is a Gem, bright and shiny in an otherwise fairly dull Church." This sort of enthusiastic reaction is definitely the exception. It seems significant that even individuals who appear favorably inclined according to the objective scale frequently insisted on adding patronizing and nasty remarks, while many of the low scorers luxuriated in comments ranging from slurs to fabrications. A surprising number of those comments are gratuitous and bear no connection with the purpose of the survey, which was clearly limited in the cover letter to eliciting clerical opinions concerning Greeley's *novels* rather than juicy bits of gossip pertaining to his personality and "psychosexual development." The same priests who are self-righteously scandalized by Greeley's tendency to portray the clergy as multifaceted human beings, prone to meanness as well as nobility, lust as well as love, weakness as well as strength, reveal themselves as petty, envious, and even vicious in their own words. Of what conceivable interest could it be for a scholar doing research on the clerical understanding of Greeley's fiction to be told by one of his seminary classmates that he used to correct the spelling in Father Greeley's themes, and by another that "Andy" used to be a "mama's boy, non-athletic but fawning over athletes"? Or to be informed that Greeley does not participate in class reunions, invented his position with the National Opinion Research Center, appears never to have experienced any true lovemaking in the bedroom(!), has no faculties and is not a priest in good standing, is "no Flannery O'Connor, Graham Greene, or C. S. Lewis," does superficial sociology, and wants to be a martyr to the hierarchy? "Poor Andy," I was told again and again, is a man to be pitied, his own worst enemy, alienated from any group of support and affirmation, talented (maybe), but insecure and paranoid, with adolescent views on sex, manipulated by and manipulating the media, insisting that every one of his thoughts emerge as a book, turning out religious soap and, generally, poorly written drivel.

Two of the clerical comments which stand out as paradigmatic of that particular type of response should suffice to make my point. Inaccurate statements which are being passed off as facts have been italicized.

Thank you for the opportunity of this survey. I would imagine that my impressions of Andrew Greeley can be seen as negative only in that he seems to portray a Church of great anger and hurt. I sense more his own frustration and hurt in the way *he* perceives the Church. But, I cannot see that his opinion is in fact a representation of the whole Church or its people. I suppose that I find untenable and unprofessional (and perhaps manipulative) the manner in which Greeley uses the media and abuses its function as purveyor of truth. Many unsuspecting people take what he writes as true. (*In his sociological Study of American Catholics, Greeley's sampling was of 1500 Catholics, 500 [of] which were in Chicago.* Not a very good random sample, is it?) I would imagine that if he were not a priest, the publishers would have taken a second look at his poor writing, unimaginative prose, and simply naive sensational-ism in the bedroom (a place where he seems best suited to sleeping rather than having experienced any sort of true lovemaking).

He has allowed (either deliberately or by omission) people to see him as a sociologist with the *North American Opinion Research Center* [sic] *(part of the University of Chicago) which has been denied publicly by its director, Wm. McCreedy* [sic]. And, Greeley has allowed people to think of him as authoritive [sic] voice of the Church, speaking for the grassroots. Both perceptions are fabrications which he chooses to allow to be maintained. For these reasons alone, one could cite him for unprofessional behavior. Lastly, as a priest (albeit in good standing with the Archdiocese of Chicago, by the kindness of Cardinal Cody and Cardinal Bernardin) who does not practice ministry in the diocese to which he has vowed obedience and service, I cannot see how he can speak on pastoral matters.

Upon receiving this response, I telephoned William McCready at the National Opinion Research Center. McCready assured me that Greeley was one of this country's most highly respected sociologists and had been associated with NORC for around two decades. Greeley had, as a matter of fact, hired him. He emphatically denied ever having made a statement to the contrary. Furthermore, Greeley had never conducted the kind of study reported by my respondent.

When I wrote to the respondent (who had signed the survey), telling him of my conversation with McCready and asking him to substantiate his charges, he suggested that I contact yet another priest who might have taped McCready's public lecture. Obviously, his allegations were based on hearsay.

Another priest writes:

I have been a priest for fifteen years. I am chaste and celibate. Most priests, far and away, are like that. I have never lived in a rectory where a priest was not keeping his vows. Is this reality accurately reflected in Greeley's books?

Andy Greeley has not been silenced but he has no "faculties." A priest
must have an assignment or he cannot preach, hear confessions or
say Mass publicly. While he may do these things in Arizona, I
can't remember when I last heard of Greeley preaching in Chicago.
He is not a priest in good standing; he doesn't have faculties.

Since for a priest the accusation of "not being in good standing" and
having no faculties is an extremely serious charge, I called Father Robert L.
Kealy, chancellor of the archdiocese of Chicago, who told me that "while
Greeley's opinions are his own, he does enjoy the faculties of archdiocese of
Chicago and is involved in a number of apostolic and pastoral activities. He
is definitely a priest in good canonical standing."

Concerning the rhetorical question as to whether the reality of "chaste
and celibate" priests is accurately reflected in Greeley's novels, I can only
say that even a cursory head count of his clerical characters reveals that,
indeed, the vast majority of them appear to remain true to their vows.

Overall, the additional remarks are overwhelmingly hostile. Only 4 to 7
percent of the comments are clearly positive, while 69 percent are negative
(12 percent extremely so). Thirty-eight percent of those scoring in the top
third (forty-four) of the survey added comments, but only 23 percent of
those comments were positive. Of the fifteen highest scorers (+16 to +26)
only four (27 percent) added comments (which constitute the total of
unambiguously positive remarks for the entire survey). Apparently, Greeley's
clerical supporters are far less inclined to go beyond filling out the forms
than his detractors, which is not surprising, since in this type of survey the
indignant are generally more likely to vent their feelings than those who
have no complaints. This imbalance in the willingness to speak out (and
possibly even to return survey forms), however, might skew Greeley's
public clerical image to appear worse than it really is.

It seems significant that 47 percent of the fifteen lowest scorers had read
none of the novels, and an additional 33 percent had read only *The Cardinal
Sins*. Yet 53 percent of them added derogatory comments, and almost
one-third of the nonreaders who wrote comments attacked the literary
quality of the works—of which they could have formed no personal
opinion. Granted, 47 percent of the readers who wrote comments (38
percent of the total clerical reader respondents) also focused on the literary-
quality issue; however, 69 percent of them had read only one or two of the
novels, and none of them offered specific backing for their opinions
concerning the supposed poor quality of writing. It appears to be taken for
granted.

In the national survey it was very clear that priests who were under the
age of fifty and had actually read at least two of the novels tended to
respond favorably to Greeley's fiction. Correspondingly, the strongest
adversaries were almost exclusively nonreaders who were on the average six

years older than their more positively inclined colleagues. In the Chicago survey this correlation, while still applicable to extreme supporters or detractors, was far less significant, while another type of correlation emerged which involved a "clerical culture" factor designed to measure the kinds of preexisting attitudes and opinions with which individuals approach Greeley and his work regardless of whether they have actually read the novels or not. The clerical culture factor relates to age and intervenes in the relationship between age and the attitudes toward the novels. Younger priests tend to be more likely to read the novels and assess them positively, because in general they are not as deeply immersed in clerical culture as the older men.

Those scoring high on the clerical culture factor tended to have negative scores on the survey and were extremely likely to add derogatory comments. Those scoring low on the clerical culture factor tended toward high scores on the survey and generally refrained from negative comments. None of those low on clerical culture thought the Church should silence Greeley, while 14 percent of the high scorers did so. Thirty-six percent of the low scorers thought the Church should encourage Greeley versus 6 percent of those high on clerical culture. Eight percent of the low scorers considered Greeley's portrayal of the Church distorted and slanderous, while 42 percent of the high scorers did so.

None of those low on clerical culture considered the fiction blasphemous, in contrast to 14 percent of those high on clerical culture. Forty-five percent of the low scorers considered the novels parables of grace, whereas only 6 percent of the high scorers thought so. Forty-four percent of those low on clerical culture said the novels were conducive to reaffirmation of faith, as compared with only 6 percent of the high scorers. Three percent of the low scorers said the novels were pornographic as opposed to 19 percent of the high scorers. Thirty-four percent of the low scorers saw the novels as theology in story form, compared with 8 percent of the high scorers. Thirteen percent of the low scorers considered the novels devoid of theological content as opposed to 33 percent of the high scorers. Sixty percent of the low scorers felt we need more books like Greeley's that teach religion in story form, while 20 percent of the high scorers thought so.

None of those low on clerical culture considered the novels a threat to the faith of young people, while 29 percent of the high scorers did. Five percent of the low scorers would discourage their congregations from reading Greeley's novels as opposed to an amazing 51 percent of those high on clerical culture. Forty-six percent of those low on clerical culture might recommend the novels and 28 percent had actually done so, compared with 3 and zero percent of the high scorers. Forty-four percent of the low scorers considered the novels helpful to the alienated in contrast to 11 percent of the high scorers.

Finally, only 8 percent of those low on clerical culture were certain the novels constituted sleazy exploitations of the mass market, compared with

64 percent of those high on clerical culture. Fifty-one percent of the low scorers considered the novels inspired by love of God, Church, and humanity as opposed to 8 percent of the high scorers.

The introduction of the clerical culture variable not only accounts for the differences between the clerical national sample and the Chicago response; it also resolves the paradoxical disparity of the opinions expressed by Greeley's nonclerical readers and the clergy in general. As one of the respondents to the Chicago survey remarked, "From my standpoint in hearing people. They put meaning into Fr. Greeley's books from their own viewpoint. Objectivity is at low ebb. It seems to me his readers are pro or anti before reading." A certain number of the clergy will be predisposed to an *a priori* condemnation of Greeley's books whether they come from Chicago or any other diocese and whether they have read the novels or not. In Chicago a greater proportion of the clerical culture segment of the clergy read the novels because of Greeley's high visibility in that region, but by itself the reading did not substantially affect their attitudes. Thus, as my respondent intuitively remarked, it appears that it is not the books themselves which matter, but what clerical readers bring to them. Furthermore, in those areas where a comparison can be done, the responses of that segment of the clergy which is least affected by the clerical culture syndrome are fairly close to those of Greeley's nonclerical readers, and I am even tempted to speculate that the adversarial readers, who, in contrast to the approving readers, tend to attend church regularly and are on the average six years older than the others, are also affected by (or infected with) clerical culture.

In conclusion, it appears that in multiple-regression analysis, the clerical culture factor made up of the following three variables, all antecedent to reading the novels, explains well over half the variance in hostile reactions to Greeley's novels: (a) the respondent's image of God, (b) the respondent's image of the Church, and (c) the respondent's attitude toward Greeley's financial success. Those who have a rigid (traditionally masculine) image of God, fear for the image of the Church, and resent the author's monetary success are far more likely to have hostile opinions concerning the books. Those who have a more flexible (traditionally feminine) image of God, see the Church as a relatively unthreatened institution, and do not suspect the author's motivation tend to react much more favorably to his books. In other words, the reaction to Greeley's novels is much more likely to be a function of what one brings to them than reading the novels themselves. If readers are rigid, fearful, and envious, they will deeply resent the author and rationalize this resentment by attacking the man and his work. Clearly, for a significant proportion of the priests of his own archdiocese, Greeley has become, as he has noted repeatedly, an inkblot upon which they can project the demons of their own unconscious—a process which may reveal far more about them than it does about him.

2

ROGER J. BRESNAHAN

The Sacramental Body: Andrew Greeley's Autobiography

I am reminded of the comic strip "Shoe." The perfesser is walking down the road with the priest and asks: "Heard any good prayers lately, Father?" The priest replies that, as a matter of fact, he has: "Lord, give me the wisdom to accept what I cannot change and the courage to change what I can." As an afterthought, he confesses he prefers the short version.

"What's that?" inquires the perfesser.

"Lighten up."

Andrew Greeley lacks nothing in courage, but it's his own peculiar cross that he cannot lighten up, except perhaps in his novels. His self-image is that of Quixote jousting at windmills: in recounting the more extreme moments of controversy he jokes that he is once more saddling up Rosinante.

Confessions of a Parish Priest is, therefore, an autobiography in which Greeley attempts to set the record straight—to explain his research as a sociologist much misquoted, to explain his intentions as a newspaper columnist much maligned, and to explain the theology behind his novels much misunderstood. Through it all he is probing his own history—his Irish-American ethnicity, his parochial school upbringing, his education and

Reprinted, with minor revisions, from *Midwestern Miscellany 15* (1987): 11–18.
See Andrew M. Greeley, *Confessions of a Parish Priest: An Autobiography* (New York: Simon and Schuster, 1986).

miseducation as a seminarian, his dedication to the Catholic Church despite "that goddamn encyclical," and his inability to ever really leave Chicago.

Greeley's opportunity to make a significant contribution to American Catholicism came when Cardinal Stritch gave him permission to write, permission which a writer-priest needed in pre–Vatican Council days. Later, Cardinal Albert Meyer gave Greeley permission to study sociology in graduate school and, on his deathbed, to live wherever he chose—with other priests in a rectory or by himself. Meyer's wisdom may readily be applauded, for the reader of *Confessions of a Parish Priest* will discover that Greeley's impatience with "clerical culture" would have made it impossible for him to endure any longer the infantilism under which young curates were then held by their pastors. Then, too, Meyer may have been thinking of the pastors, for Greeley has that Irish weakness of never backing down from a fight just because he's outnumbered, outweighed, and outgunned. That was certainly the case when he undertook his survey research of American priests. The news that most American priests were ignoring the birth control encyclical and had lost respect for the hierarchy hit the bishops like a ton of breviaries, which the priests were no longer using, either. The conservatives like Cardinal Krol and Chicago's Cardinal Cody turned the screws tighter, attempting to hedge in Andrew Greeley's freedom without actually withdrawing the permissions granted years before by Stritch and Meyer. After Greeley's survey that showed most American Catholics had ignored the birth control encyclical, while they still considered themselves in good standing with the Church, even his liberal and moderate friends among the bishops couldn't help him.

There were more studies and other battles, all recounted and refought in the pages of this autobiography. Through it all are the twin motivations of the Irish American: to fight the battle that presents itself, and to be well liked. Thus, Greeley has abhorred the practice of selecting mediocre popes and less-than-admirable bishops. Small wonder that other Irish American trait, the desire to be well loved, especially by those we criticize, is so seldom fulfilled in Greeley's life.

Greeley is a product of the old Catholic Church in America. He has championed many reforms, those that made sense. But in his view, the solid traditions of Catholicism have been swept away with the enthusiasm of post–Vatican Council theological and liturgical reform. Or have they? In fact, Greeley's surveys reveal that the stories, images, and metaphors of the old Church have remained alive within the American Catholic laity, even as the theologians have striven to expunge them. The rosary, the stations of the cross, the imposition of ashes, blessing of throats on Saint Blaise's Day, Christ the King processions, May festivals, sprinkling of holy water, burning of incense, devotion to the saints, lighting votive candles, wearing of medals and scapulars, holy cards, novenas, pilgrimages to shrines and holy places—these have all been degraded in importance. Yet in the old Church they were all sacramentals—occasions of grace.

The American Catholic laity, despite injunctions to the contrary from priests and theologians, continue to find more spiritual sustenance in these metaphors than in the propositions of the theologians. Indeed, Greeley's surveys have shown that the most powerful image for American Catholics is that of the Christmas crèche. Catholics have learned more theology from this one image than from all the propositions of all the theologians.

This is not to imply that there is a schism developing. American Catholics, even the well educated, tend to accept the propositions of the theologians and deposit them in that category of mind labeled "mysteries of the faith," thus freeing the heart and mind to focus on what may be grasped.

Greeley argues that the Church should turn its attention once more to the wellsprings of faith—to the incarnational, which people understand, rather than the eschatological favored by abstract-thinking theologians. To a theology of the sacramental rather than one of the propositional. Such a theology, tracing its roots far back in Catholic tradition, is less dependent upon hierarchical approval than propositional theology.

Though Greeley does not cite it, the encyclical of Pius XII, *Mystici Corporis*, most likely built the foundations for contemporary lay control of their own beliefs. The argument for that, which I shall make in a moment, is convoluted. Greeley says it was the birth control encyclical of Paul VI, *Humanae Vitae*, that fostered contemporary Catholic contempt of authority in the Church. The amazing thing is that though 85 percent of American Catholics acknowledge they ignore the Church's teaching on sexual ethics, they have chosen to remain Catholics. Greeley has developed a theory of religious imagination which has enabled him "to demonstrate that the critical variable is *how people imagine God.* Those who reject the Church's sexual ethic and nonetheless have an image of God as kind, gentle and loving are the ones who are most likely to go to Mass and Communion. The laity justify their continued reception of the sacraments despite the violation of the Papal birth-control teaching by an appeal from the Church to God. The Pope might not understand the importance of sex in their marriage, the laity are saying in effect, but the loving God does. The official Church has caught itself in a bind in which the laity think that God is on their side and not on the side of Papal teaching" (342–43).

How could this be, given the doctrine of papal infallibility? The answer, I think, is in three parts. First, papal infallibility was a doctrine proclaimed amidst great civil strife. Though the popes and theologians have reaffirmed it many times, the laity around the world have never been consulted. So long as papal pronouncements have not seemed unreasonable, papal infallibility has remained an acceptable tenet of propositional theology—true, perhaps, but not worth thinking about. That dry-as-dust proposition fell apart when Paul VI enunciated a doctrine which seemed unreasonable.

The second part of the answer has to do with a piece of propositional theology which has had a powerful, uplifting effect on lay people. That is, that the sacrament of marriage is performed by the couple on one another. In requiring people about to be married to participate in the so-called pre-Cana conferences, the American Church has given this proposition the widest currency. Catholics have been told, in effect, that the responsibility for their marriage, both as institution and as sacrament, is wholly their own. Of course, the birth control teaching is usually presented at the pre-Cana conference, often by a priest. But remember, Catholics overwhelmingly consider it unreasonable. Their respect for the person of the priest means they will often go along with whatever he says while holding mental reservations. Besides, Greeley's research on American priests showed that they "chose to take sides with the laity" (342), and that "more than 80 percent of the clergy said they would not enforce it [the birth control teaching] in the confessional and a slightly lower number said they did not believe the teaching was valid" (295). So with most of the priests softpedaling the birth control teaching, the attractive proposition that the couple themselves administer the sacrament of matrimony has meant that sexual ethics within marriage become, in effect, an area privileged to the couple themselves. Though we may have been offended by his crassness, few American Catholics disagreed with the quip of Secretary of Agriculture Earl Butz upon returning from the Rome food conference: "He no play-a the game, he no make-a the rules."

Finally, what enabled American Catholics to ignore the birth control encyclical and to go on considering themselves good Catholics was, in my view, Pius XII's *Mystici Corporis*, which took powerful hold on the Catholic imagination in the United States, perhaps because American Catholics had become intellectually mature and were psychologically ready for a democratization of Catholic dogma. Paradoxically, though *Mystici Corporis* reaffirmed the dignity of the lay vocation, lay people were not taken step by step through the nuances of this complex document. I would argue that what they absorbed was the powerfully attractive notion that we are all, in a mystical way, part of Christ; and that the Church does not consist of its real estate, or even of the Pope and clergy, but that we are, all of us, equally the Church. That sense of the document, which was all that was ever communicated in sermons, took powerful hold within the context of American democracy. Together with the notion that married couples are themselves responsible for the sacramental nature of their own marriage, and thus of their own sexuality, this widespread, if not wholly accurate, understanding of *Mystici Corporis* accounts for the fact that lay and clergy alike in America have rejected the birth control teaching, implicitly setting aside the doctrine of papal infallibility, yet continue to receive the sacraments and participate in the life and—ah, yes—the governance of the Church.

Andrew Greeley's novels depend heavily on his theory of religious imagination, his notions of the sociology of religion, and his use of story, rather than on propositional theology. Thus it is the narratives of the Gospels that exercise a powerful influence on American Catholics—much more than the propositions of the Pauline letters or of later theologians. Not that Greeley would make out propositional theology to be wrong, but only that it gains life with the kind of story theology that forms the more familiar episodes of the Catholic tradition and informs Greeley's own novels.

"Religion," Greeley tells us, "is an utterly secular experience in that it begins, first of all, in the ordinary events of life which renew our hope" (433). Within the traditions of the Yahwistic religions—Judaism, Islam, Protestantism, and Catholicism—there are differing images which renew hope. Religion for Greeley, therefore, is story before it is theology. He presents a living Catholic tradition as sacramental. Thus, God is disclosed "in the people, objects, and events of ordinary life" (435). Unlike Jews, Protestants, and Muslims, Catholics are not worried about slipping over into idolatry. God is not banished from the Catholic world, and so the world becomes a sacred place. "The quintessential Protestant says that the only sacrament we have is Jesus and him crucified; the quintessential Catholic says that while the crucified and risen Savior is the central sacrament, everything else is capable of becoming a sacrament. 'All is Grace'" (436).

Greeley's vision is, therefore, a sacramental one. Those who have criticized the covers of his novels as lurid and their content as lewd miss the point. These "comedies of grace" baptize the objects of the natural world, making them sacramentals. Thus my title: the sacramental body. The human body is not an occasion of sin, as taught by the heretical Jansenists of the seventeenth and eighteenth centuries, but rather a sacramental, an occasion of grace. "This flesh-affirming, life-affirming version of the Grail legend is Catholic; the life-denying, flesh-denying Arthur/Lancelot version is Manichean" (436).

Thus, in his novels, as in *The Mary Myth* and the book written by him and his sister, *How to Save the Catholic Church*, Greeley reaffirms the "traditional imaginative heritage" of the Catholic Church—"its vast and rich repertoire of experience, symbol, story and community" (437). He does not seek a return to the recent, pre–Vatican Council past characterized by the Latin Mass and the absolute power of the hierarchy. Rather, he seeks to enrich the Church of today with the older traditions: "Hopkins in the nineteenth century, Rubens in the sixteenth century, Michelangelo in the fifteenth, Aquinas and Dante in the thirteenth, Anselm and Bernard in the twelfth" (437–38).

What will all this return to Catholic tradition mean for the ecumenical movement? Greeley doesn't address this issue. Perhaps he is gun-shy after being set up by the American Jewish Committee and then accused of anti-Semitism. Perhaps, indeed, Andrew Greeley has learned that hardest of lessons for the Irish—how to walk away from a fight. Certainly ecumenism has brought Protestants and Catholics closer by eliminating the recriminations born of mutual distrust. But it has also resulted in Catholics stripping their churches of much that is right in metaphor. To approach the quintessentially Protestant ideal, much that is quintessentially Catholic has been suppressed. To take one example: the realistic, often multicolored, stations of the cross, which enabled Catholics to meditate upon the story theology of Christ's passion, have generally been replaced in Catholic churches by starkly beautiful, stylized tableaux that fail to move us.

When the goal of ecumenism is to enable us to explore the metaphors of one another's traditions, then I would judge Greeley will fully approve. But if the goal is to obliterate meaningful traditions in order to eliminate theological differences, then the Greeley that comes forth so strongly in this autobiography will not assent. For his goal is to reaffirm a sacramental view of the universe. It is a heritage too rich, he says, to ignore. Despite the fact that it has often been served up in the most "shallow and superficial" manner, Greeley's opinion research shows it has remained alive "in the experiential dimensions of the personality of the faithful" which has resulted in a finding that "Catholics were a third of a standard deviation higher than Protestants on a scale which measured the intimacy and affection of their images of God" (438).

Many of his readers have said that Greeley's novels have brought them closer to God and enabled them to understand Her. Her? Ah, yes. A significant proportion of respondents have identified God as both mother and father. And the notion goes back very far. Saint Bernard, for example, wrote that in contemplation he sucked milk from the breasts of Jesus! Catholic tradition reveals, according to Greeley, many writers "who did call God a mother (and a lover and a brother and a sister and a nurse and all kinds of relational opposites—based on the marvelous sacramental insight that all human relationships reveal something special to us about God's love)" (438).

The novels, therefore, are themselves sacramentals. And therein lies the aptness of the baffling title of this autobiography: *Confessions of a Parish Priest*. Greeley is not in any ordinary sense a "parish priest," though he does weekend parish work in those places where a bishop will permit him. But as long as Andrew Greeley continues to write novels which might give offense to those who have not read them, Cardinal Bernardin promises to withhold the privilege of performing any priestly functions within the archdiocese of Chicago. The cruelest blow! Andrew Greeley cannot consider anyplace but Chicago home. The point he is trying to make with this title is that his novels are sacramentals. That as "comedies of grace" they are occasions of grace. His parish, therefore, is his mailbox and his parishioners are his readers.

3

PATRICIA W. JULIUS

Andrew M. Greeley: Ethnic Historian or Social Reformer?

*F*ather Andrew M. Greeley is a hard man to contain—or to categorize. His writing style, even when dealing with the most serious subjects, and in the most serious way, is not that of either sociologist or historian. Throughout his writings, Greeley exhibits that wit he speaks of so eloquently in *That Most Distressful Nation*. And he uses that wit in much the same way that the Irish bards he reveres did. For example, after a learned discourse on the complexities of the Irish-English conflict, ending with the comment that England's oppression of Ireland has continued for a long time, he adds wryly and pensively, "a *hell* of a long time" (213).

This is not the language we have come to expect of a "traditional" scholar. But it is the language of a man involved. In many ways, I suspect Andrew Greeley has more in common with Vine Deloria than with Oscar Handlin. Like Deloria, Greeley's knowledge of history is considerable, as is his knowledge of sociology, of course. And, like Deloria, Greeley does more than blend the two disciplines: he adds his own vision and sense of logic, compassion, and the consciousness that pretense and pomposity are not only dangerous but, at heart, absurd. Greeley blends social science, history, outrage, and poetry in his advocacy of the fact and effect of white ethnicity.

In *That Most Distressful Nation*, for example, Greeley includes a charming and erudite discussion of fairies, banshees, and leprechauns in a chapter

Reprinted, with minor revisions, from *Midwestern Miscellany* 15 (1987): 19–24.

entitled "The Church." This kind of syncretism marks his mind generally and adds layers of complexity to what, in another, would be a straightforward disquisition of the effect of Catholicism on the Irish "soul." His analysis of the changing position of the Catholic Church, now and in the future, incisive and not always optimistic, takes the form of social (here Church) reform. He presents historical background, discusses the growth of the Irish Catholic Church in America from the early immigration to the present, and poses questions for the future that, he argues, must be answered. These questions and others of similar nature form the crimson thread which unites Greeley's nonfiction. His is a plea for, as well as an analysis of, the value of ethnicity now and in the future. His work is full of hunches, impressions, and assumptions—but if they are correct, as I suspect they are, they have great value in defining elements of ethnicity which "have made the Irish what they are today." As important, they provide a key to understanding other white ethnic groups.

In the introduction to *A Piece of My Mind*, a collection of his columns, Andrew Greeley claims, with great good cheer, to be "perverse, contentious, difficult, unpredictable, combative, difficult and outrageous." But there and elsewhere, these qualities are ever employed in the service of logic, accuracy, thoughtfulness, rationality, and love for his fellows. Always, Greeley exercises our intellect. Always, he asks the hard questions. Always, he directs our attention to work yet undone.

In *Why Can't They Be Like Us?* Greeley writes about "the diversity caused by the immigration of white ethnic groups from Europe to America between 1820–1920" (13). His basic theme is the importance—and inevitability—of ethnic pluralism, for the people who are directly affected and for the nation itself. And for the next decade or so, he continues to develop that theme. In *That Most Distressful Nation: The Taming of the American Irish* (1972), *Ethnicity in the United States* (1974), and *The Irish Americans* (1981), his plea remains pretty much the same: that while Irish Americans and other white ethnic groups are not totally explained by their heritage, understanding that heritage will help us to understand them and may even help them understand themselves.

In *Ethnicity in the United States* Greeley wears the hat of a social scientist more consistently than in any other of his investigations into European ethnic groups. Even here, however, his own intellectual diversity is clear. He quotes an Irish American mother: "I don't have a past," she said. "None of us does and I don't think I can understand myself or my family unless I can rediscover my past" (179). And Greeley writes, in part, to provide her and others like her with a past and, in part, to convince historians and social scientists that white ethnic groups do exist and their existence is a subject worth far more scholarly attention than it has hitherto been accorded.

I suspect there is a kind of national assumption in the United States that white ethnicity has been swallowed up by the whole. That is, that the act of becoming "American" has somehow eliminated the need (or even the right) to retain our ethnicity. Greeley argues, correctly I believe, that whether we recognize it or not, the ethnic element of our characters not only exists but is alive and operating in our personalities and our assumptions—those things we "know" are true, as surely as air and blood.

According to this convention, by becoming "American" we have no longer any need to be Norwegian or Russian or Irish or whatever. Our acceptance of the Myth of the Melting Pot has essentially denied the need to acknowledge our roots. It is, I think, to disprove that myth, to plead for the recognition that to be American does not demand that we give up or deny our own cultural experience, that is the message of Greeley's nonfiction. After all, those experiences made us what we are today and, unless we accept that, how *can* we be satisfied? More to the point, unless we *know* our heritage, our "ethnic origins," we cannot be sure in our identity—as individuals or as a nation.

Despite the almost conscious reluctance to admit it—a reluctance shared apparently by outside society as well as the members of the groups themselves—ethnic variations exist in American families. Certainly the nature of the family was changed by immigration. As Greeley points out, "The city replaced the village. The cultural values transmitted within the family no longer reflected the outside world and were not necessarily transmitted within it. The family was no longer insured of its traditional preeminent position in the lives of its members. Children now had to move away from their parents in order to survive and prosper. The new land encouraged independence and 'striking out on one's own.'" But the immigrant could never really leave home: that home and its values and assumptions would influence the "future growth of his children as they made their own ways" (*Ethnicity in the United States* 157). Now, a century or so later, most white ethnics have made their way in American society. They have—more or less—melted. But, Greeley maintains, they "have lost something in the process" (*Distressful Nation* 128). Certainly the Irish American mother knew that: and she had identified the nature of that loss. It was her past, her personal history.

Four years ago, at a Celtic Conference at Oxford—an occasion itself not without a certain Irish irony—a scholar from Dublin asked my national origins. When I admitted with some hesitancy that, as far as I knew, my ancestors had been English at least since about 1560, he asked my maiden name. When I told him it was Ward, he glanced triumphantly at his four fellow Dubliners, turned back to me, and fairly roared, "Ah, and wasn't there a bard named Ward in the sixth century now. I knew you had to be Irish."

Somewhere there is a connection. And I think the connection is this: Andrew Greeley has spent a good part of his intellectual life writing about the Irish Americans and their need—hence, by extension, the need of other white ethnic groups—to know their history, to have a sense of their own identity in order to understand their place in the present and the future.

My friend from Dublin surely had such a knowledge, such a sense. Alas, most of his spiritual relatives in the United States do not.

In many ways, this investigation has raised my own awareness. For example, Greeley cites pollster Lou Harris' report that about a quarter of American people "hold positions which can fairly be described as anti-Catholic" (*Irish Americans* 108). I grew up in the South where hatred of "the different" has long been a cottage industry. I attended Catholic boarding schools, listened to diatribes against Germans, Jews, Yankees, and, of course, Blacks. (We all knew the Klan hated Catholics but they hated everybody, even Episcopalians.) Certainly, in my classes on American Minority History and Literature, I have discussed anti-Catholic prejudice in the eighteenth and nineteenth centuries. Certainly, I have assigned my students to research the anti-Catholicism which discolored the Kennedy candidacies and to reach some conclusion about what that told us about the state of our Union. I had *known* this. But I had not known it was so widespread in 1981. Twenty-five percent! Somehow that number has changed the way I think, changed the things I take for granted. And such a change in his readers is, I think, what Andrew Greeley is really after.

As one considers Greeley's points and arguments and questions, one cannot escape comparison between white and racial ethnics: that is, Native Americans, Blacks, Chicanos, and Asian Americans. Indians, the only real Americans we have, and Blacks were forced to cede or at least disguise their cultural verities. Technology as well as social forces—a polite term for removal of the Indians and enslavement for the Blacks—operated to destroy their culture, language, and, in fact, their history. Mexican Americans and Asian Americans came late to citizenship, of course, but both suffered from society's assumption of white superiority. But ironically, those racial groups had one advantage. Despite the oppression and contempt of white society, they carried the impossibility of melting into some common pot on their backs—and fronts and sides. Their skin identified them. They might be oppressed, and they were. But no matter how hard mainstream society tried, it could never completely destroy their respective identities. Their existence could not be denied: there was visible evidence of their unassimilated presence, dismissed perhaps, but always there. Forced into common stereo-types, isolated by segregation laws (or custom), racial ethnic groups could maintain, no matter how tenuously or incompletely, some sense of their own pasts.

Greeley challenges scholars to turn their attention to studying the residual effects of ethnicity on the beliefs and behavior and values of white ethnic groups, in an attempt to somehow legitimize their identity. He presents statistical and historical evidence in support of that challenge. And if that were all he did, we could label him "ethnic historian" or some similarly comfortable term, and go on about our business. However, Greeley does much more. In short, he calls for a restructuring of the way we think and, so, of the society in which we live. In *The Neighborhood* (1977) his premise is that "neighborhoods are a good thing" (xiv), a belief that he has propounded in other places. But he bases that premise on a social-ethical vision which "stresses the organic, intimate, local, decentralized aspects of human life." He maintains "absolutely and irrevocably, that the dignity, worth, and value of the individual person is supreme" (167). And neighborhoods contribute to that "dignity, worth, and value" for the same reasons that our awareness of our ethnic past should. We "can't be free without belonging," we "can't be independent without being secure," and, most important, we "can't go somewhere else unless" we "can go home again" (169). And this vision of the future, this insistence on becoming, elevates Greeley above the easy labels. He is "all of the above"—priest, novelist, social scientist, historian, columnist—but most of all he is a slaughterer of sacred cows, a deflater of overblown egos, a caller of spades. Like Bernard Shaw, he asks not "Why?" but "Why not?" Greeley raises the ceiling of possibility. And in my book, that is what social reform is all about.

WORKS CITED

Greeley, Andrew M. *Ethnicity in the United States: A Preliminary Reconnaissance.* New York: Wiley-Interscience, 1974.

———. *The Irish Americans: The Rise to Money and Power.* New York: Harper & Row, 1981.

———. *The Neighborhood.* New York: Seabury, 1977.

———. *A Piece of My Mind . . . on Just About Everything.* New York: Doubleday, 1983.

———. *That Most Distressful Nation: The Taming of the American Irish.* New York: Quadrangle, 1972.

———. *Why Can't They Be Like Us? America's White Ethnic Groups.* New York: E. P. Dutton, 1971.

4

JACOB NEUSNER

No Prophet In His Own Village: Chicago and Its Bard

Once ordained, a Roman Catholic priest, like a priest in ancient Israel, remains indelibly consecrated. No sin, no violation of sacred oaths, not even a loss of faith and vocation, removes from him the indelible consecration of ordination. How, then, represent a priest saying Mass, who has left the priesthood and descended into a hell of wanton sexuality, money-grubbing, and vindictive, mean-spirited revenge-seeking? Send him to a couple that has buried a child and as yet has found no solace in the Church:

> So with his congregation gathered around the table in the kitchen overlooking the Pacific, Hugh Donlon said Mass for the first time since he'd resigned from the active ministry, with the surging blue waves of the ocean, framed in a picture window, serving as the altar-piece. He preached feelingly of Johnny Kincaid [the dead infant], now a spiritual and human giant in the life that awaits us all. He wasn't sure he believed any of it, but his congregation believed, and that perhaps was enough.
>
> All the Kincaids wept.

Then again, how would you portray the ideal of sexuality as a sacrament, as the composers of the Song of Songs would have it, a metaphor for God's love for humanity? Put your priest on television and have him say this:

Lovemaking between a man and a woman can mean many different things. Through lovemaking, lovers forgive one another, show their gratitude to one another, declare their love, renew their vows, chase their anxieties and their anger, reestablish communication, make life livable for one another, challenge, stimulate, excite, and reassure one another. Also, of course, it is the means for continuing the human race.

Paul could not have said it better today were he writing a third letter to his Christian flock in Corinth.

And, again, were you to want to portray what has happened to Christianity in the American Church, tell people what has been going on and what it means, why Christians stay Christian and what "being Christian" means to them, what do you do? Not to worry, create a whole world of Christian living, peopled with all the sorts that make up the Church today. Make them Irish, put them in Chicago, and let them go.

Not everyone can do these things, translate sociology into social life as people live it, speak the faith in story, transform doctrine into parable, through language make a world. I remember starting a novel by Andrew M. Greeley, who has done all these things, and within a half hour finding myself so engaged by his story and his people as to think I was meeting, and finding engaging, a whole new world.

Greeley is only one among many world-famous authors who live in Chicago, but, among them all, he is assuredly the most controversial. And I think he ranks way up there on two more registers: storytelling talent, but also, subjection to abuse. Sweet singer of American Eire, for his gifts he has gotten a grudging reward, but much abuse. Let me explain the sorry tale of a great man badly abused.

Not everyone has that power of storytelling, but Greeley does. In his wildly successful novels, from *The Cardinal Sins*, in 1981, he has spoken to a whole new parish: a world of Irish Roman Catholic life that turns out, when you get inside, to be the realm of the humanity we all know. It is a world we in the last half of this tormented century, we Americans, have made, endured, suffered, and survived.

Whether or not another generation will look back and find Greeley noteworthy and even still worth reading, or merely transiently famous and read only for his own day, no one now knows. He certainly does nothing to curry favor with the academic world, which serves as arbiter and mediator of the past. His portrayals of academics cut to the bone and leave out all sentimentality. While the pilgrim people of the Christian world have found in him pastor and comforter, certainly conventional and institutional churchmen and churchwomen will not always find themselves portrayed kindly. The currently fashionable in religion can find no joy in Greeley's searing vision of what counts.

When priests and nuns married and declared—speaking of themselves—

that the best of the Church was leaving, Greeley not only stayed loyal to his vows, he also wrote novels about the meaning of commitment. When, caught between an uncomprehending Tridentine hierarchy and a changing, restive laity, priests lost their way, Greeley explained what was happening, showing the enduring faith in a world in motion but not astray. His counsel, deriving from his social study of Catholic society, marked him among sociologists as a pioneer in the study of ethnicity, and this truth of social science is what he brought to the altar of the faith.

What of the literary craftsmanship? In *Lord of the Dance* Greeley transforms the description of dance steps into prose fiction, and then has each of his characters do that dance, in words. "Bolero," which is his dance seven, "danced by one dancer... includes many brilliant and intricate steps, quick movements, and a sudden stop in a characteristic position with one arm held arched over the head," has all the characters, each doing a bolero of words. The idea is not his own but for his fiction is adapted from Nietzsche, "The only God worth believing in is a dancing God." And the "Lord of the Dance" is a song by Sydney Carter. Anyone who sees Greeley's work as a series of potboilers, tossed off after midnight, will have to contend with the sheer intellectuality represented by the ambition of this one novel. And the others rest on an equally cerebral foundation of thought and theological reflection: his is a pure faith, spoken through story.

At his Mass in celebration of his sixtieth birthday at Old Saint Patrick's Church in the West Side of Chicago, just now, Greeley gave a homily woven out of the theme of Günter Grass' *Tin Drum* ("I will not turn ten") and the words of Job to tell a spellbound congregation of Catholics, Protestants, and Jews the tale of growing up, not growing old. His is not a routine intellect.

But this brief account of a considerable oeuvre of intellect and sensibility is not meant to celebrate or even defend. Greeley's novels need no defense, but demand only response of one kind or another. Rather, I want to ask, how has the man's gift of storytelling been received? In a remarkably searing passage, one of Greeley's characters explains to another the price of success. A priest in the diocese of Chicago enjoys enormous success in a television ministry. The other priests in the diocese express not admiration and pleasure at the success, which enhances the ministry of them all. The television figure asks a fellow priest's counsel. Here are the costs of success:

> "You'd better make up your mind, John," the Ace said slowly. "You're at a turning point now. If you go on with your program, particularly if it is syndicated around the country, you'll be a pariah in the priesthood for the rest of your life. . . . You'll become the victim of collective envy neurosis. Your motives will be questioned. Your personality and character will be distorted so that you will not recognize yourself. Your friends and your family will be called upon to defend you by almost every priest and nun

they encounter. Any attempts you make to reply will be twisted to
fit the neurosis. You will become a myth that many of your fellow
priests will love to hate. And even those who are free of the
neurosis will tell you that you shouldn't expect anything else. . . . Envy
is maybe the third most powerful human motive, after hunger and
sex. . . . Our reward structure is pretty thin; and we're socialized
into it in the seminary because it's a very useful means of
imposing control. Ruins talent, of course, but our leaders don't
want talent anyway. . . . Don't even count on your friends. . . . The
negative myth will stick to you for the rest of your life. Some of
your friends will secretly envy you and others will succumb to
pressure to go along with the myth."

Any doubt that the passage is autobiographical gives way before the
accumulated record of Greeley's reviewers. Here is V. De Foggia (reputed
to be the pseudonym for Philip Nobile, who more than once has supposed
to feed on Greeley's carcass) in *Penthouse Forum*, under the headline "The
Phallic Priest. The Gospel of Violent Porn According to Father Andrew
Greeley": "So amateurish is the perversity of his bestselling imagination
that only a practicing celibate could dream up such wretched sex scenes in
novel after novel." Lifting utterly out of context selected passages in which
a character in a novel shows himself a sadist, the reviewer asks, "Why does
Greeley, presumably virgin and fantasist, resort to S&M so frequently?"
The key is the "so frequently," for if you want to know how frequently "so
frequently" is, you have to have read pretty much all of Greeley's novels.
Whether or not Mr. De Foggia has I do not know, but I have, and "so
frequently" is very seldom—and always purposeful in the context of the
story. The portrayals of sexuality are diverse, as they have to be to
accomplish the narrative purpose.

True, Hugh Donlon in his descent into hell (the novel *Ascent into Hell*) is
portrayed in a passage De Foggia quotes; but in the context of the novel, the
portrait is a detail of a monster, a Picture of Dorian Gray. But, in Greeley's
world view, sin is not the whole story; there is repentance, atonement,
grace, love. In the novel at hand the monster is redeemed and made once
more a man and human, also through sexuality, this time in the person of
Maria Angelica. The contrast in love and the contrast in sex compel the
reader to the message; Greeley could not have portrayed the ascent into hell
had he not shown what hell was for Hugh. Picking and choosing to suit his
purpose, De Foggia misrepresents this among Greeley's novels, beginning,
middle, and end.

Greeley's character Ace warns about priestly envy. Here is Father
William Smith, writing in the *National Catholic Register* for 4 September
1983: "Dear Andy, . . . I write you as a brother priest . . . to ask that you
review yourself. . . ." This is a rather dramatic beginning; it certainly grabs
a reader's attention. It also denies Greeley even a modicum of respect, so
Smith:

Sometimes you say that priests are your worst critics because they are either jealous or envious. Be assured, I am neither. I write only because you are giving the priesthood a bad name. . . . Certainly you have no mandate to prove that yours was the dirtiest mind ever ordained. Consider your family—give them something better to remember than "my uncle, the priest who writes dirty books." . . . Andy, do the whole Church a favor and clean up your act; you are giving the priesthood a bad name."

So that's what it comes down to, Greeley's world of imagination encompasses men and women who go to bed with one another, and for Father Smith writing to his "friend" "Andy," that does it.

But the portrayal of sexual activity in Greeley's novels is chaste and allusive; any comparison of his description of the mechanics or plumbing of sexuality with those of other novelists of our day, say even the great genius of our age, John Updike, will absolve Greeley of the charge of pornography—and condemn his critics for malicious prosecution.

But no one has condemned Updike for placing on display, along with other components of his astonishing mastery of nearly all of human knowledge, his power to describe the anatomy and functioning, jointly and severally, of sexual parts, male and female. Things to which Greeley demurely refers, Updike sets down in the middle of Times Square. But Updike is not a Roman Catholic priest. That Greeley is titillates a few. But it precipitates a feeding friendly for the sharks in the Church.

What really bothers the critics of the sexuality of Greeley's novels? It is that he is a priest, and priests don't write that way, so Webster Schott: "Never have so many called to the cloth discovered so much glory between the sheets." And again, the notorious Father Smith, "No one was ever saved by sacrilegious adultery." That is, in fact, one of the principal points Greeley makes in the novel to which Smith refers, and which he distorts out of all recognition: sin is sin, but God's love, freely given as grace, saves.

That is not to suggest the critics have complained only about the sex, though without that to harp on, the sensation of "the priest who writes steamy novels" loses some of its sex appeal. Taking out of context a few less than well crafted sentences, Wendy Leopold, in the *Los Angeles Times*, 15 February 1987, condemns Greeley for poor writing: "Greeley does a decent job of developing his Chicago newspaperman protagonist, and his plot takes some interesting twists and turns. But writing that veers between the heady and the flat often unwittingly becomes comic and undercuts his plea for marital passion and love. . . . Worse still is the prose of the sex-as-sacrament message." Still, compared with Father Smith, Ms. Leopold is fair-minded and serious.

But, then, she is not a Roman Catholic priest writing to "Dear Andy." She is a professional and reviews like one. With her there can be argument, disagreement, negotiation. What can anyone say to Father William Smith? Greeley's fiction means to bear this message, summarized by Robert

Ellsberg in *New Age*, January 1985: "the distinctively Catholic sensibility . . . is defined as sacramental (experiencing the sacred through the concrete); analogical (recognizing similarities to God in everyday things—especially, in the authors' view, sex); comic (believing in happy endings); and communitarian. . . ." How have Catholic readers responded to this message? Very simply, they have bought his books, read them, bought more, written him letters, and then bought and read still more.

Greeley has a massive hearing among Catholics—and now a growing audience of other Americans as well—who can, if they want pornography, get more and better elsewhere. These millions do not read as "steamy" or pornographic or even titillating Greeley's rich and complex portrayals of human relationships, including sexual ones. They don't need Greeley if they're looking for voyeurism. The sensation of a priest who writes "dirty novels" is lost for these millions of readers. For that, you buy one book, not seven or fifteen in a row. These readers are just that: they read like innocents, to join in the story, they read for the story and the meaning of the story. The reason they read Greeley is very simple, so I think: in his imagination they find, and understand, their own reality.

As one reader put it in a letter to him, "After reading your novels, I find I love my wife still more, in more ways and for more reasons, than I did before. For that I thank you."

Why do I find the violent attacks on Greeley remarkable? Well, compare the reception accorded to Greeley's Jewish counterparts. Take for example two considerable storytellers in Judaism, Elie Wiesel and Chaim Potok. Potok is surely the best storyteller of Judaism today, Greeley's counterpart in the simple sense that, when Potok and Greeley tell stories, the angels stop to listen. Has Potok been condemned by rabbinical or other Jewish critics in terms applied to Greeley? No, he has been honored, received within the synagogues, accorded the much deserved respect his exceptional art has won for himself. And Wiesel? The single most popular, most influential figure in contemporary Jewish affairs in North America. Indeed, numbers of his Judaic and Christian admirers worked for many years to gain for him the recognition of the Nobel Prize he received just now. Every rabbi in Chicago would have attended a celebration of Elie Wiesel. But just now I did not see Cardinal Bernardin when people from all over the country gathered to pay honor to Andrew M. Greeley at the Hotel Nikko. The only bishop present came from Indiana, and he is retired! Quite a contrast.

So, to Father William Smith, in the spirit of his open letter to Father Andrew Greeley, one might fairly say, "Dear Bill, Drop dead."

II

Soil, Seed, Sun, and Rain: Folktales, Scripture, and Symbolic Imagination

$\mathcal{W}$hile the following essays by Michael Marsden, Roland Murphy, O. Carm., and David Tracy do not deal specifically with Andrew Greeley, they were written for a volume in his honor, and are included here to provide this anthology with a theoretical context from the perspectives of popular culture, biblical studies, and contemporary Catholic theology.

Michael Marsden focuses on the "high" culture/"low" culture dichotomy in its relation to literature. He argues that successful popular writers function in contemporary literate society the way folk story*tellers* function in preliterate societies, and are precisely for that reason generally misunderstood by print-obsessed literary critics. Possessed by their stories, these latter-day bards dialogue with their audience, weave their magic spells, and structure new-old tales to the patterns of their culture, bringing people into the warm circle of the communal hearth, the story's "fire" sparked as private imagination twirls within and against the preestablished form of genre tradition.

Roland Murphy adds a highly significant dimension to the erotic symbolism so frequently used by Greeley by arguing that the literal historical meaning of the Song of Songs as human love poem and the traditional meaning of this love poem as symbol of the love between God and God's people need not be viewed as mutually exclusive. Murphy suggests that the traditional meaning is valid precisely on the basis of the symbolism of human sexual love. He finds evidence in the Hebrew text (8:6) that sexual love as described in the Song is somehow associated with the Lord as Lover, and considers it unfortunate that the traditional meaning was allowed to eclipse the literal meaning, leading to an impoverished Christian attitude toward sex.

In his paper David Tracy lays the foundation for a postmodern marriage of art to theology, of adding aesthetic criteria as a major component in the determination of theological criteria through the uncovery/retrieval of embedded imaginative possibilities present in the analogical (albeit second-order reflective) language of Thomas Aquinas by paralleling it to metaphoric first-order symbolic language (as understood by Paul Ricoeur).

To prepare for a future which will be *both* true to the best of contemporary experience and the best of the past, Tracy joins those who urge a critically mediated reappropriation of the central stories, myths, and symbols of the religious traditions ensconced in the images and rituals of our respective communal lives. In this manner he hopes to counteract the damage done by the naive liberal rejection of the symbolic wealth of tradition, and most particularly the fact that the liberals thus "handed over the authentic symbolic resources of the tradition to those least able to appreciate them: those once embattled but now reinvigorated opponents of modernity in every tradition—those Pope John XXIII labeled the dark prophets of gloom in our culture; those whose voice—if not whose arguments— so pervade our present moment in history."

Tracy then lists three criteria which might be used to illuminate the symbolic resources of a religious tradition. The first two are aesthetic criteria: the nonreducibility of any truly symbolic reality to merely literal meanings, and the fact that a new meaning, not expressible without loss in literal terms, emerges from the very interaction and juxtaposition of words not ordinarily used conjunctively. The third criterion is religious and involves the "limit character" of genuinely religious language as projecting some "aesthetically satisfying and religiously compelling vision of the imagined possibility. . . of a final meaningfulness to human life in relationship to the whole."

                                                                          I.S.

5

MICHAEL T. MARSDEN

Chin Music: Popular Storytelling as the New Oral Tradition

Storytellers make us remember what mankind would have been like, had not fear, and the failing will and the laws of nature tripped up its heels.

—WILLIAM BUTLER YEATS

$\mathcal{F}$ew areas of human endeavor have been as misunderstood or maligned as the popular storytelling process. Yet few such areas of artistic effort have reached more people than the simple but complex art form of popular storytelling. In the minds of too many literary critics popular storytelling is located somewhere between "folklore" and "literature," with uncertitude about its location resulting in its being assigned to the scrap heap reserved for those activities deemed crass commercialism. It fails as "literature," they say, because it is not stylistically sophisticated. It fails as "folklore," they add, because it exists in the commercial world of paperback publishing. Making chin music for the mass audience is considered unartistic, pandering craftwork. No wordsmiths these scribbling entrepreneurs. The purpose of this essay is to inquire into the nature of the popular storytelling process and to assess its value for contemporary society.

One of my basic theories about popular storytelling is that the more "literary" a popular writer becomes, the more that removes the writer from the audience being served. In fact, the popular storyteller is successful in direct proportion to the closeness maintained with the oral tradition, not the literary tradition. The model is that of a dedicated popular writer "speaking"

Reprinted, with minor revisions, from *The Incarnate Imagination: Essays in Theology, the Arts and Social Sciences in Honor of Andrew Greeley. A Festschrift,* edited by Ingrid H. Shafer (Bowling Green, Ohio: Bowling Green State University Popular Press, 1987), 150–55.

his stories to a group of interested listeners. Given the economic realities of reaching a significantly large audience to earn a living, the storyteller working in the print medium keeps the focus on the oral stories as the model, not the stylized narratives of the printed page. The result is that those storytellers who succeed in the mass marketplace are those who keep true to the rhythms, tones, and structures of the oral tale. Literary critics approaching popular literature have for the most part been using the wrong tools.

The basic image which emerges from the story of any successful popular writer is that of a storyteller sharing a deeply felt tale with a friendly and willing audience. Most popular writers I have researched maintain a strong personal correspondence with a good number of their readers, because they are truly interested in the exchange and because that very exchange informs their writing. They also appear on talk shows to further encourage this audience identification. In effect, they have learned to carry on a continuing conversation with their readers by using and sometimes redirecting the mass media. They make their own rules, because continuing conversations with their readers demand it.

Popular narratives exist primarily in the world of feeling. This is not to suggest they are devoid of intellectual content. Rather, they are emotional renderings of complex human experiences and not intellectual articulations of unknowable realities. They exist to "move" people out of self-isolation and back into the warmth of human interconnectiveness.

Popular storytellers happily work within genres which are continuing, unfinished narratives. As genre theorists note, the genre story is not complete in itself; it is a gradually unfolding story which because of the complexity of the telling is never complete. Each version both reveals the past tellings of the tale and adds to those to help complete an epic narrative. The process requires constant interaction between artist, artifact, and audience, resulting in a cocreative process unmatched in the so-called high arts.

The explanation for the popularity of certain genre stories can be explained, as John Cawelti has noted, by the fact that they seem to fulfill more social and psychological needs than do other story forms. But that does not explain their origin. Evidence is strong for the proposition that genre stories are the result of collective audience sentiment and that popular storytellers are those who can interpret the pressing societal concerns and values and present them within the most effective narrative structure. Genre stories have a very special function in society because they have been developed to allow a society to "escape into" its problems by restructuring them so they can be dealt with in an acceptable and nonthreatening manner. Good wordsmiths structure their tales according to culturally preconceived patterns. (A most perceptive student pointed out to me a few years ago how the structure of UFO captivity narratives was essentially the same as that used for many of the early Indian captivity narratives.)

The popular storytelling process rekindles our sense of belonging to the human condition and helps to protect against the isolation of the study which occurred following the introduction of the printing press into Western culture. Popular storytelling is a counteractive force against the separateness print brought into the world when it allowed the speaker to become physically separated from the listener. The rise of individualism in Western culture clearly parallels the rise of print. The law becomes distant and impersonal as it relies upon the written record and not the spoken tradition. Neither an isolated figure "experiencing" literature nor a passive escapist, the reader of popular literature is a caring, feeling, and thoughtful member of a large audience who knows a good story and a good storyteller when presented with them, and who is humble enough to allow the chin music to work its magic now and then. Instead of trying to condemn popular storytellers for what they are not and what they do not do, we should be preparing an ode to those who assist in reuniting readers in both a secular and a sacred way with the human community.

The popular storyteller is more like the anonymous folk artist than the contemporary writer of "literature" who mails off his interpretations of life to the world from the confines of a hidden study. It has always been interesting to me to find out how approachable most popular writers are; they welcome contact with their readers as they strive to perfect their craft and strengthen their perceptions of the world they and their readers inhabit. Popular storytellers have learned the ultimate discipline—that of sublimating their private imaginations to the needs of the public imagination. It is, of course, the force of their private imaginations struggling for expression under the strength of inherited story traditions which gives their stories "fire." Their role as public figures is one of arbitrator and encourager. They serve to broadcast consensus values and attitudes while also narrowcasting a vision of future possibilities.

The "fire" which drives a popular storyteller is an interesting force. It is my theory that the popular storyteller's fire, which is the major tie to the oral tradition, is diminished in direct proportion to the writer's emphasis on stylistics. It is the "fire" of a popular storyteller which the readers most readily respond to as they seek out voices for their longings among the many offered on the paperback racks.

This is certainly a different perspective on the popular storytelling process than that promulgated in most literary circles. Large portions of popular literature are ignored by the literary critics and scholars because they are seen as damnably formulaic. The problem is one of not perceiving subtle but crucial dissimilarities between individual examples of a particular story form. The trained student of popular literature can perceive and assess significant differences between two examples of a particular genre. But for the untrained, prejudiced observer, it is impossible to entertain the possibility that a formulaic piece of literature could have distinctive qualities which allow it to contribute to the further development of a genre story form while at the same time reinforcing previous story patterns. The apparent and remarkable paradox of the popular narrative is that the very constraints it operates under provide it with remarkable freedom. An individual example of a genre story assumes that the reader is familiar with an elaborate story tradition and then can build upon that tradition. What is seen by most literary critics as artistic limitation in the genre story form is in fact a liberating process for the storyteller who wishes to work new magic within the context of a well-defined tradition. The formulaic writer of genre stories is thus the freest of all writers because of the rich tradition within which he/she operates.

It can be argued that because of its well-established traditions which can win and hold a large audience, the popular story form is actually able to take bolder steps toward narrative innovation than the less conventional story form which has to spend a good deal of time and space establishing the reference points for writer and reader. The popular storyteller knows his/her audience and they know the storyteller. Where an individual example of a genre story takes them depends upon the mutual understandings and agreements of storyteller and audience. Popular stories do as much to expand our understandings as they do to confirm our prior experiences. They become part of the cultural glue which binds the audience to the human community.

It is interesting how often a popular storyteller will in conversation convey the experience of the story actually taking control at a certain point in the creative process. It is almost as if the author is a conduit and not the true source of the energy. Seemingly having a life force of its own, the popular story begins and ends with the audience; the popular storyteller apparently mediates between the worlds of the collective imagination and the particular set of circumstances which define the story. As noted by Jeff Okkonen, a reviewer of a new edition of Cree Indian tales, the Cree Indians believed a story lives for a time in this world and then inhabits a person. When the story is retold by that person, it again lives. So with the popular story which lives for a time in the world, inhabits a popular storyteller, and through his/her artistry is again given life.

Popular narratives do not move people through a single experience. Rather they move people slowly through time and circumstances into a new awareness of their collective reality. There is an essential conservatism about the popular storytelling process, since its main purpose is to socialize people into the shared traditions and values of the society, to make them aware of the cares and concerns, hopes and dreams, fears and nightmares of a people, not just an individual. The role of the popular storyteller is to be a friendly voice telling the audience what they already half know. The popular storyteller provides a reasonable shape and structure for unreasonable truths. Providing linkages between our several worlds of experience, the popular storyteller brings the audience back to the communal hearth with tales which reach into the human mind and heart. No mean vocation this sacred role of human reintegration.

In addition to shoring up traditional attitudes and values, the popular storytelling process can, as several theorists have pointed out, function as a way of confronting changes in society and assisting the audience in coping with them. The fear of change is thus reduced because the change itself is presented within the context of a familiar story which seems ever so slightly new. Whether set in the past, present, or future, the popular narrative can also examine less acknowledged and often hidden areas of human experience in a way which provides the audience with a surrogate experience minus the risk which would otherwise be involved.

An often misunderstood aspect of the popular storytelling process is the necessary balance which the storyteller must strike between conventional elements and inventional elements. Certainly no one has commented more fully on this topic than John Cawelti. But it is useful to review and expand upon his analysis. Every popular artist utilizes conventional elements with which the audience is familiar. But the popular artist must also utilize inventional elements to provide the necessary challenges the audience needs to maintain interest. The artistry occurs in the balance between the "old friends" and the "new acquaintances" each storyteller strikes in the narrative. The metaphor which seems to work best at explaining this balance is that of meeting an old friend. We revel, at least temporarily, in reliving past, shared experiences with our old friend. But we also eagerly await the "new news" we expect the old friend to share with us about life between visits. A friendship can only be based on a constant balance of old understandings and new awarenesses if it is to thrive. Formulaic conventions, like old experiences, can be retold in a creative manner; often it is the juxtaposition of conventional elements in a narrative which can be highly creative and challenging for an audience. The fact that certain forms of artistic expression have a higher frequency of "invention" while others tend to be characterized by the presence of "convention" speaks not to the artistic merit of the individual works, but to the relationships between artist and the audience.

It is most unfortunate many of those in literary circles insist on suggesting that popular writers are not "serious" writers; popular storytellers could not be more serious about their vocation. And although the audience is certainly seeking entertainment, they are equally serious about the quality of their fictional lives. There is, without question, a complicated, sophisticated conversation occurring between popular storytellers and their grateful audiences. Unfortunately, not many literary critics actually listen to the conversation.

In formula stories characters tend to become personifications because they represent forces, not individuals. This particular fictional quality of the popular narrative has led many critics to condemn the world of popular fiction as inferior when in fact it is a world operating out of a different literary mode and aesthetic dimension. These "felt experiences" the popular storytellers weave are very often attempts to stretch the confines of a genre form in order to challenge the audience into new understandings in a nonthreatening manner.

As most theorists on popular story genres would agree, they are, above all else, "paradigms of ritual and order" which seek to provide important linkages between the experienced world, the felt world, and the understood world. Popular storytelling has replaced traditional oral folk culture in the sense that it now conveys the shared traditions of a people who read rather than share spoken stories. The function remains the same—bringing people into the warm circle of the communal hearth.

Theorist Leo Braudy has noted that genre should be understood to function in the same way for the popular arts that tradition has for the classical arts. Formulaic genre stories can, in fact, be perceived as necessary constraints for the artist, lest the function and purpose of popular storytelling be forgotten. One of the truly useful lines in contemporary American film occurs when Dirty Harry near the end of *Magnum Force* says to the antagonist: "A man has got to know his limitations." And why? So they can be acknowledged and exceeded. Only then can the popular storyteller lead the audience forward to new understandings and appreciations of the human struggle.

This then is an attempt to describe and define the popular storytelling process which because it serves a bardic function in contemporary society has endeared itself to many millions of readers. The relationship between the writer and the reader is a sacred one, for it involves the soul as much as the emotions or the intellect. That the process engage the intellect and the emotions is important; but that the process move people from a state of relative isolation into the larger community of human concern and understanding is more important. The popular storyteller has been embraced by everyone but the literary critics, who have consistently failed to understand the popular storytelling process and its functions in society. Lavishing praise on highly stylized narratives with little story content, these same critics have long since moved away from the warmth of the communal hearth and into the solitary forests beyond where shadows are often mistaken for life-forms. Meanwhile, people are learning, loving, and laughing as the wordsmith works the magic of the popular story.

Author's Note: I would like to thank the several enlightened theorists who have directly or indirectly influenced my own thinking on the popular storytelling process. I would also like to thank Madonna Coughlin Marsden, my wife, for sharing her insights into popular storytelling with me over the years.

6

ROLAND E. MURPHY, O. Carm.

The Symbolism of the Song of Songs

$\mathcal{S}$ymbolism, and not least of all sexual symbolism, has played a large role in the writings of the man this *Festschrift* honors. Hence it is appropriate to explore, however briefly, the symbolism of the Song of Songs. We will proceed by examining certain individual symbols within the Song, and finally the symbolism of the book as a whole.[1]

1. SYMBOLS WITHIN THE SONG

It would be difficult and perhaps unnecessary to attempt to classify the individual symbols. The most prominent category is the *wasf*, or description of the physical charms of the beloved, in which various parts of the body are singled out and praised. Much more resistant to classification is the atmosphere that the language exudes by the use of the names of animals, flowers, places, etc.

The initial reaction to the *wasf* is sheer puzzlement in many cases. How can the hair of the woman be compared to "a flock of goats that stream down Mount Gilead" (4:1; 6:5)? And her neck is "like David's tower, built

Reprinted, with minor revisions, from *The Incarnate Imagination: Essays in Theology, the Arts and Social Sciences in Honor of Andrew Greeley. A Festschrift*, edited by Ingrid H. Shafer (Bowling Green, Ohio: Bowling Green State University Popular Press, 1987), 229–34.

in rows; a thousand shields hang upon it, all the weapons of warriors" (4:4), and also "like a tower of ivory" (7:5). Her nose "is like the tower of Lebanon looking toward Damascus" (7:5). Finally, she states, "I am a wall, and my breasts like towers" (8:10).

These apparently extravagant metaphors have proved enigmatic to scholars as well as to the average reader. One solution has been to deny the representational quality and to regard them as merely evocative of a sensation. R. Soulen has argued that such images convey the delight of the beholder, without intending any comparison.[2] But this view is hardly adequate. There seems to be clear representational intent in such metaphors as the image of a scarlet thread for the mouth (4:3), or "two fawns, the twins of a gazelle" for the breasts (4:5, 7:4). Even though the precise representational is difficult to pin down, the metaphors are more than merely evocative of a subjective feeling. The problem is to capture the nuance of the symbol, if at all possible.

One scholar suggests that we should recognize the incongruities and tensions that exist in metaphorical language. Michael Fox writes that "a metaphor depends for its meaning—its full contextual meaning with its new and unparaphrasable connotations—not only on the extent of the common ground but also on the 'metaphoric distance' between image and referent: that is, the degree of unexpectedness or incongruity between the juxtaposed elements and the magnitude of the dissonance it produces."[3] This is a delicate judgment. Metaphoric distance can be stimulating, but if the distance becomes too great (Fox instances the absurdity of "your teeth are like leafy boughs"—of course this does not occur in the Song), the impact of the metaphor can be lost.

While "metaphoric distance" has a certain validity, one may also ask if the distance between image and referent is due more to our inability to understand the world view of the ancient writer. In this respect the iconographic studies of O. Keel have been fruitful.[4] He starts with the premise that dynamics, not form, are the prominent feature of the ancient biblical symbol. That is to say, the point of the comparison lies not in form or shape so much as in the function and power of the symbol. For example, there is the well-known biblical idiom in which 'ap ("nose") symbolizes anger; 'ayin ("eye") has to do with a glance (cf. 5:9), rather than the shape of the physical organ. Keel goes on to discuss the difficult symbols which have already been mentioned. Thus, with respect to the comparison to a tower, he asks, what is its function? It suggests protection, due to its firmness, height, and inaccessibility. It is not surprising then that these aspects of the woman be celebrated by this metaphor. Iconography of the ancient Near East sheds light on the "shields" (4:4), for there are representations of women with necklaces in the form of rows of beads, suggesting a certain majesty and pride. Women are also depicted with a diadem in the form of a wall with towers. Hence to compare the neck to David's tower is to suggest the pride and majesty of the woman, who is also as inaccessible as David's tower.

In 4:8 the man invites his beloved,

> *With me from Lebanon, O bride,*
> *with me from Lebanon shall you come!*
> *Come down from the top of Amanah,*
> *from the top of Senir and Hermon,*
> *From dens of lions,*
> *from ramparts of leopards.*

In context he has just finished a description of her physical charms, and now he appears to be addressing her as if she were in some mountain fastness (cf. also 2:14) surrounded by wild animals. What does this picture suggest? Keel illustrates it with ancient art that portrays goddesses enthroned on mountains with lions and other types of animals. Again, the effect is to underscore the inaccessible character of the woman.

A common comparison in the Song, and apparently the simplest, is the association of eyes with doves (in the case of the woman, 1:15, 4:1; and of the man, 5:12). Interpreters have gone in several different directions with this comparison, mainly in terms of shape and color. However, Keel has recourse to the dynamic use of "eye" as in Proverbs 23:31, where the "eye" of the wine refers to its sparkle, or in Ezekiel 1:7, where the "eye" of bronze represents its gleam or luster. Hence the reference is rather to the glance than to the physical organ of the eye. What is the point scored by the mention of doves? Keel points out that in the ancient Levant the white dove is associated with the goddess of love as a love messenger. Hence he paraphrases "your eyes are doves" as "your glances are messengers of love."

The speed with which the lover comes to the beloved seems to be the reason why she compares him to "a gazelle or a young stag" in 2:8–9, and in an inclusio at the end of the reminiscence in 2:8–17 she invites him to be "like a gazelle or a young stag upon the mountains of Bether," a reference that can mean only her own person, just as in 8:14 she invites him to be "like a gazelle or a young stag upon the mountains of spices," that is, herself. The metaphor has moved from the speed of the animal to its roaming in favorite haunts.

Some metaphors deserve delicate treatment, such as the comparison of female breasts to "two fawns, twins of a gazelle, browsing among the lilies" (4:5; in 7:4 the browsing is omitted). The reader can be spared the odd interpretations that have accumulated over the centuries. Even in recent times there have been clumsy references by insensitive commentators (e.g., the breasts compared to a static vision of the backsides of fawns nuzzling among flowers). M. Pope thinks that "the youth of the fawns bespeak the youthful freshness and small size of the mammary orbs." But he interprets the woman's words in 8:10 as referring to her "towering *mammae*."[5] It is a mistake to take size as the key to the passage. More imaginatively, Keel suggests that the playful motion and mobility of the breasts are suggested by the grace of these animals. He has also pointed out the association of gazelles and goats with the lotus (the "lilies" in the Song of Songs) in Egypt and Palestine.

If there is a climax in the Song, it may be seen in the superlative lines of 8:6,

> *Place me as a seal on your heart,*
> *as a seal on your arm.*
> *Strong as Death is love,*
> *intense as Sheol is ardor;*
> *Its shafts are shafts of fire,*
> *a flame of Yah.*

This is obviously intended as a compliment to love, but what is the point of the comparison of love/ardor to Death/Sheol? The Hebrew understanding of Death and the netherworld supplies the answer. Israel's understanding of Death was influenced by the Ugaritic deity Mot (=Death). Although Death was not divine for the Israelite, it was felt to be a dynamic, not a static power. It was pictured as pursuing a human being through life. Its presence was particularly felt when any degree of nonlife (pain, distress, hostility, etc.) afflicted a person. Thus the psalmist cries out in gratitude to the Lord, "You brought me up from Sheol" (Psalm 30:4). Metaphorically, the psalmist was in the grip of the power of Death, but now he experiences restoration (not resuscitation). And Sheol/Death is the great enemy who will eventually claim one's life. But love, too, can make its own claims.

2. THE SONG AS SYMBOL

What is the symbolism of a love poem? By itself does love poetry mean more than its fruity lines, and express an idea or vision that transcends itself? I think that a case can be made that the love poetry of Israel aspires to more than it directly says. Expressions of love can be merely self-centered, but at their best they express some degree of commitment and mutuality, as the Song certainly does. The role of the self is inescapable, but it is redeemed by concentration on the beloved. And here what is left unsaid or even unfathomed is part of the outreach of the poem itself. The beloved does not hear or read love poetry as though it were an encyclopedia. The experience of being in love is the atmosphere of the poem. In the case of the Song one might claim that there is nothing unusual in its celebration of human love. But the history of the interpretation of the Song suggests that in itself this love poem is a symbol of another love.

The striking fact is that the two communities of faith that preserved and read the Song understood it on a level different from human sexual love. Centuries of Jewish and Christian tradition have rarely given such an example of a unified understanding of a book of the Hebrew Bible. Both traditions, as far back as evidence will lead us, interpreted the Song as dealing with God and God's People. Divine/human love, not human sexual love, is the referent of the Song. Of course, significant variations immediately occur. In the Jewish tradition the Song reflects the tortuous but blessed relationship between God and Israel (in the Targum, from the Exodus to the messianic eschaton). In Christian tradition the Song was understood in the light of Christ and the Church, God and the individual soul. It was Origen (d. *ca.* 253) who was the lodestar for Christian interpreters. A genre of spiritual/mystical commentary was born and nourished, especially in the monasteries. It has been noted that in the twelfth century some thirty commentaries on the Song appeared—more than for any other biblical book. The trend came to a climax in the eighty-six "sermons" which Bernard of Clairvaux wrote for his Cistercian brothers—and he never got beyond the first two chapters! The influence of this heritage can be seen in the famous "Cántico Espiritual" of San Juan de la Cruz, and in recent times in the writings of Paul Claudel.[6]

Is all this tradition just a brilliant mistake? One can point out at least two reasons that justify the traditional interpretation as a valid meaning. The first is the bold fact that Israel made human love the symbol of the mutual love of her Lord and herself. One need only recall Hosea 1–3, and this theme appears consistently in other prophets (Isa. 1:21; Jer. 3:1, etc.). True, it occurs more often in the context of Israel's infidelity. But the ideal remained, as Isa. 62:5 testifies:

> *As a young man marries a virgin,*
> *your Builder shall marry you;*
> *And as a bridegroom rejoices in his bride*
> *so shall your God rejoice in you.*

The covenant formula, "you shall be my people and I shall be your God," was understood as more than a binding legal agreement. It was a marriage. As Deuteronomy put it, "It was not because you are the largest of all nations that the Lord set his heart on you and chose you, for you are really the smallest of all nations. It was because the Lord loved you . . ." (7:7–8). Hence the protestation in the Song was heard by Israel and eventually by the Church on a deeper level: "My lover belongs to me and I to him" (2:16, 6:3, 7:11).

Perhaps a serious reservation about the traditional meaning as it developed in the communities of faith should be expressed here. The allegorical method of interpreting the text is not essential for the validity of the traditional meaning. Symbolism is involved in the allegorical process, but unless a poem is written precisely in the allegorical mode (as, for example, Ezek. 17; Eccles. 12:2–6), allegorical method is subject to arbitrary *ad hoc* interpretations that detract from the vitality of the traditional meaning.

The second reason in favor of the traditional interpretation is a hint contained within the Song itself in 8:6, where the shafts of love (already compared for its power to Death/Sheol, as seen above) are described as "fiery shafts, a flame of Yah." It is grammatically justifiable to translate the Hebrew *šalhebetyah* (literally, "Yah[weh] flame") as "a most vehement flame" (so the RSV, and similarly many other translations, such as the New Jewish Version). In this case, the short form of the divine name, *yah*, is taken as a kind of superlative (divine, mighty, etc.). But a literal translation is "flame of Yah," rendered emphatically in the New Jerusalem Bible as "a flame of Yahweh himself." It is frequently said that the divine name is absent from the Bible only in the books of Esther and the Song of Songs; much depends on the rendering of 8:6.

If one adopts this possible translation, there is a clear affirmation that sexual love as described in the Song is somehow associated with the Lord. That association is left unspecified, but it should not go unmentioned. It is part of the symbolism of human love. Human love suggests an outreach to (an origin from, or a participation in?) the God who is described as love (1 John 4:8).

The validity of the traditional meaning is to be affirmed on the basis of the symbolism of human love. A misfortune of history has been the fact that the traditional meaning was allowed to snuff out the literal historical meaning which expressed love between the sexes. The Christian attitude to sex suffered from this impoverishment. It should not have been so, and it remains for the communities of faith which accept the Song as canonical to nourish themselves in the inner symbolism of human love which the poetry breathes, as well as the outreach to the divine which it provides.

In his exciting study of Mesopotamian religion Thorkild Jacobsen singled out central religious metaphors which he detected in the culture. Among them is a view of the gods as parents, and also as providers. Analogously, we want to claim that one religious metaphor in Israel is God as lover. This is unmistakably shown in the prophetic writings, and it is rooted in the Song of Songs as well. As Jacobsen remarks, "a religious metaphor is not truly understood until it is experienced as a means of suggesting the Numinous."[7]

NOTES

1. This is not the place to expand on a philosophy of symbolism. The prejudices of the writer will doubtless be apparent to the reader, who may

be referred to the helpful treatment of Avery Dulles in *Models of Revelation* (Doubleday, 1983), especially 131–54.

2. R. Soulen, "The Wasfs of the Song of Songs and Hermeneutic," *Journal of Biblical Literature* 96 (1967): 183–90.

3. M. Fox, *The Song of Songs and the Ancient Egyptian Love Songs* (University of Wisconsin Press, 1985), 276.

4. O. Keel, *Deine Blicke sind Tauben. Zur Metaphorik des Hohen Liedes* (Stuttgarter Bibelstudien 114/115; Katholisches Bibelwerk, 1984).

5. M. Pope, *Song of Songs* (Anchor Bible 7C; Doubleday, 1977), 470; 683.

6. The works of Origen, Saint Bernard, and Saint John of the Cross are easily available in translation. For Claudel, see his *Paul Claudel interroge le Cantique des cantiques* (Paris, 1948).

7. T. Jacobsen, *The Treasures of Darkness* (Yale University Press, 1976), especially 3–5, 20–21; the quotation is from p. 5. In the case of Mesopotamia one is of course working with another set of symbols; Israel worshipped a lover, but not a fertility god.

7

DAVID TRACY

Theology and the Symbolic Imagination: A Tribute to Andrew Greeley

*I*n the course of his remarkable intellectual career, Andrew Greeley has illuminated the pervasiveness of symbols in our social and personal, our secular and religious lives. As one who shares that belief, I will use the welcome occasion of this *Festschrift* to reflect on the reality and permanence of symbol in theology.

Indeed, a distinguishing characteristic of the contemporary period in religious studies and theology is the continuing recovery of the symbolic imagination. As represented, for example, by those several theologies which employ story, metaphor, image, symbol, myth, and ritual as their central categories, the emergence of the centrality of the imagination for the study of religion, and thereby of fundamentally aesthetic criteria[1] for interpreting and appropriating the symbolic possibilities of our several religious traditions, seems a legitimate inference. Sometimes this concern is articulated by the imaginative genius of a genuine storyteller with a theological bent as with Elie Wiesel or Walker Percy or John Updike or Andrew Greeley or by artists of drama, dance, music who employ their art forms in strikingly contemporary—that is, both aesthetically satisfying and religiously compelling—forms of worship. More often constructive theologians are concerned

An earlier version of this essay appeared in *The Incarnate Imagination: Essays in Theology, the Arts and Social Sciences in Honor of Andrew Greeley. A Festschrift*, edited by Ingrid H. Shafer (Bowling Green, Ohio: Bowling Green State University Popular Press, 1987), 235-55.

not to develop new rituals and symbols, but to appropriate an analysis of symbol and imagination into more familiar forms of theological argument. In brief, basically theological-aesthetic criteria have joined more familiar philosophical, ethical, and historical criteria as relevant to the theologian's task.

Amidst the conflict of interpretations on the exact meaning of symbol, theologians from several traditions now unite to urge a critical reappropriation of the enriching possibilities for our present situation provided by the central stories, myths, symbols, and rituals of our Western religious traditions. There is every reason for all those in the liberal traditions in theology to affirm and to aid this new resource. Indeed, there seem good reasons to believe that only those theologians formed by both a religious and an aesthetic sensibility and by a critical attitude in theology can achieve the kind of aesthetic and religious "second naiveté"[2] toward the symbolic resources of the religious traditions which these sometimes rather disparate theologies of symbol and these new attempts at worship really represent. To be sure, it does seem to be the case that we now live in what has often been named a postmodern period of life and reflection.[3] Yet another truism also remains the case: postmodern need not mean a retreat to that kind of obscurantism which masks an intellectual failure of nerve reveling in the present, real dilemmas of liberalism and sometimes meretriciously wishing to impose a merely conservative first naiveté on our present situation. Rather for those who have truly appropriated the modern, critical tradition, the term "postmodern" implies that the modern tradition should remain firm in its basic belief in the need for continued critical fidelity to the best of both contemporary experience and the tradition. Only such firmness will assure the success of a move forward into a situation wherein the richness of the tradition, including its forms of worship, can now be restructured and reappropriated by a fuller and critical concentration upon the emancipatory possibilities of the major symbolic expressions of the religious imagination encapsuled in the images of its communal life, in the metaphors, stories, and myths of its writings, in the rituals of its forms of worship, in the analogies of its theologies.[4] Yet that very reappropriation of the symbolic imagination, I believe, will probably prove fruitful only in the context of the continuing critical reexamination of the modern heritage, namely, tradition and critique.

CONTEXT OF THE DISCUSSION: TRADITION AND CRITIQUE

As Hans-Georg Gadamer, perhaps more than any other modern thinker, has insisted, the concept "tradition," so suspect by Enlightenment thinkers, may bear a fully positive meaning (235–74). To be sure, the merely authoritarian concept of the tradition was correctly challenged by Enlightenment thinkers in favor of a model of critical autonomy. That latter

model, incorporated both personally and communally in the various reformed and modern traditions in contemporary religious life, has surely
proved one of the important and, one hopes, enduring characteristics of the
modern period.[5] Unhappily, as Gadamer persuasively argues in philosophical terms, this modern achievement often became the occasion for a
dangerously naive rejection of the very realities of tradition and thereby
tradition itself. Naive, because we can deny in theory but cannot really
reject in fact the radical historicity of our social selves. Dangerously naive,
because by their own partial failures at appropriation of symbolic reality,
many liberals in effect handed over the authentic symbolic resources of the
tradition to those least able to appreciate them: those once embattled but
now reinvigorated opponents of modernity in every tradition—those Pope
John XXIII labeled the dark prophets of gloom in our culture; those whose
voice—if not whose arguments— so pervade our present moment in history.

Neither a romantic—today we say nostalgic—explosion of praise for the
tradition nor a merely hostile hermeneutics of suspicion upon the very
concepts and reality of tradition and its central component, the symbolic
imagination, seems an appropriate response to the present situation.[6] Indeed, the vanishing art of the old scholastic distinction seems in order here.
If one means by tradition simply to accept without question the *tradita* (i.e.,
the handed-down and unexamined conclusions of any intellectual or religious heritage), then, with our Enlightenment forebears, one must, in
conscience, simply say *nego*. If, however, one really means tradition as
traditio (i.e., the living, liberating, and resourceful modes of inquiry,
sensibility, and imagination of any intellectual or religious heritage), then
every critical inquirer can applaud the continuing fruitfulness of critical
inquiry and retrieval of all the major traditions, rituals, and symbols of our
tradition.[7]

Precisely this postmodern concept of tradition as *traditio* seems the
driving intellectual force behind the contemporary theological reexamination of the resources of the several possible modes-of-being-in-the-world
disclosed by such expressions of the traditional religious imagination as
story, symbol, myth, ritual, metaphor, and analogy. Yet the question recurs:
how can one assure that even this notion of tradition does not become the
occasion to disown the needs for critical inquiry into all claims to truth, to
disclosure, to emancipation; does not, for example, simply become the
occasion to insist upon worship services as mere repetition, untouched by
contemporary concerns for authentic reappropriation: for a second, not a
lost first naiveté? In the midst of a revival of interest in symbolic forms,
how can one avoid the kind of historical romanticism that has clouded many
a liturgical renewal?[8] How can one assure that spirit of the examined
life—including our lives at worship—which still defines the genuinely
emancipatory character of the reformed liberal religious and theological
traditions?

In one sense, of course, the question is a self-answering one. For insofar as one really means tradition as *traditio*, not *tradita*, one affirms the route taken by so many in our period: a return to symbol, but *only* by means of the mediation of critical inquiry; a continued recognition, for example, that a first naiveté in worship seems forever lost to us; a continued search to see whether a second naiveté is indeed an authentic possibility, not a strategy of desperation. Only a genuinely critical attitude, I suggest, now directed to aesthetic and religious criteria for assuring a second naiveté will allow that possibility. For only a continued fidelity to critical inquiry seems to allow an ethical way of retrieving the enriching disclosures upon our common lives of traditional expressions and rituals of the religious imagination. As a consequence, far more than was previously the case, most modern theologians now seem more willing to admit that tradition and symbol, like their ethical correlates loyalty, fidelity, patriotism, are too rich in reality, too disclosive in possibility, to be handed over to the purveyors of sterile condemnations of modern innovation and autonomy.

In another sense, the question of a proper attitude to a revival of interest in symbol is not self-answering at all. For the postmodern theologian is faced with the further and familiar dilemma that the Enlightenment notion of critical reason, once so liberating, now seems too often in practice a narrowing of possibilities. Rather the contemporary situation, as those revisionist Marxists known as the Frankfurt School among others have argued,[9] now seems one where reason itself may too often become merely technical reason; where the finest expression of autonomous human inquiry, scientific reason, can result in the mere fetish of scientism and expertise; where concepts too often seem not to bear the emancipatory power of truly critical reason. More to our present point, as Ernst Bloch observes, a merely technical reason can misunderstand itself as critical reason and thereby disallow symbol and ritual imagination and emancipating possibilities. A merely technical reason can reify reality and serve merely to legitimate the prevailing status quo. It can disown the symbolic needs of the human spirit and domesticate aesthetic and religious sensibilities into a kind of global ritualistic Muzak. Too often even avant-garde art no longer seems to serve a genuinely communal function, but rather can retreat into self-imposed "reservations" of the spirit where one is momentarily freed from the wider technocratic culture.[10] In that context, how can we continue to hope that the modern genius at critique may not impede rather than enhance the disclosive and emancipatory powers of these retrieved symbolic forms? How can we continue to hope that the very power of authentic critique released by liberalism does not become captive to an *ethos* of technocracy?

This is, of course, a familiar charge laid at modernity's door: most often by such conservative critics of the modern experiment as Russell Kirk and Michael Oakeshott, or on the question of religion by the latter stages of several new theological formulations of "postliberal" theologies.[11] What is of greater interest to those who fundamentally affirm the modern experiment of commitment to full-scale critique and emancipation, however, is not so much the familiar cannon blasts from the right (although they too have hit many a target) as the more nuanced and ultimately more serious attacks from one's natural allies on the left.

For example, the Marxist social theorist Jürgen Habermas argues that our present societal situation is one where modernity's possibilities for critique are severely limited by a situation he describes as one of systematically distorted communication on every level of our complex culture—the political, economic, social, cultural, and intersubjective.[12] In such a situation it seems clear that conservative critics of the culture, whatever their other difficulties, are naive to hope that classical hermeneutical reflection upon the remaining and fragmented symbolic resources of the tradition will suffice. The more important question for us is how a liberal critique can best function in that kind of situation.[13] If the problem is really no longer one of mere social error but of far more radical societal illusion, our approach to religious questions can be neither merely a conservative return to symbol nor even such classic liberal strategies as the critical exposure of traditional errors with very little effort toward a constructive reappropriation of symbolic resources. Rather we need theories, practices, and symbols which, precisely by their fidelity to the critical spirit of modernity, can develop contemporary symbolic forms to help unmask the distortions and illusions of our societal lives in the same manner as the theories, practices, and symbolic systems of psychoanalysis provide an opportunity to unmask systematic distortions on an individual level. More specifically—and in more Anglo-American language—we need more, not less, commitment by the entire community of inquirers into religion on the need for publicly available discourse, for argument—criteria, evidence, warrants, backing; for the increasingly sophisticated recognition of context-variant standards for so wide-ranging a subject matter as religion and so field-encompassing a discipline as theology.[14]

For our present question on the revival of the symbolic imagination, I suggest, this situation implies that we need to concentrate more attention on unpacking the claims to existential significance and disclosive truth of the symbolic resources of our heritage. In that manner, the modern theological tradition would develop its fidelity to critical reason and argument in a direction where explicitly aesthetic and religious criteria could be more publically addressed. The critical resources of the modern tradition would direct their attention to the revival of interest in the symbolic imagination in such manner that the creative but not merely private resources of art and religion could be brought into the public light of critical reason and re-appropriated for public disclosive and emancipatory use. As a single and limited example of that possibility, I will turn to an exposure of the kind of analysis and resources presently available for that task.

THE SYMBOLIC IMAGINATION:
METAPHOR, ANALOGY, RITUAL

In the context of affirmation of both tradition and critique, a plea for the relevance of the symbolic imagination may take a general or a more specific form. When contemporary philosophers and theologians approach the reality of *traditio* through the resource of the symbolic imagination, they are wont to appeal to the central category of possibility. More exactly, these thinkers no longer approach the reality of imagination in its classical philosophical form as merely another faculty of human knowing.[15] Indeed several contemporary philosophical and theological positions now approach the reality of the imagination as a central reality in all religious discourse and action. Moreover, the power of the creative imagination can now be understood not in merely general terms, but in a context where a wealth of scholarly studies from several disciplines can actually provide the retrieved symbolic material needed: the actual nonlinguistic images and rituals used in worship, the linguistic metaphors, stories, and myths of religious language, the models and analogies of theology.[16] Whenever a particular image, ritual, metaphor, myth, or analogy discloses some *permanent* possibility for the human spirit, it may bear the distinctive title "symbol." Symbol, therefore, has become the generic name for all those permanent imaginative possibilities for our common humanity disclosed in the reigning images, rituals, metaphors, myths, and analogies of our several traditions.[17] The appeal of symbols, to be sure, is an appeal fundamentally to the imagination and thereby to a redescription of possibility.[18] More specifically, symbols appeal to those kinds of imaginative redescriptions of human possibility which critical reason can illuminate by aesthetic analysis and can learn to discriminate through the development of explicitly aesthetic criteria analogous to those criteria already developed by classical liberalism in the metaphysical, ethical, and empirical realms.[19]

In Paul Ricoeur's well-known slogan to describe this situation, "The symbol gives rise to thought, but thought always returns to and is informed by symbol" (*Symbolism of Evil* 347–57). This slogan, as too many of its admirers fail to note, does not simply give a *carte blanche* to the symbolic imagination; it insists that our best critical reason *must* be employed on all our symbols (the symbol gives rise to the thought), before suggesting that through such critical mediation, thought returns again to symbol. On the further side of demythologizing, we still find a disclosive and imaginative power to the Adamic myth over the Orphic and cosmogonic myths (330–47). After the best historical-critical analysis of the central events and images of the tradition, we do seem to rediscover the still emancipatory force of the Exodus symbol.[20] After all the surely necessary critical restructuring of traditional forms of worship, we find that many traditional words and rituals bespeak transformative possibilities for our everyday lives.[21] After the most rigorous contemporary philosophical and theological critiques of the inherent difficulties in the conceptual analogies developed by a Maimonides, an Aquinas, a Calvin, we still find that these great symbolic-as-analogical visions of our theological traditions continue to disclose an imagined vision of human life as a whole which we ignore at the unwelcome price of self-impoverishment.

I will now risk showing how this new possibility may occur rather than simply stating that it does. I shall do so by appealing to an initially unlikely candidate for the symbolic imagination, the symbolic-as-analogical vision of Thomas Aquinas.[22] By concentrating the analysis on one acknowledged Western classic of theological language, I also hope to encourage similar studies now occurring on the analogical language of a Maimonides or a Calvin. Although I have, in fact, made forays into the analogical language of the latter two theological giants, I will concentrate my own efforts here on trying to recover the imaginative possibilities present in the analogical language of Aquinas. That attempt, I trust, will prove resonant to those familiar with the better known studies of such symbolic forms as image, ritual, and myth. At any rate, the choice of Aquinas' analogical language should have the advantage of suggesting the kind of aesthetic and religious criteria relevant to any study of any rendering of the symbolic imagination, even one as highly conceptual as that of Aquinas.

The key to understanding the recent modern Catholic reappropriation of Aquinas by means of symbol and the imagination is to note that the study assumes earlier and more standard philosophical analysis and criteria (especially metaphysical and ethical criteria) and then turns to specifically aesthetic and religious criteria to analyze the symbolic dimensions of the analogical language of Thomas as disclosive of certain possible modes-of-being-in-the-world.

It is important to note, however, that this present example of analogy in Thomas is confined to theological language. I understand that language to be a second-order, reflective language which claims fidelity to the originating religious languages of image, metaphor, symbol, myth, and ritual. Although much reflection has recently been devoted to analyzing those originating religious languages—for Catholicism ordinarily under the rubrics of the Catholic use of image, ritual, and sacrament in worship—very little work seems addressed to explicating the symbolic form of life disclosed in that properly theological language of analogy, so widely used by Catholic theologians and employed in Catholic creedal statements and worship services. Yet I have come to believe that even this highly conceptual language of Thomist analogy[23] may also profitably be studied by uncover a symbolic dimension which discloses certain possible modes-of-being-in-the-world, certain symbolic forms of life, certain distinctive projects for the imagination.

In order not to assume that everyone may prove as interested in Aquinas' use of analogical language as I am myself, however, I will discuss his usage by paralleling it to the more familiar work on that classical aesthetic figure of speech, the metaphor.[24] By that parallelism procedure, I hope to be able to suggest what kind of aesthetic and religious criteria can in fact be developed by theologians in any tradition to illuminate the symbolic resources of that tradition.

In fact, a partial consensus seems to have emerged in recent studies of symbols.[25] A major part of that consensus can be delineated by noting three characteristics of the religious use of that primary kind of symbolic language we name a metaphor so dominant in both ritual and scripture. The first characteristic is a negative one: the traditional assumption (often shared by conservatives and liberals alike) that metaphors are merely rhetorical devices in the sense of decorative substitutions for the true-as-literal meaning has been effectively challenged by much recent linguistic and aesthetic study. On the question of the logic of the "Kingdom of God" language in the New Testament parables, for example, the implications of this criterion have challenged both traditional (usually allegorical) and earlier liberal (often purely ethical) interpretations of the central Christian language forms of parables for a new generation of New Testament scholars.[26] The recognition of this peculiar aesthetic phenomenon of a more than literal meaning in metaphor suggests, therefore, the presence of a first aesthetic criterion: the nonreducibility of any truly symbolic reality, whether linguistic, as in metaphor, or nonlinguistic, as in ritual, to merely literal meanings.

The second characteristic is a more positive one: whatever theory of the logic of metaphor is employed by its various proponents, the analyst will still note that a new meaning, not expressible without loss in literal terms, emerges from the very interaction of words not ordinarily—that is, in terms of their "literal" meanings—used conjunctively. Good metaphorical usage, as Aristotle observed, cannot be learned by formulating rules: the capacity to recognize similarity in dissimilarity is a mark of poetic genius. Good ritual, we might add, demands the same power of aesthetic and religious discrimination. As new emergent meanings explode in a culture's consciousness, the older and spent ones become merely dead metaphors and thereby enter our dictionaries. As we learn to hear in a more discriminating fashion the emergent meanings in any truly symbolic expression, whether metaphor, ritual, or analogy, we find a second aesthetic criterion for symbols: the presence of the peculiar logic of a nonreducible emergent meaning achieved through the interaction of literal words and actions whose conjunction is unlikely. This criterion may serve as the central positive clue to noting good aesthetic usage of metaphor and ritual.

The third characteristic is, from the viewpoint of the symbolic dimension of both theological language and religious action, the most important one. Since I have tried to defend this conclusion at length elsewhere (*Blessed Rage for Order*, especially 91–146), here I will simply state it. The conclusion can be variously formulated. In its more familiar form in contemporary linguistic philosophy of religion, one may recall Ian Ramsey's attempt to show what he nicely called the "odd logic" of religious language.[27] In its less familiar but, for my part, more adequate formulation, one may cite the theory of Paul Ricoeur that the specificity of religious language lies in its character as a symbolic limit-language ("Specificity" 107–45). Alternatively, if I may presume to cite it, one may note my own attempted development of that limit-language tradition which suggests that careful attention to any explicitly religious use of symbolic forms shows the presence of two languages at work: a language expressive of a "limit-to" our ordinary language and experience; and a second limit language which, precisely by stating that limit-to, is also able to disclose or show a "limit-of" language— that is, a language which projects some aesthetically satisfying and religiously compelling vision of an imagined possibility for human life as a whole. More summarily, a genuinely religious use of any symbolic form seems to involve a limit-character wherein precisely by *stating* a limit-to the ordinary use of the language, there is also *shown* and *partly stated* a symbolic language expressive of an imagined limit-of possibility, some vision expressing a final meaningfulness to human life in relationship to the whole. An explicitly religious use, as limit-use, of symbolic forms, therefore, seems to serve as a third criterion to add to the two aesthetic criteria already advanced for appropriate theological discrimination.[28]

It is of some interest to note, moreover, that these same three criteria seem relevant to analyzing the symbolic dimension of the more conceptual and reflective language of theology itself. Allow me to return, therefore, to the question of Thomas Aquinas' actual use of analogical language with these same three criteria in mind.

In relationship to the first criterion, one may note that the same kind of initial move of negation is made by several contemporary linguistic inter- preters of Thomas. Indeed, the most important criticism of the older Thomist tradition is not really that on most theological issues their position proved too often antimodern, but that the classical modern Thomists failed to understand Aquinas' own highly pluralistic uses of analogical language in their own narrowly scholastic attempt to systematize a single Thomist doctrine of analogy.[29] That latter and almost canonical doctrine ended, ironically, in disclosing some form of a Scotist univocal language of "common being" to "bolster" what seems to be the too elusive, too pluralistic, and even too symbolic use of analogical language by Thomas himself. Just as religious metaphors were once considered mere substitutions for literal meanings, so theological analogies—now implicitly rather than explicitly— were robbed of their symbolic function and considered substitutions for the real—the univocal—meaning. The first criterion, which negates mere literal substitution language, thereby seems to hold even for the highly conceptual language of Aquinas.

The second and more positive point of these theological studies of Thomas' analogical language parallels the second criterion, namely, the "emergent meaning through interaction" theory of metaphor. For good analogies, like good metaphors and good rituals, depend on the capacity to recognize what Aristotle called similarity-in-dissimilarity. This capacity, so natural to the natively symbolic mind, allows us to break out of accustomed and deceptively univocal usage to describe either the unfamiliar or a forgotten dimension of the familiar. More specifically, analogical usage in both Aristotle and Aquinas is fundamentally a matter of good usage of "focal meanings"—ordinary meanings expressive of human purpose and possibility—which provide a primary focus of meaning that is then proportionally employed in properly symbolic fashion for more extended usage.[30] In sum, the emergent meanings of analogous terms are not substitutions for a real—a univocal—meaning. Rather they are good language usage, which, precisely as symbolic, relates all other uses to the focal meaning of the hopes, purposes, strivings, and imagined possibilities of the human being.

The third criterion likewise is relevant. For the final clue to the proper use of analogical and symbolic language in Thomas may be found in noting how he, too, uses limit-language, now for strictly conceptual and reflective purposes. Recall, for example, that familiar analogical language of "perfection terms" used by Aquinas to speak of God. The logic of perfection, as Aquinas knew, is an "odd," even a "limit" logic precisely as involved in the logical differences of all—some—or—none. Metaphysical criteria are thereby not merely relevant but necessary to adjudicating Aquinas' truth claims. At the same time, the religious as limit-character of that very use of analogical language in theology should also turn an analyst's attention to the kind of focal meanings employed for these "perfection-terms." For the final symbolic focal meaning of those odd perfection-terms used for Thomist God-language may be found in the philosophical anthropology, the symbolic self-understanding of human possibility—its purposes, hopes, and desires—present in any particular religious and aesthetic tradition.[31]

Even in the highly conceptual language of Thomist analogy, therefore, a vision of properly theological speech for God-language is articulated which begins by a choice of aesthetic and religious criteria to describe human possibility as a focal meaning and ends in limit-language declarations, as Karl Rahner showed, of the disclosure of the radical mystery and intrinsic incomprehensibility of human existence itself and of the God religiously encountered in authentic faith.[32] Yet the basic route to this theological declaration is a familiar modern one with the addition of aesthetic criteria, now added to the more familiar metaphysical and ethical criteria: a route which insists that reason can be trusted to bring one to just this point of disclosure of the symbols as relevatory of mystery and of aesthetic and religious criteria as appropriate to analyzing those symbols. This theological route also insists that even the reflective language of theology—if properly analogical language—can, by its fidelity to the logic of the symbols reflected upon, be trusted to lead the language-user to that aesthetic and religious self-discovery. Just this kind of development of aesthetic and religious criteria for the symbolic dimension of the analogical language of theology has led some contemporary Catholic theologians to an initially surprising enterprise: namely, the attempt to retrieve the embedded symbolic resources in Thomas' articulation of focal meanings disclosive of one imagined and possible way-of-being-in-the-world before God. For in its final moment, I think, any really masterful analogical vision in theology contains dimensions of the symbolic imagination well worth retrieving: dimensions which, once religiously engaged, seem to provide their proponents with a clearing, indeed what Hemingway called a clean, well-lighted place, which allows for a partial glimpse of the surrounding darkness and its possibly encompassing light.

If this example of three kinds of aesthetic and religious criteria relevant for the religious language-use of metaphor and the theological language-use of analogy is at all correct, it seems to shed some criteriological light on the wider question of all symbolic expressions. Any properly theological reflection on appropriate forms of worship and ritual, for example, will also seem to need these same kinds of aesthetic and religious criteria for its own process of discrimination: the first criterion to eliminate any temptations to literalization; the second criterion to retrieve those truly emergent meanings in the images, metaphors, myths, and rituals of the particular worship traditions; the third, religious-as-limit-language criterion to discriminate a properly religious-as-limit-use of the particular symbolic forms employed in the ritual. With the aid of those three criteria, we may then attempt to imagine the possibilities for contemporary worship services that would be both aesthetically satisfying and religiously compelling. Yet that desired possibility seems unlikely to prove other than a project for the imagination unless theologians employ their critical powers, on other than an *ad hoc* basis, to understand the still-enriching possibilities of the symbolic imagination embedded in every worship tradition by developing some such set of aesthetic and religious criteria as the three suggested here.

As the theological retrieval of the symbolic imagination continues on several fronts—on the realities of images, myths, metaphors, analogies, stories, and rituals—we may well find an increased interest among theologians for adding aesthetic criteria as a major component in the present postmodern determination of theological criteria. Indeed, such a possibility seems, to me at least, one of the most promising in the present revival of interest in the symbolic imagination and in linguistic, sociological, and anthropological studies. If that does in fact continue to occur, then the ever-delicate attempt of postmodernity to unite both critique and tradition, both emancipation and fidelity, both ritual and reflection, may find needed new ways to retrieve the symbolic resources of the tradition in a truly critical fashion.

In the meantime, some may justifiably wonder whether this kind of search for aesthetic and religious criteria can really—that is, practically—suffice. The answer, of course, is no. Any theological determination of criteria never suffices. Yet the development of criteria, however partial—as

these are—does serve by providing more appropriate modes of discrimination. The constructive theologian must usually rest content to work out a
partial criteriological contribution to the larger whole and then turn to aid
and be aided by those aesthetically and religiously creative spirits in any
community who do not work out criteria but instinctively use them. At that
point in the wider community's dialogue, the theologian finds that she/he
has made, as best as one can, the partial contribution of developing criteria
relevant to the question at issue. When asked for more specific advice, the
same theologian may well feel rather like Saul Bellow's central character in
his novel *Humboldt's Gift*, who, in the final lines of the novel, is asked just
what is the name of a certain flower spotted in the early spring: "Search
me," Bellow's protagonist says, "I'm a city boy myself. They must be
crocuses" (487).

At least that is all this "city boy" can say. It is a moment of no small
amazement that another "city boy," Andrew Greeley, has not only named
but produced crocuses. How? Search me. I'm a New York city boy myself.
It must have something to do with Chicago.

NOTES

1. The choice of the word "aesthetic" may prove confusing here. The
argument may also be described as an argument on the "logic of the
symbol." However, I have chosen to retain the adjective "aesthetic" to
highlight the function of the imagination and thereby clarify the ontological
locus of the discussion in relationship fundamentally to "the beautiful"
rather than "the good" or "the true." My hope is that precisely such a
concentration may lead to the use of "ethical" and "metaphysical" criteria as
well—but now in relationship to these earlier "aesthetic" criteria. In all
these cases, of course, the form of argumentation is philosophical. In this
specific case, to repeat, the basic argument is correctly described as
argument on the logical status of symbolic language (criteria 1 and 2) and
the logically "odd" or "limit" status of the religious use of symbolic forms
(criterion 3). The last criterion, of course, should indicate that the position
represented by this argument is not, *in principle*, open to the charge of
"reducing" religious to aesthetic experience. Whether *in fact* that occurs can
only be decided on the basis of the analysis of the argument itself.

2. The expression is Paul Ricoeur's. *Inter alia*, *The Symbolism of Evil* (New
York: Harper & Row, 1967), 352. A less evocative but perhaps more
accurate expression is a "critically mediated immediacy."

3. For my own attempt to outline the basic contours of that "postmodern"
situation, see *Plurality and Ambiguity: Hermeneutics, Religion, Hope* (San
Francisco: Harper & Row, 1987); for an alternative reading of "postliberal"
theology, see George Lindbeck, *The Nature of Doctrine: Religion and Theology
in a Postliberal Age* (Philadelphia: Westminster, 1984).

4. Throughout this essay, I am employing the term "symbol" in a generic sense expressive of *permanent* human possibilities. Symbolic expressions, therefore, may be formed in either nonlinguistic images and rituals or linguistic metaphor, stories, myths, and rituals or even linguistic but second-order reflective concepts and analogies.

5. For a good contemporary theological formulation of this insistence from an ethical perspective, see Van A. Harvey, *The Historian and the Believer: The Morality of Historical Knowledge and Christian Belief* (New York: Macmillan, 1966).

6. The dual assumption is, therefore, that the *symbolic* expressions of any particular tradition bear further analysis in the light of the possibilities for reimagining human existence they may disclose.

7. The distinction between *tradita* and *traditio* is a familiar one in Roman Catholic theology since the pioneering work on "development of doctrine" and "tradition" of John Henry Newman and Maurice Blondel. For a survey here, see James Mackey, *Modern Theology of Tradition* (New York: Herder & Herder, 1962).

8. In my own Roman Catholic tradition, the early work of Don Gueranger is the most obvious example of this liturgical romanticism.

9. *Inter alia*, see Max Horkheimer and Theodor W. Adorno, *Dialectic of Enlightenment* (New York: Herder & Herder, 1972); Herbert Marcuse, *One Dimensional Man* (Boston: Beacon, 1964). For a history of the Frankfurt School up to but not including Jürgen Habermas, cf. Martin Jay, *The Dialectical Imagination: A History of the Frankfurt School and the Institute of Social Research. 1923–1950.* (Boston: Little, Brown, 1973).

10. The problem is not stated to be technological but the *ethos* of technology as technocracy. For analyses here, see Carl Mitcham and Robert Mackey, "Bibliography of the Philosophy of Technology," *Technology and Culture* 14, no. 2 (1973), and the debate between Habermas and Luhmann in note 12.

11. The clearest example in Christian theology remains the difference between the Karl Barth of *Romans* and the "later" Barth of the *Dogmatics*.

12. Jürgen Habermas and Niklas Luhmann, *Theorie der Gesellschaft oder Sozialtechnologie?* (Frankfurt: Suhrkamp, 1970), especially 119–20. In English, cf. "On Systematically Distorted Communication" and "Toward a Theory of Communicative Competence," *Inquiry* 13 (1970): 205–18, 360–75.

13. For Habermas' latest articulation of this possibility, see *Legitimation Crisis* (Boston: Beacon, 1973).

14. Note Habermas' own appeal to the work of Stephen Toulmin (*Crisis* 107). For Toulmin's notion of discipline, see *Human Understanding*, vol. 1 (Princeton: Princeton University Press, 1972), especially 145–200, 364–412.

15. For the clearest example of this shift in the contemporary reemergence of major interest in Kant's Third Critique, see Allan Megill, *Prophets of Extremity: Nietzsche, Heidegger, Foucault, Derrida* (Berkeley: University of California Press, 1987).

16. For example, Paul Ricoeur's attempts to develop a modern philosophy of the imagination appeals not merely to the Third Critique but also to the creative work on specific religious images in several traditions in the

work of Mircea Eliade. For a clear example of Eliade's wide-ranging work here, see *Images and Symbols: Studies in Religious Symbolism* (New York: Sheed & Ward, 1969). On ritual, see also the suggestive work of Victor Turner, especially *The Ritual Process: Structure and Anti-Structure* (Chicago: Aldene, 1960).

17. I am employing here the linguistic conventions developed in the work of Paul Ricoeur.

18. On "fiction" as a redescription of possibility, see Wayne Booth, *The Rhetoric of Fiction* (Chicago: University of Chicago Press, 1961), especially 3–67.

19. See the attempt at clarification and caution in note 1. For a fuller spelling-out of this position for hermeneutical theory, see my *The Analogical Imagination* (New York: Crossroad, 1981).

20. Recall, for example, the appeal to the Exodus symbol as the primary symbol needed for a contemporary theology of liberation in Gustavo Gutierrez, *A Theology of Liberation* (Maryknoll: Orbis, 1973), 155–60. See also Michael Walzer, *Exodus and Revolution* (New York: Basic Books, 1985).

21. *Inter alia*, cf. Victor Turner's development of the notions of "liminality" and "communitas" in *The Ritual Process*, 94–131, or Mircea Eliade, *Rites and Symbols of Initiation* (New York: Harper, 1958), especially ix–xv.

22. See John Cobb and David Tracy, *Talking About God* (New York: Paulist, 1983).

23. In the terms of the internal-Thomist discussion, my emphasis on "concepts" here is not meant to encourage the "conceptualism" that has plagued many forms of neo-Thomism. For a clear criticism of that danger and an argument for "intellectualism" (i.e., insights "over" concepts in Thomas), see Bernard Lonergan, *Verbum: Word and Idea in Aquinas* (Notre Dame: University of Notre Dame Press, 1969), especially vii–xv. My own interpretation of the meaning of "concept" and "insight" in Aquinas continues to be influenced principally by Lonergan's masterful interpretation.

24. See Paul Ricoeur, *La Métaphore Vive* (Paris: Editions du Seuil, 1975), for the most constructive expression of this interpretation. My own interpretation, unless otherwise cited here, is heavily dependent upon this work.

25. For the most comprehensive survey-analysis of this emerging (if still partial) consensus, cf. *La Métaphore Vive* 87–321; in the English-speaking context, cf. the representative work of Max Black, *Models and Metaphors* (Ithaca: Cornell University Press, 1967); Frederick Ferré, "Metaphors, Models, and Religion," *Soundings* 51 (1968): 327–45; Mary Gerhart and Allan Russell, *Metaphoric Process* (Fort Worth: Texas Christian University Press, 1984).

26. For a summary-analysis of this discussion in the work of Dominic Crossman, Robert Funk, Norman Perrin, and Dan O. Via in New Testament parables, see my *Blessed Rage for Order* (New York: Seabury, 1975), 126–31.

27. See especially Ian Ramsey, *Religious Language: An Empirical Placing of Theological Phrases* (New York: Macmillan, 1963).

28. Hence, if this criterion of a "religious" of aesthetic forms holds, the position presented is not reducible to a Santayana-like identification of "religion" and "art." I regret, of course, that present legitimate limitations of

space force me to state my conclusion rather than argue it. Any reader interested in the argument proper may find it in my *Blessed Rage for Order.*

29. Amidst the vast literature in the Thomist meaning of analogy, see especially the pioneering linguistic work of David Burrell, *Analogy and Philosophical Language* (New Haven: Yale University Press, 1973). Although I reformulate his position in relationship to the present discussion, my interpretation of Thomas on analogy, unless otherwise cited here, is heavily dependent upon Burrell's work.

30. This "focal meaning" approach to analogical language is, in my judgment, the correct route to take; if taken, it challenges the Cajetan tradition of interpretation via "the analogy of proper proportionality." A modern logical defense of that latter tradition may be found in James F. Foss, "Analogy as a Rule of Meaning for Religious Language," in Anthony Kenny, ed., *Aquinas: A Collection of Critical Essays* (New York: Anchor, 1969), 54–93.

31. A critical comparison of the Thomist and process tradition on each one's respective analogical God-language, therefore, should concentrate initially on the distinct anthropologies providing the "focal meanings" for the "perfection-language" employed and then upon the question of whether the "odd logic of perfection" is adhered to. It seems incorrect for Burrell to employ a similar logical series of steps to analyze Thomist analogical God-language, only to fail to do the same for the process-analogical language of Charles Hartshorne and Schubert Ogden. Since I believe that the anthropology informing the "focal meanings" of the process tradition is more relatively adequate for contemporary self-understanding than the Thomist, and since Hartshorne clearly meets the third criterion on the "odd logic" of perfection terms (see *inter alia, Man's Vision of God and the Logic of Theism* [Chicago: Willett, Clark, 1941], this failure of Burrell's seems a central one for anyone desirous of a critical conversation between these two contemporary analogical languages. For further discussion, see my essay in the above-cited *Talking About God.*

32. Clear expression of this familiar Rahnerian theme may be found in his "The Concept of Mystery in Catholic Theology," *Theological Investigations* 4 (London: Danton, Longman and Todd, 1964), 37–77, and *Foundations of Christian Faith* (New York: Crossroad, 1978).

WORKS CITED

Bellow, Saul. *Humboldt's Gift.* New York: Viking, 1975.

Black, Max. *Models and Metaphors.* Ithaca: Cornell University Press, 1967.

Booth, Wayne. *The Rhetoric of Fiction.* Chicago: University of Chicago Press, 1961.

Burrell, David. *Analogy and Philosophical Language.* New Haven: Yale University Press, 1973.

Cobb, John, and David Tracy. *Talking About God.* New York: Paulist, 1983.

Eliade, Mircea. *Images and Symbols: Studies in Religious Symbolism.* New York: Sheed & Ward, 1969.

———. *Rites and Symbols of Initiation.* New York: Harper, 1958.

Ferré, Frederick. "Metaphors, Models, and Religion." *Soundings* 51 (1968): 327–45.

Foss, James F. "Analogy as a Rule of Meaning for Religious Language."

Gadamer, Hans-Georg. *Truth and Method*. New York: Seabury, 1975.

Gerhart, Mary, and Allan Melvin Russell. *Metaphoric Process: The Creation of Scientific and Religious Understanding*. Fort Worth: Texas Christian University Press, 1984.

Gutierrez, Gustavo. *A Theology of Liberation*. Maryknoll: Orbis, 1973.

Habermas, Jürgen. *Legitimation Crisis*. Boston: Beacon, 1973.

———, and Niklas Luhmann. *Theorie der Gesellschaft oder Sozialtechnologie?* Frankfurt: Suhrkamp, 1970.

Harvey, Van A. *The Historian and the Believer: The Morality of Historical Knowledge and Christian Belief*. New York: Macmillan, 1966.

Horkheimer, Max, and Theodor W. Adorno. *Dialectic of Enlightenment*. New York: Herder & Herder, 1972.

Jay, Martin. *The Dialectical Imagination: A History of the Frankfurt School and the Institute of Social Research. 1923–1950*. Boston: Little, Brown, 1973.

Kenny, Anthony, ed. *Aquinas: A Collection of Critical Essays*. 54–93. New York: Anchor, 1969.

Lindbeck, George. *The Nature of Doctrine: Religion and Theology in a Postliberal Age*. Philadelphia: Westminster, 1984.

Lonergan, Bernard. *Verbum: Word and Idea in Aquinas*. Notre Dame: University of Notre Dame Press, 1969.

Mackey, James. *Modern Theology of Tradition*. New York: Herder & Herder, 1962.

Marcuse, Herbert. *One Dimensional Man*. Boston: Beacon, 1964.

Megill, Allan. *Prophets of Extremity: Nietzsche, Heidegger, Foucault, Derrida*. Berkeley: University of California Press, 1987.

Rahner, Karl. *Foundations of Christian Faith*. New York: Crossroad, 1978.

———. *Theological Investigations* 4. London: Danton, Longman and Todd, 1964.

Ramsey, Ian. *Religious Language: An Empirical Placing of Theological Phrases*. New York: Macmillan, 1963.

Ricoeur, Paul. *La Métaphore Vive*. Paris: Editions du Seuil, 1975.

———. "The Specificity of Religious Language." *Semeia* 4 (1975): 107–45.

———. *The Symbolism of Evil*. New York: Harper & Row, 1967.

Toulmin, Stephen. *Human Understanding*. Vol. 1. Princeton: Princeton University Press, 1972.

Tracy, David. *The Analogical Imagination: Christian Theology and the Culture of Pluralism*. New York: Crossroad, 1981.

———. *Blessed Rage for Order: The New Pluralism in Theology*. New York: Seabury, 1975.

———. *Plurality and Ambiguity: Hermeneutics, Religion, Hope*. San Francisco: Harper & Row, 1987.

Turner, Victor. *The Ritual Process: Structure and Anti-Structure*. Chicago: Aldene, 1960.

Walzer, Michael. *Exodus and Revolution*. New York: Basic, 1985.

8

INGRID SHAFER

The Virgin and the Grail: Archetypes in Andrew Greeley's Fiction

Of all the symbols in Andrew Greeley's novels, none is more pervasive or powerful than that of the Holy Grail and/or the Magic Princess, the source, inspiration, and goal of the human pilgrimage. In the fall of 1984 I conducted the first phase of a study investigating the attitudes of American diocesan priests toward Andrew Greeley and his novels. A personal acquaintance of Greeley's from Indiana wrote that in his opinion, Greeley was motivated by two fierce loves, the Catholic Church and his Irish heritage, an opinion which can be objectively supported by any survey of Greeley's extensive scholarly work. And nowhere do those two loves coincide more forcefully than in the mysterious Holy Grail, particularly in its original, active, and generally flesh-affirming Celtic form. In addition, the Grail provides Greeley with a ready-made vehicle to communicate his theological vision of the sacramentality of sexual love and the womanliness of God, as well as his psychological vision of the human psyche as a transforming journey toward integration and wholeness. In this latter sense, the Grail contains what Carl Gustav Jung calls "the living spirit... the perennial water, the water of life, the virgin's milk, the fount,... and [whoever] drinks of it shall not perish" (*Mysterium Coniunctionis* 500). It is the "divine

A much shorter version of this essay was presented under the title "Woman-God, Sex, and the Celtic Grail in the Fiction of Father Andrew Greeley" at the Mid-America Medievalist Association's annual meeting in Wichita, Kansas, 1 Mar. 1986.

krater" filled with "the Nous . . . so that those mortals who wished to attain consciousness could renew themselves in the baptismal bath" (503). In this context it is interesting to note that Henry and Renée Kahane argue that the word "grail" can be derived from the Greek *krater*, significant to the Hermeticists. By writing contemporary Grail stories, initially without even realizing he was doing so, Greeley unwittingly tapped one of the most powerful symbol clusters of the religious imagination. In Jungian terms, beneath the surface of Greeley's stories, this particular archetype represents a primordial image he and his public share, a symbolic reality which can become consciously appropriated through the process of reading.

In his exhaustive study of world mythologies, Jung discovered not only that there was something like a universal symbolic language which united the imaginative realms of geographically and chronologically distant ancient peoples, but that these same primordial images continued to appear in the dreams and artistic creations of modern Westerners. Most of these men and women knew little or nothing (on a conscious level) of the mythic structures which informed their dreams, drawings, and stories. Jung concluded that the individual psyche is suspended in the ocean of the collective unconscious which contains the elemental symbols connecting people of all eras. He calls these primordial ways of grasping reality archetypes. By archetype he means a "primordial image" which is "common to entire peoples or epochs" (*Psychological Types* 443). It is a dynamic fragment of the psyche, representing a "mode of psychic behavior" and an " 'irrepresentable' factor" which unconsciously arranges the psychic elements so they fall into typical configurations, much as a crystalline grid arranges the molecules in a saturated solution" (*Symbolic Life* 483). Individuation or self-actualization occurs through the recognition and assimilation of certain archetypes, thereby becoming conscious of at least some of the activities of the collective unconscious. Thus, paradoxically, we attain a higher level of individual selfhood, become more unique, precisely by extending our personal roots into the common waters nourishing all of humanity. Even if we do not accept Jung's hypothesis that those archetypes are part of our biological genetic endowment, it seems reasonable, given Greeley's lifelong fascination with Celtic mythology, that his is an Irish Grail.[1]

Greeley's first published novel, *The Magic Cup*, is a carefully researched and historically faithful variation on the Irish Grail legend of Art the Son of Conn. In subsequent stories Greeley introduces contemporary literary "reincarnations" of Cormac, his versions of Bran, Conn, Fann, Maelduin, and Saint Brendan in search of the Blessed Land of the Ever-Living Women, the Celtic Heaven according to Jean Markale (*Women of the Celts* 52). Greeley's men (and with appropriate adjustments, his women) spend their lives in quest of the "magic cup," relentlessly pursuing and pursued by the "magic princess" (Brigid/Biddy of *The Magic Cup*) of the "shining castle" originally known by such names as Morgan, Morrigan, Modron, Cuchulain, Debchaen. They were in turn aspects of the Celtic goddess

Brigid who would in due time be reborn as the Christian Saint Brigid of Kildare.

Among the numerous medieval versions of the Quest for the Holy Grail, Mircea Eliade considers Wolfram's *Parzival*[2] "the most complete story and coherent mythology of the Grail" (*History of Religious Ideas* 3:105). Eliade was particularly struck by the fact that Wolfram deliberately includes numerous oriental motifs, and did so with respect. Wolfram claimed that the original source of his tale was a Muslim-Jewish sage; Parzival's father lived for a while in Africa, where he had a Muslim wife and son; Parzival's uncle had traveled to Asia and Africa; Parzival's half brother's son would become Prester John, priest/king in India. In summary, Eliade notes:

> Whatever one makes of the works of Wolfram and his successors, it is evident that the symbolism of the Grail and the scenarios it inspires represent a new spiritual synthesis that draws upon the contributions of diverse traditions. Behind this passionate interest in the Orient, one detects a profound disillusionment aroused by the Crusades, the aspiration for a religious tolerance that would have encouraged a rapproachement with Islam, and a nostalgia for a "spiritual chivalry" . . . (107).

The Grail is obviously an immensely powerful symbol of primal female fecundity/nurturance/wisdom/divinity. The Grail-bearer is generally a young woman, and the luminous Grail often contains the image of a child either by itself or within a eucharistic wafer. It takes little imagination to see the symbolic connection between the Grail as vessel/womb being fertilized and the Christian story of the Incarnation/Annunciation, symbolized by the Eucharistic Cup. It also seems more than merely coincidental that popular and poetic fascination with the Grail burst forth at exactly the time when the most hotly debated doctrinal issue concerned the mystery of the Eucharist, a controversy which culminated in the promulgation of the dogma of transubstantiation by the Fourth Lateran Council in 1215. In liturgical practice the Eucharist becomes Communion, the sacramental sacred meal, spiritual food in the form of bread and wine, the Christian adaptation of the pagan eating of the god. It reinforced the Christian emphasis on the Incarnation, in contrast to the Cathar insistence that the world and matter, including marriage and procreation, were wholly evil, and that the body of Christ was illusory.

Basic motifs of the Grail legend include a magic castle, inhabited by the emasculated Fisher King and a virgin who serves as the Grail-bearer. The Grail itself is variously identified as luminous cup, bowl, jewel, and (by Wolfram) stone, capable of providing unlimited food and drink. It is a fountain of youth and health, a source of wisdom and truth. In its baptized form, the Grail has been identified with the cup Christ used at the Last Supper and the vessel in which Christ's blood had been caught by Joseph of

Arimathea. The Maimed Fisher King is generally also associated with a fiery or bleeding lance, which has in turn been linked to the Celtic god Lug's spear and the blade which pierced Jesus' side.

Reflecting on those motifs, Roger Sherman Loomis concluded that the Grail tradition is Celtic in origin, that it "violates the most elementary proprieties of Christian ethics and ritual," and thus could "not have originated in a pious fabrication" (*Arthurian Tradition* 272). To clinch his case, he asks, "Would a holy relic or even a common paten or ciborium have been placed in charge of a lovely damsel, not of a priest or a sacristan?" adding, "No wonder the Church has never recognized the Grail romances as authentic and has displayed a shrewd suspicion about their unorthodox background" (272).

Obviously, the Grail story, particularly in its Celtic origins and as related by Wolfram, is at odds with a theology which insists on the masculinity of God and the inferiority of women and an ethos of sexual asceticism. In Loomis' pre–Vatican II days (the study was initially published in 1948), the image of a ciborium placed in charge of a lowly *woman* must have appeared both blasphemous and heretical. The Catholic tradition, however, also contains a popular strain, which emphasizes the role of Mary as the Mother of God, the *theotokos* or God-bearer, and, in function if not in doctrine, the manifestation of the nurturing, healing, maternal, passionately and tenderly loving aspects of divinity.

It is in this perspective that Greeley's use of the Grail Quest motive must be understood. Rather than simply assuming that the Grail is non-Christian, we might more properly inquire what it can teach us concerning the fullness of God and the true meaning of the Christian message. The Grail symbol seems particularly well suited to the present age, which may finally be ready to deal with the sacramental potential of woman and sexuality. As Mircea Eliade noted, "the spiritual message of the scenario elaborated around the Grail continues to excite the imagination and reflection of contemporaries. In sum, the mythology of the Grail is part of the religious history of the West. . . ." (108).

Some of the conflicting ways the Grail has been portrayed and interpreted can be explained by the fact that it began to captivate the medieval popular imagination during a time of intense intellectual and religious ferment and turmoil. While the doctrine of the transubstantiation reflected a sense of God-in-the-world, dualistic Manichaeanism had reemerged in the form of the Cathar heresy which combined legitimate contempt for clerical corruption with extreme hatred of material life and the human body. After ruthless official persecution, the Cathars (Albigensians) were exterminated, but ironically, some of their dualism managed to infect the already partially non-Platonic Catholic tradition with a new dose of life- and world-negation. Thus it can properly be argued, as Pauline Matarasso does, following Etienne Gilson, that the Quest for the Holy Grail is closely linked to Cistercian ecstasy, God's love manifested as grace eliciting the human response of pure and spontaneous love leading to the *unio mystica*, entirely purged of all carnal dimensions (15). In a perversion of the early troubadour ideal, the earthly goal of yearning must now always remain beyond reach. Love of God and the God of Love, chaste Agape and passionate Eros, were at war; and the latter was temporarily defeated.

In the original Celtic tradition, however, and in Wolfram's tale, human love and the yearning for sexual fulfillment were portrayed as positive values. In contrast to Chrétien's Galahad (who achieves the Grail through ascetic denial of the flesh, because he is a *virgin* knight—and hence supposedly spiritually perfect), Parzival attains both his beloved, Cond-wiramurs, and the spiritual Grail. Wolfram portrays nuptial love as a mysterious and immensely powerful secular sacrament.

In addition there is strong evidence in the text that it is precisely conjugal passion (along with the willingness to abandon literal obedience to law for life under the sign of loving humaneness) which renders Parzival worthy of the Grail. Not only does the memory of his wife, Condwiramurs, sustain him in his wanderings, but his election to Grail King is followed almost immediately by prolonged and enthusiastic lovemaking in Condwiramurs' forest tent. Wolfram reports: "As far as I know he enjoyed his wife's delights until almost noon. But then the entire army arrived to find out what was going on. . . . Now sleep was out of the question. The king and queen got up, and a priest said early Mass" (629–31). Since one suspects that "early Mass" was not generally celebrated at noon, it is obvious that Wolfram considered the sexual sacrament a proper reason for the delay of services. Here, as elsewhere in the epic, Wolfram rejects the clerical claim that the Church is the only mediator between God and humanity. This anticlericalism may have led to the absurd suggestion that Wolfram was a Cathar.[3]

Thus Wolfgang Spiewok, the German translator (from Middle High German), notes in his commentary: "Wolfram transforms courtly romantic love (*Minne*) into genuine, conjugal love: the foundation and fulfillment of marriage" (699) and, for Wolfram, "God is not encountered (as clerical ideologues still insist) through asceticism and denial of the world, but rather through meaningful social relationships in the service of God" (701–2). According to Spiewok, it is Wolfram's nondualistic acceptance of the material world which accounted for the immense popularity of his work during the subsequent pre-Reformation centuries. If Spiewok is right, then Wolfram's story may well have represented a popular antidote to the prevailing dualism of the late Middle Ages. It is not surprising that Spiewok's comments apply to Greeley's Grail stories as well.

The sacramentality of sexuality, far from being Greeley's invention or a cheap sellout to contemporary preoccupation with sex in all its forms, reveals itself instead as a major religious theme, an unchanging aspect of Christianity as founded by God-become-Flesh, thus sanctifying for all time the material world.

The marriage symbol is associated with the Grail in yet another highly significant way. Jung found major clues to individuation in the writings of the alchemists,[4] particularly Gerard Dorn's *Theatrum Chemicum*. He considered the concept of the *mysterium coniunctionis* (the complete merging of all opposites), called *chymical marriage* by Dorn, the equivalent of the individuation process (*Mysterium Coniunctionis* 469). Jung points out that Dorn, in seeing the consummation of the *mysterium coniunctionis* as the union of the *caelum* with the *unus mundus*, expressly meant a *unio mystica* with the potential world, not an adaptation of the individual to the environment. This realization, Jung argues, is the result of Dorn's underlying assumption that ultimately all divisions and differentiations arise out of and return back into the One. Furthermore, this intuition of unity rests on the "basic psychic structure common to all souls, which, though not visible and tangible like the anatomical structure, is just as evident as it" (537). Jung notes that "in contradiction to the modern prejudice that self-knowledge is nothing but a knowledge of the ego, the alchemists regarded the self as a substance incommensurable with ego, hidden in the body, and identical with the image of God" (499).

The chymical marriage of the alchemists takes place in a crucible, often referred to as *krater*, containing mercury or quicksilver, a liquid metal/mineral. Jung quotes a lengthy passage from Albertus Magnus' treatise on the philosopher's stone, the *Liber octo captiulorum de lapide philosophorum*: "Quicksilver. . . alone is the living spirit . . . the perennial water, the water of life, the virgin's milk, the fount, the alumen, and [whoever] drinks of it shall not perish. . . . As it is transmuted, so it transmutes. . . ." (500). Jung interprets the passage in psychological terms: "By introducing the modern concept of self we can explain the paradoxes of Albertus without too much difficulty. Mercurius is matter and spirit; the self, as its symbolism proves, embraces the bodily sphere as well as the psychic" (503).

If we stop for a moment and consider the above statement, we must surely realize that it cannot possibly refer to "facts" in the ordinary sense. Mercury *is* a metal. In itself it has nothing to do whatsoever with either the "Really Real" or the self. It becomes significant only after it has first been made into a symbol and consequently has been transformed into a metaphor pointing to another level of reality. Jung continues: "In the course of time, . . . it took on the significance of the Nous, with which the divine *krater* was filled so that those mortals who wished to attain consciousness could renew themselves in this baptismal bath; . . . its maternal aspect as the matrix and 'nurse of all things' makes it an insurpassable analogy of the unconscious" (503–504).

And so, in a twentieth-century tale of a woman's journey toward authentic selfhood, one in which the word "Grail" is never mentioned, Kathy Collins of *Virgin and Martyr* finds herself implacably pursued by "quicksilver mists" (401–2), Greeley's active, passionate version of the Grail. Yes, indeed, *all* of Greeley's stories are variations on the Grail Quest theme.

As I have already noted, Greeley's first novel, *The Magic Cup*, is an undisguised Grail quest, complete with an early medieval setting and a scholarly note on the Irish Grail Cycle. Jim O'Neill in Greeley's second novel, *Death in April*, is described by his psychiatrist friend Monique as "the last of the knights of the round table, a red-haired Lancelot forever seeking his Grail, his sacred vessel" (21). Teenagers Kevin Brennan and Ellen Foley of *Cardinal Sins* "touch each other's bodies, as though [they] were touching the sacred vessels in an ancient sanctuary" (18), while their friend Patrick sees "a soft bowl of light, rising up from the water of the lake," feels invaded by "peace, joy, forgiveness, love," and "cleansed and renewed" by "all the women in the world . . . ," women who eventually merge "into a woman in a white and gold gown" (29–30). Obviously, Greeley not only uses the Grail symbol but associates it with the Virgin Mary and the Great Mother of the ancient world. While contemporary Catholics might be puzzled or offended by this association of the Virgin with the pre-Christian goddess and a mysterious, numinous object of pagan origin, this nexus is historically grounded, and clearly woven into numerous officially sanctioned liturgical and ritual practices pertaining to the Mother of Jesus.

Consider, for example, the traditional Litany of the Blessed Virgin in the 1960 edition of the *Maryknoll Missal*, in which Mary is addressed by the following names (among others):

> *Holy Mother of God* . . .
> *Mother of our Creator,*
> *Mother of our Savior.* . .
> *Virgin most powerful* . . .
> *Mirror of justice,*
> *Seat of wisdom* . . .
> *Spiritual Vessel,*
> *Vessel of honor,*
> *Singular Vessel of devotion,*
> *Mystical rose,*
> *Tower of David,*
> *Tower of ivory,*
> *House of Gold,*
> *Ark of the covenant* . . .
> *Health of the sick,*
> *Refuge of sinners* . . .
> *Queen of peace* . . . *(1670–71)*

The imagery in this medieval litany, particularly the reference to Mary as *both* "vessel" and "tower," can be unpacked to reveal mythic strata taking us all the way back to the gynandrous prehistoric Cosmic Mother of the gods and all of creation. She is called "Mother of God," and to make sure we don't miss the point, not only "Mother of our Savior" but also "Mother of our *Creator*" (emphasis mine). This figure of speech clearly identifies Mary as the ground of being, the cosmic unity which is ontologically prior to the trinity, and which is called the *Tao* by the Chinese and the *Brahman* in Hindu tradition. This interpretation is supported by Mary's title of *theotokos* (God-bearer) in theological speculation, and in the late medieval artistic convention of carving her image in the form of the *vierge ouvrante*, a pregnant woman, often wearing the crown of the Queen of Heaven, whose belly could be opened to reveal within its hollow the trinity.

"Virgin most powerful" presents woman as not only *independent* from male domination but man's superior. Ancient goddesses, like Isis, Ishtar, and Diana, were called virgins to indicate not chastity, but autonomy and strength. The matriarchal virgin archetype is diametrically opposed to the patriarchal spouse archetype which (mis)represents woman as her husband's possession with no purpose or identity other than that achieved through union with the male and passive motherhood. She lies at the base of the Taoist world view which refuses to be shackled by the rigid rules of civilized, androcentric Confucianism. As Ishtar, she inhabits Mount Sinai long before the children of Israel hear the thunderous voice of Yahweh, and Moses receives the law engraved in stone (to be placed into the Ark of the Covenant, yet another one of Mary's names).

The name "seat of wisdom" reminds us of both the Old Testament convention of referring to Sophia/wisdom in feminine terms and the popular medieval tradition of imagining the Holy Spirit as female. In addition, the image evokes echoes of the life-giving and matter-transmuting philosopher's stone sought by the alchemists as the means to achieve the *mysterium coniunctionis*, the absolute unification of all opposites.

The appellation "mystical rose" recalls the rose of Aphrodite and Isis, as well as the central position given to the rose in Gothic church architecture (in cathedrals usually dedicated to "Our Lady") and in late medieval allegories of love from the *Romance of the Rose* to Dante's *Divine Comedy*, where the Virgin and the Rose are fused in the final revelation in paradise.

As "ark of the covenant" Mary is symbolically linked with the Greek term *kibotos*, which in the Septuagint is used for both the Ark of the Covenant and Noah's ark. Both *kibotos* and *kiborion*, the cup-shaped seed vessel of the Egyptian water lily and a drinking cup, are derived from the root *kibos*. *Kiborion* was eventually transformed into the Latin ciborium, the covered chalice used to store the consecrated Host, and may in that sense be associated with Latin *cibus* (food).

"Health of the sick" obviously refers to Mary as the one who heals, not only physical ailments but spiritual afflictions as well, as her role as "refuge of sinners" indicates. Finally, the "Queen of Peace" is the female corollary of Christ, the "King (or Prince) of Peace."

Peeling back the strata of the multivalent Mary symbol is not only intriguing in itself but becomes particularly evocative in the present context, once we realize that except for "Mother of the Creator," the Marian attributes I have cited could be applied to the Holy Grail as well. Like

Mary, the Grail is associated with the fragrance of blossoms and described as numinous and luminous vessel (from cup to bowl or platter) with the powers of generation, wisdom, and healing, and at times portrayed containing the infant Jesus. We simply cannot get around the indisputable fact that the medieval popular imagination and the troubadours who both reflected and shaped that imagination chose to link the Virgin and the Grail.

In *Die Grosse Mutter* (cited by Greeley in his *Mary Myth*) Erich Neumann comments on Bartel Bruyn's sixteenth-century *Annunciation*: "Next to Mary there stands the vessel which is she. The body of this vessel bears the Host with the name of the Divine Son; above it towers the lily of the Cretan Virgin-Goddess. The vessel is the Goddess Herself bearing the Divine Child of the Sun, and without the artist's conscious intention, Mary becomes again the Goddess of the Beginning" (308).

The Grail theme is forcefully sounded in *The Magic Cup*, which introduces Cormac MacDermot, the Celtic Parzival, and mysterious Brigid/ Biddy, his "Magic Princess" in disguise. In a scenario typical of the preconscious realm of dream and myth, Brigid, the slave/princess heroine, merges with both the pagan Mother Goddess and the Christian saint, thus symbolizing the actual historic fusion of roles which took place in seventh-century Ireland. It was during that time that the mighty pagan triadic goddess Brigid (patroness of poetry, metalwork, and healing) and mother/ wife/daughter of god Dagda (the Celtic equivalent of the Roman Saturn) became Saint Brigid, who was also identified with the Virgin Mary and called Mary of the Gael.

Saint Brigid, abbess at Kildare, Christian patroness of learning, crafts, and medicine, continued to inspire folk customs closely tied to Celtic ritual designed to preserve harmony in nature. Her feast day is the first of February, the pre-Christian fertility festival of Inbolc. In the thirteenth century the poet Giolla Brighde (ca. 1210–72) addresses both her and the Virgin Mary in a touching poetic plea to grant him and his wife at least one child. He addresses Bridget as "faithful sweetheart of God" (Williams 223) and Mary as "three Maries" (217) (unconsciously and innocently preserving the ancient Celtic motif of a triple goddess), which in connection with the trinity form the "six proving letters of knowledge," in the balancing of masculine and feminine forces typical of pre-Christian Ireland. It is precisely this nondualistic vision of reality which is beginning to reemerge forcefully in the present age and which is reflected in Greeley's analogical imagination.

Cormac MacDermot and Brigid are reborn in *Death in April* as Jim O'Neill and Lynnie Conroy. "Lynnie and the lake. The girl is the lake is the Grail is God . . ." (64), Jim muses early on in the story, preconsciously aware of the path prepared for him, the invitation extended.

Cormac and Brigid become Kevin Brennan and Ellen Foley of *The Cardinal Sins*. While their love remains unconsummated, it allows Kevin to mature into an empathetic, caring priest precisely because he learns to accept his sexual nature. "If my faith means anything to me, it means that the electricity between us survives death, just as the sun survives the night" (281). It is not until this point that his choice of celibacy becomes truly meaningful, since it now involves a transformation/transcendence of lust into spiritual passion.

They are Sean Cronin and Nora Riley in *Thy Brother's Wife*, a novel which shows intriguing thematic parallels to the medieval Persian *Wis and Ramin*, an early version of *Tristan and Isolde* with its sacramental (though illicit) lovemaking scene so maligned by Denise de Rougemont. Sean has spent his entire life struggling to be a saint by denying much of his essential humanity. Like Parzival on Good Friday, he feels distant, alienated from God. He is alone, going through the routine motions of being a good priest, but zeal and passion are lacking. With Nora he dares accept the divine invitation to radical intimacy, he dares take the ultimate risk, a leap of faith into the unknown. For a long time he fails to grasp the true significance of this *felix culpa*. He is haunted by guilt, torment, self-contempt, until eleven years later he finally comprehends the pattern. "You damn fool," he writes into his spiritual journal. "You missed God's sign for thirty years." He finally realizes that "because he had lost his mother, God had sent him Nora, the best sign of God's love he would ever. have.... Talk about the twisted lines of God" (302).

They are Hugh Donlon and Maria Manfredy in *Ascent into Hell*. Hugh's odyssey has taken him from the active priesthood to the heights and depths of worldly involvement. A man on the run, from himself, life, fate, God, he is drained and hollow, the ghost of who he might have been. He is in hell. Then, after his release from prison, Maria literally kidnaps him for a weekend of loving and healing. "I love you," she says. "I have always loved you and always will, no matter how much you hide from me" (356). Eventually, he realizes that he had to die before he could live. And so he enters Maria's "house of gold," God's mansion, "a pleasant house, inviting, reassuring, comforting. And once you went into its light you never left" (367).

They are Red and Eileen Kane in *Patience of a Saint*, a Christmas-Pentecost story of a man reborn and a marriage renewed. While Red has lived with his Grail for twenty years, Monsignor Blackie cautions him that "the Grail is never fully possessed, but must always be pursued—that's the agony, the joy, and, to be candid, the fun" (413).

They are, finally, Brendan Ryan and Ciara Kelly in *Rite of Spring*, which in many ways transposes the medieval fairy world of the *Magic Cup* into a contemporary setting, complete with numerous allusions to pagan fertility rites and a climactic conclusion on the Strand of Inch. Brendan's Grail inspires him, revitalizes him, literally gives him the spine to refuse a supposed "friend's" demand that he put his career on the line to protect another "friend" who has betrayed him. "No way," he says. He has other things in his life now. "Like Ciara Kelly. My Holy Grail" (66). More powerfully than in any other story, Brendan Ryan's Grail represents the symbol in its archetypal womb-fertility aspect, including the strange vision of the child already contained within the vessel (115). In his imagination he and Ciara are ancient mythological figures. He even identifies himself with the Celtic hero Finn (Fionn) McCool, who along with Cuchulain, supplies one of the main sources for Parzival's childhood (Loomis 337–38).

The Magic Cup, the Holy Grail, thus emerges as the central and most significant symbol in Greeley's writings, for, even more than the literary form of the romance (though inseparable from it), the Grail theme allows him to combine his two loves for the Catholic Church and his Irish heritage, while simultaneously permitting him to pursue the theological topics of the sacramentality of sexuality and the womanliness of God.

The mysterious Grail sounds literally countless archetypal associations, womanly as well as androgynous, pagan as well as Christian. Some of those associations include the Celtic feminine principle of birth, death, and immortality; a mysteriously ill Fisher King, evoking images of Jesus and the *ichthys*/fish as symbolic of nourishment and fertility; the Last Supper; an infant descending into the eucharistic wafer contained in the Grail; the vessel/womb being fertilized, and the Christian event of the Annunciation/Incarnation; the philosopher's stone and wisdom as feminine aspect of divinity; a lance bleeding into a silver cup or cauldron; the Eucharistic Cup or the ciborium placed in charge of a woman, and thus Mary as Great Cosmic Mother, the *theotokos*, manifestation of the powerful, nurturing, healing, maternal, passionately and tenderly loving aspects of divinity.

Greeley's use of the Grail motif shows the erotic dimension as inextricably intertwined with the uniquely human struggle to wrest meaning from a reluctant cosmos, to break out of isolation and alienation and merge with the universal forces of life. Ultimately, our God, Yahweh-Wisdom-Jesus, primal Mother-Father, Holy Grail and Magic Princess, reveals Himself/Herself to each one of us in and through those we love and by whom we are loved. This is the message of Father Andrew Greeley, twentieth-century Irish bard and knight-errant, a faintly comic Celtic Lancelot in green armor, astride his Compaq 286 computer, a Brigid's cross tied to his lance, faithfully doing battle in his Lady's service.

NOTES

1. A pre-Christian story tells how Connla, the son of King Conn, meets a beautiful young woman who professes her love and asks him to follow her to the Land of the Living, a joyous region of immortality and perpetual feasting. While she is only visible to him, others can hear her, and his father commands his Druid to banish her with a mighty spell. Connla lingers, sick with love and longing, until one day she returns in a glass boat and repeats

her invitation. He leaps into the boat which sets sail toward the land of joy inhabited only by women.

That Land of the Ever-Living Women is also visited by Maelduin, who has been sailing the oceans in search of his father's killer. Like Odysseus, he and his companions find themselves on an island of perpetual youth and immortality, inhabited by a lovely Amazon queen and her seventeen daughters. She makes Maelduin her consort and offers her daughters to his crew. Eventually, the crew members become homesick, and Maelduin sadly leaves with them despite his love for the queen. This version, presumably under Christian influence, has partially transformed the life-giving erotic woman into the beguiling *femme fatale*, not originally part of the Celtic heritage.

In *Women of the Celts* Jean Markale relates an earlier version of Maelduin's journey involving Bran, the Son of Febal, who ends up spending eternity upon the marvelous Island of Women. In this pre-Christian legend women's charms are still considered entirely beneficent. A later, fully Christianized variation introduces Saint Brendan on his ultimately futile voyage in search of the fabled land in the West.

During a visit with God Manannan, King Cormac Son of Art and his family are entertained at a table set with a tablecloth which instantly produces any food demanded. The god produces a magic cup which will break if a lie is spoken, and restore itself if the truth is said. As parting gifts, the god presents Cormac and his wife with the magic cup, the magic tablecloth, and a magic branch which will restore fruitfulness to Ireland.

Markale also tells the story of "The Adventures of Art, Son of Conn" (199), which in pre-Christian form contains most of the major themes of the Grail quest as recorded by Chrétien de Troyes, Wolfram von Eschenbach, and countless others. It is this version of the Grail story which Greeley cites in *The Magic Cup* as basis for his own retelling of the legend.

2. Wolfram's *Parzival* is the story of an innocent young man, brought up in forest isolation. His mother, a widowed queen, has given up her realm in order to keep her posthumously born son from the lure of combat and adventure. As a teenager Parzival sees three "knights in shining armor" and against his mother's express wishes, naively sets out to pursue the chivalric ideal. He does not know that his mother dies of a "broken heart." On his travels he encounters all sorts of adventures, most notably Condwiramurs, a young queen, whose castle is under siege from a determined suitor and his knights. Parzival saves her; they fall in love, make love, and are married. Soon, however, Parzival rides off again, yearning for adventure and concerned for his mother. Eventually he arrives at a fabulous mountain fortress surrounded by water and owned by a languishing fisher king. He is welcomed as an honored guest. A magnificent banquet is served from the bountiful, luminous Grail, carried by a lovely young woman. Still, all the inhabitants of the castle seem strangely sad. Out of naive courtesy Parzival fails to inquire concerning his host's mysterious illness, the significance of the Grail, or the spirit of sadness clouding the castle. He has been advised to stop asking so many questions and has not yet learned to go beyond the mere literal meaning of words. The following morning he discovers the castle deserted and hears a disembodied voice chiding him rudely for his

insensitivity. If he had asked the fateful question he could have lifted the enchantment from the castle and cured the ailing king. The fortress gates bang shut. He spends years in futile quest to reclaim it, and becomes one of King Arthur's knights. Finally, after numerous further adventures, and longtime loss of faith, purified by suffering and healed of doubt and despair, he discovers that he is the fisher king's nephew. Sustained by the image of his wife, he is allowed to return to *Munsalwäsche* (Mount of Salvation, the Grail precinct), makes friends with his Muslim black half brother (who converts in order to marry the Grail-bearer), is reunited with Condwiramurs, meets his twin sons, and assumes his preordained position as the new King of the Grail.

3. See John Matthews, *The Grail: Quest for the Eternal*, 22. While there is evidence that some versions of the Grail story did indeed show Cathar characteristics, Wolfram's *Parzival* is far less dualistic than even orthodox Christianity of his day.

4. The importance of alchemy in the study of the self lies for Jung not in the particular claims made concerning the nature of the physical world nor the experiments themselves or the surface denotations of the writings. It lies in its *symbolic* significance, that toward which it points rather than that which is directly stated. Jung studies the *Theatrum Chemicum* as he might analyze the psyche of one of his clients. As a cultural phenomenon it provides him with clues concerning the mysterious depths of the collective unconscious.

WORKS CITED

Eliade, Mircea. *A History of Religious Ideas*. Vol. 3, *From Muhammad to the Age of Reforms*. Translated by Alf Hiltebeitel and Diane Apostolos-Cappadona. Chicago: University of Chicago Press, 1985.

Greeley, Andrew M. *Ascent into Hell*. New York: Warner, 1983.

———. *The Cardinal Sins*. New York: Warner, 1981.

———. *Death in April*. 1980. New York: Dell, 1984.

———. *Patience of a Saint*. New York: Warner, 1987.

———. *Rite of Spring*. New York: Warner, 1987.

———. *Thy Brother's Wife*. New York: Warner, 1982.

———. *Virgin and Martyr*. New York: Warner, 1985.

Jung, Carl Gustav. *Collected Works*. Bollingen Series XX. Vol. 6, *Psychological Types*. Princeton: Princeton University Press, 1971.

———. *Collected Works*. Vol. 14, *Mysterium Coniunctionis*. Princeton: Princeton University Press, 1970.

———. *Collected Works*. Vol. 18, *The Symbolic Life. Miscellaneous Writings*. Princeton: Princeton University Press, 1976.

Kahane, Henry and Renée. *The Krater and the Grail: Hermetic Sources of the Parzival*. Urbana: University of Illinois Press, 1965.

Loomis, Roger Sherman. *Arthurian Tradition and Chrétien de Troyes*. New York: Columbia University Press, 1961.

Markale, Jean. *Women of the Celts*. Translated by A. Mygind, C. Hauch, and Peter Henry. London: Gordon Cremonesi, 1975.

Maryknoll Fathers, eds. *Daily Missal of the Mystical Body*. New York: P. J. Kennedy & Sons, 1961.

Matarasso, Pauline M., trans. *The Quest of the Holy Grail*. New York: Penguin, 1984.

Matthews, John. *The Grail: Quest for the Eternal*. New York: Crossroad, 1981.

Neumann, Erich. *Die Grosse Mutter: eine Phänomenologie der weiblichen Gestaltungen des Unbewussten*. 1974. Olten: Walter-Verlag, 1985.

Williams, N. J. A., ed. *The Poems of Giolla Brighde Mac Con Midhe*. Dublin: Irish Texts Society, 1980.

Wolfram von Eschenbach. *Parzival: Mittelhochdeutsch/Neuhochdeutsch*. Translated by Wolfgang Spiewok. 2 vols. Stuttgart: Philipp Reclam Jun., 1981.

III

Opening the Gate: Critical Parameters

9

MIRIAM ESPINOSA

Andrew Greeley and the Author = Narrator Fallacy: Confessions of an English Professor

*C*ollege teaching, like any profession, has its metaphorical ups and downs. The ups happen when a pair of happy eyes dance with pleasure or amusement at something I have said, or when a pair of concerned eyes reflect the puzzled thought I have made happen within the brain. The downs are the eyes of boredom even though the topic (I know) is fascinating and the dull eyes belong to someone who doesn't want to think. If the class taught is literature, the ups and downs correspond to students' grappling with something that should be as natural to them as the breaths they take—the creative imagination. From the time they first learned to walk and talk, these now classroom-bound, core-curriculum-mandated young adults begged that stories be read or told to them—and then in turn they made up tales themselves. Perhaps a child's innocence included an unquestioning acceptance of the flights of fancy—the beauty of fiction—the "rough magic" Shakespeare's Prospero creates throughout the Bard's finale, *The Tempest* (5.1.50). One does not have to go quite so far as espousing Rousseau's doctrine of the Noble Savage, accepting Wordsworth's contention that "The Child is father of the Man" ("The Rainbow"), or Tolstoi's thesis that society

---

An earlier version of this essay was presented under the title "Satire in *God Game:* A Clue to Andrew Greeley's Literary and Theological Beliefs" during the third of four sessions dealing with Andrew Greeley's fiction at the Popular Culture Association Meeting in New Orleans, Louisiana, 26 Mar. 1988.

corrupts in order to recognize the fact that in the rite of passage from innocence to experience something of the youth's comfortable rapport with the art of fiction is sullied and made inexplicably complicated.

I was about to leave temporarily the problems of the classroom in order to prepare a publishable text on the nature of satire in one of my favorite works, *God Game*, of one of my favorite novelists, Andrew M. Greeley, when I was brought back to the responsibilities of my overworked and underpaid profession by an article in my local diocesan newspaper. The news item, appearing in the section of the paper directed to teenage readers, quoted Father Greeley as praising the metaphorically religious music of Bruce Springsteen, particularly his album *Tunnel of Love*. In holding up the power of a musician, along with all troubadours and storytellers, over the more limited influence of a doctrinal authority, even the Pope, Greeley cited the religious realities naturally included in Springsteen's music: "sin, temptation, forgiveness, life, death, hope" ("Catholic Imagination" 112). Although reading this article reminded me of Andrew Greeley's own use of creative imaginative talent and reinforced my strong opinion that many contemporary song lyrics affirm divine as well as human love (and are the two totally separate anyway?), it was not untnil the following week that I realized fully and also reluctantly the connection between my profession and the status of the fiction of Andrew Greeley. In the following week's *Texas Catholic*, a letter to the editor reared its self-righteous head:

> I was surprised and disappointed to see quotes from Father Andrew Greeley on the "Young Catholics" page in your Feb. 19 issue. Don't you know that many of this priest's novels are rated "X" by the leading book clubs?
> I never know how to reply to friends of other faiths who ask how a bishop would allow one of his priests to publish X-rated novels. (I don't know the answer.) Isn't this a case of giving scandal?
> I would appreciate some help in your comments, and please, let us quote worthier sources in our newspaper.
>
> M. Bracken
> *Greenville* ("Greeley 'Z-Rated'" 5)

M. Bracken's problem with Andrew Greeley's fiction is partly theological and partly moralistic in nature. However, it can also be addressed and solved from the standpoint of literary pedagogy. The rebuttal to Bracken's letter to the editor may be found in the syllabus of any self-respecting freshman Introduction to Literature course in any college in the country.

One of the most often repeated mini-lectures of the English instructor from middle school to college concerns the distinction between the author and the narrator of a piece of fiction. After they have passed the innocent, wonderful young age when they can *admit* that they like to pretend to be someone else and speak in that voice, students forget that uninhibited pleasure and want to assume that every narrator of every fictional work is the author. They must be reminded that Frank O'Connor is only the author of "Guests of the Nation." Yes, he was Irish, but not necessarily the young, antiwar, inexperienced soldier named Bonaparte who touchingly yet one-sidedly narrated the short story. Surely, O'Connor saw both sides of war and wanted his readers to do the same. The student of literature believes it is obvious to assume that Edgar Allan Poe *is* the mad, plotting murderer of the old man in the classic short story "The Tell-Tale Heart." After he has made that false assumption, he draws the further unwarranted conclusion that the man known as Edgar Allan Poe was most assuredly high on drugs, alcohol, opium, or *something*, and obviously nothing short of a madman himself. Since the student has self-confidently equated the author Poe with the narrator-murderer, he is not inclined to change his opinion as he reads—if he ever does—Poe's cogent and rigorously logical literary criticism.

The case of mistaken identity, once begun, persists: Mark Twain becomes Huck Finn, Herman Melville becomes Ishmael, F. Scott Fitzgerald becomes Nick Carraway, etc. This literary problem extends to poetry as well. The speaker in "My Last Duchess" is heard as Robert Browning's voice, rather than as the voice of the egotistical duke; John Donne is considered to be revealing his own experience in "The Ecstasy" rather than to be giving a poetic explanation of the nature of true love between two human beings. And Shakespeare's sonnets—students feel a greater compulsion to discover to whom the author wrote them and the types of autobiographical relationships which are implied by the lines than to discover through these timeless poems what the narrator is revealing about the nature of life and love. Left unchecked, this error makes it impossible for a reader to see a distinction between the "real person" who takes pen to paper or disk to computer and the fictional character who relates the story. What happens to such a student who somehow missed this elementary lesson in analyzing literature? He or she persists in ignorance, smugly sitting at home some years after graduation writing letters to the editor, unable to see any other possibility besides equating Andrew M. Greeley with Kevin Brennan in *The Cardinal Sins*. Greeley wrote the book; Kevin Brennan says "I" throughout; therefore the two must be one and the same. Whatever Kevin does and thinks and feels in the story, Andrew Greeley is certainly admitting can be attributed to him. Furthermore, they are both priests—need the reader say more?

A slightly different but often more misleading version of this literary error is the identification of the author with the main character of the work of fiction. The difficulties inherent in making such an identification between the two should discourage the attempt altogether, but instead, some students persist in their errors. They assume that Katherine Anne Porter must have been dying in order to write "The Jilting of Granny Weatherall": she wasn't; she was not even old or ill. A check of Porter's autobiography would reveal the impossibility of making the identifying link, but the guilty students prefer to assume their own facts. Stephen Crane is equated with the young Henry Fleming of *The Red Badge of Courage*; in truth, Crane wrote the novel never having been near a battlefield. There are students who wonder how a man named John Steinbeck could possibly get inside the thoughts and emotions of a woman. Accept the fact that he did, the professor says for again another semester: he is a great writer. He can create a narrator omniscient, who can in turn play God, and in so doing can tell the reader how a woman thinks—the workings of creative imagination— remember?

With Andrew Greeley's fiction this error is persistent and quite misleading. Greeley has been identified with Patrick Donahue in *The Cardinal Sins*, with Sean Cronin in *Thy Brother's Wife*, and with Hugh Donlon in *Ascent into Hell*. The readers who make such identifications are more concerned with who wrote the novels than they are with the totality of plot within the works. Priest/author and priest/protagonist must imply author/protagonist. Maintaining on the one hand that no priest should know about the passions and weaknesses described in the novels and on the other that Greeley must have experienced the entire plot in order to write it, these readers are once again exhibiting the classroom fallacy involving the author/narrator/protagonist vicious triangle.

The fallacy is indicative of a serious failing: a failure to analyze and evaluate the work as a whole. Just as TV viewers called their local stations to register shock at the language used by Colonel Kincaid (portrayed by Henry Fonda) in Preston Jones' *The Oldest Living Graduate* instead of trying to understand what Jones was really saying about the selfishness of Kincaid's son and the difficulties of old age; just as parents and teachers in the 1950s banned *The Catcher in the Rye* on the basis of language alone, not on the basis of the society or the characters which J. D. Salinger sought to portray; and just as some shallow readers attack the language and life-styles in such sociological novels as Hemingway's *The Sun Also Rises* and Larry McMurtry's *All My Friends Are Going to Be Strangers* without realizing that the Lost Generation of the twenties and the Beat Generation of the sixties cannot be accurately portrayed unless their words and drifting, purposeless actions are given prominent attention; so do many of Greeley's readers reduce his works to whatever physical weakness they choose to dwell on. For such persons Greeley's novels consist only of Patrick Donahue's sudden and uncontrollable bursts of passion, Kevin Brennan's persistent (enduring would be a kinder and better word) love for Ellen Foley, Sean Cronin's week with Nora in Amalfi, and Hugh Donlon's flirtations with Helen Fowler and his days with Maria at Lake Geneva.

The readers who narrow their focus to the weaknesses of Andrew Greeley's characters—to the incidents they like to say are the shocking parts of the fiction of a daring priest/writer—are committing more than a theological error. They grossly misread fiction, like a moviegoer who decides against seeing a film on the basis of an eye-catching advertisement of a four-second scene, or like a student who hasn't read the assignment and wants to talk in class about a single minor part he happened to stumble upon or hear about secondhand and thus knows only out of context. What such readers miss while they are busy censoring the author for his so-called sex scenes is in most instances the heart of the matter.

It is as if no one ever taught them the meaning of the term "well-rounded character" as opposed to "flat character." A character, any character, priest or otherwise, who plods through the pages of fiction with a single attribute, good or bad, with no change, no contradiction, no conflict, is a flat character, his story dull, his writer/creator deadly untalented. Not so Greeley's characters or Greeley's ability. Did such readers miss Patrick Donahue's frantic, desperate regrets after his passionate or greedy failures, skipping over the "God forgive me . . . please, please forgive me" (*Cardinal Sins* 61) after he thrust himself upon Ellen, overlooking his sobs and act of contrition after he took Georgina Carey brutally, forgetting the sob Kevin barely hears before Pat hangs up the phone after hearing his daughter is dying? Did they forget Ellen's assurance to Kevin that he would be a wonderful priest and her promise to pray that he would make it through the hard times? Are they unmoved by love at its truest, its best, on this earth, the only place we can find it, for a while anyway? Were they asleep as they read the pages of Kevin's rebound-tipping, of his bringing Mo back to life after the deaths of her parents? Didn't they recognize human kindness when it jumped off the page? And didn't human kindness remind them of Someone Else's kindness, of which Kevin's was a beautiful counterpart? Were they only skimming pages in *Thy Brother's Wife* when Sean Cronin, with Nora painting the rectory kitchen, spoke to a convert class about God's abiding love, even toward the poor, the hungry, and the homeless? Didn't they want to jump off whatever they were on and shout with delight and relief as first Angèlica and then Nora assured Sean that it was quite all right to be imperfect, as each in turn welcomed him to the human race? Did they totally miss the point that Nora's love sustained Sean throughout decades of fighting the dragons of Church and government politics and working against frightening odds to make a difference in people's lives? Where were they when Nora and Sean kept their commitments, opting for a noble decision that took more courage and self-denial than most of us mortals could ever muster? And were they napping when it was obvious that God used each of them to keep the other from weakening? Don't these readers need love in their own lives, don't they want to see that God works wonders through aging, weary, frail humans like us? And as they read *Ascent into Hell*, were they able to take in only Hugh's desire for Maria and for Liz? Where were they when Hugh gave the homily at Marge's wedding and assured his listeners that forgiveness is the essence of love—human and Divine—and that the love between bride and groom would teach them both about God? How could they have missed both the guilt which consumed

Hugh after he and Liz first made love and the despair which engulfed him after he knew his love for Maria would prevent his ever desiring his wife again? Most readers of *Ascent into Hell* have heard sermons or meditations on the Last Words of Christ before His death on the cross. Can they honestly say they have ever heard a more pertinent commentary than Hugh's life?

One of the most elementary yet essential fundamentals of the study of fiction is the nature of theme in any work. A theme is not a moral, but a meaning, an underlying truth, pervading a literary work. In any work of the length and depth of Andrew Greeley's there will be multiple themes, each of which is defensible through a careful analysis of the whole. In no case is sexual love as an isolated entity a theme of any one of Andrew Greeley's novels. First, in no case is it made by the author to be the key part of the overall work; second, a theme, the truth portrayed through fiction, is a statement, a fact, a conclusion induced or deduced through careful literary creativity. In Greeley's fiction what the shallow reader wants to call "the sex scenes" are there as part of a wider truth, just as sexual love is in itself a part of a broader scope of love, or Love. Of course, sexual love exists, both in and out of fiction. It is a constant, a given. Greeley is not attempting to prove or justify its existence, for priests or for anyone else. What *is* Greeley setting forth as fundamental truths? What if you were assigned an analytical essay on the theme of a Greeley novel (two to three pages, typed, double-spaced, complete with cover sheet, outline, thesis statement, at least three supporting paragraphs with topic sentences, a conclusion, due at the beginning of class next Friday)? Couldn't you argue that Kevin's words to Ellen (after she has admitted to him that she blamed the Church for everything that went wrong in her life) are the theme of *The Cardinal Sins*? Aren't they what the book is really about after all:

> [Ellen:] "I blamed the Church for Tim's death. I loved him so much. I couldn't save him, and I thought the Church should have saved him. Even when I was doing it, I knew I was wrong and that someday I'd be kneeling on the floor before you and pleading to be let back in."
>
> [Kevin:] "And now you have done it," I said, feeling a huge burden lift away and go spiraling off into space. "And the damn-fool Church says, 'Ellen Foley Curran Strauss, we really didn't notice you were gone, because we never let you go.'" (350)

Remember that Ellen repeats the same wisdom to Mo as she joins Kevin in comforting the dying woman:

> Maureen opened her eyes again. I became aware of how tightly I was holding her limp body. "Does he really love me?"
>
> "Pat?" I said uncertainly.
>
> The old grin. "No, silly, God. I've tried . . . I usually make a

mess of things... but I try... at least sometimes." She winced with pain.

Ellen knelt beside me, her face twisted in terror and grief. "God loves you so much, Mo, that He never lets go of you."

She nodded. I was holding one hand, Ellen the other. God was getting a lot of help. (496)

If you chose to write on *Thy Brother's Wife*, wouldn't you choose love, not sex, as the topic, and argue that through the novel all love, human, physical, familial, selfish, lustful, passionate, compassionate, power-seeking, sublimated, dutiful, exhilarating, is but a metaphor for the perfect love of God for all men? You would need to consider Sean's debate with the pious Jesuit:

"Lovemaking between a man and woman... can mean many different things. Through lovemaking, lovers forgive one another, show their gratitude to one another, declare their love, renew their vows, chase their anxieties and their anger, reestablish communication, make life livable for one another, challenge, stimulate, excite, and reassure one another. Also, of course, it is the means for continuing the human race."

The pious Jesuit who shared the panel with Sean was outraged. "Even if you are a bishop, I must be frank, Your Excellency. Those are tasteless, vulgar words." (364)

Nora's love for Paul:

Nora would spend a long time trying to understand her own grief. She had loved Paul. A strange love, perhaps, but still a true love in its way. (481)

Sean's words at his mother's funeral Mass:

She was not, as far as we could tell, lonely, but she was surely alone, a lost soul. And yet, we know that God loved Mary, and that now all the joys of life are part of a bright, glowing joy that will never grow pale, never be dimmed, never end for all eternity. There is only one thing we can understand today. God loves Mary, and he loves all of us. (397–98)

And Sean's recognition of the nature of Nora's love for him:

"You damn fool," he wrote. "You missed God's sign for thirty years."

He crossed out the words, tore the paper into little pieces, and threw them into the wastebasket. Because he had lost his mother, God sent him Nora, the best sign of God's love he would ever

have. The same father who had taken away his mother brought
the shy little girl into his life so long ago. Talk about the twisted
lines of God. (493)

If you chose *Ascent into Hell* as the novel on which to write your paper, you
could weave the theme into the very structure of the work, linking the life
of Hugh Donlon to the mystical ascent to union with God described by
Teresa of Ávila and John of the Cross. Another student could relate the title
of the novel and the plot structure of Hugh's life to the truth expressed by
Dante in the *Divine Comedy*: the way up is the way down. With each topic,
as with each of the three novels, what sexual scenes there are, are subsumed
under a more universal truth about God, man, and the relationship between
them.

   Part of a student's inability to look beyond the forefront scenes of a novel
into its overall meaning is his all too frequent inability to comprehend the
nature of good and evil in the fictional work. It is ironic that censored works
are deemed unfit or scandalous almost always because of what someone
considers to be "improper" sexual passages. It is the puzzling but undeniable
truth that too often sins of the flesh loom as the unspeakable and "unwritable"
sins, while the greater evils in the work exist unnoticed or at least
unprotested. Dante realized this fact yet solved the theological difficulty by
placing the incontinent in the upper region of hell while sentencing the
violent and the treacherous souls to the lower echelons of premeditated evil.
Wasn't Nathaniel Hawthorne showing through *The Scarlet Letter* that the
bigoted self-righteousness of the American Puritans is a far worse sin than
the frankly admitted sin of adultery committed by Hester Prynne? And
isn't Roger Chillingworth's deliberate torture of the Reverend Arthur
Dimmesdale a more serious crime than the minister's sin of the flesh? Yet
readers and censors do not always see the author's intention.

   Flaubert's *Madame Bovary* was ruled forbidden reading because of the
adulterous acts of Emma, while the selfish provinciality of Homais, the total
stupidity and lack of commitment of the parish priest, and the maliciousness
of the moneylenders and shopkeeper went unprotested. The controversy
surrounding the novel *Madame Bovary* is further proof, when compared with
the controversy surrounding Andrew Greeley's fiction, that some of us have
not progressed much in our ability to analyze literature since the nineteenth
century. When Flaubert was brought to trial concerning his "scandalous
novel," the prosecuting attorney accused him of praising the lewd actions of
an adulteress; the defense attorney argued that, on the contrary, Flaubert
was teaching his readers a moral lesson by depicting the punishment of
Emma Bovary for her sins. In reality, Gustav Flaubert was doing neither;
he was writing a finely crafted fictitious piece about how one woman might
react to very real conditions in her background and in the nineteenth-
century provinces of France.

   When attempting to analyze the fiction of Andrew Greeley, many readers fall into the same either/or fallacy as did the two nineteenth-century French lawyers. Either they believe that the priest/author is teaching a class in moral ethics and that he will obviously show all evil punished in the form of a moral at the end of every work, or they rise up in active, self-righteous protest of this creator of salacious, scandalous behavior—a priest writing about sexual immorality! What they fail to see is a truth which is made apparent by Greeley in novel after novel: the greatest human evil lies not in man's failing to keep his sexual powers in check, but in his failure to control his pride, to love others, and to live up to his responsibilities to his fellowmen. How can a reader miss the true Greeley villains: head usher Leonard Kaspar, who had stolen a thousand dollars every Sunday for years from his parish, yet who held himself up as the model parishioner; Leo Mark Rafferty, who disliked all parishioners except those with sufficient money to support his expensive taste; the grim-faced missionaries who threatened the faithful with hellfire for their sins and bad confessions and pitted family members against one another in a campaign to cleanse the blackness of their vile lives; members of the Roman Curia, whose every move and vote was to enhance their power; Daniel Cardinal O'Neil, who could turn the facts into fiction, with himself as hero; Paul Cronin, remorseless after masterminding a political break-in and the hired killing of a longtime enemy; Monsignor Augustine Ambrose Aquinas Sullivan, who hated change, had not read a book in thirty years, avoided all work and controversy, called Sister Elizabeth Ann a "nigger lover" (*Ascent into Hell* 93), believed that "those parishioners who had the most money were closest to God" (106), insulted widows and children at funerals, avoided nuns and schoolchildren, believed that sex was the worst sin of all and therefore should not be discussed in his parish, believed that he, the cardinal, and the Pope shared infallible authority, and drank heavily; Father Lloyd Kilbride, who was vulgar when sober and obscene when drunk, and saw Sister Elizabeth Ann as the nun with great knockers; and Ben Fowler, who didn't know how to handle his daughter, beat his wife mercilessly, and betrayed Hugh Donlon and his fellow parishioners. Yes, the true Greeley villains— given a close reading, the novels do seem to make them obvious.

As with other problems of "what to do with Greeley's fiction," the issue of good vs. evil as depicted in individual human lives has its precedents in literary tradition. The Greeks realized that man must assume the blame for his actions in a moment of truth, alone (think of Greeley characters in similar situations); atone for his wrongdoing; and emerge victorious even in tragedy. Sophocles showed both Oedipus and Creon rise above their frailty to a kind of natural sainthood; without the benefit of biblical revelation, Sophocles knew that man sins, repents, atones, and is forgiven. His tragedies are metaphors for the Divine forgiveness that is central to the fiction of Andrew Greeley. Andrew Greeley's depth of understanding of the nature of tragedy is evident in his article on the music of Bruce Springsteen. Greeley says that Springsteen writes often of the tragic human

condition. Greeley, though, like Sophocles, Shakespeare, and Arthur Miller
before him, realizes that tragedy is not hopelessness: "Tragedy, however, is
not pessimism, not despair. It is still possible to fight back" ("Catholic
Imagination" 113).

Medieval writers, too, knew how to incorporate the very real dichotomy
of good and evil in their works. Gawain was given three trials and was
forgiven by his host, who was a symbol of God the grace-giver. Everyman,
whose Good Deeds lie in a pathetic heap on the ground, too weak to rise, is
given the sacraments and salvation because his Good Deeds, meager as they
appear, are sufficient to gain him God's forgiveness and redemption.
Remember Chaucer's *Canterbury Tales*: the Miller and Reeve, earthy pil-
grims to be sure, tell bawdy yet funny tales; the Wife of Bath has had five
husbands and is on the pilgrimage to look for a sixth, yet she is written up
as a comic character; Chaucer's ideal characters are those who, like the
Parson and the Plowman, love God and neighbor and follow the precepts
which they expect of others; Chaucer's real villains are those who have
failed in their commitments and duped their innocent victims; they are
precursors of Greeley's pompous and vile churchmen: the Friar, the Monk,
and the Pardoner (parallels, to be sure, with Greeley's Larry, Curly, and
Moe—or the Archbishop, the Cardinal, and the Roman Curia).

Recall Goethe's *Faust*. Faust forsakes his religious tradition for the loftier
goal of attaining all knowledge, the secrets of the universe, the elixir of life;
Faust and Gretchen, very much in love, give a sleeping potion to Gretchen's
mother and spend the night together; her mother dies, as does their
illegitimate child. But Goethe's God, a model for Greeley's God, speaks to
Mephistopheles in the Prologue:

> *Although he [Faust] serves me now confusedly,*
> *I soon shall lead him forth where all is clear.*
> *The gardener knows, when verdant grows the tree,*
> *That bloom and fruit will deck the coming year. (11.69–72)*

The Goethe/Greeley God does not fear for Faust's soul as he gives
Mephistopheles permission to tempt Faust:

> *As long as on the earth he shall survive,*
> *So long you'll meet no prohibition.*
> *Man errs as long as he doth survive. (11.76–78)*

Remember, too, that Faust is brought back to life away from suicide by
the sound of the Easter bells. The Church is so much a part of him that he
cannot resist it. Faust exhibited the same loyalty to his sacramental Church
that Greeley attributes to American Catholics of the twentieth century
("Why Catholics Stay in the Church," "Empirical Liturgy: The Search for
Grace," "The Catholic Imagination of Bruce Springsteen"). Like Greeley's

characters at their lowest points, Faust knows he is unworthy of grace; yet he, like Pat Donahue, Kevin Brennan, Hugh Donlon, Red Kane, Ellen Cronin, and Maureen Cunningham, is lifted by its presence. Grace and forgiveness persevere to the end, grace and free will cooperate one with the other, as Gretchen is redeemed because of her weak but sincere prayer for redemption, and Faust is saved because he relentlessly kept seeking truth, never finding rest or peace in anything less than the Truth of the Other One. The fiction of Andrew Greeley is often criticized for depicting for its readers the vivid, immoral, and widespread existence of sin in the world. Don't these critics realize that the fiction also shows over and over again that these sins, whatever they are, can be forgiven *ad infinitum* by a God who wants to forgive so much that He/She stands waiting to be asked?

Finally, a word about satire. Proof that this literary technique has caused problems for readers may be found in the puzzlement of students over Jonathan Swift's "A Modest Proposal," Shirley Jackson's "The Lottery," and Franz Kafka's "Metamorphosis." In fact, the prominent words "A Novel By... Andrew M. Greeley" on the covers of his early novels is reminiscent of the line of print preceding the first frame of the film "The Lottery": "The following is fiction." It is interesting to note that children have had through the centuries little difficulty deciphering the animals and their corresponding traits satirized in Aesop's *Fables*. Adults in the 1700s, however, could not read Molière's *Tartuffe* and figure out that the playwright was criticizing moral hypocrisy, not the Church or true piety.

The solutions to the problems discussed in this article are laid out, clearly, ingeniously, at least for a child, perhaps, in *God Game*, Andrew Greeley's 1986 satiric fantasy which weaves magic out of a computer game into serious theology. The solutions lie in what—and how—Father Greeley satirizes.

Father Greeley sharply, harshly, caustically—after the manner of Juvenal and Lucian—satirizes war, warriors, the love of war ("The gore on my screen was unsuitable for anyone" [21] or 'Rasia's comment "There have always been wars. There will always be wars. That's what we have warriors for" [80]) in much the same manner that Old Man Warner in Shirley Jackson's "The Lottery" argues "There's always been a lottery" (215). Greeley mocks and caricatures government bureaucrats (Greeley's narrator calls Malvau a "pompous bastard if there ever was one" [*God Game* 72], members of the Roman Curia (whom he calls sociopaths while matching up some of the principal and most unsavory clerics in his fantasy with their real-life names), and, particularly, Church leaders who misrepresent the love, forgiveness, and exuberance of Jesus. Cardinals in *God Game* are stupid, pompous, cruel, unbending, self-seeking, as when one argues for restraint of the "ilel"—actually, he had no moral qualms about eliminating her, but it would have been impractical to do so; furthermore, the narrator of *God Game* preferred this fictitious cardinal over the God-created real ones; priests who are bigoted, cruel, power-hungry, and nonreligious; and mad scientists—satirically named Larry, Curly, and Moe. Indeed, Greeley is a literary master at depicting many higher-ups in the world as clear examples of stooges. These are precisely the groups that are hit the hardest in Greeley's other novels. In *God Game* he simply explains that the Other One sees them, too, for what they really are: here's the real evil in Greeley's fiction, what you would not want anyone to imitate. In fact, according to the *God Game* narrator, these types are the impossible ones—even for God: "Conclusion: you can as an author shake those who are open to lust of one kind or another, but not those who are into power" (90). Again, remember Dante. The lustful are barely in Hell and are far up the mountain of Purgatory, whereas at the center of the earth, the deepest recess of Hell, are three of the most powerful human beings ever to live: Brutus, Cassius, and Judas.

Father Greeley mildly, gently, informatively—after the manner of Horace—satirizes the Jesuits (who are watching the tape of this game while "wondering what B'Mella and Lenrau would do about the high-school education of any potential offspring" 30); the theology department of Notre Dame (upon which the narrator wishes a good drenching); the unbearably distinguished appearance of officials like Malvau; the botanist's assumption that our world is "right" and any other world would naturally imitate ours; the pre–Vatican II Church (the unthinking Ice Maiden would have made a good pre–Vatican II novice, and the Duchess on one occasion mumbled as did pre–Vatican II kids at Thursday confession before First Friday); and the stubborn humans whom God has to *push* through the workings of grace. Such groups as these, plus the fictional priests' friends from time to time in the earlier novels, are playfully, humorously, mildly, yet pointedly satirized in Greeley's fiction.

And there are some things which are spared the Greeley satire. He never scoffs at or puts down human nature in its essence. He makes it very clear from the outset that God agonizes over, worries about, and loves Her/His creatures. If that belief of the author could possibly be doubted after a reading of Greeley's other fiction, certainly it cannot be anything short of affirmed after a reading of *God Game*. The narrator, as a temporary God, a metaphor or sacramental symbol of the Other One, fell in love with the Duchess at once, liked the Duke immediately, believed he needed the characters on the screen as much as they needed him, loved the two main characters, representative of all men: "I loved them both. Flawed, arrogant, stupid, they still had courage and flair. And curiosity" (201); told the Ice Maiden, "God is overwhelmed by the appeal of the creatures he has made" (224); looked at the newlyweds and thought, "Why else be God unless you can help such folks?" (240); and gave the clearest statement this professor has ever encountered of the exuberance and love which God shows forth to all men: "I was in fact having the time of my life. And in love with everyone. Just like God" (109).

The God-love which was implicit in the other novels is at the forefront of

God Game through the words of the God-like narrator about his characters. Human nature is lovable; God cannot keep Herself/Himself from loving mankind. Again, consider what a Greeley reader is shown with clarity and wit: God is waiting at the controls, waiting for a sign from us to press His/Her Enter key, so that the next onrush of grace can begin.

The very parts of the earlier novels which are scorned by some readers are clearly given their place in the scheme of things by the narrator of *God Game*. When the Duchess tells him that she wants to cuddle Lenrau's poor weary head against her breasts and asks if that is wrong, the narrator assures her: "Not wrong, but remarkably honest" (68). He makes the earlier Greeley novels even clearer on this point by refusing to allow Kaila to separate love and lust: "Nonsense. We are designed so that the two cannot be completely separated and ought not to be" (170). Clearest of all, though, is the narrator/God's comment as he watches the Duke and Duchess begin to make love: "Watching them was not like viewing an X-rated tape but rather like participating in a powerful liturgy. I wondered why there was not the music of pipe organ, trumpets, and drums in the background" (213). The *God Game* God is reminiscent of Kevin Brennan's encouraging words to Mo: "God will find you as irresistible as everyone else does, especially in a bikini" (*Cardinal Sins* 119). No, Andrew Greeley never satirizes the sexuality of a human being.

If sexual powers, with all their complications in tow, are exempt from Greeley's satire, so are all of human frailties. The author's sensitivity to man's nature can be seen clearly in the scenes—and there are many of them—in which man turns to God in prayer. This is the communication between creature and Creator, and the natures of both parties are key doctrines of the theologian-sociologist Andrew Greeley. Man prays often and hesitantly. Kaila is said to pray with "more than routine piety" (*God Game* 47) for safety and protection; there is an actual ritual that the characters in the God Game carry out in their praying: the removal of their outer garments suggests both the goodness of their bodies and the stripping away of all concealment before their Lord. (Remember that the God/narrator also notes that Ranora looks chaste despite her nudity and that Mo comments comfortably to Kevin that God can see her in the shower whenever He wants.) No matter how many failings human creatures may have, Greeley shows them stripped of evil and pride as they pray. Even the Duchess is not arrogant, but seems childlike in prayer. Ranora is without guile in all her actions; at prayer she is irresistible. After she prays for things to work out with the Duke and Duchess, and adds her contrition for impatience and a "please" at the end, the computer God wonders "how good the Other Person is at resisting such appealing little connivers" (197). The point to the reader and definitely to God is that man keeps on praying. This doctrine is taught not by a logical diatribe (recall Greeley's point about troubadours and storytellers), but rather by repetition within the plot. This God (and his permanent counterpart) says what Goethe and Faust's God

said over a century before: as long as man strives, God will listen, and as long
as God listens, man can be saved. It works with everyone. There is always
hope: for Faust and Gretchen, Ellen, Pat, Sean, Kevin, Mo, et al.

God is won over by prayer, Greeley reiterates often. After B'Mella and
Lenrau pray that their love will never turn cold or that if it does, it may
become even warmer than before, the priest/God responds in thought: "A
prudent and discreet prayer" (228). Man's ambiguous notion of prayer is
exemplified by Maureen in *The Cardinal Sins*: " 'Please, dear God, help me,'
she prayed, wondering if God bothered to listen to the prayers of sacrilegious fornicators" (263). After B'Mella berates herself in prayer ("You of all
people know what a miserable and vile woman I am—arrogant, proud,
ill-tempered, vindictive, moody, vicious" [*God Game* 235]), concluding that
God should not allow her to exist, ending her prayer with the judgment: "It
would be better if you slay me this night instead of sending me to his
wedding couch" (235), her God replies, "No way, kid" (235), and he wisely
ignores the Duke's protests that he is unable to pray on his wedding night,
smiling as the Duke and Duchess try to pray with other things on their
minds. Greeley's greatest truth about prayer is that when men tell God
they can't pray, they are of course doing it. Kevin says it, as do Ellen, Sean,
Pat, and the Duke, yet they are turning to God in their despair and
frustration. In the Lost Generation days at the beginning of our century,
Hemingway had Jake Barnes do the same thing. Jake said that the Catholic
religion is a grand religion but he didn't think he could believe in it
anymore, but he did want to pray for money and his friends and the
bullfighters, if he could, and God listened (*Sun Also Rises* 97). Jake prayed as
he told God he didn't know how anymore. (Weren't we all taught in our
Baltimore Catechisms that prayer is holding a conversation with God?
Hemingway and Greeley don't show men conversing perfectly—but at
least they keep on trying, with God at the other end straining to hear.) Just
as John of the Cross put the Dark Night of the Soul, or spiritual dryness, as
a step in the process of mystical union with God, so these frail human
beings are making the attempt to turn to God even as they say they can't.
And even the negative prayers count.

If that's not hope, and a continuation of the Gospel truth, I don't know
what is. The point for Greeley is: God is always there, so whenever and
however man turns to find Her/Him, man is not disappointed. Even when
the creature does not know he is seeking, God and the Church are there.
Greeley continues the literary and theological tradition of Christ forgiving
the adulteress, no questions asked, and pursuing the soul even while the
soul is fleeing down the nights and down the days and years; of God being
in His heaven—or at His computer terminal—so all must be right with the
world, any world. (I wonder if anyone ever protested the works of Francis
Thompson or Gerard Manley Hopkins. I also wonder how many people
read their works compared with the number of Greeley books sold.)

One final untouchable, unsatirized quality of man—and of God: a sense of humor. Although people are usually rather willing to accept a sense of humor as a desirable and perhaps even as a necessary characteristic of other human beings, people are often leery of ascribing it to God. In my parish in Irving, Texas, a Greeley-type priest (that is, open, fun-loving, drawn to young people, more likely to talk about God's love than His punishments, and more likely to praise his fellowmen than to judge or condemn them) preached a sermon recently which contained the following words:

> Jesus enjoyed parties. He loved people, and He went to their dinner parties. He loved to laugh. He changed water into wine, and if that's not a party, I don't know what is. Jesus would be the type of person that we would want to take with us everywhere. If we were going skiing, then we would want to take Him with us to the ski slopes. (Monaghan)

Many of our parishioners do not like such sermons. They don't like to hear God made light of—that sounds disrespectful. Furthermore, they believe that this priest talks too much about skiing. He should be more serious when he talks about Jesus to our young people—everyone knows Jesus would not ski. It is not clear how these parishioners know so much—I guess they just do.

In Greeley's fiction a sense of humor is essential to man and to God, and it is bound up with happiness. In *God Game* Ranora is the redeemer, Messiah, Shakespeare's Fool, Ariel, nymph, child, teenager. She brings laughter, innocence, and love into the world. Man needs more of her spirit, the story shows, and God must be laughing with her because she is irresistible to him. Then are we irresistible to God when we laugh? Is that what makes Her/Him irresistible to us? Isn't that what we want teenagers to know? (My parish priest talked about snow skiing to Texas teenagers; Father Greeley writes about Chicago teens going waterskiing. Good evidence that they both know young people.)

Greeley's fictional world is a place where laughter redeems and sanctifies. The child with the creative imagination knows it. Noreen knew it:

> On Palm Sunday, Noreen, Sean, and Nora rode to Oakland Beach to visit Mike. The two adults were moody and preoccupied, paying little attention to the wonderful spring day. Noreen considered talking about Easter and resurrection and decided against it. She knew that teenagers didn't teach sermons to bishops. (*Thy Brother's Wife* 484).

But of course they do—Ranora and Noreen were excellent teachers. Perhaps they could do a better job of it than English professors, for we don't seem to have fared so well.

WORKS CONSULTED

Bracken, M. "Greeley 'X-Rated.'" *The Texas Catholic*, 26 Feb. 1988, 5.

Goethe, Johann Wolfgang. *Faust*, Part 1. Baltimore: Penguin, 1960.

Greeley, Andrew M. *Ascent into Hell*. New York: Warner, 1983.

———. *The Cardinal Sins*. 1981. New York: Warner, 1982.

———. "The Catholic Imagination of Bruce Springsteen." *America*, 6 Feb. 1988, 110–15.

———. "Empirical Liturgy: The Search for Grace." *America*, 21 Nov. 1987, 379–83, 390.

———. *God Game*. New York: Warner, 1986.

———. *Thy Brother's Wife*. 1982. New York: Warner, 1983.

———. "Why Catholics Stay in the Church." *America*, 8 Aug. 1987, 54–57, 70.

Hemingway, Ernest. *The Sun Also Rises*. New York: Scribner's, 1954.

Jackson, Shirley. *The Lottery*. New York: Popular Library, 1949.

Monaghan, George. Sermon delivered at Holy Family Church, Irving, Texas, 19 Mar. 1988.

10

INGRID SHAFER

John Updike and Andrew Greeley: Two Visions of God and Humanity

*I*n their novels and stories, both John Updike and Andrew Greeley link religious experience and sex, but they do so in very different, one might even say diametrically opposed, ways. Updike, coming from the Protestant dialectical tradition of Søren Kierkegaard and Karl Barth, considers all attempts of the fallen human being to experience God through affirmation of everyday life vain. In the temporal sphere Updike's absolutely transcendent God can only be intuited through His absence. For Greeley, rooted in the Catholic analogical tradition of Saint Thomas and Karl Rahner, God reveals himself precisely in and through a world redeemed by the Incarnation.

In the following, I shall limit my main argument to the analysis of one extended, theologically crucial sexual passage toward the end of Updike's *Roger's Version* (1986) and three internally related passages from Greeley's *Patience of a Saint* (1987) which portray the male hero in situations similar to those experienced by Updike's protagonist but show him responding to those situations in a strikingly different manner. The two novels are excellent candidates for comparison. In both works the central characters are introduced as well-educated, fundamentally passive and passionless men

An earlier version of this essay was presented during the second of four sessions dealing with Andrew Greeley's fiction at the Popular Culture Association Meeting in New Orleans, Louisiana, 25 Mar. 1988.

in their fifties, closet daydreamers, successful yet dissatisfied in their professions, alienated from their strong and attractive wives, narcissistic and cynical, and suffering from a combined strain of midlife crisis and "existential despair." Their one essential difference is their religious background. While both have fallen away from active involvement in parish life, one is a Protestant and reads Tertullian and Paul Tillich; the other is a Catholic and reads the Song of Songs and Richard Rolle.

While neither hero should be identified with his author, each lives in the context of what his respective creator considers an accurate working model of the relation of this world and God. In keeping with Greeley's Catholic faith in God's active presence in the world, Red Kane of *Patience of a Saint* undergoes a profound process of change and renewal in the course of the book. He does not as much speak for Greeley as he responds to the loving "meddling" of other characters, most especially that of the *Real* protagonist: *God Her/Himself*. Red Kane's Chicago, invaded by the fire of divine passion, is at once the ancient Israel of the Song of Songs and County Sligo in Ireland.

In keeping with Updike's assumption of a distant, majestic, transcendent God, Roger Lambert remains the same throughout *Roger's Version*, finding in his experiences only confirmation of the Immutable Truth he already knows, the Truth of human depravity and divine perfection. Since this "Truth" is one which Updike consistently explores in his novels, it seems justifiable to assume that Roger's theological comments are at least a partially accurate reflection of Updike's position. Roger's anonymous New England city seems a contemporary ironic version of Roger Chillingworth's somber and frigid Puritan Boston, complete with Esther/Hester and Dale/Dimmesdale. Hence, thematically, *Roger's Version* is reminiscent of Updike's "turning Dimmesdale's Puritan dilemma upside down into that of Marshfield" (Hunt 185) in *A Month of Sundays*.

Before proceeding to the main argument, it is helpful to examine the flyleaves of the novels. In both works theme-setting citations suggest theological objectives while leaving no doubt concerning their authors' disparate perspectives. Updike introduces his book with Matthew's question "To what purpose is this waste?" as well as Kierkegaard's insistence that he (a lonely and bitter bachelor) would still continue to love God's infinite cold majesty even if it were devoid of love, and Barth's argument that the majesty of God implies the hopelessness of all human activity. Greeley presents God, the Passionately Pursuing Lover, by quoting from the Song of Songs, Fred Fisher's "Chicago" with "I saw a man, he danced with his wife," Francis Thompson's "The Hound of Heaven," Jeremiah's verses describing God present like fire in his heart and bones, and Gerard Manley Hopkins' tender image of the Holy Ghost brooding over the "bent world with warm breast and ah! bright wings."

The first selection is taken from *Roger's Version*. Roger Lambert, Professor of Divinity and former minister, who has long ago given up talking about

God (300), submissive, seemingly passionless son of "love-miserly Alma"[1] (353) and husband of green-eyed, long-nailed Esther, his former mistress, whom he now likes best "in that iconic view of a woman from the rear" (306), has taken unending delight in graphically imagining his limber wife whom he rarely beds in assorted adulterous positions with a devout Christian graduate student. He has also grown perversely fascinated with Verna, his niece, a high school dropout druggie and the mother of an illegitimate part-black little girl. One night, when Paula, Verna's daughter, is in the hospital after her stoned mother has accidentally broken her leg and whacked her for howling after she was down, he finds himself, his attire reduced to socks and boxer shorts, in bed (though still chastely on top of the blanket) with his niece.

> . . . Verna's plump and naked arms had snaked out from beneath the covers and she was pulling at my maligned undershorts, trying in clumsy sorrowful fashion to undress me, while her uncovered breasts slewed about on her chest. At her attack, the delicious flutter of ambiguity beat its wings, necessarily two, through all my suddenly feminized being. Not either/or but both/and lies at the heart of the cosmos. "This isn't right," I ventured, limp in some parts, stiff in others. (301)

As George W. Hunt, S.J., points out in *John Updike and the Three Great Secret Things: Sex, Religion, and Art*, it is indeed possible exegetically to interpret the story of the Fall wholly in sexual terms complete with the phallic serpent borrowed from the Canaanite fertility cult (127). This is obviously what Roger is doing. He imaginatively projects himself into the Garden of Eden, reverting to his primal nakedness, albeit without being able to recapture primal innocence. Verna, whose name sounds like spring and who throughout the novel is portrayed as at once sluttish, crude, and innocent, turns into Evil Eve, the familiar temptress of misogynist lore, clumsily bent upon undressing Roger with her "snaking" arms. The "flutter of ambiguity," particularly in association with "either/or" dissolved into "both/and," is closely related to Kierkegaard's concept of dread, the delightfully repulsive, repulsively delightful fear of the not-yet, the unknown possible, which is "simultaneously *both* attractive and repugnant" (Hunt 122). At this moment Roger becomes Everyman about to reenact Adam's first transgression and choose sin, at once his personal sin and what theologians call original sin.

After a deliberately unappealingly clinical description of the sexual act replete with terms such as "cunt" and memories of a long-ago plastic vagina (Updike 302), Roger reflects upon the theological implications of the experience:

> When I was spent and my niece released, we lay together on a hard floor of the spirit, partners in incest, adultery, and child

abuse. We wanted to be rid of each other, to destroy the evidence, yet perversely clung, lovers, miles below the ceiling, our comfort being that we had no further to fall. Lying there with Verna, gazing upward, I saw how much majesty resides in our continuing to love and honor God even as He inflicts blows upon us—as much as resides in the silence He maintains so that we may enjoy and explore our human freedom. This was *my* proof of His existence, I saw—the distance to the impalpable ceiling, the immense distance measuring our abasement. So great a fall proves great heights. Sweet certainty invaded me. "Bless you" was all I could say. (302)

As Christians, how do we find God according to Kierkegaard? To start out with, the question is itself illegitimate. We do not, we *cannot* actively find God; at best we can choose to be open to the possibility of being found by, grasped by God. This openness is like a gaping wound, despair at the ultimate meaninglessness of all things finite including the self, a despair which pits against the inherent imperfection of the material world an infinite and eternal standard of unity in the light of which we, the human "other," are judged and found wanting. We know ourselves as a concrete unity of irreconcilable opposites, spirit painfully stretched between the temporal and the eternal, battleground and tenuous synthesis of body and soul, sick unto death; through that very sickness raised above the beast, through that very consciousness distinguished from the non-Christian. Human life, precisely because it is finite, individual, and torn by contradiction, presupposes an absolute ground of being as its negation, the shadow-void positing the sun-fullness, and yet, since shadow is essentially absence, incapable of comprehending that which is its source. "To be sharply observant of this sickness constitutes the Christian's advantage over the natural man; to be healed of this sickness is the Christian's bliss" (*Fear and Trembling* 148).

How to be healed? We tremble at the very thought of sustaining a relationship with the eternal and unchanging and demanding God (*Bretall* 479) experienced negatively as the abyss of nothingness, a relationship which entails surrender to His Absolute Holiness, a surrender which in turn implies the absolute sinfulness of the human being (*Either/Or* 2:354). And so Roger and Verna find themselves "on a hard floor of the spirit, partners in incest, adultery, and child abuse," filled with mutual distrust and dislike, yet perversely clinging to one another, "lovers, miles below the ceiling," comforted by the realization that they "had no further to fall." "Lying there with Verna"—the tangible evidence of his fallen state—Roger, gazing upward, sees "how much majesty resides in our continuing to love and honor God even as He inflicts blows upon us—as much as resides in the silence He maintains so that we may enjoy and explore our human freedom."

For Roger/Updike as for Kierkegaard, God is accessible, if at all, only through His silence—*Deus Absconditus* intuited in the "Dark Night of the Soul"—and the blows he might inflict upon us. "For the thought that he is always in the wrong is the wing whereby he soars above finitude, it is the longing wherewith he seeks God, it is the love wherein he finds God" (*Either/Or* 2:354). Yet even this wing, this poverty-born Eros, would be of no avail were it not for God's infinite love for us, a love like that of a King for a scullery wench, a love for the sake of which the King transforms Himself into a servant (*Bretall* 168) in order to draw the wench on high, beyond herself. It is precisely through insistence on humiliation and degradation—"partners in incest, adultery, and child abuse"—as prerequisites for faith that we are given the choice to respond to the offer of salvation. The paradox can "be relevant only to the very nature of the absolute difference that distinguishes man from God" (*Concluding Postscript* 195) and thus is meaningless unless it is grasped in the inwardness of faith with the passion of the infinite (192), which, though not the annihilation of the earthly (*Journals and Papers* 382), nevertheless constitutes a transvaluation of all human values, and is paradoxically found in that "distance to the impalpable ceiling, the immense distance measuring our abasement." And so, postcoitally invaded by "sweet certainty," Roger candy-coats the caustic horror at the heart of things, as he once routinely used to placate his childishly hopeful congregations, with a simple and sincerely insincere "Bless you," before starting to express his worries (rather belatedly) that Verna might end up pregnant. "Relax, Nunc," is her nonchalant reply. "I just had my period a couple of days ago. Anyways I could always get another abortion now that you've showed me how" (Updike 303). Roger's God-consciousness-through-sin is no more lasting or fruitful or authentic than the brief, solitary coupling he has just experienced. The force of love is severed from primal erotic power and both are as barren as the abovementioned artificial vagina.

The following selections are taken from *Patience of a Saint*. Red Kane, a middle-aged, competent but cynical Chicago newspaper reporter, unfaithful husband, indifferent father, and fundamentally bitter, unhappy man, has a tremendously powerful mystical experience at the busy downtown corner of Wacker and Wacker after imaginatively associating a new elegantly curved glass skyscraper with his wife's ice-green eyes and alluring figure (12–13), and almost being run over by a Cadillac limousine. In subsequent days and weeks Red proceeds instinctively, and to his own utter amazement, from this merry dance "on a flaming sea of ecstatic love" (14), toward a renewed zest for life, the determination to unmask a corrupt politician, thoughtful civility toward his stunned colleagues, and most particularly the determined pursuit of his wife, whom he has neglected for years. Contrast the following scene, also told from the male partner's point of view, with serpentine Verna's attempts at removing her uncle's shorts:

For a fraction of a second he thought he heard the cosmic baseball
bat. Irritably he told it to go away. The Holy Ghost ought not to
be a voyeur. Ought He? Or She?

"What if the kids—"

"We'll run." She tossed his shirt aside and knelt next to him,
fingers on his belt buckle. "I don't know what's happening, Red
Kane, but you started this and I"—she opened the belt and at the
same time pressed a breast, warm and slightly moist, against his
face—"I intend to love you from now on the way you deserve to
be loved." (166)

On the surface the images are similar. Though this particular manifestation of the Paraclete has discarded dove wings for the force of a cosmic
baseball bat, Red's Swooshing Spirit is still a variation on the theme of
Roger's "delicious flutter of ambiguity," an invitation by the Other, experienced as dread by Protestant existentialist and delight by the Catholic
Incarnationalist. Both Red and Roger offer no resistance to their women's
hands, but one is conscious of "fingers" (symbolic of human technical and
cultural creativity), the other of primordially "snaking" arms. Both also
report reactions to their partners' breasts, but one describes a feeling of
moist warmth against his cheek, an intimate, kisslike touching of skin; the
other dispassionately reports uncovered breasts slewing about on the girl's
chest, an image which somehow evokes visions of raw beef livers slithering,
shifting, and turning on a butcher block.

Red is totally open to his wife's ministrations; Roger remains behind an
armor of invisible fig leaves despite his nakedness. The uniquely human
association of genital union with permanent commitment and the powerful
emotions of love and friendship inextricably link sexual *love* to our perception of ultimate Reality. Red envisions the divine as gracious and the cosmos
as essentially benign; thus he finds it easier than Roger to take the risk of
radically disclosing himself to another, not only, or even primarily, by
literally allowing his sexual partner to see him in his physical nakedness but
also by daring to expose the most tender and vulnerable inner core of his
self. Roger, on the other hand, who conceives of the Really Real as coldly
indifferent, remains in his protective shell, particularly since he is incapable
of separating the concepts of sin and sex. Both authors follow their visions
consistently. Red and Eileen (as almost all of Greeley's couples) make love
with the lights on, as befits the celebration of a saving sacrament of life;
Roger and Verna have sex, a shameful, secretive activity, in the dark, as
befits the reenactment of the death-bringing Fall.

Time-honored dualistic traditions and abovementioned exegetes notwith-
standing, the Catholic theologian Karl Rahner points out that the Christian
should not identify original sin with concupiscence. Original sin is the loss
of our supernatural union with God and our primal holiness. Thus, genuine
asceticism is never based on the "false and cowardly minimization of the
good it renounces" (60). The Christian ascetic "becomes free, not in order

to wall up his heart but to give it away, to God and the world" (59). Most of
what used to be negatively dismissed as sinful concupiscence is actually (as
Saint Thomas already noted) legitimate God-given self-affirmation. In this
perspective, erotic love, the "nuptial embrace," the earthly, temporal interhuman
re- and preenactment of the eternal divine-human love affair, is—as Saint
Paul admitted, albeit somewhat reluctantly—a sacrament.

Both Roger and Red experience a descent in connection with coupling.
For Roger the "fall" is lonely and follows the completed, equally solitary act
in which Verna seems little more than an uninvolved but appropriately
disreputable receptacle. For Red "submersion" is integrated early into the
cycle of lovemaking itself, followed by joint ascent described as merging of
"two firestorms" (84). Still, even Roger starts out smelling in Verna's breath
"the innocence of mint," though "innocence" is quickly unmasked as
illusion—"a whiff of antiseptic mouthwash"—while she inquires, "How
shitty a person do I seem to you?" (299), an observation with which her
soon-to-be "lover" secretly agrees. Eventually, after the completed act, he
plummets to "the hard floor of the spirit." Eileen, on the other hand, takes
Red (in an earlier sexual episode)

> down into a primal swamp or not quite fulfilled desire, a swamp
> that smelled of lavender liquid soap, sweat, aroused woman, and
> Scope mouthwash and was inhabited by demanding kisses and
> gentle but persistent fingers and darting electrical impulses that
> exorcised his guilts and regrets, his convictions of failure and
> worthlessness, his self-hatred and self-contempt. He sank into the
> sweet, savory, and tenaciously strong warmth of mother earth. (83)

For different reasons, Roger and Verna consider the sexual embrace a
human version of casual canine coupling in a back alley. Verna is portrayed
as almost pure id, functioning primarily on a material infantile and egotistical
plane, while Roger's dualistic theological superego permits him no other
perspective. In this connection it is significant to note that Roger experienced no difficulties enjoying his present wife's physical charms while he
was still married to his first wife (and in the active parish ministry). For
such individuals, and there are many, sex is essentially tainted and cannot
be fully "enjoyed" *unless* it is illicit. Recent widely publicized "revelations"
concerning two fundamentalist television preachers fit the pattern perfectly.
Like Roger, they may well have found evidence of the Divine Judge, or at
least proof for the sinfulness of human nature, in their very abasement.
And what deeper abasement than one resulting from *sex*, that most powerful
and hence (from the dualist's point of view) most suspect and potentially
blasphemous of all human activities? It is reasonable to assume that a God
who is primarily identified with the rod or absence cannot be experienced
except when humans act to offend Him, and cannot be spoken of *except* for
the language of radical otherness. This is certainly a realistic position; all we
have to do is read the daily paper and watch the evening news to gather

evidence for cosmic indifference and human depravity. It is also a censorious position which seeks to "raise human consciousness" while dismissing faith in natural human goodness, cosmic meaning, happy endings, and hope in the face of evil and adversity as simple-minded self-delusions unfortunately perpetuated by popular culture.

Still, much like the proverbial glass which can be described as both half empty and half full, it is not the *only* possible position. For Andrew Greeley, as for Saint Thomas (who confidently incorporated the writings of non-Christian thinkers into his system), the earthly, natural, material sphere is not primarily the absence-shadow of divine transcendence but rather participates in divine essence the way the moon mirrors the light of the sun. According to Saint Thomas, human knowledge and Christian revelation, the world and God, are aspects of a single truth originating in God and thus cannot be in conflict with one another. Consequently, he argues, human beings have the right to use their imagination, reason, and language to speak analogically of God's nature and to look for traces of the divine in their daily lives. Applied to the contemporary situation, this means that we may confidently explore the entire spectrum of human learning, action, and experience (including popular culture) to recover God for the Present. There is no "secular" sphere automatically opposed to divinity, and sexuality, precisely because of its immense power as Romantic love, is a prime candidate for an immensely forceful sacrament of divine passion.

Thus, Red and Eileen (along with Uranos and Gaia, aka Yahweh and His Shekhinah) allow themselves to be absorbed into the cauldron of primal chaos, in order to reenact the ancient and ever-new *hieros gamos* of creation, at once violent fusion of elemental forces, solemn, sacred ritual, and creative play appropriate to a God who enjoys a romp with His pet Leviathan and His Bride, Israel, and, who almost two millennia ago made love with a dark-eyed olive-skinned Semitic girl.

In contrast, Updike's primary theological mentor, the early Karl Barth, considered the *analogia entis* (the appeal to being in general shared by God and all that is) the "invention of the Antichrist" (x) insisting on an infinite chasm between God and World, the radical otherness and transcendence of a God whose revelation comes down upon us exclusively from on high, challenging and shattering *all* of our humanly acquired notions, even (or especially) those concerning religion. Human beings are evil throughout, sinners, totally blind to divine truth. From such a point of view both Thomist natural theology and the ways of the mystic are not merely frivolous and useless, they are blasphemous and idolatrous. Thus Greeley's scenario of a cosmic baseball-bat-swinging Divine Voyeur vicariously participating in a human lovemaking interlude and his insistence that in and through this "carnal" act the sexual partners actually increase their knowledge of God, must from a Barthian perspective be denounced as compromising divine majesty and erroneously investing the natural (post-Fall) human being with the capability of reaching out toward God or at least posit the possibility of divine-human interplay and reciprocity. But Red and Eileen are Irish and Catholic. Thus, undaunted by stern Protestant neo-orthodoxy, they cheerfully imitate *their* God and do what comes naturally, in Her name:

> Then, as she guided him . . . to the shining mountaintops of their lovemaking, Red knew that he had finally unlocked the secret of his magic, green eyed wife just as she had unlocked the secret of healing his accumulated pain.
> . . . His insight went far beyond physical skill. He would not only make love to Eileen but he would love her, and being loved, she would be happy and his. The pride, the enormous shattering that went with that realization, was not a pride of possession, but rather the pride that comes from knowing at long last who one must be and what one must do. (342)

As Karl Rahner and Herbert Vorgrimler put it, in their *Kleines Theologisches Wörterbuch* (imprimatur: Freiburg i. Br. 2 December 1975), loosely translated and paraphrased: God is love. For humans, love is radical self-actualization in response to God's grace-conferring self-communication; loving is the most fundamental of all human acts; in love everything is integrated—"knowing at long last who one must be and what one must do"; if we love others, we want to possess and enjoy them and do our utmost to foster their self-actualization—"being loved she would be happy and his" (262). Thus it is entirely consistent with the Catholic imagination to portray Red experiencing lovemaking as ascent as well as descent.

> He was drowsily slipping along the down side of ecstasy into a contented afterglow. . . . Dreamily Red noticed how spectacularly beautiful she was after lovemaking and felt a vague but powerful contentment that he finally knew how to love her in bed and out.
> The light from the emerald grew in power and filled the room. (342)

To continue Rahner, in love infinity appears in finite form. Love has the power to transform worlds. Whenever we actively love another we also love Christ. Authentic love for a specific person opens that individual up to universal love; genuine love is a dialogue which involves give and take, and though the one we love may be quite imperfect, she or he is nevertheless God for us if our love is truly unconditional and grounded in grace (*Wörterbuch* 262)—"The light from the emerald grew in power and filled the room."

Having just engaged in God-like behavior, and given his mystical tendencies, Red's God-consciousness, unlike Roger's fleeting "sweet certainty" based on the infinite distance between wormlike man and majestic God, turns into a full-blown mystical encounter, initiated by God, the implacably passionate Lover: "The bed, the room, the Doral Plaza, the Chicago skyline, the cosmos turned into fluid chaos. Desperately Red reached for his wife, a last wild grasp for stability and protection" (343).

Both Roger and Red are conscious of the night city, but again in different ways. While Verna undresses in the other room, Roger stands at the living area window "looking toward the tall crystalline center of the city, marvelling at how many of the skyscraper windows were lit." It is not the sublime beauty of the moment, however, which strikes him. With characteristic pessimism he comments only on "the waste" (298), thus reintroducing the Matthew citation on the flyleaf. While Greeley confidently speaks of sanctifying the city, Updike resists any such delusion.

> Then, again, the swooshing sound of the cosmic baseball bat. It was not exactly a sound because it was nothing you heard, but rather a signal, an advance warning, a loud primal cry that perhaps might be translated, upon later reflection, "Look out, buster, old Yahweh is here again!" ... Then the love that had lurked behind the green glass skyscraper at 333 Wacker Drive swooped with ah! bright wings into the small studio apartment and took possession of him.
>
> No, rather the Holy Ghost, or Whatever, erupted from the emerald and from his wife's swelling breasts. Yes, of course, warm breast. Eileen was not merely the occasion of this new love that invaded their room and their bed of pleasure. She and the love were temporarily bound together in one eternal love. (343)

Red Kane's Chicago has literally been invaded by that Spirit of Fire and Love who almost two millennia ago transformed a motley group of first-century Jews into the vital, passionately committed shock troops of a new faith. Chicago, the earthly city, is utterly transfigured and becomes the *civitas dei*. Again Red experiences a foretaste of the beautiful vision in eternity. Teilhard's noosphere has broken into the everyday of the sidewalk in front of the 333 Wacker building and continues to pursue its "prey." Chicago, Everycity USA, is the New Zion, aglow with the radiance and power of love. For Red, the atemporality and ecstasy of lovemaking have somehow opened the "gate" to the *nunc stans*, the Eternal Now, of synchronicity. The end precedes the beginning in much the same way as the fully developed oak tree is already implicitly present in the tiny acorn. Red is given the chance to contribute to the full realization of the Kingdom of God by recognizing the here and now as the hidden presence of the ultimate future. It seems an added and significant irony that Updike's hero is playfully called "Nunc" by his niece, a word supposedly a contraction of "Uncle" but also Latin for "now."

In contrast to Red, Roger recovers quickly from both sex and religious insight. He lets himself out of Verna's shabby apartment, noting, "The hall shocked me by being lit, as if its glaring vacuity, lined with shut doors, had been all this time eavesdropping" (303). Updike, like Greeley, introduces the image of the voyeur, or at least the third-party listener. In Updike's iconic cosmos the "glaring vacuity" of the hall with its shut doors (closed eyes) may well represent God, the distant Majestic Judge who listens to the evidence and deals out blows with blind dispassion. Greeley's Divine Voyeur, on the other hand, has been intimately involved all along. It is She, bright-winged and soft-breasted, who, "like a barrage of sky rockets exploding over Grant Park on the Fourth of July" (77), had issued the rather forceful invitation to the divine banquet/wedding feast initially, and who has since insisted on "hanging around" wanted or not.

Roger reports, "I danced, considerably lightened, down the vibrating project stairs and into the Audi, its tan paint sucked empty of color by the sulphurous streetlamp overhead" (303). Again, images also found in *Patience of a Saint* appear with different connotations. After Red's original mystical encounter on the Chicago street corner, he is described as "a creature who used to be Red Kane . . . now dancing merrily on a flaming sea of ecstatic love" (14). For Red, lovemaking, its afterglow, the green-glass curvaceous, contemporary architectural "goddess," Eileen's green eyes and swelling breasts, and the crystalline, trance-inducing emerald all fuse into a word-transforming and mind-shattering encounter with the Holy Spirit of Absolute Love. The entire experience is consistent with Rahner's comments on Christian mysticism. "Since in his love Jesus Christ redeemed all of creation along with humanity, the Christian mystical experience is ultimately neither rejection of the world nor meeting with the infinite. Instead, it is taking the world along toward and into a loving encounter with the personal deity" *Wörterbuch* (290).

> Later, trying to analyze the experience, Red felt that someone was saying to him, in effect, "You like her, huh? I'm glad you do, because I made her for you. I like her too. She's mine. In fact, she's Me."
>
> It was like Wacker Drive: light, heat, fire, overwhelming, invading, possessing love; dazzling truth, beauty and goodness; confidence, hope, joy, the promise that all would be well; a love so unspeakably powerful that, in the instant it possessed Red, he knew he could never escape from it. Nor would it ever allow him and Eileen to escape from one another. When the joy seemed so intense that he knew he would die, the operator of this transcendental Concorde jet turned on the afterburners and Red thought he had died and was in heaven, a golden city whose ivory walls were his wife's breasts (Greeley 343).

In Greeley's Catholic cosmos, the Heavenly City reveals itself not as a distant place, but rather as a different dimension of the here and now, a state of the soul touched by God Himself (or more appropriately Herself). Both Updike and Greeley use the color symbolism of shades of green and yellow—the former to evoke hell and the latter heaven—beginning with their respective protagonists' wives' color of eyes. In addition, contrast Red's experience first of the seductive green glass building and then of ecstatic, joyous, golden, emerald inspired luminosity in a "transcendental Concorde jet" with Roger's descent to his tan Audi, its "paint sucked empty of color by the sulphurous streetlamp overhead," a description reminiscent of hollow-toothed vampires, pale, bloodless husks, and the devil complete with sulphur. Note also that while the 333 Wacker building actually exists, the street number fortuitously represents the trinity (while being exactly half of the demonic 666 generally associated with the Antichrist).

In *Roger's Version* the human being is finally alone because Roger's theology is neither fully incarnational nor fully trinitarian and certainly not sacramental (as his fascination with the eventual Montanist Tertullian indicates). Unless God is envisioned as Loving Presence, we can indeed know God only in His absence or fury, and Roger's lip service given to "both/and" rather than "either/or" lying at the "heart of the cosmos" remains precisely that: empty rhetoric. This admittedly incarnationally humanistic Catholic writer is tempted to quote from *Inherit the Wind*, substituting Roger Lambert for Matt Brady: "But [Roger Lambert] got lost. Because he was looking for God too high up and too far away" (Lawrence and Lee 780). The screaming fiery fundamentalist and the resigned cold cynic are two manifestations of the inability to accept that God is Unconditional Love.

The association of love and knowledge is rooted in the mystery of the trinity and a sacramental view of the world. Karl Rahner and other Catholic theologians speak of God as the absolute Mystery, a mystery which chooses to communicate Itself to us and interact with us in time and history. In this radical self-disclosure God imparts Himself as Himself in such a way that the divinely immanent Trinity, the eternally ineffable, infinitely distant Mystery, intuited by humans as the Wholly Other, is simultaneously the Trinity of saving grace and liberating action, the reality of how God relates to the world in time, the Mystery at the very center of our own being, experienced by humans as divine Presence, the call from within to be the best we can be, something we might call the Utterly Us. The absolute self-disclosure of God to the world, the mystery-come-near through grace, this active divine pole of the divine-human dialogue, is called Father as Its own primal source. As Incarnate activity in history, It is called Son; as abiding presence given to us and accepted by us, It is called Spirit.

At the very core of The Mystery of the triune God there lies the ultimate Mystery of Passionate Love (cf. Tracy 443, n. 30). Passionate in the dual sense of the term: ardent and suffering. Love which created the universe and every living creature. Love which took on flesh in a woman's womb; Love which was born, lived and taught the message of God's love; Love, which taught us to call God *Abba* (Daddy); Love which died on the cross and rose from the dead, all for the love of sinful humanity. Love which promised to be with us always and poured itself into human vessels at Pentecost. Love which instructed us to baptize all of humanity in the Name of the Father and the Son and the Holy Spirit.

In a sense, both Updike and Greeley consider sex and woman avenues to God. In the work of the former, however, sex, even between married partners (cf. *Couples*), can never symbolize more than the *via negativa*, the "dark night of the soul," which dialectically points toward its absolute negation, the ineffable, infinitely distant perfect fullness of divine light far above the carnal shadow realm. Correspondingly, woman is either Eve, the temptress, or, viewed from behind, walking off, reminiscent of Yahweh passing Moses in the desert and allowing Himself only to be seen from the back, not face-to-face. If we apply Rudolf Otto's categories of God-experience to Updike and Greeley, the former focuses on the Holy as *Mysterium Tremendum* while minimizing the *Fascinans* or at least subordinating it to terror: the flame about to consume the fascinated moth.

Greeley, on the other hand, balances the two aspects, though he emphasizes the positive, life-engendering power of divinity as Fascination/Invitation. Terror at the Wholly Other is subordinated to delight at hearing the Call of Love. Grace will allow the responding moth to experience no more of the flame than it can bear. Thus sex, if joined to love and commitment, even if technically adulterous but particularly within marriage, generally represents the *via positiva* of ecstatic mystical union which can and should be a powerful sacrament of divine passion and springtime renewal. In the same spirit, the very seductiveness of woman toward man (*and* man toward woman) is interpreted positively, as a human reflection of divine passion seeking to draw Her/His creatures into the divine embrace.

In the Judeo-Christian cosmic calendar, Updike focuses primarily on the dread-full past, the darkness of the new moon: his characters reenact the loss of Eden, the Fall, understood as sexual transgression in the Augustinian tradition. Greeley takes his people full cycle through and beyond the dark phase of the Fall toward the grace-full future: in ecstatic sexual fusion they are allowed to preenact the ultimate reunion of God and the world which might be visualized as the sun-intoxicated disk of the full moon.

And so the stories of two couples, Roger with green-eyed, long-nailed, vaguely satanic Esther, and Red with green-eyed, warm-breasted, definitely God-like Eileen, end with going to church. When Esther appears in the kitchen all dressed up in a "crisp dark suit, with lace at her throat" (354) one Sunday morning, Roger wonders where she is going.

> "Obviously," she said, "to church."
> "Why would you do a ridiculous thing like that?"
> "Oh—" She appraised me with her pale green eyes. Whatever emotions had washed through her had left an amused glint, a hint or seed. In her gorgeous rounded woman's voice she pronounced smilingly, "To annoy you." (354)

It is Christmas Eve in the Kanes' world. Red, whose mystical interludes terrified Eileen and resulted in a series of professional and personal disasters including his short-term committal to a mental institution, is determined to get rid of the bothersome Spirit once and for all and withdraw into his old cynical shell. Driving his family to Midnight Mass is a meaningless routine activity. Thus he is less than delighted when he notes Eileen's seductive white and red Christmas dress and the dangerously flickering emerald. The congregation sings "Adeste Fideles." "Next to him, Eileen was singing softly in her sweet, clear voice. Amazingly, Red was singing too" (440).

> Chaos swept through St. Clements, blurring the whole church and the whole world. The cosmos once again dissolving. He reached for Eileen's hand, to protect her, no, to seek her protection. Unaccountably her arm was already around him. (440)

In Updike's fundamentally unredeemed world, salvation consists of accepting ourselves as the makers of our own hells on earth and being open to God's deserved wrath or undeserved grace. God is intellectually envisioned as Transcendent Ruler and Judge. Romantic love and the passionate closeness of married life are foolish and dangerous delusions. Human communities, such as families or church, provide no support. Each one of us is ultimately alone. Realistically, relationships are founded largely on mutual distrust, exploitation, and the need to torment another. There is, to quote Sartre, "No Exit."

In Greeley's fundamentally redeemed (though, of course, imperfect) world as experienced by Red and Eileen we are cradled/embraced by God's nurturing love and invaded/engulfed by divine passion. God is the Wholly Immanent Transcendence, at once in "Heaven on High" *and* pervading every atom on earth, the "Both/And" at the heart of the cosmos which Roger intuits, seeks, but finally rejects. God wants to be known as our Mother/Father, Lover, Friend. Divine Love, however, is demanding; it challenges us to abandon our insecurities and fears of failure. It challenges us to embrace the Cross, to look at the world and ourselves honestly, the "landscape" illuminated by the radiance of unconditional love, the darkest, most hidden corners, all those terrible secrets we least want to face, thrust upon us. It challenges us to resist the lure of cynical apathy and accept a life of hope and passion, to remember that accepting the Cross also means joyfully yielding to the resolution of Easter Sunday already implicitly contained in the promise of Bethlehem. As Red Kane was to discover, this very opportunity is fraught with danger and supremely terrifying. It demands continued choices, decisions which might and probably will result in being ridiculed, persecuted, misunderstood. Becoming a source of light for others, confidently living one's life on a day-by-day basis in the Presence of God, is at least as difficult as groveling in the dark abyss, certain that we have been abandoned to cruel fate by a distant God. Jesus came to show us the Father as *Abba*, Daddy, who acts in the world, who wants us to be happy, who loves totally and freely, and whose love cannot be earned, because, no matter how immoral and even godless, we already have it. No strings attached. No questions asked.

Updike helps us overcome the no longer possible childish stance of the uncritical innocence of what Paul Ricoeur has labeled the first or "primitive naiveté" (351). One suspects he would agree with Flannery O'Connor that "a child's faith [is] all right for the children, but eventually you have to grow religiously as every other way. . . . What people don't realize is how much religion costs. They think faith is a big electric blanket, when, of course it is the cross" (354). Both Updike and O'Connor, however, along with the majority of theologically sensitive contemporary writers, fail to differentiate between "childish" and "childlike" and stop short of the next step, the progress/return to Tracy's "critically mediated immediacy" (sup. 58n. 2), Ricoeur's "second naiveté," which in the Christian symbolic universe consists in becoming child*like*. After all, Jesus said, "The kingdom of God belongs to such as these" (Matt. 19:14), mature men and women who are not afraid to accept God's love and emerge from the crucible to celebrate the Easter birthday party/marriage feast of human rebirth and redemption. No, God is not the counterfeit warmth of an "electric blanket"; God is the live Flame of Creation calling us to the primordial hearth.

For different reasons, Updike and Greeley agree that salvation cannot be earned; they disagree on the earthly effects of that theological position. The former drops his readers down into the frozen pit of Dante's hell and demands they focus on what lies beyond the cold infinity which separates them from God; the latter leads his readers to the brightly colored hot-air balloon a loving Dad has provided for those who become like children, and dares them to take a flying leap into the gondola, cut the ropes of fearful distrust, and allow themselves to be carried up, across the void, toward their home.

NOTE

1. Ironically, the Latin word *alma* means "nourishing"—thus the traditional name of the Madonna as "*Mater Alma*." Updike misses no trick in this carefully crafted parody of the Romantic and Catholic vision.

WORKS CITED

Barth, Karl. *Kirchliche Dogmatik*. Vol. 1, *Die Lehre vom Worte Gottes. Prolegomena zur christlichen Dogmatik*. München: Chr. Kaiser, 1927.

Bretall, Robert, ed. *A Kierkegaard Anthology.* New York: Random House, n.d.

Greeley, Andrew M. *Patience of a Saint.* New York: Warner, 1987.

Hunt, George W. *John Updike and the Three Great Secret Things: Sex, Religion, and Art.* Grand Rapids: Eerdmans, 1980.

Kierkegaard, Søren. *Concluding Unscientific Postscript.* Translated by David F. Swenson and Walter Lowrie. Princeton: Princeton University Press, 1941.

————. *Either/Or.* Translated by Walter Lowrie and revised by Rev. Howard A. Johnson. 2 vols. Garden City, N.Y.: Doubleday, 1959.

————. *Fear and Trembling* and *Sickness unto Death.* Translated by Walter Lowrie. Garden City, N.Y.: Doubleday, 1954.

————. *Journals and Papers.* Vol. 1: A–E. Edited and translated by Howard V. Hong and Edna H. Hong. Bloomington: Indiana University Press, 1967.

Lawrence, Jerome, and Robert Lee. *Inherit the Wind. America on Stage: Ten Great Plays of American History.* Edited by Stanley Richards. 693–781. New York: Doubleday, 1976.

O'Connor, Flannery. *Habit of Being.* Edited by Sally Fitzgerald. New York: Farrar, Strauss & Giroux, 1979.

Rahner, Karl. *Theological Investigations.* Vol. 3, *The Theology of the Spiritual Life.* Translated by Karl H. and Boniface Kruger. Baltimore: Helicon, 1967.

————, and Herbert Vorgrimler. *Kleines Theologisches Wörterbuch.* 14th ed. Freiburg: Herder, 1983.

Ricoeur, Paul. *The Symbolism of Evil.* Translated by Emerson Buchanan. New York: Harper & Row, 1967.

Tracy, David. *The Analogical Imagination: Christian Theology and the Culture of Pluralism.* 1981. New York: Crossroad, 1986.

Updike, John. *Roger's Version.* 1986. New York: Ballantine, 1987.

11

KIRBY WILCOXSON

The Sociologist as Storyteller: Science and Fiction in the Novels of Andrew Greeley

$\mathcal{M}$y task here is to reflect upon the sociological character of the novels of Andrew Greeley. My personal experience, however, is that sociological reflection upon Greeley's novels is always secondary, always a conscious rereading of stories that are satisfying for more basic reasons.

Although I became interested in Greeley's novels because he is a sociologist, I read them first for the story's sake. Enjoyment, not theological or even sociological insight, is the primary motive for reading fiction. Yet the stories became a catalyst for theological reflection.

As an evangelical Baptist, my own theological tradition is considerably removed from that of Greeley. Through my own reflections on scripture and on life, I had become increasingly convinced that the problem of systematic theology is that God is not very systematic. Instead, I came to know a God of surprises, a God continually tearing asunder all of our carefully constructed categories. In the discovery of Greeley's fiction I found stories of the God I was coming to know—a Lover pursuing us with unrelenting tenderness, graciously offering to us a love that can never be earned, a God who, according to Father Blackie, breaks all Her own rules in order to lure us to Herself. This was an ironic lesson, since we

An earlier version of this essay was presented during the second of four sessions dealing with Andrew Greeley's fiction at the Popular Culture Association Meeting in New Orleans, Louisiana, 25 Mar. 1988.

evangelicals learn early in life that Catholics try to earn favor with God through works and rituals while we receive it as a gift of God's grace—although it does help to not drink, dance, or smoke.

I read Greeley's stories first for the sake of the story, and therein find myself caught up in Greeley's religious imagination. But neither story in itself nor story theology is my concern here. Rather, it is to consider the role of the sociologist as storyteller. Greeley makes it clear in his own reflections that the theologian and the storyteller are one. My question concerns the extent to which the sociologist and the storyteller are the same person.

Greeley heralded Bruce Springsteen's album *Tunnel of Love* as perhaps a "more important Catholic event in this country than the visit of Pope John Paul II" ("Catholic Imagination" 112). Greeley's contention is that the Pope uses the language of propositional theology, but Springsteen uses the language of the imagination, a much more powerful means of appealing to the whole person. It is useless to debate Springsteen's intentions in this matter; Greeley's point is simply that whether Springsteen intends it or not, *Tunnel of Love* is "profoundly Catholic" and is so because of the effect of the Catholic imagination which Springsteen has absorbed and from which he cannot escape.

Religious imagination does not, however, exhaust our imaginative lives. Sociologists, especially those of Greeley's caliber, are necessarily possessed by a sociological imagination as well. This sociological imagination is perhaps not so deep or significant as our religious imagination—although for some sociologists it is undoubtedly more significant—but it is inescapable nonetheless. Like the religious imagination, it colors all that we engage in.

This is not at all to suggest that writing novels is simply another way to do sociology, nor that Greeley intends the same outcomes from his novels as he does from his empirical studies. Instead, it is to suggest that Greeley's novels are Catholic songs—given the functioning of the imagination, it is difficult to believe that they could be otherwise.

In his *Confessions*, Greeley himself raises the question of the relationship between the sociologist and the storyteller. He states that "sociology forced me eventually to become a storyteller" (222). There is an obvious interpretation of that statement. Greeley's own research in the sociology of religion is concerned with the functioning of the religious imagination. He argues that people develop their religious understandings primarily as the result of the stories they hear and that propositional theology is, in fact, a by-product of the imagination. In Western culture, however, we exalt rationality and convince ourselves that the rational is prior to the imaginative in both experience and significance. The obvious relationship, then, is this: given the evidence provided by Greeley the sociologist, Greeley the priest, who desires to communicate God to people, decides he should tell them stories. These should be stories about God and people; there is no *prima facie* requirement, however, that these be sociological stories.

On the other hand, Greeley himself suggests that sociology is involved in his stories in a much deeper way than merely as empirical justification for his particular priestly endeavors. For example, in his autobiography Greeley quotes an exchange between Ellen Foley and Kevin Brennan in *The Cardinal Sins*:

> "All right, Kevin, I'll say it, and you'll have to mop up the tears on this hard floor of yours. I blamed the Church and God for things that were inside me and my family. I focused on all the ugly things and forgot about Father Conroy, Sister Caroline and first Communion and May crownings and High Club dances and midnight mass and all those wonderful things that I love so much. I gave them all up because I was angry. I blamed the Church for Tim's death. I loved him so much. I couldn't save him, and I thought the Church should have saved him. Even when I was doing it, I knew I was wrong and that someday I'd be kneeling on the floor before you and pleading to be let back in."
>
> "And now you have done it," I said, feeling a huge burden lift away and go spiraling off into space. "And the damn-fool Church says, 'Ellen Foley Curran Strauss, we really didn't notice you were gone, because we never let you go.'" (209–10)

Greeley calls this passage the "central moment" of the book, and then contends that "all my theology and my sociology and my pastoral experience and my life are crammed into the symbols and loves in those two paragraphs." And in the same context, Greeley approvingly quotes social scientist Ken Prewitt, who says that he will read no more of Greeley's technical works, because "all the sociology is in the stories and far more palatable there" (*Confessions* 442).

So then Greeley, and evidently others, recognizes his novels as sociological stories as well as religious ones. Yet they are not, except in fleeting instances, sociological treatises. Father Blackie does, for example, have something of the sociologist in him. In one instance in *Patience of a Saint* (65) he quotes to journalist Red Kane the basic findings—statistics and all—by Greeley and McCready on the sociology of mystical experiences; these findings are amplified in the sociological note which concludes that novel.

Furthermore, despite his recognition of the sociological nature of his stories, Greeley rightly denies that they should be read as treatises. *Ascent into Hell* is not, according to Greeley, "a sociological study about marriages between priests and nuns" (ix). In the note introducing *Virgin and Martyr* Greeley states, "I have written a story, not a sociological study of North American Catholicism or a political science study of Latin American Catholicism" (ix). One presumes that disclaimers of this type apply to all of Greeley's stories. And thus the dilemma: all of the Greeley novels are products of a sociological imagination as well as of a religious imagination, but none are sociological treatises; yet reputable social scientists such as Prewitt approve of the novels at least in part because of their sociological content. So how do Greeley the storyteller and Greeley the sociologist fit together?

My first contention is that the scientist (including the sociologist) and the artist (including the storyteller) are much more closely related than is sometimes supposed: both have as a primary goal the understanding and illumination of reality.

As a sociologist, I might, for any of a variety of reasons, choose to study ethnic Catholics. I might even produce a treatise called *The American Catholic: A Social Portrait* (Greeley, 1977); and it might even occur to me that a portrait is something an artist produces. In the study I carefully delineate a research strategy, construct hypotheses, and test those hypotheses using the best available methodological and statistical techniques. I cannot, of course, help bringing to the study my own preconceptions of what Irish Catholics, for instance, are like. In fact, those very preconceptions may prove to be important sources of insight, albeit insight that must be empirically tested. If I am careful in my work, the methods and statistics that I use do not depersonalize or somehow obliterate the Irish Catholics; instead they lead me to a richer and more accurate understanding of what it means to be Irish Catholic. And the proper reward of the work comes when the sociologist (and the reader) says, "Aha, that's what the Irish Catholics are like."

Now suppose that I decide to write novels as well as monographs, and by coincidence I decide to write about Chicago Irish Catholics. My goal is to write a good story, not to make sociology more palatable. Therefore, I do not make my characters into types (not even "ideal types," to use the sociological lingo) which are somehow representative of Chicago Irish Catholics. Instead, if my stories are "true," the characters are flesh-and-blood people who take on a life of their own (as Greeley points out, the novelist cannot be responsible for the moral behavior of his or her creatures). As novelist, I once again bring my own preconceptions to the story. But if I am sensitive to the lives of my characters, the result is not a stereotype, but a deeper and more accurate understanding of what it means to be Irish Catholic. Again, the reward comes when the storyteller (and the reader) says, "Aha, so that's what the Irish Catholics are like." And the novelist who is possessed by a sociological imagination does not need to intend to write a sociological novel. Rather, he or she is by nature sensitive to the social webs in which the characters are entwined.

According to Robert Nisbet, both the sociologist and the storyteller have as a main goal *verstehen*, understanding which penetrates to the realm of feeling, motivation, and spirit. *Verstehen* is a generalized understanding that is not stereotypical but is rooted in the concrete, in the particular. Novels and the sociological treatises do not, of course, have the same status within the scientific community where the logic of verification and codification is of primary concern. Nonetheless, it must be seen that art and science—when well done—are but two ways of seeing the same truth, of understanding the feeling, motivations, and spirit of human behavior.

So what fruits of the sociological imagination are evidenced in Greeley's stories?

Most obvious is the centrality of ethnicity. Greeley has done as much as any sociologist in emphasizing the continuing importance of ethnicity. The novels do not explore the many varieties of being ethnic in the United States, or even the possible ways of being an ethnic Catholic. But one cannot read the novels without developing some sense of what it means to be an Irish Catholic. The beauty of novels—especially multiple novels dealing with related themes—is that one can "know" in a fuller and richer sense what it means to be Irish Catholic without being tempted into stereotypical knowledge. One cannot come to know the Ryans, the Collinses, and the Farrells without realizing that despite "assimilation" and "upward mobility," Irish Catholicism retains its significance and will continue to do so across generations. On the other hand, no one who comes to know the Ryans, the Collinses, and the Farrells through Greeley's novels can ever believe that Irish Catholic ethnicity is reducible to a cliché or formula. One learns instead that there are many different ways of being indisputably and irrevocably Irish.

Perhaps a more subtle but no less significant sociological theme that permeates the novels is a concern with the social construction and maintenance of reality. Reality, in life and in the novels, is always mediated by social groups. This is to say that knowledge is never accepted or rejected simply on the basis of its "truth value." Rather, what we know and regard to be true is in no small part the result of the communities in which we live. No sociological insight is of greater importance than this.

The communities in which our knowledge is constructed and maintained include, but are certainly not limited to, the geographic locations where our lives center. Neighborhood is always an important shaper of consciousness. A move from the city to the suburb is much more than a change in location; one is transformed in more basic ways, for the change in location necessarily involves a change in thinking as well. In the stories, characters are careful to identify their status as "South Side" or "West Side" Irish, for each location entails an entirely different way of being Irish. Place is important in Greeley's novels—Twin Lakes, Forest Lawn, the Loop—not merely for the memories that places evoke, but because place is at the center of consciousness.

Geographic communities are not, of course, the only communities which shape consciousness. Others of at least as great an importance in the stories include ethnic group, family, church, and occupational group (e.g., journalist, psychiatrist, missionary, bureaucrat). Without the Catholic Church as a whole, there are smaller communities which are important in shaping consciousness: parish (e.g., Saint Praxides), religious organizations (e.g., Teen Club), and especially self-contained religious bodies (e.g., seminary, Our Lady of the Hill).

Within communities, one does not so much become persuaded by the truth of an idea as one becomes socialized in that truth. Hence, one does not simply possess knowledge but is possessed by it; therefore, one seldom accepts or rejects knowledge simply on the basis of rational argument.

Red Kane and his psychiatrist can be in perfect agreement on the description of his ecstatic experiences, but the meanings each attaches to those experiences are at loggerheads. Furthermore, the correctness of the meanings cannot be established by appeals to rules of logic or empirical evidence; rather, each makes perfect sense within the context of the correct community.

This notion that reality is socially constructed does not imply that all views are equally viable and that persons consciously pick the appropriate view according to the social context. I do not pick and choose among alternative views but am socialized into particular views as the result of participation in various communities. My vision of the world is structured by the preconceptions I have internalized, and I cannot help but see the world through those preconceptions.

This leads to the next sociological theme that permeates Greeley's novels—the persistence of basic categories of socially constructed thought even when the social context that produced those categories no longer holds. This is the key to understanding Greeley's remarks about Bruce Springsteen and to understanding what happens to the characters in his stories.

Greeley states that Catholicism "inundates the preconscious of its members very early in life with intense, powerful, pervasive and durable images that shape that activity of the agent intellect for the rest of life. . . . The preconscious is certainly Catholic by the time one is six and, arguably, after one's first conscious Christmas experience" ("Catholic Imagination" 112).

According to Greeley, Springsteen's imagination is permeated by Catholic symbolism as the result of his early socialization in the Church, and specifically because of the sacramental nature of the Church. Springsteen may consciously reject the Church, but he cannot escape his own preconscious, and it is this preconscious which provides the basic categories and symbols which organize and make sense out of the world. Because of this working of the preconscious, Springsteen is "both a liturgist . . . and a superb example of why Catholics cannot leave the church" (111).

For Springsteen and for the Greeley characters this preconsciousness is shaped communally—within the family, within the neighborhood, and within the Church—through conversations and symbols and stories and sacraments. Or, in Ellen Foley's more particular list, the preconscious is shaped by "Father Conroy and Sister Caroline and first Communion and May crownings and High Club dances."

The communities and structures which shape the preconscious inevitably shift. Geographic location, occupational position, religious group membership may all change, and each of these changes implies a psychical shift as well. One may even consciously abandon the community, as do Ellen Foley and presumably Bruce Springsteen. But the truth is that one may, so to speak, take the person out of the Church, but not the Church out of the person. The preconscious continues to shape one's view of the world even in the absence of the communities which originally shaped the preconscious.

Ellen Foley blames the Church for the tragedies in her life, but, she tells Kevin, "Even when I was doing it, I knew I was wrong and that someday I'd be kneeling on the floor before you and pleading to be let back in." And Bruce Springsteen writes and sings Catholic songs regardless of his intention in the matter. In theological terms the Hound of Heaven continues to pursue, and even those in the novels who attempt to reject the Church— some for very good reasons—continue to meet God at every corner.

That this phenomenon is not limited to Catholicism is perhaps best evidenced by the existence of groups such as Fundamentalists Anonymous. Although fundamentalism does not share the sacramental nature of Catholicism, it is still a powerful shaper of the preconscious. Fundamentalists Anonymous recognizes that to reject the Church on rational, intellectual grounds does not necessarily free the psyche, the preconscious, the imagination from the bonds of the Church.

A final and related sociological theme which permeates the Greeley stories concerns the manner in which his characters come to know and experience God. Both his sociology of religion and his theology find religion mediated to persons through two primary means: metaphors and relationships.

Catholicism, Greeley says, is a religion rich with metaphors, none of which are more powerful than the sacraments ("Catholic Imagination" 112). These metaphors are meaning-producing; they make sense out of our lives and mediate our experience with God. Catholic minstrels (like Springsteen) and storytellers (like Greeley himself) are metaphor-makers, telling the old stories in new ways and thereby reengaging the imagination of the hearers.

Human relationships become metaphoric, even sacramental, in Greeley's fiction. Such a view is substantiated by Greeley's research in the sociology of religion. Proposition 11.6 of *Religion: A Secular Theory* states: "There is an empirical correlation between human love and divine love" (154). Religious stories, biblical or otherwise, are always stories of relationships. It is through these relationships that one develops images of God. The fictive relationships between characters in the novels evoke the religious imaginations of the reader. The story of Anne Reilly, for instance, becomes a story of God in which the priest, lover, psychiatrist, and cop become the "angels" of September, representing the "Church at its most effectively caring best" (*Angels of September* 452). The stories can be epiphanic for the reader because the characters of the stories experience their epiphanies (although not all have such experiences) in a very human manner: not through the doctrinal catechism, but through stories, sacraments, and relationships.

A final note must be made concerning Greeley's sociological storytelling. Greeley's statement that *Tunnel of Love* is a more important Catholic event in America than the Pope's visit is premised on the contention that "troubadours always have more impact than theologians or bishops, storytellers more influence than homilists" ("Catholic Imagination" 112). My guess is that they also have more impact and influence than sociologists and that if the sociological imagination is ever to become a public imagination, it will be due in no small part to sociological storytellers such as Greeley.

WORKS CITED

Greeley, Andrew M. *The American Catholic: A Social Portrait*. New York: Basic, 1977.

———. *Angels of September.* New York: Warner, 1986.

———. *Ascent into Hell*. New York: Warner, 1983.

———. *The Cardinal Sins*. New York: Warner, 1981.

———. "The Catholic Imagination of Bruce Springsteen." *America* 6 Feb. 1988, 110–15.

———. *Confessions of a Parish Priest*. New York: Simon & Schuster, 1986.

———. *Patience of a Saint*. New York: Warner, 1987.

———. *Religion: A Secular Theory*. New York: Free Press, 1982.

———. *The Religious Imagination*. New York: Sadlier, 1981.

———. *Virgin and Martyr.* New York: Warner, 1985.

Nisbet, Robert. *Sociology as an Art Form*. New York: Oxford, 1976.

12

PHILIP H. KELLY

The Reader as Hero: Reader-Response Criticism and Greeley's Fiction

This paper grows out of three notions, each of which is concerned with what happens to the person who reads fiction. In that respect, this paper is an essay in reader-response criticism.

The first notion is T. S. Eliot's proviso in "Religion and Literature" that "popular" reading needs to be considered as carefully and critically as does reading of the classics. I include this notion for two reasons: (1) because some people question whether we should be spending energies studying "popular" novels and (2) because Eliot has some special words for the religious and moral formation that derives from "popular" reading.

> I incline to come to the alarming conclusion that it is just the literature that we read for "amusement," or "purely for pleasure" that may have the greatest and least suspected influence upon us. It is the literature which we read with the least effort that can have the easiest and most insidious influence upon us. Hence it is that influence of the popular novelists . . . requires to be scrutinized most closely. And it is chiefly *contemporary* literature that the majority of people ever read in this attitude of "purely for pleasure," of pure passivity.

An earlier version of this eassy was presented during the first of four sessions dealing with Andrew Greeley's fiction at the Popular Culture Association Meeting in New Orleans, Louisiana, 25 Mar. 1988.

> . . . Though we may read literature merely for pleasure, . . . this
> reading never affects simply a sort of special sense: it affects us as
> entire human beings; it affects our moral and religious existence.
> (350)

I imagine that many people read Greeley's novels for pleasure rather than
for serious intellectual engagement. According to Eliot, whether we read
Greeley's novels for pleasure or for intellectual engagement, the effect on us
is substantial. Eliot argues that when we read a classic we are attuned to the
influence it will likely have on us. And since we don't have any special sense
that we can turn on and off at will, we will be equally influenced by that
which we read purely for pleasure. In fact, Eliot suggests that we probably
need to read popular works more carefully than we do the classics, because
in reading "purely for pleasure" we are less likely to be conscious of the
emotional, psychological, moral, and intellectual impact.

The second notion is Robert Scholes' description of what happens to us
as we read fiction. In *Elements of Fiction* Scholes sees the reader as one who
suspends participation in the activities of this world while partaking in
those of the world created by the fiction:

> When we are reading a story we . . . have stopped the ordinary
> course of our existence, severed our connections with friends and
> family, in order to withdraw temporarily into a private and unreal
> world. Our experience of fiction is more like dreaming than like
> our normal waking activity. It makes us physically inert but
> exercises our imagination. In terms of our performing any action
> in it, this special world is absolutely unreal, whether we are
> reading a history book or a science fiction story. We can do
> nothing to affect either the Battle of Waterloo or the War of the
> Worlds. And yet, in a way, we participate. We are engaged and
> involved in the events we are reading about, though powerless to
> alter them. We *experience* the events of a story, but without the
> consequences—emerging from John Hersey's *Hiroshima* without a
> scratch on our bodies. Emotionally, however, and intellectually, we
> are different. We have experienced something. (4–5; emphasis on
> "experience" is Scholes'.)

When we read, we participate imaginatively in the new world created by
the author. That participation changes us. If what we experience is morally
sound, we are likely to be made better for having read.

The third notion is from Joseph Campbell's sketch of the typical journey
of the hero in *Hero with a Thousand Faces*. Campbell sees the hero as one who
is called to adventure by a herald. The adventure takes the hero out of the
regular world we know and into a private unreal world. When the hero
crosses the threshold into that unreal world, he is reassured by supernatural
agents. The adventure is usually a series of trials and terrors that drive him

down, often to the brink of despair. The true hero survives the trials and overcomes the terrors to win a treasure—a boon with which he can return to the regular world and make it a better place.

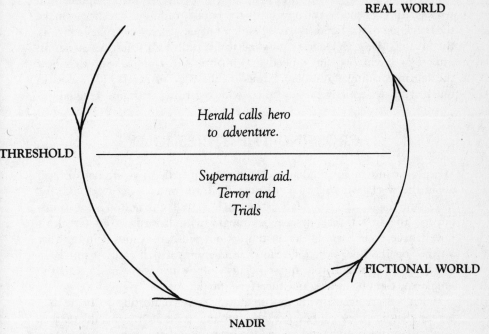

Adapted from a diagram in Joseph Campbell, *Hero with a Thousand Faces* (Cleveland: World Publishing, 1949), 245.

Campbell summarizes the hero's journey as follows:

> A hero ventures forth from the world of common day into a region of supernatural wonder: fabulous forces are there encountered and a decisive victory is won: the hero comes back from this mysterious adventure with the power to bestow boon on his fellow man. (30)

In this paper I will argue that in a sense Greeley's work has the potential to make heroes of us all. Like the hero, we venture into the moral world of Greeley's fiction. The good effect of the time spent in Greeley's moral world can empower the reader to return to the world at large with a renewed faith in the presence of God and the moral nature of man.

The next few headings in this paper are from Joseph Campbell's *Hero with a Thousand Faces*. Implied in my use of the headings is that the reader partakes in the same journey as the typical hero described in Campbell's book.

CALL TO ADVENTURE

In Campbell's schema the hero is summoned to adventure by a herald who ushers the hero across the threshold and into the world of supernatural wonder. In my schema the novelist is the herald, calling the reader to make the transition to the fictional world. Father Greeley is particularly effective as the herald. Many feel safe responding to his call. As a priest he carries an important credibility, an implied imprimatur. He is not a wild-eyed new theologian treading those outer limits on the edge of heresy. He seems in touch with what many are wrestling with regarding faith and religion.

CROSSING THE THRESHOLD

When we contemplate reading a classic piece of fiction, we are not worried about the world we are about to enter. The waters have been charted; the maps are made. But popular fiction is less well charted. The territory beyond the first threshold can be fraught with hazards. And Greeley's novels have their hazards—rape, mutilation, murder, even a painting that writhes on the floor when shredded. Sometimes it is literally a jungle in there. But the real heroic quest begins only when we venture into the unknown, the uncharted, and therefore the dangerous.

When we are faced with the unknown, it is comforting to be with a herald that inspires confidence. We put out trust in the herald (Father Greeley in this case); and we cross over into that second world, that fictional world of fabulous adventure. As we read, we give ourselves over to the experience of the characters that populate that other world. Scholes says, "We are engaged and involved in the events we are reading about, though powerless to alter them" (4). Typically, once we set foot across the threshold, a Greeley novel engages us quickly. Suspense often whisks us along.

SUPERNATURAL AID

Once we have been whisked into the world of the fiction, we might feel like Alice tumbling down the rabbit's hole. We need a guide, a helper who can make sense out of all this rush and tumble of adventure. In Greeley's novels this figure is often one removed from the direct action (Blackie Ryan) or one who is able to maintain a special equanimity even in the midst of frantic action (Nora in the midst of her affair with Sean Cronin; Maria Angelica in relation to Hugh Donlon's self-torture; Kevin Brennan in the face of Pat's absurd carrying on or Kevin again when sharing a bedroom with Ellen). Whether a priest or a layperson, that character seems somehow specially touched by God. This character calms us and gives us confidence. The reader comes to rely on that person as a kind of anchor of calm rationality. We can, for example, depend on Blackie to provide a clear textbook explanation for Red's cosmic baseball or for the curious effect of Father Desmond Kenny's painting on Anne Reilly.

THE BELLY OF THE WHALE

According to Campbell, the hero at the nadir of the adventure "discovers for the first time that there is a benign power everywhere supporting him in his superhuman passage" (97). Similarly, Greeley's novels picture God as ubiquitous and irrepressible. Vicariously, we accompany the characters as they sink to their darkest depths of sin and guilt. Rising from that nadir will require a superhuman, supernatural effort. In a Greeley novel that supernatural aid will always be there, often in the person of one of God's agents, like Nora, or Blackie, or Noele, or Maria.

THE ULTIMATE BOON

In the classic hero story there is a payoff for all the terrors and trials that the hero survives. The classic hero garners some grand treasure—the golden fleece, a beautiful maiden, the way to peace and prosperity. Whatever the tangible treasure, at its root it is literally or symbolically the secret of life, the key to living better. In a Greeley novel the reader comes to understand a secret to life. That secret usually constitutes an increased understanding of mankind's relationship with God.

Campbell refers to the hero's boon as "uninterrupted residence in the Paradise of the Milk that Never Fails . . ." (176). The hero experiencing this paradise is comfortable and contented. In reading a Greeley novel the reader comes to appreciate God in Her manifestation as woman and mother. In Greeley's novels God is ordinarily a woman, always comforting, always nourishing. She is the world's navel, the nipple that never fails to nourish. The reader discovers a peace based on a feminine God whose love is unconditional, unbounded, and ever-present.

THE RETURN

In Campbell's schema the hero who discovers such unbounded peace is sorely tempted to remain in that second world content with simply having made his discovery. But in order for the discovery to be more than selfish contentment, the hero must return to the first world.

Campbell calls the boon a life-transmuting trophy, the runes of wisdom

(193). The boon that Greeley presents his readers with can be similarly life-transmuting. With Greeley's runes of wisdom, the reader leaves the world of fiction to return to the world of everyday life.

Scholes says, "We *experience* the events of a story, but without the consequences—emerging . . . without a scratch on our bodies. Emotionally, however, and intellectually, we are different. We have experienced something" (4–5). The reader of a Greeley novel has "experienced something" and leaves the novel with a better way to understand himself, his humanity, his flesh, and his failings. Such understandings are true runes of wisdom. The Greeley novel is likely to provide the reader with a more balanced view of his humanity, a view that recognizes sexuality as equally important with the intellectual and the spiritual. Campbell says that the typical hero has gained a "freedom to live," a freedom that is tinged with neither guilt nor self-righteousness, "a reconciliation of individual consciousness with the universal will" (238), thus affecting an at-one-ment with the divine. Reading a Greeley novel puts the reader in the position of attaining a greater understanding of God and of his relationship to that God.

APPLICATION: *VIRGIN AND MARTYR*

Consider how the schema of the reader-as-hero might apply to the reader of a specific novel, *Virgin and Martyr.* In responding to the call to adventure, those already familiar with Greeley's fiction approach the novel confident that they will be treated to a good story and that the reading has the extra excitement of a priest talking about life in a relatively fast lane. Upon crossing the threshold, we are met with the horrific description of Catherine's dismemberment. We have seen some brutality in Greeley's other novels, but nothing this severe. The opening is disturbing, but the skepticism of Blackie Ryan with his semidetached disposition provides a calming effect. Blackie's disposition makes it seem safer for the reader to proceed; we seem in relatively safe hands. The balance between the brutality and what we feel comfortable with creates an important tension. Blackie with his calm rationality mediates that tension. The novel's retrospective view of Catherine shows her sinking into the belly of the whale on at least three occasions, notably her novitiate, her time in New York with Roy, and her time in Costaguana. Each time, she separates herself from her native world of Grand Beach and environs and proceeds to a separate, sometimes unreal world; each time, she sinks further and further into the depths; and each of her ventures is capped with some mad rushing return. The most notable return is from Costaguana because it is the only one on her own initiative and it is the only one wherein she has gained a boon for herself. She seems to have come to terms with herself, at least partly. She has seen what she can't do; she has seen what Ed can do. The escape was a test in itself; a discovery of some potential strengths, some animal cunning that she had not used before.

Although her escape from Costaguana is certainly exciting, the important perspective in terms of reader response is the reader's trip into the belly of the whale, the reader's discovery of a boon, and the reader's return from the fictional world to the real world. What the reader sees in the depths of Catherine's trials and during her mad dash from Costaguana is that there is an abiding presence everywhere. The image of that presence is the "quicksilver mists" that "had dogged her down those railroad tracks, swirled around her in the plaza . . . and finally, just so there would be no doubt, flashed into view in the church at Rio Secco" (401–2). The description of that presence in the church is particularly pointed: Catherine "had asked for nothing, wanted nothing from whatever might lurk in the church. . . . But that which was in the church intruded just the same, assuring her that she was loved, deeply, powerfully, passionately loved. . . . Then there was no more time or space, only a vast and reassuring peace" (394–95). Such a reminder of God's ever-presence is both reassuring and comforting.

In Mobile, Catherine has discovered that it is more comfortable simply to live with the discovery, to live with the boon, rather than return with it to the old life she left in Chicago, a life that would embody commitment to Nicholas and to her inheritance. It is more comfortable simply to be Angela rather than to become Catherine again. What she further discovers is that there is an agent of the supernatural on earth, in the person of Blackie Ryan. It is Blackie who is almost as unrelenting as the divine in his pursuit of Catherine. The payoff for all the trials for Catherine is a seven-million-dollar estate, and in some respects that payoff is a paltry thing in comparison with the payoff for the reader. The reader may come to understand better the relationship between the rich and the poor in the world. The reader may even understand why one might like to change one's identity. But most important, the reader comes to understand that God doesn't abandon us, even if we seem to abandon God.

Generally, what the reader discovers in a Greeley novel is a positive Catholic theory, what Greeley at one point describes as "the Church at its most effectively caring best" (*Angels of September* 452). While individual characters will sin, the sins are consistently regarded as redeemable human failings rather than the wherewithal for eternal damnation. Clearly Nicholas and Catherine fornicate. Though it is a sin, it is an act between two people in love, two people who we assume will eventually marry one another. And even this illicit sexuality is regarded in a positive light, given the particular circumstances between these two.

While Greeley's novels attempt to reinforce a positive Catholic theory, we have to be careful that we don't look to them as models for living. The people in his novels are particular characters in particular contexts. Given the specifics of their cases, they act as they do. In terms of considering reader response, we need to focus on the overall impact of the novel rather than on the specific happenings. A comment on poetry by T. S. Eliot may help clarify this focus. Eliot suggests that in some instances the prose sense of a poem is useful in keeping the reader's mind "diverted and quiet, while the poem does its work upon him" (*Points of View* 51). In one sense, the surface tale in a Greeley novel is there to keep you distracted while the essence of the novel's theology does its work on you. As readers, then, our response is twofold. We respond to the surface story consciously, while the whole ambience of the story operates on our reflective intellect. We come back from a Greeley novel not with a tidy lesson nor with a model for living, but with a positive sense of God's presence in the world.

SUMMARY

The world that Greeley creates in his novels is characterized by a nurturing theology embodied in an understanding priesthood and a forgiving deity. For many readers, this is a comforting counterbalance to the stern, unrelenting, condemning, repressive theology of the pre-1960s. For all readers, I suspect, it is a liberating theology; one that empowers rather than cripples; one that enables and encourages the believers to realize their fullest human potential.

In spite of this divine empowering and nurturing, there is no equivocating on sin. Sin is a very real phenomenon in the life of these novels. The sin, however, is not so much the breaking of rules as it is the breaking of people. In an early nonfiction work, *Letters to Nancy*, Greeley defined grace as "God calling us to be as thoroughly human as we can possibly be." Sin, by contrast, occurs "when you turn away from yourself," when you fail to realize your full human potential (Kotre, 22).

In a Greeley novel we consistently feel a divine presence, a continual reminder of God as irrepressible. More important than the constancy of that presence is its comfortable and comforting equanimity. The good priests seem never to condemn and are concerned continually with reassuring the sinner of God's forgiveness. In *Angels of September* Father Blackie Ryan sees God falling all over herself to find ways to forgive our transgressions; this is a God willing to break Her own rules to assure our salvation. Blackie defines hell, for example, as "a place where God puts people until She figures out a way to give them a second chance" (7). With that as a prospect for our final disposition, we are more likely to focus on what we can do right rather than worry about avoiding wrong. Such a disposition is empowering. With such power, we can all be heroes.

WORKS CITED

Campbell, Joseph. *Hero with a Thousand Faces*. Cleveland: World Publishing, 1949.

Eliot, T. S. *Points of View*. Edited and selected by John Hayward. London: Faber & Faber, 1941.

————. "Religion and Literature." In *Selected Essays*. New ed. New York: Harcourt, Brace, 1950.

Greeley, Andrew M. *Angels of September*. New York: Warner, 1986.

————. *Virgin and Martyr*. New York: Warner, 1985.

Kotre, John N. *The Best of Times, the Worst of Times: Andrew Greeley and American Catholicism, 1950–1975*. Chicago: Nelson-Hall, 1978.

Scholes, Robert. *Elements of Fiction*. New York: Oxford, 1968.

13

JAMES M. HARKIN

A Reader Responds: Andrew Greeley and the Magic Flaw

$\mathcal{W}$ith the enormous success and mixed critical reception of *The Cardinal Sins* Father Andrew M. Greeley established a presence as a novelist of note. This was not Greeley's first novel; it was preceded by the widely (and unfortunately) unread *Magic Cup* and *Death in April*. And, goodness knows, this was not the first foray into seeing his words in print for Andrew Greeley, who is justly renowned for the scholarly work embodied in his voluminous academic output.

However, the novels of Andrew Greeley have set a special course in his career. The developing popular reaction to Father Greeley's novels, as one effort has succeeded another, appears to have taken somehing of the following route:

–"This priest is a guy who writes about sex!"
–"This priest is a guy who writes!!"
–"This guy writes!!!"

Greeley's readers have moved through this progression at their own pace. Most of them caught on somewhere before the end of *The Cardinal Sins*. Others may have taken a while longer. Of course, there are still those,

---

After noting Greeley's reference to Mr. Harkin's astute and sensitive reading of his manuscripts, the editor of this volume asked Harkin to write an informal essay summarizing his interpretation of Greeley's stories. It seems a perfect opportunity to include a paradigmatic nonacademic reader in this anthology.

unable to overcome the inhibitions of the first step, who have read little or none of the Greeley literature. Their loss. It must be gratifying for Greeley to have worked himself from the status of phenomenon (with shock on the fringes), through respected novelist (with a growing readership consuming the current work and hanging on the appearance of the next one), to legitimately important storyteller with major themes, powerfully developed, through intriguing characters.

The present paper aims to consider the patterns of storytelling in Greeley's novels as I have found them. I judge Father Greeley to be after big fish in his novels. He writes not to provide escapist entertainment. His intent is not to titillate. He is not in it for the money. At the same time, his stories are entertaining, a dash of titillation is probably good for the soul, and I presume that he cashes his checks.

Andrew Greeley's high ambition, as I read his work, is to write within the context of the popular novel (the more popular the better, as Dickens might say) to develop his own notions of love and redemption. Greeley's stories are full of purpose. The purpose is to delimit the work of "God" by means of "love," to effect the "redemption" of those folks whom I call "Greeley's People." This paper explores the meaning of the words that are offset in the previous sentence.

This is done through the consideration of the concept of the "Magic Flaw." Greeley's People are damaged goods. Their deficiencies go beyond their own will or ability to resolve alone. But, through the working out of the implications of the Magic Flaw, in each case Greeley's People can find the path to their own redemption.

Since I have had the opportunity to read Father Greeley's novels in manuscript, some of the comments in this paper are drawn from works not yet in print as this is written. I think it necessary to take this approach because Greeley continues to grow as a writer.

Indeed, by the time this paper appears, some work now in manuscript will be published and some good stuff not yet formulated will be in manuscript.

I make this point in both hope and expectation. By the evidence of his own work, Greeley has not exhausted his creative juices. Indeed, it remains to be seen how far he can stretch his considerable talent with writings yet to come.

The earlier works, starting with *The Cardinal Sins* and the first two works coming under the heading of the "Passover Trilogy," *Thy Brother's Wife* and *Ascent into Hell*, can be faulted as stories for their excessive linearity—first this happened and then that happened and so forth—and for their determined effort to tie up every loose end.

Beginning with the last work of the Passover Trilogy, *Lord of the Dance*, followed by *Virgin and Martyr* and *Angels of September*, comes more complexity: stories follow a more crooked path. They are full of twists and turns and uncertainties.

Just what is at the bottom of the bizarre familial relationships of the Farrell clan of *Lord of the Dance*? Indeed, for heart-thumping excitement it would be difficult to surpass the adventure of assassination in that book's closing pages. Moving on, who is Cathy Collins—"Not quite virgin; not quite martyr," as Blackie Ryan has it—and where is she and what does she want? Is Anne Reilly of *Angels of September* really loony and, if so, does she have good reason to be loony? These kinds of questions keep pages turning. With these books Father Greeley established without question his claim as a popular novelist deserving of widespread acclaim.

More of a challenge in his recent stories—and still more of an accomplishment—Greeley is prepared to exit, the tale unfinished. *Patience of a Saint* leaves Redmond Kane more or less upright at Christmas Midnight Mass having reencountered Greeley's "cosmic baseball bat." Swoosh. Brendan and Ciara sit frigid on Dingle Bay Beach at the end of *Rite of Spring*. Jean emerges to first embrace—Ciara. But much, much indeed, remains to be worked out.

The novels which I have seen in manuscript (*Angel Fire*, "Love Song," "War in Heaven," "A Comedy of Errors," and "St. Valentine's Night") carry on this device of entrusting the completion of the story to the mind of the reader where it can take place chronologically after Greeley has finished the story on paper. This is a demanding gambit on Greeley's part. It also shows considerable confidence in a readership that cares enough to ponder outcomes that live beyond the particular book.

But, to be specific, what of Greeley's People? What do they bring to their stories? How do they change through their experiences—and highly dramatic experiences at that? What do they take away from their stories to carry into the future?

It is in this context that the concept of the "Magic Flaw" is useful to help us understand what Greeley is about and what he has to offer as storyteller. Thus, the task is to determine what the concept of the Magic Flaw can do to enhance the reading of Andrew Greeley's novels.

A strength of Andrew Greeley's stories from the very first has been the power and depth of his characterizations. Greeley's People, as I call them, are full-blown human beings. These People are always in movement. They bring a history to their stories: they have come from someplace (more on this matter later), and they have done things in coming to the crisis point in their lives to be related in their story.

Greeley's People commonly appear to the world at large as "beautiful people." They are invariably attractive and intelligent. They are largely talented and they have had the occasion to apply their talents to the effect of substantial accomplishment. This accomplishment has often been recognized and rewarded by the world.

Indeed, some of Greeley's People are at the highest level of public visibility for their career aspirations. Cormac MacDermot of *The Magic Cup* is in line to become King of Ireland. Sean Cronin of *Thy Brother's Wife* is a bishop of the Church on a fast track to the archbishopric of Chicago. Red Kane in *Patience of a Saint* is twice a Pulitzer Prize winner and a widely read columnist. Sean Desmond of *Angel Fire* is a Nobel laureate.

However, these folk and the others of Greeley's People are seriously flawed. Their past has brought them to the point of becoming dangerously dysfunctional: they violate their own wonderful human capacity and risk aborting their own potential for life.

There is an irony in all this that underlines Greeley's skills as a storyteller. It is often at the point of widest recognition and acclaim for career accomplishment that Greeley's People approach their personal crisis.

If anything, Greeley's women are more deeply damaged than his men. Ellen Foley of *The Cardinal Sins* grows a serious and debilitating antagonism toward the Catholic Church. More distressing still, Cathy Collins, virgin and martyr, works most diligently to toss away her life. Anne Reilly of *Angels of September* carries a heavy load of misplaced guilt from her child-hood, compounded by a brutal marriage experience. She may be the most threatened of Greeley's women. But there are others: Maggie Ward is on the run, mostly from herself, in "War in Heaven." Rosemarie Clancy, by contrast, is trapped by her family in "A Comedy of Errors." So, too, is Diana Lyons of "Love Song." The stories are different: Rosemarie is in literal fear for her life; Diana is consumed by filial obligation to a cruel and emotionally abusive father. The implication of this observation is that Greeley's women, allotted a heavier load to carry, are more courageous than his men in facing their problems. They need to be so!

But what is the problem? This is the Magic Flaw, the hinge on which Greeley turns his stories. Greeley's People are full of pride. They have good reason for just pride, as suggested above, in the real achievements they have realized in their lives.

However, at some time in some fashion, this pride has turned on itself. Greeley's People have come to the point of attempting to see themselves as free-standing and fully self-sustaining and self-sufficient. Yet, there is a tickle in the brain to tell them this is a lie. So legitimate pride of self and accomplishment becomes pathological.

The pridefulness of Greeley's People can take different forms. This is to be expected in an Andrew Greeley story: these are individuals and each is a unique person.

Kevin Brennan of *The Cardinal Sins* is very smart. More, and potentially worse, he knows he is smart. He translates his intelligence into an intellec-tual arrogance that condescends to others and offers nothing of self. Sean Cronin of *Thy Brother's Wife* knows his own talent full well but is afraid of it. What better solution for him than to push aside his obligations and take refuge in humility carried to a prideful extreme?

Another example: Hugh Donlon of *Ascent into Hell* is consumed by shame for the mess he feels he has made of his life. He has reduced his image of self to zero-point, while taking pride in his ability to understand and accept himself flat-on without equivocation or apology. Conor Clarke of "Love Song" was raised with the proverbial silver spoon in his mouth. He has taken his inherited wealth and he has done much good while doing very well. But he had nothing of family along the way. He faces guilt for what he believes he acquired without merit and for what he intuits he lost without reason. He takes pride in the recognition of his own worthlessness.

As noted above, Andrew Greeley is especially adept at creating multifaceted characters: real human beings with all the shadings of desire and will and motivation that come with the species. There is some danger in the kind of analysis done here of oversimplifying and, indeed, trivializing Greeley's work by appearing to reduce his People to single images. However, there is value in seeing the tendency in Greeley's People to seek escape from the responsibility of realizing the best of self through overweening pride, as a reaction to that combination of experience, condition, and circumstance that has brought about the personal crisis related in the story.

This is the Magic Flaw that moves Greeley's storytelling. The tension in the stories lies in the potential of his People for true evil. Having allowed themselves to be consumed by their pridefulness in their own straightened situation, they can begin to consume others.

But Greeley is a cautious optimist, and his People are survivors. They have an essential internal balance. They fall far but no farther. The drive for life is too intense to let it slip or be snatched away. The heart of the matter for Greeley is the redemption of his People.

If the Magic Flaw is the misplaced pride of Greeley's People in believing that they can stand alone, then redemption is found in recognition that such belief (the next words are to be taken quite literally) is damnably dangerous. Redemption is never easy for Greeley's People. The sense of it is very much of the order of one step forward, two steps backward; then two steps forward for two steps backward; followed by three steps forward for a single step backward.

Then four steps forward . . .

Ultimately, for redemption's sake, Greeley's People must come to terms with the reality that life cannot be lived in isolation. Self-redemption is an oxymoron. As people create sound relationships, they create dependencies, and these dependencies are equally healthy. The grease that turns the wheels of human dependency is love. For Greeley's People, love becomes the passionate (always passionate!) and ultimately inescapable embrace of other people.

In Greeley's storytelling, love, as the means of redemption—the vehicle to channel the enervating energy of the Magic Flaw in productive directions—operates through a "significant other." In the earlier stories the Person in need of the redemptive powers of love is generally clear enough. The more recent stories, including those still in manuscript at this writing, follow a more ambitious line. Redemption through the power of human love is a more mutual experience. Redemption for Greeley's People becomes profoundly interactive.

Cathy Collins was fortunate to have such a committed lover as Nick Curran. A less resolute person than Nick would have abandoned Cathy long before the culmination of *Virgin and Martyr.* This would have been a great loss for Nick but he would have survived and, in time, flourished. However, it would have been the end of Cathy. In *Angels of September* Mike the Cop surely needed Anne Reilly to find fulfillment in life. But he had a life of accomplishment and he could look to a future of more accomplishment. The issue of redemption was Anne's to face.

On the other hand, Brendan Ryan and Ciara Kelly make it together or not at all in *Rite of Spring.* One apart from the other, Jerry Keenan and Maggie Ward in "War in Heaven" have no life that means anything. Ditto, Chuck O'Malley and Rosemarie Clancy of "A Comedy of Errors," as well as Neil Connor and Megan Keefe Lane of "St. Valentine's Night."

The exchange between Conor Clarke and Blackie Ryan at the end of "Love Song," begun after Diana Lyons has walked out on Conor, shows Greeley at his absolute best on this issue:

> "Did I say anything wrong?" Con pleaded desperately.
>
> "Absolutely not." Glasses still on his forehead, Blackie collapsed into his battered Victorian easy chair.
>
> "She's cut herself off."
>
> "Certainly."
>
> "If she acts that way I should get rid of the ring and the Mercedes and the house I bought for her last autumn."
>
> "Assuredly," the priest didn't seem to be giving Con his full attention.
>
> "She has the right to resist grace."
>
> "Undoubtedly."
>
> "I can't force her to change."
>
> "No way."
>
> "She's not sorry about what happened."
>
> "Definitely not."
>
> "She rejects my forgiveness and my love."
>
> "Totally."
>
> "She is burying herself in her own icy hell."
>
> "Unquestionably."
>
> "Then I should forget about her?"
>
> "Certainly not . . . How did you come to that conclusion?" . . .
>
> "She's made her decision," Con was beginning to realize how deeply he had been humiliated.
>
> "Certainly."
>
> "She's made her bed, let her lie in it. . . ."
>
> "A cliche unworthy of a potentially great poet, but the logic is unarguable."

"If I should put on my Burberry... and run after her, she will reject me again."
"In all probability."
"I'd be insulted and humiliated."
"A reasonable projection."
"Then I don't have to do it."
Blackie Ryan looked at him in amazement. "That does not follow." (406–8)

Some of the flavor (indeed, too much of the flavor) of the exchange has been edited out for reasons of space. But the depth of Conor's need for Diana and, in the response that follows, Diana's recognition of her need for Conor mark the quality of mutual love as a means for redemption in Greeley's stories.

Love as a means for interactive redemption for Greeley's People always takes place in context. The context is the community, or more narrowly expressed but much richer in meaning, the "Neighborhood." Greeley's People at their most elemental level are "folks from the Neighborhood." The Neighborhood does not merely facilitate the creation of the crucial dependencies of Greeley's People with and for each other, but is at the heart of the entire nurturing process.

Let it go this far. For Greeley's People there is no redemption outside the Neighborhood, because the Neighborhood is the setting for his People to do what they must do to realize their redemption. The Neighborhood is a setting for life, because the Neighborhood itself lives. As Greeley's People have a history, so too does the Neighborhood have a history. The Neighborhood begins in a place and grows from a place. Its people take the Neighborhood with them wherever they go and whatever they do. And, in time, they repair to the Neighborhood to address and answer the questions they have not resolved in life.

The repair to the Neighborhood may be in an actual physical sense, as for Danny Farrell of *Lord of the Dance* and Neil Connor of "St. Valentine's Night." The recognition of what the Neighborhood is all about may actually come from far afield. Brendan Ryan's discovery in *Rite of Spring* is that he can hope—and expect—to go home again. He must go to Ireland to explore his deepest roots to discover this prospect. Sean Desmond of *Angel Fire* voyages through Europe on his Nobel trek; Cathy Collins survives the fire of Costaguana in *Virgin and Martyr.* For some of Greeley's People, the understanding of the Neighborhood involves much movement of emotion and psyche but no physical relocation. So it is for Anne Reilly in *Angels of September* and Redmond Kane of *Patience of a Saint*.

Greeley's Neighborhood has the confidence of its own identity. The Neighborhood is not tied up by fear and self-doubt. Therefore, the Neighborhood not only can afford to be tolerant of individual differences, it flourishes on the strength of these differences. The Neighborhood encourages deviation as a means for its People to realize the best in themselves. For this reason it can be a place of repair and renewal for its People.

Greeley's Neighborhood itself is proactive. The Neighborhood pursues its intended. This is followed by pursuit and pursuit and pursuit. Greeley's People resist the pursuit, but they do perceive, however dimly at first, that herein lies personal redemption. In time the intuition becomes a fully articulated understanding that the Neighborhood demands much but gives ever more as a place to live life. Either Greeley's People will surrender to the redemptive power of the Neighborhood carried out through the interaction of his People on, with, and through each other, or the Neighborhood will lose its People on these very terms.

It is true that the Neighborhood can be fairly faulted for producing such foul creatures as the Clancys of "A Comedy of Errors" and the Keefes of "St. Valentine's Night." However, the Neighborhood also provides the means for sustenance and ultimately redemption for Rosemarie Clancy O'Malley and Megan Keefe Lane.

Greeley himself has had his say on the Neighborhood (and, in so doing, outlined his own agenda on the matter with crystal clarity) in an exchange between Kevin and Ellen in *The Cardinal Sins* (1981):

> "All right, Kevin, I'll say it, and you'll have to mop up the tears on this hard floor of yours. I blamed the Church and God for things that were inside me and my family. I focused on all the ugly things and forgot. . . . Even when I was doing it, I knew I was wrong and that someday I'd be kneeling on the floor before you and pleading to be let back in."
>
> "And now you've done it," I said. . . . "And, the damn-fool Church says, 'Ellen Foley Curran Stauss, we really didn't notice you were gone, because we never let you go.' . . . So Ellen's worst sin was against Ellen. . . ." (209–10)

The Neighborhood is a place of ceremony, most typically involving the Church as place and the Mass as event. Noele Marie Farrell sings the praise of the Lord of the Dance with desperate energy at Sunday Mass. Red Kane's last encounter with the cosmic baseball bat (at least in the course of the formal story) in *Patience of a Saint* takes place at Christmas Eve Mass. In "Love Song" Conor Clarke and Diana Lyons face the ultimate implications of a future together and apart during and after Good Friday services. Neil Connor is reintroduced to his roots at the reunion Mass of his eighth-grade class in "St. Valentine's Night."

There is no dimension of wimpishness in the Neighborhood. The Neighborhood defends its own. Danny Farrell and Jaimie Burns of *Lord of the Dance* must do away with Rocco (the Marshall) Marsallo to foreclose further attack on Noele Marie. They do it. Ciara Kelly in *Rite of Spring* must cut the throat of Rory McLafferty to save Brendan Ryan, after Brendan himself has eliminated McLafferty's henchmen. There is no hesitation in Ciara. Jerry Keenan must leave Wade McCarron a bloody hulk on a snowy street to save Maggie in "War in Heaven." He does it. Gabriella Light is faced with erasing the better part of East German evil to protect Sean Desmond in *Angel Fire*. Well, they brought it on themselves. Neil Connor and Megan Keefe Lane of "St. Valentine's Night" are not safe while Lou Garcia lives. He dies, violently.

This all serves to underline again that Greeley is, first of all, a whacking good storyteller. And as Greeley has written more stories and as he has deepened his own art, the quality of redemption in his People has become more complex as his stories have become more complex.

The hand of God is both transparent and ambiguous in Greeley's storytelling. There is no clumsy *deus ex machina* in Greeley's stories. Indeed, God's hand is somewhere in the proceedings as Greeley's People take the step forward and two steps backward (as already outlined above) in their voyage. But God writes straight with a crooked hand, as Sean Desmond of *Angel Fire* quotes Blackie Ryan.

The Neighborhood, so much of its life spinning around the Church, is the convenient vehicle for God's work. But God operates through human instrumentalities. God creates opportunity and then hovers over it all. Then God creates another opportunity. Then come two steps forward for two steps backward. And another opportunity. And, indeed, Greeley's God will provide as many opportunities as his People need. A useful model to understand Greeley's God might fall under some quasi-technical heading, like a "Holy Spirit."

But it is the ultimate point of Greeley's storytelling that in time even his People figure out his purpose.

The aim of this paper has been to outline an interpretation of Andrew Greeley's stories by considering the patterns of human behavior and the development of human relationships related in the stories. The key concept of the Magic Flaw has been examined as a core character trait that Greeley's People bring to their own stories. The Magic Flaw involves some dimension of misplaced pride which threatens not only to be self-destructive but to be destructive of others.

The Neighborhood creates a setting of single-minded—even crazed—pursuit in which Greeley's People can learn and operationalize love in their lives for themselves and others as the means of redemption.

Through it all, there is Greeley's God, visible and hidden, for his People to understand a little better and to appreciate a little more and to live the best that life can offer.

Greeley's stories are his message. The stories are his means to communicate with his readers about his view of life; to show them what a quite literally marvelous experience life can be, where there are other people to give and take and to give to and take from.

The gratifying reality is that in doing all this, Greeley has shown himself to be a wonderful storyteller, and has intimated by his growth that the best is yet to come. This is indeed a happy and hopeful prospect.

"FLAWED HEROES"
IN THE WORK OF ANDREW GREELEY

BOOK	HERO	MAGIC FLAW	SALVATION
The Magic Cup	Cormac MacDermot	Shame	Biddy
Death in April	Jim O'Neill	Fear	Lynnie
The Cardinal Sins	Kevin Brennan	Arrogance	Ellen
Thy Brother's Wife	Sean Cronin	Fear	Nora
Ascent into Hell	Hugh Donlon	Shame	Maria
Lord of the Dance	Danny Farrell	Fear	Noele Marie
Patience of a Saint	Red Kane	Cynicism	Eileen
Rite of Spring	Brendan Ryan	Shame	Ciara
Angel Fire	Sean Desmond	Fear	Gabriella

"FLAWED HEROINES"
IN THE WORK OF ANDREW GREELEY

BOOK	HEROINE	MAGIC FLAW	SALVATION
Virgin and Martyr	Cathy Collins	Fear	Nick
Angels of September	Anne Reilly	Guilt	Mike the Cop

INTERACTIVE REDEMPTION
IN THE WORK OF ANDREW GREELEY

BOOK (UNPUBLISHED)	HERO/HEROINE	MAGIC FLAW	SALVATION
"Love Song"	Conor Clarke	Guilt	Diana
	Diana Marie Lyons	Guilt	Conor
"War in Heaven"	Jerry Keenan	Despair	Maggie
	Margaret Ward	Shame	Jerry
"A Comedy of Errors"	Charles O'Malley	Ignorance	Rosemarie
	Rosemarie Clancy	Shame	Chuckie
"Saint Valentine's Night"	Neil Connor	Despair	Megan
	Megan Keefe Lane	Shame	Neil

IV

In the Garden: Novels

14

INGRID SHAFER

The Catholic Imaginative Universe in the Novels of Andrew Greeley

One of the most striking examples of the deliberate use of literature as means of conveying a religious ideology can be found in Andrew Greeley's popular novels. Greeley presents the Catholic *Weltanschauung* by incorporating elements of the medieval morality play, miracle story, and the traditional romance (as a *legitimate* literary form to be distinguished from Harlequin formula type pablum) into contemporary fiction which he himself refers to as "parables of grace" and "romances of redemption." Though the former are presumed to proceed from the unconscious mind and the latter are consciously designed (analogous to Schiller's "naive" and "sentimental" categories of poetry), there exists a fundamental congruence between Greeley's work and that of the generally anonymous forgers of countless legends elaborating on the "lives of the saints." Like those analogical embroideries upon the Christian theme, Greeley's stories are rooted in popular devotional piety and ancient folk traditions which reflect the Catholic insistence on intertwining the sacred and the profane, or, as Karl Rahner might say, the Catholic tendency to interpret the Incarnation in terms of the "sacramentality of the world." Intentionally or accidentally, Greeley has transformed the medium of mass-appeal fiction into an alternate pulpit designed to reach precisely that segment of the Catholic population which does not attend

Reprinted, with minor revisions, from the *Quarterly Journal of Ideology*, 10.3 (1986):71–83.

church regularly and feels cut off from the sacramental life of the Church (*Confessions* 469).

It is impossible to separate Andrew Greeley the novelist from Dr. Greeley the sociologist or Father Greeley the parish priest. The material in his fiction flows directly from his sociological findings which in turn confirm the continued power the God-concept exerts upon the religious imagination of contemporary human beings and chronicle the American Catholic experience from the "Garrison Church" beyond Vatican II. In sharp contrast to the prevailing assumption of the secularization of the contemporary world, Greeley insists that "the basic human religious needs and the basic religious functions have not changed very notably since the late Ice Age" (*Unsecular Man* 1). He has persistently and eloquently advocated this position in such additional nonfiction works as *The Religious Imagination* and *Religion: A Secular Theory*. As a sociologist he views religion as a symbol system which mediates our encounter with the ambiguities of life, while disclosing at least some reason for hope, some justification for assuming that human life has significance. As a priest he posits the presence of a living, gracious, personal God who passionately cares about each and every one of us. Like the theologian John Shea, Greeley realizes that "people are interested in their own personal stories. We must begin with contemporary stories and bring forward the story of Jesus, the premier sacred story of Christianity, to interpret the depth of what is happening" (12–13). It is for this reason, one presumes, that Greeley not only introduces "spiritual guide" characters into his tales to help his readers go beyond the narrative surface but also (to the inevitable chagrin of art-for-art's-sake purists) insists on providing introductory remarks and/or postscripts.

The religious ideology presented in Greeley's novels is not his private invention, distinct from the Christian and most specifically the Catholic tradition. It represents, instead, an attempt to recover precisely that tradition by exploring its relevance to the contemporary scene. "Religion," remarks Whitehead, ". . . is the transition from God the void to God the enemy, and from God the enemy to God the companion" (16–17). The central Judeo-Christian insight consists in recognizing the personhood of God, in acknowledging that the ultimate, ineffable, totally other creative ground of being is simultaneously a genuine "Thou" who relates to us the way we relate to one another. Among the ancient Hebrews, this personal God was experienced primarily as a passionately pursuing but often terrifying and generally masculine Presence, demanding absolute obedience to the divine will. Jesus not only put God's fatherhood into focal position but by using the familiar term *Abba* (Daddy) invited all of us to approach God in a far more intimate manner than had been the Old Testament pattern, psychologically preparing the way for understanding, accepting, and internalizing the Incarnation, the final reconciliation of God and humanity, spirit and nature. By introducing Mary as tender mother and *theotokos*, medieval popular piety and theological speculation laid the foundation for recovering the Great Mother aspects of divinity largely redacted out of the Hebraic androcentric tradition.

Greeley's religious paradigm is constructed by combining the pragmatic notions of religion as experience of the sacred developed by Rudolph Otto and William James with the sociological theory of religion as a set of fundamental models or templates which both determine our understanding of ultimate Reality and give shape to that Reality. Religion thus represents a constitutive element in the worlds we create. The image precedes theological reflection and analytical reduction. Fundamentally, religion is not something to be learned and rationlly assimilated. It is rather an alternate way of seeing, a form of enlightenment which allows us to commit ourselves to a special kind of world-transforming action, rooted in a special kind of world-understanding vision.

In all of his stories Greeley allows the noumenal and phenomenal realms to interpenetrate with sufficient plausibility to provide a sense of the space-time continuum being rooted in *illo tempore,* to use Mircea Eliade's expression. It is this kind of blurring of boundaries or limit-experience which is exemplified in Noele's encounter with the Really Real in *Lord of the Dance.* Virgin archetype Noele, at once contemporary American teenager and "a pre-Christian deity, a visitor from the many-colored land of Irish antiquity" (11), visits her "sacred grove" (reminiscent of her Celtic heritage) of the tennis courts, a space at once terrifying, holy, comforting, *and,* due to her recent rape, demonic. It is there that she must renew her personal covenant relationship; it is there, her private Mount Sinai, that she "hears" the voice of God and encounters the Mystery, not, like Moses, in a burning bush, but in the form of a cheerful sunbeam lighting up a familiar street. Like the people of Israel, she has experienced slavery and violent defilement, and, like Moses (or Christ), she must be true to her secret parentage and bring her family out of spiritual bondage. Hers is a new-old story, a story of sin, despair, and redemption through faith in the ultimate graciousness of Reality. The theme of laughter is sounded. Noele's God, like Nora's God in *Thy Brother's Wife* (276), is a God-who-Laughs, a God who loves her like a mother. "Laughter, not crying, is the deepest purpose that God wills for man," notes theologian Edward Schillebeeckx (178). We see ourselves in a world in which beauty and ugliness, sin and grace are next-door neighbors, each revealing the other, a world which would be absurd if it were not for our wisely foolish pervasive faith in love and the ultimate graciousness of the Really Real, which does not cause or condone evil but allows it to exist as a void or absence of goodness, the price we pay for the gift of freedom.

Divine revelation is disclosure of the hidden, gratuitous, positive forces which challenge us to confront evil and enable us to move creatively into the future. God is present within our lives as a call, a beacon, a horizon, assuming an infinite variety of forms. He/She assaults us with a "cosmic baseball bat" (*Patience of a Saint* 13), appears as the "Cheshire Smile" (66), seeps like a combination of "mist and quicksilver" (*Virgin and Martyr* 13)

into the crannies and interstices of our personalities. For Noele, Grace skips
or slouches down Jefferson Avenue in the shape of a giggling sunbeam (*Lord
of the Dance* 378). Instead of conceptualizing God as a remote, distant agent
over and above history who intervenes at His convenience, or a hidden and
numinous Ground of Being residing serenely in abstract isolation, Noele
encounters divine reality as the innermost dimension of her life, the
eternally creative and benevolent Matrix-Mother out of whom she, her
parents, the entire Farrell clan, and ultimately every human being, every
bird and bug and blade of grass, came into being.

Significantly, Noele is named not only in honor of Christmas, the feast of
the Incarnation, but also in honor of the Virgin Mary and her alter ego, the
Irish Saint Brigid (Mary of the Gael). Like the Church, she was conceived
at Easter and born at Christmas; like the Church, she is the future while
remaining solidly rooted in the past and present; and like the Church, it is
her mission to challenge each deeply beloved member of her family to
become the best he or she can be. As in two earlier novels, *Thy Brother's
Wife* (Holy Thursday) and *Ascent into Hell* (Good Friday), *Lord of the Dance*
(Easter Sunday) moves within the analogical universe of Holy Week, adding
to the themes of commitment and crucifixion the theme of resurrection, the
consummation of Christ's marriage with the *Ecclesia*, symbolically recalled
in the Easter Vigil liturgy of blessing the baptismal font by plunging the
lighted candle into the waters, in a "baptized" version of the ancient pagan
spring fertility rite of joining fire and water to ensure fruitful fields,
livestock, and wives.

As long ago as 1961, Greeley, then curate at Christ the King Church and
a graduate student at the University of Chicago, wrote in *Strangers in the
House: Catholic Youth in America*, "Our young people have retreated into a
world of fantasy and non-involvement because they, like the rest of Western
civilization, have lost faith in the world and in themselves" (15). He
attributed this metaphysical malaise largely to the failure of Christians and
most particularly the clergy to provide effective solutions to a prevalent
sense of despair and alienation. Yet, he insisted, "The human spirit is not
defeated. The longing for meaning and significance is still very much with
us" (22). The twentieth-century loss of self rooted in what he called the
collapse of community was not an irreversible condition. "If man is not
related to God," he argued, "then he cannot be related to nature and his
fellow man; but on the other hand, by using natural signs, physical symbols
to relate to nature and his fellow man, he can relate to God" (61). After
deploring the lack of meaningful symbols in modern society, he put the
central problem in a different form: "To harmonize the city and nature, the
technical and the numinous, the profane and the religious is never easy; in
the world of Einstein and Planck it is terrifyingly difficult" (64). The
"sanctification" of the contemporary world, he suggested, should be the
task of "the poet, the metaphysician, and the theologian" (64).

As Northrop Frye noted, ours is a transitional era characterized by "an energy common to subject and object which can be expressed verbally only through some form of metaphor" (*Great Code* 15–16), a new-old "hieroglyphic," "*kerygmatic*," or "proclamatory" use of limit-language designed to release God from a linguistic cenotaph, a language which can be "uncoded" by exploring the polysemous meaning (archetypal, metaphorical, and allegorical levels) of the stories told.

It is this kind of limit-language of the analogical imagination (identified by David Tracy as the way to dissolve the Gordian knot of dualism)[1] which Greeley uses in his stories, as shocking to us as Jesus' parables of the employer who refuses to adjust his pay to merit and the father who welcomes back his runaway son with a party must have been to His Torah-steeped contemporaries. "Surely, our God cannot be this *unfair*," one imagines the disciples grumbling, particularly when their foolish rabbi insists on sending the woman taken in sin on her way without demanding she be stoned or even express regret. "Surely, it is blasphemous to think of God as a physical lover, as enthusiastic voyeur and participant in a *ménage à trois*," mutter and scream contemporary clerical culture critics of Greeley's novels. "God as a naked woman chewing a cross, how disgusting!" The point in all those images is the same. God loves us so much that Her/His passion explodes all the commonsense categories of reason and ever good taste. "The trouble with the God that Jesus claimed to represent is that he loves too much" (Greeley, *Jesus Myth* 45) and becomes a scandal and embarrassment to the good, solid, righteous, law-abiding members of the congregation. "Never, I repeat, NEVER fuck with the Lord God" (*Patience of a Saint* 414), Blackie advises Red Kane. Shocking? Definitely. Poor taste? Not in context. Effective? Most assuredly. And that is precisely the point. With Peter Pan contrariness and leprechaun irreverence, Greeley uses *any* expression, *any* image, *any* story which might conceivably break through the safe categories of conventionally dead piety and spread the "Good News" of the implacably loving, passionately pursuing androgynous Deity. By linking God, Woman, and Sex, and sprinkling the resulting mixture generously with both violence and tenderness, he arrived at the magic formula: whether infuriated or delighted, offended or enthralled, people will be forced to listen and think—about themselves, their friends and family, their love lives, their Church, and their God. For ultimately, the *real* protagonist of all of Greeley's stories is—Herself.

She appears in many archetypal incarnations, as Mother Goddess, the womb-tomb source and goal of physical life, the tender fountain of nourishment and protection; as Virgin, aloof and independent, the eternal promise of spring and youth; as Spouse, gently yielding and implacably pursuing, the "Daughter of Jerusalem" turned "Mother from Sligo" (*Patience of a Saint* 80). She manifests Herself in the clear and yet unfathomable depths of Kevin Brennan and Patrick Donahue's Lake, at once mysteriously alluring and profoundly threatening (*Cardinal Sins* 40–43, 59–62). She lurks in the House which is also Home, its interior warmly lit by the twentieth-century equivalent of Hesta's hearth, a "lighthouse" beacon of sorts, inviting, reassuring, comforting. "And once you went into its light you never left," realizes Hugh Donlon, "Mason Avenue, Lake Geneva, Bethlehem" (*Ascent into Hell* 486). She lies in wait within the protectively captivating walls of Jim O'Neill's fascinating, dazzling, ever-changing, and surprising City, the *civitas dei*, Chicago-Camelot (*Death in April* 244–45).

She both operates through and is reached by the path of Eros, the primal force of love and life, the highest and most potent form of fusion energy. The new birth (of ourselves as individual, actualized, God-related human beings, *and* the "community of the faithful") cannot occur until the real demons of sexuality (the flesh *denied* as enemy) have been exorcised, and sexuality is accepted as positive sacrament of creation and generation. The nuptial meaning of the body, the sacramentality of the flesh, must be recognized and affirmed. Properly understood, sexuality represents an invitation to physical *and* spiritual intimacy, which in turns demands that we overcome our pessimistic dread of dependence and vulnerability, rooted in suspicion of others (including the cosmos), and self-hating self-pity which insist that we can't be lovable. The empirical datum of sexual attraction and attractiveness allows us to approach ultimate reality as fundamentally loving and gracious.

In Jungian terms the journey toward psychic wholeness involves the romantic descent into the libidinal underworld of chaotic instincts and violent, often deadly passions, the recovery of archetypes in the depths of the unconscious, a turning point (symbolized by Dante as literally passing through the satanic anus), and the ascent toward renewed and consciously appropriated psychic integration.

All of Greeley's stories, even the mysteries, can ultimately be described as spiritual pilgrimages beginning with the main character's departure from a state of identity and ending by his or her return to wholeness and integration. On a literal level his heroes and heroines journey across time and space, from the fantastic future world depicted in the science fiction fantasy *The Final Planet* and the bogs and mists and fairy glens of sixth-century Ireland of *The Magic Cup* through Chicago in a bewildering variety of moods, to the sidewalk cafés of Paris, the dark corridors of the Vatican, a jungle river of Africa, Joseph Conrad's Costaguana in Latin America, and Ashford Castle, Galway City, and the Strand of Inch in contemporary Ireland. They descend into underground caves and crypts and skim the waves in sailboats. But far more important than their physical, external journey is their internal odyssey through the vast expanse of allegorical and psychological space and time. Like Jesus-Dante-Faust, each one of them must empty the bitter chalice and pass through darkness, sin, and death before the possibility of rebirth and salvation even arises, and like Jesus-Dante-Faust, the mysterious, inexhaustible energy source which sustains and inspires them, and ultimately propels them through and beyond the realm of darkness toward the upper regions of joyous ecstasy and realized union, is the greatest of all spiritual forces—Love, passionate, cosmic, absolute Love, which "moves the sun in heaven and all the stars" (Alighieri 600).

Their world is split into two distinct realms, a region of perfection, purity, childhood, spring and summer love, a paradise on earth, apparently untouched by the Fall, and a nether region of humiliation, suffering, alienation, violence, and adventure, of conflict between the forces of good and evil, light and shadow, dream and nightmare, sleep and reality. They achieve full humanity only by temporarily forsaking the idyllic world of vernal innocence for the dark, demonic labyrinth of lived experience and Darwinian or Hobbesian strife, by eating of the forbidden tree and abandoning the *civitas dei* for the *civitas diaboli*, thus coming to know themselves and others as potentially demonic as well as sacramental. This subterranean libidinal world of *eros* and *thanatos* presents a nightmare scenario of ferocious beasts and demonic ordeals, terrifyingly portrayed in Anne Reilly's psychic absorption into the netherworld of "Divine Justice," painted by Father Des Kenny, a lunatic latter-day Hieronymus Bosch, whose artistic abomination portrays his naked victim, trapped in a swamp, a demon's claw buried in her breast "writhing in terror as the devil's pitchforks plunged toward her fresh young flesh" (*Angels of September* 1). Daniel finds himself cast into the lion's den, and Plato's prisoners inhabit an underground cave waiting to tear their returning savior limb from limb.

Their journey parallels that of human consciousness in Hegel's *Phenomenology* or Goethe's *Faust* which is unable to achieve full self-actualization and/or yield to "salvation" without first having traveled the "path of doubt and despair" (*Hegel* 71) and entered a "pact with the devil" in order to comprehend the futility of all finite positions. The process of becoming fully human according to Hegel (as well as Goethe and Jung) inevitably involves the agonizing task of appropriating and transcending one's own otherness or opposite, "in a way that negates itself and yet passes through that negation into a new stage, preserving its essence in a broader context, and abandoning the one just completed like the chrysalis of a butterfly or a crustacean's outgrown shell" (Frye, *Great Code* 222).

Yet ultimately and ironically, no matter how terrifying and exciting the adventures, how immense the distances covered, how apparently remote the goal sought, and how unattainable the lover pursued, the end of the journey, the focus of all our yearnings, invariably turns out to be as commonplace and familiar as the neighborhood McDonald's with its golden arches (*God Game* 156), the boy or girl next door, or even, as Red Kane discovers, our very own spouse from whom we have drifted away in years of taking each other for granted (*Patience of a Saint*). Paradise Lost reveals itself as Paradise Regained, and the power of our first love carries us literally full circle to the place of our origins. The Promised Land in the West, the Many-colored Land, is both ten thousand light-years away *and* in our own backyard or marriage bed.

Space limitations do not permit the discussion of all or even most of Greeley's variations on the descent and ascent themes. I shall limit myself to two paradigmatic examples, Hugh Donlon's "fall from grace" in *Ascent into Hell* and Cathy Collins' emergence from the underworld in *Virgin and Martyr.*

Hugh Donlon enters the priesthood primarily (though quite unconsciously so) to please his mother and prove himself capable of doing his best even, "indeed especially, when it is difficult" (*Ascent* 27). Three times he is given the opportunity of allowing grace in the form of Maria to transform him (once even in an appropriately named *Chris* craft), of accepting the divine invitation to be happy, and three times he denies the call to live, in a misdirected effort to preserve *his* virginity and abide by the rules of his vocation.

It should be obvious by now that Greeley makes selective use of the structuring principles of the traditional romance. Thus, while the descent and ascent themes figure prominently in his stories, he replaces the inevitable preoccupation with the defense of feminine virginity found in romances from Heliodorus' *Ethiopica* to Spenser's *The Fairie Queene* with a decidedly contemporary Western or possibly ancient Celtic insistence on affirming rather than denying flesh. Sexual attraction to the social scientist priest represents both an evolutionary device for binding men and women to one another in permanent relationships and a psychological motivator inspiring them to persist in pursuing that which they already seem to possess. Sexual union is no longer the hidden event which happens after the story is over, but the decisive event which threatens to happen when the story begins. It is Aristotle's and Saint Thomas' actuality which ontologically precedes potentiality. Maria is God for Hugh, passionately loving, implacably pursuing, ready to save him from himself long before he realizes that he might possibly be in trouble. But Hugh is determined to do the will of his Manichaean kind of God, and remains perversely convinced that He could not possibly want him to do the natural and easy thing.

Nineteen years have come and gone. Hugh has left the priesthood to marry a former nun (after a lovemaking episode one Christmas night), haunted by her own demons. In preparation for an academic career, he attained a Ph.D. but instead entered the business jungle of the Chicago Board of Trade, characteristically to please his father and keep an eye on his irresponsible brother. He is desperately unhappy and drugs his sense of futility, self-loathing, and horror in fleeting, painfully intense adulterous relationships with an old enemy's daughter and wife. Maria, his guardian angel (appropriately named Maria *Angelica*), seems gone, except for occasional happy dreams of sailing with her on the Pegeen. And so, on yet another Christmas Eve, Hugh has sex with his older mistress. They are discovered by the husband, whose fury is cut short by a near fatal seizure leaving him "spread eagled under the tree. . . . His face was decorated with evergreen and tinsel and his accusing right hand, still brandishing the cigar, had shattered the pieces of the Christmas creche and smashed to bits the manger and the little figure within it" (338–43). In a perfect inversion of images, Christmas, the celebration of the Incarnation, turns into Hugh's Golgotha, his spiritual death preceding his descent into the very pit of hell. The symbols are overpowering: demonic sex (dimly intuited as a loathsome disease, a fatal addiction) in the basement room; Fowler's stroke and collapse into the Christmas tree; the smashed crèche and figure of the Christ child.

As Pat Cleary, Hugh's wise priest friend, recognizes, Hugh is still running, still falling into the void. His external circumstances appear to improve. Ben's stroke has saved him from exposure, business goes well, he finds himself ambassador to an unstable African republic. He is brutalized by native soldiers. His wife and a female Peace Corps volunteer are tortured, humiliated, and almost raped in a nightmarish jungle scene. His brother betrays him in a silver market scheme, selling him for the contemporary equivalent of thirty pieces of silver. "Poor Hugh, Tim thought. He would get one with a poker up his ass" (409). The bitter cup must be emptied to the last drop. True to the romance motif of the hero falsely accused of a major crime and separated from the heroine and his friends, Hugh Donlon is convicted of stealing five million dollars' worth of his clients' money and ends up in federal prison. He has reached bottom and entered his dark night of the soul. In a gracious universe any further spiritual development and narrative movement must and will be an ascent.

Virgin and Martyr is in many ways a companion piece to *Ascent into Hell* and may structurally be the purest romance Greeley has written since his Celtic Grail quest, *The Magic Cup*. Both Hugh Donlon and Cathy Collins (the heroine of *Virgin and Martyr*) are compulsive perfectionists desperately trying to earn salvation while simultaneously searching for a maternally loving, passionately tender God who does not demand that sanctity be purchased at the expense of their personal integrity. Both decide on the religious life for the wrong reasons. Both are brutalized by psychopathic, authoritarian, and incompetent religious superiors. Both eventually leave their respective communities and marry immature psychosexual cripples. Both are betrayed by someone they love and trust, Hugh by his brother for silver, and Cathy by Father Ed, a revolutionary priest, with a kiss, for money and "the Cause." Both are imprisoned. Hugh's torment at Lexington (which compares favorably with conditions at his old seminary) consists of self-imposed isolation and profound depression. Cathy, on the other hand, is physically abused. Her experience is both a parody of the perverted preoccupation with torn and bleeding female flesh found in traditional hagiography and a serious comment on the violence to which women have been subject since times immemorial. On the way to the *comandante*'s seaside villa, García and López, two sergeants, assault her in the back of the car with her arms extended in the form of a cross. "Just like Jesus," grins López (*Virgin and Martyr* 380). A few hours later she has managed to break her straps and is free, in her purse a rosary wrapped around a loaded .45. She is in control of her own fate for the first time in weeks, possibly for the first time ever.

The themes of healing, reintegration, and ascent are sounded. First Cathy kills her tormentors. In López and García she figuratively annihilates Evil Incarnate. Not only does she exorcise those who have brutalized her, but in a sense she shatters two thousand years of institutionalized spiritual, emotional, and physical battering of women. The .45, an instrument of death, has been symbolically sanctified by its association with her rosary, the last of three left blessed by Pope John, who once, an eternity ago, suggested that she try to be a "good teacher" rather than a frustrated saint. She leaves behind the mountains of death and walks across the wilderness toward the cleansing waters of the sea. She rests in the shadow of a rock. We are reminded of the "spiritual rock" which relentlessly pursued the Hebrews through the desert, the rock from which the water flowed "for the people to drink," the rock which "was Christ" (1 Cor. 10:14). the Nursing Mother sharing Her liquid of life with Her children, the rock which is the Church. She swims in the clear waters of the gulf, submerges herself in the natural sacrament, allows herself to be cradled and healed. Once again she touches the primal roots of her inviolate self, that fragile core which somehow, mysteriously, has remained intact throughout all those years of ever-increasing disintegration.

Cathy's alternate identity buried in the crypt at Río Secco sounds a universal, archetypal motif of death and rebirth, of the nightmare-illusion of the tomb revealing itself in waking reality as the fecund womb engendering new life. The theme of the apparently dead and buried heroine can be traced to the Mesopotamian myth of moon goddess Ishtar, who periodically descends into the underworld to "raise the dead," an admittedly ambivalent effort which might result in an upper world populated by zombies, since she also threatens to devour the living to make room for her partially reconstituted dead. "Keeping in mind the Christian parallel, it is as though there were two aspects to the sacrificial victim, one in which she is a hostage for death, and so exposed to death herself, and another in which she is what has come instead of death. In the latter aspect she is, potentially, the conqueror of death and the redeemer of its captives" (Frye, *Secular Scripture* 89). Thus she appears in a contemporary incarnation as Bob Fosse's Angélique, the terrifying, captivating, inescapably tender, passionately loving, and supremely beautiful angel of death Woman-God played by Jessica Lange in *All That Jazz*.

In one sense Cathy has died in the course of her imprisonment, torture, and rape, a death symbolized by her alter ego's "burial" in the Río Secco crypt. In a second sense that very death constitutes, through the process of double negation, the death of someone already killed, the death of Cathy, the empty human shell left after her novitiate, and thus actually represents a new birth, the leaving behind of the chrysalis as the butterfly emerges. In a third sense Cathy herself, having passed through death and rebirth, reveals herself as sacrament of redemption, a living conduit of love and grace. Cathy's ascent is finally completed, Paradise Lost is reclaimed, as she decides to listen to what Carl Rogers might call her organismic valuing process, and accepts Nick's freely offered love, allowing Eros to be hallowed by commitment.

Greeley's Eros is not the selfish, vulgar fellow bent upon nothing but a quick and preferably adulterous roll in the hay, set up and attacked as a "straw man" by de Rougemont (*Love in the Western World*) and countless generations of well-meaning flesh-hating celibate confessors. Instead, "he" symbolizes divine passion, pure and simple, the "Love," as Blackie puts it, "that launched the universe in a vast BANG" (*Virgin and Martyr* 438), the love to which each one of us owes our individual existence, the loyal and committed yet endlessly surprising and delightful love which lies at the basis of all genuine friendship and marriage as a sacrament, as D'Arcy brilliantly demonstrated (*Mind and Heart of Love*). Once Eros has been recovered, despair yields to hope and death to life, as the chrysalis of the human tragedy breaks open to reveal the overarching divine comedy of grace.

All of Greeley's protagonists must go through a symbolic reenactment of the passion, death, and resurrection of Christ. None of them are alone on their odyssey, their personal quest for the Grail. The Grail turns out to be an actively pursuing force, drawing them on toward the fulfillment of their yearning. Like Goethe's archetypal hero, Faust, or Dante in the *Divine Comedy*, that are supported, urged on, and ultimately saved through divine caring, tenderness, and affection, qualities traditionally connected with the womanly aspects of an androgynous deity, and symbolized in the novels by a flesh-and-blood lover, who generally turns out to be the original girl or boy next door, their first and long-forsaken/betrayed love. The end of our explorations, as T. S. Eliot put it, is to return whence we started and recognize it for the first time. The God whom we seek also seeks us and turns out to have been living in our neighborhood all along. "Lynnie and the lake. The girl is the lake is the Grail is God . . ." muses Jim O'Neill in *Death in April* (64).

Greeley's Grail is certainly no "coy mistress." In honored Celtic tradition She is an enthusiastic and active participant, wearing Her "spells" with wisdom and vigor. She is the Light which pierces our darkness when least expected, touching sinners and saints alike. For Hugh Donlon She appears in the guise of Maria.

> golden and glowing in the late afternoon sun, wearing only her glasses and a plain gold cross at her throat. . . . Sacred love offering her benediction. . . .
> "Maria . . . I must climb out of hell . . . I can't. . . ."
> "No, you don't. You can't escape that way. You should stretch

out your hands to God."... "And let Him pull you out." She
pulled him back to her. "This way."

"Why do you bother with me?" he asked.

Her eyes filled with tears. . . . "Because I love you, you crazy so
and so. I have always loved you and always will, no matter how
much you hide from me." (*Ascent into Hell* 471–72)

She is Grace à la William James, totally gratuitous and given, described
by Blackie in *Virgin and Martyr* as a "combination of mist and quicksilver"
(13). She is the source and object of dozens of big and little "epiphanies"
scattered throughout Greeley's novels, moments of divine self-revelation
and human response, of vocation, conversion, and marriage celebration.

The Grail/Magic Princess represents both God and the Church. Nora, in
Thy Brother's Wife, who supports and "mothers" all those she touches, is an
obvious Church analogue,[2] as are Noele in *Lord of the Dance* and Eileen in
Patience of a Saint. The Grail/Communal Womb aspect of the Church as
source, nourisher, and goal of the faithful appears in the indefatigable Ryan
clan with its Madonna penchant for not only cherishing and protecting each
and every member of the family but also adopting an assortment of needy
strays, deserving or otherwise.

According to the Catholic doctrine as restated in *Lumen Gentium* of
Vatican II, "The origin and growth of the Church are symbolized by the
blood and the water which flowed from the open side of the crucified Jesus
(cf. Jn. 19:34)" (351), a symbol also connected with the Grail. The Church
is "a sheepfold, the sole and necessary gateway to which is Christ (Jn.
10:1–10), . . . the Holy City" (353–54). To reinforce those archetypes of
femininity, the Church is called "a bride adorned for her husband (Apoc.
21:1f.) . . . the spotless spouse of the spotless lamb, . . . 'our mother'" (354).
In her identity as exile, "while on earth she journeys in a foreign land away
from the Lord (cf. 2 Cor. 5:6)" (354), and as such also represents the pilgrim
on his/her way home. She "encompasses with her love all those who are
afflicted by human misery, . . . [and], clasping sinners to her bosom, at once
holy and always in need of purification, follows constantly the path of
penance and renewal" (358). She is compared to "the mystery of the
incarnate Word" (357). By being identified both with the Mystical Body of
Christ, "a single mystical person" (66), and His Bride, she is envisioned
primarily in terms of sexual imagery, called to "reveal in the world,
faithfully, however darkly, the mystery of her Lord until, in the *consummation*,
it shall be manifested in full light" (358; emphasis mine).

In *The New Agenda* Greeley includes a chapter on the Church entitled
"From Ecclesiastical Structure to Community of the Faithful" (209–34). This
"headline" summarizes Greeley's ideal Church. It is this kind of Church
which is envisioned as emerging in the conversation of pagan Brigid with
Jesus and Mary in *The Magic Cup*. Brigid finds herself in an unredeemed
world, a world of barren cliffs rearing from a melancholy, churning sea

toward an angry sky, a world of emptiness and howling winds, a world without hope in which the ultimate defiant challenge of human dignity *vis-à-vis* cosmic futility consists in suicide. "Their" laughter transforms the tragedy into comedy. "They" have arrived bringing joy and hope. Brigid's proudly desperate "I don't believe in hope" (168), the fatal leap from the rearing cliffs into the yawning void, yields to the Christian "leap of faith" into the embrace of God represented on earth by the supportive community of the Church. "Do you think, child, that matters to us?" (168) is the gentle reply. At the core of Christianity there lies a spirit of loving acceptance. The ancient gods have served their purpose; their season has passed; they are preserved and fulfilled, not annihilated.

It is this kind of Church manifested in Kevin in his crucial conversation with Ellen (significantly, a Catholic married to a Jew) in *The Cardinal Sins*. The real Church emerges as a medley of warm images of communal life and shared humanity, as "Father Conroy and Sister Caroline and First Communion and May crownings and High Club dances and midnight mass and all those wonderful things that I love so much" (349–50). The real Church (like Jesus and Mary) wraps us all up in her blue cloak of hope and love. "And the damn-fool Church says," in Kevin's words, "Ellen Foley Curran Strauss, we really didn't notice you were gone, because we never let you go.'" (350)

While constructive criticism of the institutional Church constitutes a major thematic strand in *The Cardinal Sins*, *Thy Brother's Wife*, and *Ascent into Hell*, it takes on even greater significance in *Virgin and Martyr*, which deals not as much with weaknesses in the Church as manifested by individuals, as it constitutes an assessment of basic institutional policies of the contemporary global Church. Greeley's position throughout is one of loyal dissent. "I reserve the right to criticize as Paul criticized Peter, 'to his face,'" notes Blackie Ryan, "but I can't be contemptuous of the church. It may not be much of a church now, but it's the only one I have" (*Virgin and Martyr* 276). As Greeley notes in his memoir, his friend and fellow-priest Bill Grogan insists that "Blackie and Maria are Andy's vision of God" (*Confessions* 457). God on earth, God Incarnate, the Mystical Body of Christ, becomes the Church, and as such the Maria/Blackie syzygy symbolizes not only the androgynous God but also the ideal Church, the *ecclesia semper reformanda*, at once, to use a Hegelian image, combatants, battle, and battleground, the process of her own genesis.

In many ways *Virgin and Martyr* seems a literary version of *How to Save the Catholic Church*, by Greeley and his sister, the theologian Mary G. Durkin. Neither the reactionary Counter-Reformation Immigrant Church of the first half of the twentieth century nor the post–Vatican II Church of the past two decades is immune to scathing criticism. The message is clear: the American Catholic Church is in trouble. The Global Church is in trouble. The twentieth century in the form of a post–Vatican II hurricane has invaded her hallowed halls with a vengeance. The forces of change must be harnessed and controlled lest they sweep away the structure. Still, and this essential point must not be forgotten, *Virgin and Martyr,* in keeping with Greeley's faith in a loving and gracious God, is a work filled with hope. The end of Catholicism and the Church is never a real possibility. The Church will survive. In an altered form, and yet, mysteriously, eternally, the same. Many of the birth pangs of transition, however, could be alleviated, the period of readjustment could be shortened, if certain problems are identified and solutions put into effect. A head-in-the-sand ostrich policy will only prolong the agony.

Reflecting on this sad state of affairs, Blackie notes, "Most priests and nuns are not very well educated. They are not trained in disciplined intelligence, careful reflection, precise expression and respect for the grey, complex nature of reality. Indeed, such qualities are thought to be unnecessary for virtue if not a serious obstacle in it" (*Virgin and Martyr* 191).

In the wake of the Second Vatican Council this mixture of enthusiasm and incompetence leads to a "humid jungle of (half-assed) ideas and schemes" (183), Blackie observes with his usual tact. Manic social and political zeal took the place of careful, passionately dispassionate reflection. *Virgin and Martyr* constitutes a full-scale assault on banners raised in the name of flash-in-the-pan relevance. Popular versions of liberation theology (adapted from Marx), charismatic renewal (borrowed from Pentecostal Protestantism), self-actualization (stolen from Maslow, albeit misunderstood), Third World rhetoric, encounter groups, women priests, married priests, gay liberation, hastily deposed saints . . . the list seems endless. Nevertheless, the work presents an indictment, not of issues, but of the inept and amateurish manner in which these issues have been approached. Why is it, for example, Greeley wonders, that so many theologians insist on seeking solutions to very real and urgent problems in alien traditions, neglecting to look for answers in a rich and promising heritage? What makes Marx so much more appealing than Pope Leo XIII? Why does it appear that there is so little middle ground between the extremes of blindly tenacious, rigid fundamentalism and wholesale rejection of the past? "I think it's too much too soon," Blackie comments concerning the manic frenzy of the sixties. "We can't replace a culture that's at least five hundred years old in a few months. We have to proceed slowly, give it time, resist the temptation for the quick fix, the overnight update, the easy solution" (197).

Thus, ultimately, *Virgin and Martyr* is a passionate plea for quality, honesty, sanity. Cathy, who has spent most of her life running away from herself by embracing "big causes," and who spouts traditional "sweet bridegroom Jesus" pieties as convincingly as "male-pig" feminist and "Amerikan Imperialist" revolutionary rhetoric, finally comes face-to-face with reality in the form of a young woman, one of those she and her group have supposedly come to save. "Why cannot you North Americans leave us alone? Why must we be exploited by both your capitalists and your Marxists? Why do you impose on us your religion? . . . Who asked you to be our advocates? . . . Who voted for you?" (350). Interesting question.

Greeley never tires of contrasting the Church in her two destructive contemporary manifestations, as authoritarian, reactionary, rule-ridden fossil and as manic incarnation of sloppy social activism dedicated to change for the sake of change with the *Real* Church of Christian Love. It is to this Church that Red Kane turns in his hour of need. "Where do I go for help? he asked himself again. The answer was still obvious. The only institution in the world that could help him now was the Roman Catholic Church—the *real* Catholic Church. . . . 'Holy Name Cathedral,' he told the driver" (*Patience of a Saint* 406; emphasis mine). One might even argue that by installing Monsignor Ryan as the rector of the cathedral, the parish church of the entire city, the bishop's own church, Greeley implicitly affirms his support of the institutional Church. He is not waging war against the hierarchy as such, merely against excessive authoritarianism, mediocrity, and incompetence in leadership. More than eight centuries ago, Bernard of Clairvaux suggested that those in ecclesiastical power might be well advised to act more like mothers and less like masters. "Grow gentle," he wrote, "divest yourselves of ferocity, spare the rod and offer your breasts—breasts filled with milk not swelled with pride" (Dinzelbacher and Bauer 56). Maybe, Greeley seems to suggest, the time has finally come for that kind of transformation.

Meanwhile, Andrew Greeley, part latter-day "Defender of the Faith," part Parzival, part Don Quixote, part Peter Pan, continues to share his vision, conjuring up above and beyond the chaotic jungle of errant human passions and a Church corrupted by authoritarianism, envy, and lust for power, a bright, warm image of God as passionately caring and sustaining Presence and the "real" Church as a community of equals, a genuine mother whose nurturing love enfolds every last one of her children within her tender embrace. As a novelist, this priest without a parish now ministers to a congregation of millions, teasing the Christian comedy of grace out of the new-old symbols presented to us in contemporary life, and weaving ever-new variations on the central Christian motif of the Incarnate God revealing Himself/Herself through the dynamics of divinely human love.

NOTES

1. See, *inter alia, The Analogical Imagination: Christian Theology and the Culture of Pluralism* (New York: Crossroad, 1981).

2. Nora's nurturing and cherishing Woman God and Church roles have paradoxically gone almost entirely unnoticed by reviewers and critics, such as James E. Johnston in "Priests, Prose, and Preachments," *Theology Today,* July 1984, 161–70.

WORKS CITED

Alighieri, Dante. *The Vision; or Hell, Purgatory, & Paradise of Dante Alighieri.* Translated by Henry F. Cary. New York: Hurst, 1844.

D'Arcy, Martin C., S. J. *The Mind and Heart of Love. Lion and Unicorn: A Study in Eros and Agape.* Cleveland and New York: World Publishing, 1956.

Dinzelbacher, Peter, and Dieter R. Bauer. *Frauenmystik im Mittelalter.* Ostfildern bei Stuttgart: Schwabenverlag, 1985.

Flannery, Austin P., ed. *Documents of Vatican II: A New Authoritative Translation of the Conciliar Documents—Including Post Conciliar Papers and Commentaries.* New rev. ed. Grand Rapids: William B. Eerdmans, 1984.

Frye, Northrop. *The Great Code: The Bible and Literature.* New York and London: Harcourt Brace Jovanovich, 1981.

———. *The Secular Scripture: A Study of the Structure of Romance.* Cambridge: Harvard University Press, 1976.

Greeley, Andrew M. *Angels of September.* New York: Warner, 1986.

———. *Ascent into Hell.* 1983. New York: Warner, 1984.

———. *The Cardinal Sins.* 1981. New York: Warner, 1982.

———. *Confessions of a Parish Priest: An Autobiography.* New York: Simon & Schuster, 1986.

———. *Death in April.* 1980. New York: Dell, 1984.

———. *The Final Planet.* New York: Warner, 1987.

———. *God Game.* New York: Warner, 1986.

———. *Happy Are the Meek.* New York: Warner, 1985.

———. *The Jesus Myth.* Garden City, N.Y.: Doubleday, 1971.

———. *Lord of the Dance.* New York: Warner, 1984.

———. *The Magic Cup.* 1979. London: Futura Publications, 1984.

———. *The New Agenda: A Proposal for a New Approach to Fundamental Religious Issues in Contemporary Terms.* Foreword by Gregory Baum. New York: Image, 1975.

———. *Patience of a Saint.* New York: Warner, 1987.

———. *Strangers in the House: Catholic Youth in America.* New York: Sheed & Ward, 1961.

———. *Thy Brother's Wife.* New York: Warner, 1982.

———. *Unsecular Man.* New York: Schocken, 1972.

———. *Virgin and Martyr.* New York: Warner, 1985.

———, and Mary G. Durkin. *How to Save the Catholic Church.* Preface by David Tracy. New York: Viking, 1984.

Hegel, Georg Wilhelm Friedrich. *Sämtliche Werke: Jubiläumsausgabe in zwanzig Bänden*. Edited by Hermann Glockner. Vol. 2, *Phänomenologie des Geistes*. Stuttgart: Frommann, 1927.

Rougemont, Denis de. *Love in the Western World*. Albert Saifer, 1940.

Schillebeeckx, Edward. *Jesus, an Experiment in Christology*. New York: Seabury, 1979.

Shea, John. *An Experience Named Spirit*. Chicago: Thomas More, 1983.

Whitehead, Alfred North. *Religion in the Making: Lowell Lectures, 1926*. New York: Macmillan, 1926.

15

PHILIP H. KELLY

Sin, Guilt, and Forgiveness in Greeley's Passover Trilogy

SPECTACULAR SIN AND SPECTACULAR GUILT

For Catholics few sins are more spectacular than a priest's fornication or adultery. In Andrew Greeley's *Thy Brother's Wife* Father Sean Cronin's adultery with his brother's wife at the European resort of Amalfi is certainly spectacular, but for pure spectacle that sin is easily outdone in Greeley's *Ascent into Hell* when Father Hugh Donlon fornicates with a nun at her apartment on Christmas morning. These are patently spectacular and patently Catholic sins.

The popularity of these fictions might be attributed to the novelty of a priest writing fiction that features the clergy's sexuality as a substantial theme, but that novelty would certainly wear off after a novel or two. To date, Greeley has published nine novels, and each has maintained a measure of popularity. I suggest that something more substantive may account for the popularity. That substance may be the theology of forgiveness that his works vivify.

Although the novels of the Passover Trilogy create substantial and spectacular sins, the novels do not focus on the sins so much as on the sinners' response to them. Greeley uses the spectacle of the sins and the

Reprinted, with minor revisions, from the *Journal of Popular Literature* 4 (Spring/Summer 1988): 37–48. An earlier version of this essay was presented in a session on living authors chaired by Allienne R. Becker at the Northeast Modern Language Association Convention, Boston, 2 Apr. 1987.

attendant guilt as an opportunity to work out in fiction a theology of
forgiveness based on God's unbounded love. Although there is nothing
essentially new about a theology of forgiveness, it takes on a fresh appearance and fresh impetus in these fictions.

In *Thy Brother's Wife* Sean confesses his sin of adultery, but does not feel
free of it. He is concerned that the absolution did not reach the depths of
his pain and confusion. He is having trouble feeling sorry for having done
something that was so enjoyable. To complicate matters further, remember
that adultery is not only physically pleasurable, but it is also the only sin
that is potentially life-giving. The adultery in this case results in the birth
of a son to Nora, and it also seems to have contributed to Sean's personal
strength in enabling him to stand up to the Pope (ironically, over the Pope's
stand on birth control). Sean's dilemma is the curse of adulterers trying to
repent: he finds himself ashamed, confused, and dismayed, yet "he could
not escape from a sense of enormous satisfaction and complacency" (177).

The satisfaction and complacency, however, are short-lived, and the guilt
he develops is crushingly oppressive. The affair with Nora cripples him
emotionally, leaving him a victim of his own self-contempt:

> But the guilt, the torment, and the self-contempt he now felt
> because of their experience would never go away, it seemed, nor
> would the shattering memories of its pleasures. "Oh, God!" he
> sobbed, burying his head in his hands. "What have I done?"
> (185–86)

The guilt malingers, maybe too much so, for Jimmy, Sean's fellow priest, is
prompted to exclaim:

> "Sean, are you going to revel in guilt for the rest of your life? The
> truth is, you damn fool, that what bothers you is not the sin,
> which God forgives, but the mark on your stainless white record.
> Sean Cronin isn't perfect. He's a sinner like the rest of human-
> kind." (205)

A crucial point here is the distinction between forgiving a sinner and
forgiving a sin. God forgives sins; that is, he forgives a sinner's sinning, but
he can't absolve one from being a sinner, for being a sinner is part of being
human. Sean continues wrestling with and resisting the need to come to
terms with his own humanity for almost one hundred pages more.

In *Ascent into Hell* Hugh Donlon has a similar response to his affair with
Sister Liz:

> Then as he emerged into full awareness, he felt enormous guilt.
> Mortal sin, sacrilege, violation of his priestly vows. He was a
> beast, an animal. "God in heaven, forgive me," he pleaded, "I'll
> never do it again." (158)

Clearly, this is a man fully conscious of his sin, begging forgiveness and making a firm resolve not to sin again. But fornication is an ambiguous sin: it is difficult to feel sorry for something so pleasurable. Seven pages later, his prayer reflects the ambiguity: "Dear God, he prayed . . . I don't know what I should do . . . I don't want to give her up, not yet anyway" (165). The ambiguity (in clear contrast to the "mortal sin, sacrilege, violation of his priestly vows" above) increases his disgust with himself. Notice the harshness with which he regards his plans for a weekend with Liz:

> Self-contempt and lust battled inside him as he hung up the phone. He knew he would hate himself even more after the weekend idyll. . . . how low could he get? (166)

Hugh's confession, like Sean's, is not wholly satisfactory, but it does highlight what is wrong with his increasingly morbid sense of self and his sense of guilt. Hugh's confessor pinpoints the core of the problem:

> "You seem less willing to forgive yourself than God is. . . . Some disgust is appropriate. But you have a purpose of amendment, you intend to end the relationship. You would do much better to atone by hard work instead of self-hatred." (168)

Hugh completes his confession with a measure of resolve; his "I'll try, Father" is much less emphatic than his earlier "I'll never do it again." News of Liz's pregnancy, however, undermines any good intentions he had of ending the relationship.

While Hugh feels compelled to marry Liz, his friends see the contemplated marriage not as a noble gesture, but as a damning self-punishment ensuring his descent and degeneration. Father Xav Martin is especially insistent against the marriage. He sees that the marriage is bound to be an unhappy one, one that will foster Hugh's infidelity and contribute to his further decline. Xav feels Hugh has trapped himself into an "irrational sense of obligation." The marriage, according to Xav, would be a self-made punishment, "a man-made hell" probably more punishing than what God would exact for his sins: "Marry that woman and you'll take the first step on your own descent into hell" (170). Hugh goes through with the marriage and does indeed descend into his own self-punishment, his own man-made hell.

Both Sean Cronin and Hugh Donlon have committed sins, but rather than allowing God's forgiveness, both overstate their guilt and institute their own overly harsh, man-made hell on earth. As stated above, God forgives sins, or he forgives a sinner's sinning, but he can't absolve one from being a sinner, because being a sinner is part of being human.

Sean and Hugh both let themselves fall prey to a kind of double jeopardy: they feel guilt for their sins and then they also feel guilt for being sinners—as Sean's friend suggests, that's like feeling sorry for being human.

The effects of this double jeopardy are seen most clearly in Hugh's case as the novel chronicles his descent deeper and deeper into the hell of his own making.

SIN AND HUMAN NATURE

The only relief for such abject guilt, such self-degradation, is to recognize one's own humanity. In a light moment Hugh counsels a friend by saying, "We're all terrible sinners, Kathy. But God must like us because he made so many of us" (223). This statement suggests a couple of key truths: that sinning is apparently part of human frailty and that God loves us even though we are frail and do sin.

Recognizing the frailty of one's humanity is the first step in Greeley's theology of sin and forgiveness. Hating sinning is hating oneself. Rather than hating oneself, Greeley seems to suggest that one is better off simply to hate the sin and then open oneself to God's forgiveness, something we may not inherently deserve but something that God in His loving mercy dispenses nonetheless.

The central women in these novels (Nora and Maria) seem to understand that sinning is human and therefore forgivable. These two women sin substantially, but they contend with the guilt much better than the priests do. The women seem to understand more readily that while sin is something we do, we can separate ourselves from the sin; we are not the sin.

In *Thy Brother's Wife* Nora's response to her affair parallels Sean's response in some key respects: she, too, is disappointed that she is no longer fully "self-possessed and self-controlled" and that she is prey to "irrational passion" (194). Unlike Sean, however, she is able to recognize that her adultery was simply the result of her own humanity: "Welcome into the human race, she told herself bitterly" (194). Her self-understanding allows her to be instrumental in Sean's coming to terms with his own humanity. In talking with Sean about their adultery and their respective commitments, she distinguishes between transgressing a commitment and dissolving it. Both she and he have made promises—her marriage vows and his Holy Orders—and in spite of their sin, the commitments and vows are still intact. The sin did not dissolve the vows. The sin is evidence of their human weakness, and God forgives sins.

Nora's notion here that the momentary transgression does not dissolve the commitment is a paradigm for how God's love works. We sin, but God's love for us endures, just as the commitments implied in Nora's and Sean's respective vows endure. Nora helps Sean recognize that he, too, is simply human and that God loves him in his humanity without condition.

Maria, Nora's counterpart in *Ascent into Hell*, serves a similar end as she helps Hugh recognize that his own humanity, frail though it may be, is still an object of God's love. Hugh's descent has been deeper and the reclamation project is more involved, but the rule of God's love is the same.

THE MOTHERLY PRINCIPLE OF LOVE:
LOVE FOR SIMPLY BEING

Nora and Maria help Sean and Hugh to recognize a broader conception of God's love, a conception that is often characterized as the motherly principle of love which is found in the normal relationship between mother and child. J. J. Bachofen, Erich Fromm, Jane Ellen Harrison, and others describe that relationship. Motherly love is unconditional, unearned, undeserved. Motherly love comes simply because one is, rather than because of what one does. Fatherly love, on the other hand, is dispensed to those worthy, to those who deserve it. Obedience to authority and acting to fulfill the expectations of that authority are primary means of earning fatherly love.

According to Erich Fromm in *The Art of Loving*,

> Unconditional love corresponds to one of the deepest longings, not only of the child, but of every human being; on the other hand, to be loved because of one's merit, because one deserves it, always leaves doubt; maybe I did not please the person whom I want to love me, maybe this, or that—there is always a fear that love could disappear. Furthermore, "deserved" love easily leaves a bitter feeling that one is not loved for oneself, that one is loved only because one pleases, that one is, in the last analysis, not loved at all but used." (41–42)

The insecurity and potential bitterness engendered by the fatherly principle seems to underlie much of the guilt and torturous behavior in Father Sean and Father Hugh.

Hugh's insistence that he leave the priesthood and marry Liz is characteristic of that despair and self-punishment, that feeling of having lost out by no longer deserving God's love. Such despair and alienation seem warranted according to the fatherly principle of love. The reasoning runs like this: "I engendered God's love by doing good. I've done evil; therefore, God doesn't love me anymore." That's the fatherly principle at work.

The motherly principle as advocated by and embodied in key women in the novels bears none of that harshness. Nora, for example, insists that her and Sean's adultery does not close the door on God's love, nor does it nullify the commitments they have made—her marriage and his Holy Orders. They have deviated from authority, but adherence to authority is not the source of God's love. According to the motherly principle, love is unconditional. In that light, God loves Sean simply because Sean is.

Maria tries to bring this point home to Hugh when she chides him for always wanting to "Do, Do, Do." She calls for him simply to "Be."

The third novel of the trilogy, *Lord of the Dance*, extends and elaborates the emphasis on simply being. The metaphor of the dance in this novel is in fact a celebration of simply being. Dance is primarily embellishment.

Dance is certainly no efficient means of locomotion; rather, it is a celebration of movement for its own sake. In the novel dance is a celebration of being.

Noele embodies that celebration of being as she encourages the entire guilt-ridden Farrell family to forgo the guilt they have been harboring and to celebrate their lives. She seems to say that God loves us for our dancing, for our simply being.

WOMEN AND DIVINE PRESENCE

Key women in these novels seem to have a special association and kinship with God. In some respects, Peggy Donlon, Hugh's mother, is the prototype for these women. A particularly poignant scene early in *Ascent into Hell* portrays Peggy as a kind of Earth Mother. In the scene Tom, Hugh's father, suddenly wakes from his sleep to see Peggy nursing their son for his night feeding. Tom finds the tableau of mother and child strangely fascinating. Peggy's smiling eyes are fixed on the nursing child with "infatuation" and "delight." She clearly loves providing her own milk as nourishment for the child: "A light was radiating from them, soft and misty and very bright." When she sees that Tom is watching, she "smiled at him too, inviting him into their communion." She draws him to her and administers "her sacrament to him. The light crept around him too."

> "I have enough love for both of you," she said complacently.
> No longer a child bride with a live doll, Peggy was age-old woman, mysterious, absorbing, life-giving, totally captivating. (7)

A number of points in this passage are worth highlighting. In this scene Peggy is mother, nurturer, and sexual lover. She provides the normal sustenance to her son, Hugh, a sustenance that in nursing is a real giving of oneself. The nursing also engenders touching and its attendant physical and psychological comforts. Since a woman's breast is erogenous, the touching associated with nursing is both sexual and practical. When Tom partakes in the nursing, the sexual is more prominent, but the nursing is still physical nurturing as well. The point of combining the sexual and the physical nurturing is to heighten the sense of the woman's and mother's love as simultaneously intimate, comforting, and exciting. Beyond these practical considerations, the scene layers on an additional dimension with the trappings of the sacramental. She is a chalice; the exchange is communion. In these terms she is the embodiment of the life force; she is the Earth Mother. She shares the life force without discrimination; she is the world navel. She is no longer "a child bride"; she is "age-old woman." She is a worldly manifestation of motherly love.

The notable light in this scene, "radiating from them, soft and misty and very bright," develops in the rest of the novel as a motif associated with the Divine Presence.

Nora, Maria, and Noele exhibit a similar kinship with God, though it is presented less dramatically than in the emotion- and symbol-laden scene cited above.

In *Thy Brother's Wife* Nora experiences the Divine as something she refers to simply as the Presence. This Presence is palpable to Nora. In one scene she reflects on her relationship with Sean and her husband and concludes that both are really little boys and that she would "mother them both, each according to his needs . . . and leave the rest to God." With that she felt the Divine Presence "enveloping . . . caressing, encouraging, reassuring" her. She talks to the Presence, even chides it:

> Rarely did the Presence say anything. Rather it absorbed, bathed, and soothed her. Tonight, however, it laughed . . . the way she often laughed at Noreen when that teenage tomboy did something particularly wonderful.
>
> Everyone, sighed Nora, wants to be a mother. Even you. (276)

Notable here is not only Nora's relationship with the Presence but also the matriarchal traits of that Presence. The Presence is motherly, "caressing, encouraging, reassuring," much as Nora was in her relationships with her husband and with Sean. The Presence is also a joyful parent rather than a stern one.

In *Ascent into Hell* Maria is the triple embodiment of mother, lover, and channel for the Divine Presence. She is a carefree spirit, and she engenders some of that spirit in others as she brings God's joy into the lives of those around her. Tom and Peggy, Hugh's parents, early in the novel recognize a special sensuality in Maria, sensual in the sense that she helps them realize God's grace in all they do. Maria has that special ability to remind people of the sacredness of such things as the moonlit lake and the night sky. The nighttime swim that she suggested stimulated Tom's and Peggy's sexuality, prompting Tom to say, "That little Italian girl made a simple thing like swimming a sacrament, a revelation of God's grace" (21). On more than one occasion, Maria Angelica, an angel on earth, brings to the Donlons and others a greater awareness of God's presence in the world. She is a conduit for the Presence.

Maria seems exactly the right person to act as this conduit. After offering Norma Austin a job in exchange for testimony to support Hugh's exoneration in security fraud, she refers to herself as "Maria Angelica . . . lady bountiful" (334), thus picturing herself as a grace-giving presence. Furthermore, Maria understands the essence of motherly love; she explains to her son that a "mother's love doesn't have to be earned by pleasing her" (329). Like Maria, the Divine Presence is bountiful with unconditional love. The final scene of the novel articulates most directly the special association between Maria and the Presence. Here Hugh administers the Last Rites to Maria's elderly neighbor, Grace Monaghan. The scene, bathed in the glow of warm, comforting light, harkens back to the light associated with his mother, Peggy, as she nursed Hugh in the night. The novel ends with Hugh joining Maria at her home, seemingly bringing him full circle and confirming that the farther Hugh removed himself from Maria, the less he seemed in touch with the Divine. Ending with Maria is both comfortable and comforting.

Lord of the Dance, like the previous novels in the Passover Trilogy, features believers overburdened with guilt. In this novel three generations of Farrells harbor the guilt of dark sins, some hidden, some quite public. And again it is a woman, the fay sprite Noele, who is instrumental in delivering them. Noele is structurally and symbolically the embodiment of the Divine Presence and of divine motherly love. She is born on Christmas. She brings Daniel back from the dead. Before Easter, she suffers for the sins of others with no malice toward those who rape and torture her. On Easter morning she rises from her sickbed to lead the celebration. Her love for the sinners around her is unrelenting, and it seems tinged with the same sensuous joy for life that Maria exhibited in the previous novel. For example, Brigid Farrell regards her long-term affair with Burke Kennedy a sin beyond forgiveness, but Noele's attitude is generous and uncritical: "They would be forgiven much because of their devotion to each other. And, Noele supposed, as cute as they were with each other, there probably was a lot to be forgiven" (64). It is through the workings of Noele that all the Farrells face up to and overcome their individual and collective guilt.

There seems to be a progression in the three novels. Nora is as much a sinner as Sean, thus making her both the central woman and the major female sinner in the novel. Maria, the central woman in the second novel, is not the central female sinner; Liz is. And in the third novel Noele is not sinner at all, though the novel is peopled with a number of female sinners. Paralleling that progression, Nora is the least in touch with the Presence; it seems her close friend, but it is clearly separate from her. Maria is more closely identified with that Presence. Her life and vitality seem to bring the joy of God into others' lives, from the midnight swim at the beginning of the novel to the glow that Hugh feels at the end. She is not the Presence, but she seems an avenue, a conduit for that Presence in the world. Noele is clearly a Christ-figure—she seems an embodiment of that Presence. In creating this progression, Greeley makes God and woman more closely identified. He brings home the feminity of God. In so doing, he argues for broadening our perception of God to include the feminine principle of love.

The key women in the novels may be imperfect realizations of that motherly principle, but they bespeak the potential for a broader conception of God. Alhough God is surely sexless, we in our limited wisdom have always found it helpful to think of God in anthropomorphic terms. Traditionally, we have anthropomorphized God as the father; Greeley's novels suggest we should also anthropomorphize God as the mother. Doing so enhances self-tolerance and helps make sense of God's unquestioning willingness to forgive. Doing so is crucial to Greeley's theology of sin, guilt, and forgiveness. This theology encourages us to celebrate God as the complete parent: mother and father. Amen.

WORKS CITED

Fromm, Erich. *The Art of Loving*. New York: Harper & Row, 1956.

Greeley, Andrew M. *Ascent into Hell*. New York: Warner, 1983.

———. *Lord of the Dance*. New York: Warner, 1984.

———. *Thy Brother's Wife*. New York: Warner, 1982.

16

KATHLEEN ROUT

Renew Your People, O Lord: Andrew Greeley's Passover Trilogy

In March of 1986 *The New York Times Magazine* printed part of Father Andrew Greeley's introduction to the new paperback edition of Lloyd C. Douglass' *The Robe* under the title "'The Robe' and I: The Making of a Christian Storyteller." There, Greeley explains that it was his experience in reading *The Robe* at the age of fourteen that formed the nucleus of his later inspiration: the desire to convey Christian truth in a manner as exciting and involving as a good narrative can be. The intensity of the experience and the realism of the presentation of the characters of the Bible seemed to him then and now to be the optimum way to present the insights of faith to readers who were beyond the reach of theological analyses. *The Robe* was attacked, as Greeley's novels have been to an even greater extent, because the powers that be in Church preferred, alas insisted, that the characters be, in Greeley's words, "saints, not sinners in need of salvation," and that the events be inoffensive to even "the most timid of the faithful."

All of his novels lend themselves to criticism of this nature: there are those who believe that any work written by a good person must be about good persons; only G ratings, as it were, receive their stamp of approval. But Greeley does what he does, and he defends what he does on the grounds that he tries to describe the action of grace and the effect of God's

Reprinted, with minor revisions, from *Midwestern Miscellany* 15 (1987): 25–32.

love in a world of sinners, Catholic or not, who often fall into despair. An examination of three of his recent novels, which are grouped together as the Passover Trilogy, will serve to illustrate the grounds of his critics' complaints and of Greeley's justifications.

Thy Brother's Wife (1982), *Ascent into Hell* (1983), and *Lord of the Dance* (1984) constitute a grouping in which the major events in each work occur during Holy Week: specifically, *Thy Brother's Wife* centers around Holy Thursday, the day in the Christian calendar when a priest recommits himself to his vocation; *Ascent into Hell* has various Good Fridays serve to mark the passage of time and the occurrence of major events; and *Lord of the Dance*, Holy Saturday, particularly the Easter Vigil Mass on Saturday night, which looks forward to the Sunday Masses of the Resurrection.

There is some duplication of characters and themes in the first two novels in the trilogy. Further, while the span of time in each volume covers several years, the dates often overlapping, the Holy Week events are always prominent, especially as they increase or create the symbolism of rising action and dénouement. In each case, an introductory page explains the significance of the Judeo-Christian season of liberation and renewal in terms most appropriate to that particular novel. The note preceding *Thy Brother's Wife*, for example, specifically mentions that on the first Holy Thursday, while eating the Seder with his followers, Jesus "committed himself to them irrevocably." Throughout the novel, which commences on Holy Thursday in 1951, with Sean Cronin, the young seminarian, experiencing misgivings about his vocation, and ends on Holy Thursday in 1977 with his acceptance, at long last, of God's will for him, the books, or sections, are each preceded by a relevant passage from the Gospel of John, including two from the description of the Last Supper. The connection is not always easy to perceive; for example, one can see as ironic his use of the lines "I leave to you my own peace, I give you a peace the word cannot give; this is my gift to you" (John 14:27), because the chapter opens with the assassination of Martin Luther King and includes Bob Kennedy's assassination, the suicide of a rejected woman, and the death of a little boy, as well as the discovery that the mother of Sean and Paul, whose gravestone reads 1908–1934, is in fact alive but locked away.

The prologue to *Ascent into Hell* begins the story on Good Friday in 1933, with the main action picking up in 1954. Here, each of the six books is preceded by Last Words of Christ on the cross, beginning with "I thirst" and ending with "Into thy hands I commend my spirit." Each line is a sort of double entendre which refers not only to Christ's torment but to a stage in the emotional anguish of the central character, the young priest Hugh Donlon, who ultimately accepts God's will on Good Friday of 1981.

The first two novels are interrelated in that Sean Cronin's and Hugh Donlon's crises overlap in time, although the results are different, and in that Sean is Hugh's superior with whom he must consult at several points in the novel. Each priest's crisis is threefold: the temptations a normal heterosexual life offers a celibate clergyman, conflicts with the same sorts of incompetent or capricious administrators one could find anywhere, and a questioning of both faith and mission that lasts most of their lives. In Sean Cronin's case, his and his brother Paul's acceptance of their dictatorial father's will that one go into the clergy and the other into politics as the husband of the orphaned Nora, who grew up with them, is the root of all the later conflict. Paul is willing to marry Nora, although he doesn't really love her, while Sean has been deeply in love with Nora for most of his life, but rejects her in favor of the priesthood, because he cannot yet say no to a parent-figure.

Sean's most serious crisis occurs in 1966, when he is in his early thirties; weeks after Nora and Paul's tenth wedding anniversary, which they have spent apart, the three of them on vacation in Amalfi, "the old threesome," as they call it, back together again. Soon, Paul is called back to Chicago by Mayor Daley, and Sean's and Nora's attraction for each other finally has its expression in a brief affair which fills him, at least, with endless guilt. As according to Nora's plan, however, the union produces her fourth child and only son, Mickey Cronin. Over the next few years occur the traumas of Book six mentioned above, and in the midst of all of this Hugh Donlon enters the office of the now Monsignor Cronin in a chapter from *Ascent into Hell* to tell him that he plans to leave the priesthood in order to marry a nun whom he has impregnated during an affair that would otherwise have ended. While Hugh has repressed his doubts about the marriage, Sean has repressed his doubts about the priesthood; he suffers from guilt over Nora and has trouble with the priests and papacy over the issue of artificial birth control. It is no wonder that he treats Hugh with acerbity, and that Hugh regards him as "a cold, ambitious bastard." After years of increasing estrangement, in which Liz Donlon and her Christ Commune group of left-wing radical ex-priests and nuns alienate everyone possible and Liz alienates Hugh from his children, Hugh is framed and imprisoned for activities in the Chicago Board of Trade, and he feels convinced that he is also alienated from God, down in the cold pit that is at the very bottom of hell. Ultimately, however, Liz is killed in a plane crash and Hugh is free to commit himself to the priesthood should he so choose.

Hugh's time in the pit of hell is his "time on the cross." Whereas Thursday, the day of commitment to the community, dominates Sean Cronin's story about a priest who remains in the priesthood after a quarter of a century of doubt, Friday, the day of Freedom Through Forgiveness, marks the days of Hugh's life. Born on Good Friday in 1933, consecrated to God from the start, he finally accepts God's plan for him on the final Good Friday of the novel in 1981, when he realizes he has been forgiven for his sins and has been offered one more chance to accept Maria, the girl he fell in love with and rejected in 1954 because of his mother's plan for his vocation. Hugh is still struggling with his soul that last afternoon, during his audience with Sean Cronin, who agrees both that Maria may indeed *be*

God's will for Hugh and also that Hugh is now and ever shall be a priest. "The choice," Hugh is told, "is between active ministry and being a priest in some other way no one has yet figured out."

But Hugh considers himself an ordinary "lost soul," and he finds it hard to accept the message of the hymn "Vexilla Regis," sung during the veneration of the cross, which assures us that the lance that pierced the side of Christ released the saving fluid that will wash us free of all our sins. This forgiveness and love has always been the hardest thing for Hugh to accept for himself personally, although he has delivered sermons on it; it is, in fact, the dominant theme of the novel.

Whereas the *Ascent into Hell* is about one priest undergoing a crisis of the soul that caused him to leave the priesthood, in both *Thy Brother's Wife* and *Lord of the Dance* the priest, Sean, or John, is part of a pair of brothers in which the elder is a politician like Paul Cronin or a professor and would-be politician like Roger Farrell. Whereas Sean and Paul were joined by an adopted child in the family (Nora), John and Roger are raised with their first cousin Danny, whose mother was killed by a Mafia hit man when he was four, because she asked too many questions about wills and shares in the family business.

There was a minor mystery in *Thy Brother's Wife;* Nora takes over much of the family business as well as the Cronin Foundation when her husband becomes more and more deeply involved in politics, and thus stumbles onto the discovery that Sean and Paul's mother, Mary Eileen, is not in fact dead, as had been assumed, but insane. She has been kept in a Catholic nursing home by her husband since her complete breakdown in 1934 following the birth of Sean. His father, it turns out, is not Paul's father, her husband, but a priest with whom Mary Eileen had had an affair; her guilt, her husband's reaction, and her naturally susceptible temperament caused her to try to kill her baby, after which she lapsed into psychosis.

In *Lord of the Dance* the quest for a supposedly long-dead relative is the mainspring of the action. When Noele Farrell must write a family history for a high school assignment, she begins to ask some of the questions that got Florence Farrell killed years before, and that will lead to her own rape and beating as a warning to her and to her family. Almost accidentally, through the medium of her boyfriend Jamie's father, Congressman Burns, she effects the release of her Uncle Danny Farrell from a Chinese prison camp, where he has been held incommunicado since his plane lost power and went down in 1964, the year of her birth. Danny's appearance precipitates several crises: it is revealed that his plane went down by prearrangement through a powerful family member (his step-uncle, Aunt Brigid's second husband), who feared Danny would kill him as he had been rumored to have murdered his Uncle Clancy, Brigid's first husband and the father of John and Roger, for beating her, Danny's aunt and foster mother. It is further revealed that Danny was the husband (first and now *only* husband) of Roger's wife, Irene, and beyond *that*, he is the true father of

Noele herself, who was conceived before he left on his last mission and born early, on Christmas Day. Improbably, Noele had never been informed of the truth, because the whole family had deceived everyone into thinking Noele was Roger's daughter in order to cover the fact that briefly, the widowed and disinherited Irene had given Noele up for adoption and then reclaimed her after she met Roger again while working in California and married him.

Noele does not have a murderer for a father yet, though; the killer of the violent old Clancy was Uncle Monsignor—John Farrell. Believing his vocation as a priest to be threatened by the revelation of such a crime, the family covered up for him, allowed the rumor to persist that Danny had done it, and got a doctor to sign a certificate of accidental death. John's killing of his father is a convenient way for Greeley to bring up the subject of the morality of killing someone to protect loved ones; not only is John's conscience clear, but so is Danny's when he and Jamie, using German-made precision rifles with telescopic lenses, blast the faces off three Mafia chiefs just as they are ready to tee off one lovely Sunday morning.

Lord of the Dance is a mystery because it is about a mystery—the Resurrection of Christ. It begins in the fall of 1981 and ends on Holy Saturday of 1982, at the Easter Vigil Mass. Father Greeley's selection of the Vigil Mass preserves the Thursday-Friday-Saturday sequence established by the first two books, but it also permits him to make good use of the phallic symbolism of the Easter candle and the newly blessed holy water used only at that particular Mass. Saturday is the day set aside to commemorate new life. Throughout the trilogy, he has consistently emphasized the concept of human sexuality as a metaphor of Christ's love for his Church, and here the symbolism and the reality are articulated by one of the characters, the long-lost Daniel Farrell, newly reunited with his wife, Irene.

We have seen renewal in the novels all along: On the final Holy Thursday of *Thy Brother's Wife*, Sean Cronin realizes that his brother's wife, now widow, Nora, has been the sign of God's love for him all his life, with or without a marriage taking place; he renews his priestly vows with the other priests, and he will accept the Pope's designation of him as the new archbishop of Chicago. Hugh Donlon, after following the wrong way ever since he refused to leave the seminary and marry Maria when he was young, sees that she is correct in her conviction that she is what God wants for him, and chooses, somewhat ambiguously, to marry her and somehow to see himself as a priest as well. His time on the cross ended, he enters an earthly paradise. But the clearest and most sweeping of all renewals is that which takes place in *Lord of the Dance*. Through the events that unfold when Noele begins to ask the probing questions that no one wants to answer, old secrets are brought to light, suffering and sin are further endured, and ultimately everyone is changed. Noele, the analogue for Christ, is born on Christmas Day, scourged on the Friday of Passion Week when she is beaten, raped, and sodomized, avenged in the purging of evil on the golf course on

Palm Sunday, and given her due as a reader of song and bringer of grace at the Easter Vigil Mass. All the Farrells were renewed by the events described, we are told, and the novel ends on a stronger note of affirmation and divine love than any of the others, with the singing of the hymn "Sons and Daughters."

What, then, to return to the case of *The Robe,* are we taught in this trilogy of renewal and rebirth? And why has Andrew Greeley chosen to present the concept of God's love and forgiveness through the unsavory sorts of tales we find here? One might well wonder, after a few of his books, whether most of the priests in the country aren't conducting secret affairs with favorite parishioners, or even their in-laws. The answer, as Greeley takes pains to point out at the end of each book, is that his stories, for one thing, are little worse in their basic subject matter than the parables and stories in the Bible itself, which regularly feature sinners of small or grandiose proportions. He merely develops the potential in those, he would say, into a full-blown modern narrative. But more important, he writes about what he sees and knows, and what the modern Catholic writer often sees, as Flannery O'Connor repeatedly pointed out, as a grotesque world full of people who are lost precisely because they worship false gods, are prey to most of the seven deadly sins at once, and choose to violate a handful of commandments if they get in the way of their plans. She usually wrote about southern Protestants because those were around her; they were what she could render. Greeley's stomping grounds are where the rich Irish Catholics of Chicago live; is that his fault? The point he makes over and over is that much of our suffering is of our own making, the result of our blindness and failure to understand God's will, while all of the forgiveness is God's, who is often easier on us than we are on ourselves.

17

MICHAEL T. MARSDEN

The Feminine Divine: A Search for Unity in Andrew Greeley's Passover Trilogy

There is little doubt that Father Andrew M. Greeley is writing modern religious parables in his best-selling fiction which certainly seem to have found a large audience among both the Catholic and non-Catholic populations in the United States. His tales are a wonderful crazy quilt of theology, sociology, psychology, and everyday human sensibility. It is important to note that while Father Greeley may be writing sociological novels, he is working from a basis of what can be referred to as "felt sociology," a process which reengages the emotions along with the intellect in the storytelling process. Within this matrix is to be found his emphasis on the womanliness of God:

> My sociology drove me to novel writing, and, if the essence of priesting is to offer religious comfort and religious challenge, novel writing turned out to be demonstrably the most priestly work I have ever done—a result, which, if I had paid sufficient attention to my sociological theory, I would have anticipated. And I would also have not been surprised, had I heeded my sociology, that one of the dominant themes of my storytelling is the womanliness of God. ("Making of a Storyteller" 391)

Reprinted, with minor revisions, from the *Journal of Popular Literature* 4 (Spring/Summer 1988): 13–24. A version of this paper was presented at the 1987 Popular Culture Association/ American Culture Association Meeting in Montreal, Quebec, 28 Mar. 1987.

This concept of the feminine divine is central to Father Greeley's storytelling process and perhaps to his popular success. In the first major critical work to date on Greeley's fiction, *Eros and the Womanliness of God: Andrew Greeley's Romances of Renewal*, Professor Ingrid Shafer notes that Greeley's thesis is linked to time immemorial:

> In the universal religious code, the fertile womb is associated both with the image of a container or sacred vessel and with life-giving, purifying waters. Not only Brigid and Mary but *every* woman has the potential to appear as the Great Mother, of symbolizing God in her femininity. (39–40)

The application of these concepts into daily life results in perceiving sexuality as a potential sacrament. Greeley writes:

> ... other people are the most important sacraments of grace, particularly one's parents and one's spouse.
>
> The more satisfying the sexual relationship with one's spouse, the more gracious is one's image of God—Saint Paul has finally been empirically validated: sex *is* the Great Sacrament. The religious imaginations of husband and wife converge over time, especially if their sexual relationship is satisfying. Your story and my story merge into our story. ("Making of a Storyteller" 393)

This focus on human sexuality has, of course, transformed Father Greeley from a controversial but well-respected sociologist into a noted and sometimes controversial best-selling storyteller who breaks all the stereotypes Americans (and Europeans as well) have evolved of priests cast in the Bing Crosby or Fulton J. Sheen mold.

Almost in the same breath that he notes the importance of the womanliness of God and the sacramentality of sex, Father Greeley underscores the importance of place—the Neighborhood—in his fiction. The Neighborhood is the place where all grace is found and the place to which all people must return. He writes:

> I find myself preoccupied by the Catholicism of neighborhood rituals, or parish buildings, or kids in the schoolyard. . . .
>
> Do I mean basketball courts and May crownings and Midnight Mass and a priest in back of church on Sunday morning and a high club dance are more important religiously than a statement of the national hierarchy or a rescript from Rome?
>
> You bet I do.
>
> And what's more, the empirical data shows that when people do come back it is precisely for the symbols that Ellen sought again. Good reasons to come back, it seems to me. (396)

At its very essence, Greeley's fiction is religious, a point he feels many of the critics seem to miss or ignore. He writes:

> Such political and social and ethical issues, admittedly important and surely derivatively religious, have become a substitute for what is fundamentally religious—the meaning of human life and death. (400)

The literary/creative muse is the means by which the human imagination can be elevated to the religious imagination. In a recent commencement address Father Greeley commented on the muse's qualities, exhorting the graduates to embrace her:

> For the muse, spouse, handmaiden, siren, lover, is a gracious and charming lady—imperious in her invitations, but deeply hurt if ignored. She pleads with you to listen to her, watch her, dance with her all the night long and into the morning.
> And recount, charmingly, your love affair with her.
> For the Muse is also the Lord of the Dance. Or at least her agent in the spirit of each of us. The Spirit, St. Paul tells us, speaks to our spirit. ("Muse")

Thus is the stage set for a discussion of Father Greeley's first fictional trilogy, the Passover Trilogy. As the name implies, the stories are tied to the past, but they also look to the present and the future as they attempt to provide meaning for human life and death within the contexts of the religious imagination, human learning, and human sexuality. The importance of Easter and spring rituals within the world of Andrew Greeley cannot be overemphasized. That he would seek their beginnings within time primordial and trace them through the pre-Christian rituals of the season up to contemporary Catholic liturgy is both understandable and necessary. In his *Religion: A Secular Theory* Greeley wrote of Passover and Easter:

> Easter and Passover (in most languages the feasts have the same name) are fascinating because they represent layer upon layer of religious experience, the unleavened bread representing the pre-Sinai spring festival of an agricultural people, the paschal lamb representing the pre-Sinai experience of a pastoral people, the fire and the water representing the male and female elements in the Christian liturgy of Holy Saturday (in which the fire of the candle is plunged into the water), clearly following the pagan spring fertility rite. (The fiery cloud and the water of the Red Sea are a somewhat more obscure Israelite allusion to such pagan symbolism.) Thus, one has fire, water, paschal lamb, and unleavened bread as pagan pictures to which has been added the Jewish

symbolisms of people, liberation, and new life over which has been added a Christian interpretation which does not so much change, but deepen the meaning of peoplehood, liberation, and new life. All three symbols are used precisely to stir up spring images of life beginning again for a new people, a new humanity. Such symbols reach deep into the past, and deep into the human preconscious and unconscious. (88)

And in his introduction to the single edition of the three novels which constitute the Passover Trilogy he even further clarifies the sexual symbolism of the Easter ritual:

The first manifestation of this new attitude in the celebration of the Christian Passover was the addition in the fourth century of the rite of fire and water. While there was justification in the Exodus story for such a change (the pillar of fire hovered over the waters of the sea), in fact the rite was a Roman spring fertility rite: the fire represented the male organ, as it does in most nature religions and in the depths of the human unconscious; and the water, the female organ. The union of the two, in a symbolism patent to anyone familiar with the ancient religious symbols of humankind, represents sexual intercourse. Moreover, the words spoken as the candle was plunged into the water left little doubt about the meaning intended: "May this candle fructify these waters." (In the new Catholic rite of the Easter vigil, the ceremony has been bowdlerized: the priest may not plunge the candle into the waters and the text is deprived of all sexual implication. For fear of shocking the laity, the liturgical reformers have cut the heart out of a ceremony that is fifteen hundred years old.) (viii)

Andrew Greeley's Passover Trilogy is a complex modern parable of the meaning of Easter. Even the cover designs of the three novels speak to the point: *Thy Brother's Wife* (1982) depicts a sensuous woman, toying with a crucifix on a chain with her teeth while set against a strong, red background; *Ascent into Hell* (1983) presents a more complete image of sexuality with a woman in white, crucifix firmly on her neck, reaching out against a red backdrop to a male arm in imitation of Michelangelo's "Creation" painting; finally, *Lord of the Dance* (1984) depicts a virginal young woman with red hair against a white backdrop—only the lettering is red. The Easter message is clear—from the red lance of Good Friday to the white Dance of Easter morn the tale is complete.

Thy Brother's Wife begins with a quotation: "*Ubi caritas et amor, ibi Deus est.*" ("Where there is charity and love, God is always present.") It is from the hymn sung at the washing of the feet on Holy Thursday. So, most appropriately, begins the Easter trilogy. The organizational structure of the novel is that of Holy Thursday, the feast of the unleavened bread, the Last Supper. After the death of his wife, Mary Eileen Morrisey Cronin, Michael

Cronin struggles to raise his two sons in the Kennedy fashion, one to be a president, the other to be a cardinal. Along the way he instructs them to remember that there is nothing more important than family. Nora Riley, an orphan, is adopted by Michael Cronin and brought into his family. Michael Cronin uses people and especially women; his sexuality is superficial and unfulfilled. The adopted Nora eventually becomes the wife of one of Michael's sons, Paul, who is destined to be a politician, while Sean, the other son, becomes a priest and enters a different political arena. Paul, like his father, Michael, does not understand the sacrament of sexuality, only the fleeting pleasures it brings to those who manipulate it. Paul becomes special assistant to Attorney General Robert Kennedy during the Kennedy administration, while Sean is sent to Rome by the Chicago archbishop to become the Church historian for the diocese.

Throughout the novel there is an emphasis on maintaining a continuity with the past, especially with the traditions of the past. In part it is a statement of love for lost rituals and in part it is a statement about the necessity of connections for meanings. Sean becomes a monsignor because he is successful and brave at his tasks, and he preaches the value of commitment to even his sister-in-law Nora. Later in Europe he and Nora have an affair, and in the words of his confidante, Angèlica, Sean Cronin is welcomed into the human race. Of Nora, Greeley writes:

> She, who had so prized her own fidelity to commitments, had blithely violated the central commitment in her life and led another to do so too. That Mickey was probably the result of such a shattered commitment did not change the facts. Self-possessed and self-controlled Nora Riley Cronin was as much a victim of the fires of irrational passion as were her husband, and Uncle Mike, and Mary Eileen and Maggie Shields. (312–13)

Sean Cronin, in the face of a papal ruling on birth control, learns to become a heroic priest who can take a stand. Little Mickey Cronin, the probable product of the illicit affair between the now Bishop Sean Cronin and Nora, dies of leukemia at the age of two and a half, just before Christmas when the poinsettias are already decorating the altar. The light has not yet come into the world; we must wait and go through Good Friday. Nora and Paul's daughter, Eileen, is one hopeful light on the horizon, a prefiguring perhaps of Noele in *Lord of the Dance*. Of Eileen, Greeley writes: "She was a typical high school senior: bright, attractive, happy, her whole life stretching out ahead of her in promise" (386). But of Nora he writes:

> Part of Nora was dead. She presumed it would remain dead, killed by the poison of guilt, pain, and regret. Nora accepted the verdict. The part of her that still lived would pass out its years, doing its best, lamenting that which had been lost but refusing to quit. She would continue to be a wife, a mother, and a businesswoman until the comedy was finished. (393)

When Eileen asks her mother Nora why she remains with Paul when the light of love is no longer there, Nora replies, "Because if people don't keep their commitments, no one can trust anyone else" (396). When Sean and Nora realize their commitments will keep them from becoming regular lovers, they have a mystical experience. The Presence is experienced:

> Then, without warning, the Presence was there, enveloping the two of them, caressing, encouraging, reassuring. You never told me it was to be this way, Nora silently chided the Presence. Rarely did the Presence say anything. Rather, it absorbed, bathed, and soothed her. Tonight, however, it laughed. Not a sardonic laugh; rather it laughed at her in the way she often laughed at Noreen when that teenage tomboy did something particularly wonderful. Everyone, sighed Nora, wants to be a mother. Even you. (448)

At the end of the novel Sean loses his brother, has the opportunity finally to have a life with Nora but chooses not to because he realizes he needs to love her forever, and comes to realize the true sign from God. The final passage of the novel is noteworthy: "Sean Cronin walked down the steps of the rectory to go into the cathedral and repeat with his priests his vows of commitment. He sang softly the words of the hymn to himself" (494). He has just accepted the offer of the position of archbishop of the diocese of Chicago and has made peace with himself and his God.

If *Thy Brother's Wife* is a reenactment of Holy Thursday's liturgy, then *Ascent into Hell* is a restaging of the Good Friday liturgy. Once again, the novel begins with a foreword from the author about the significance of Passover and a focused comment on Good Friday:

> Or perhaps the story of men and women who have spent much of their lives in the misguided crucifixion of themselves with misunderstood passions, discovering at last that their God is not a God of rules but a God of love, a God whose forgiveness cannot be earned since it is already given. (xii)

The novel opens with the marriage of Tom Donlon and Peggy Curtin, who soon have a son, Hugh. In an almost mystical scene at the beginning of the novel, Peg shares her mother's milk with both infant Hugh and father Tom. Hugh grows up to enter the seminary and to become infatuated one summer with Maria, a bewitching family guest. Maria, an Italian, turns even the simple act of swimming at a summer resort into a sacrament, "a revelation of God's grace" (21). The blond Maria Angelica is described by Greeley: "The girl had the elegance of a Dresden doll, the drive of a union organizer, and the quick intelligence of a high-priced lawyer for the defense—the kind the mob employed" (32). While Maria brings Hugh to spiritual life, she also almost woos him out of the seminary. Hugh becomes a priest but finds he is not happy in his vocation because it does not fulfill him the way he was led to believe it should. But he does love his priestly parish work, save for the tyrant pastor Gus Sullivan. This novel provides an inside look at the complexity of parish life, with its school problems and even attempts to remove the pastor.

Those attempts only result in a new assignment for Father Hugh Donlon—to get an advanced degree in demography and study population trends. Hugh subsequently falls in love with an ex-nun, Liz. Torn between his love for Liz and his priestly vocation, Hugh begins his ascent into hell:

> He also wanted to assure himself that, no matter how strong his doubts and no matter how much he would enjoy the things he was going to do with Liz, and no matter how much he would loathe himself for his lust after he left her, he was still a priest and would remain one. (163)

Hugh's confidant tells him that if he marries Liz, he will enter his own man-made hell from which he will not be able to escape. Despite the fact that it tears his family apart, Hugh marries Liz in a simple, civil ceremony. In order to support himself, Hugh begins to work for the Chicago Board of Trade. Despite his new vocation, he is occasionally called upon to perform the priestly functions of comforting the afflicted.

His marriage to Liz sours as he seeks more money and power and she falls into her own hell, physically represented by her slovenliness and unfeeling responses to circumstances. His long-ago affair with Maria Angelica is rekindled in the Mediterranean. But he is convicted of business fraud and is sent to the penitentiary, only to be rescued by Cardinal Cronin, whom we met in *Thy Brother's Wife*. When he is released from prison and finally consummates his love with Maria Angelica, he experiences "Sacred love offering her benediction" (355). Hugh experiences the mystical Presence at the end of this novel just as Sean and Nora had in the previous novel: "Hugh tried to flee from the Lover's majestic instancy and unperturbed grace, escape from it, hide from it, turn away from it. There was not exit" (366). And the novel ends with the Greek Easter greeting—"Christ is risen, Maria, alleluia" (367).

The union of the male (fire) and the female (water) occurs most clearly in Greeley's final novel in the Passover Trilogy, *Lord of the Dance*. The result is the dance divine of the feminine divine. Noele Farrell, a Christmas child with the ability to read people's minds, becomes the main force in the novel, even a surrogate Church. In the process of doing a family history project for her schoolwork, she uncovers many unanswered questions involving her parents, grandparents, Uncle Monsignor, and another uncle lost over China some twenty years before. Noele also loves Latin and directs the folk liturgy at her parish, Saint Praxides. The novel is a series of stories about the inability of human beings to forgive and love again. The possible murder of the grandfather some twenty years before and the many unanswered questions surrounding the death become the Good Friday with which the Farrells have to deal in their "ascent into hell." Like Hugh Donlon before them, they have to spend their time in purgatory and rise on Easter Sunday. And it is the Christmas child who leads them from the tomb into the light.

The mystery of the grandfather's death is further complicated by wills and the family business. The motives are many, the cover-ups several, and the results disastrous. Noele's father, Roger, becomes a candidate for governor, and mysteries surrounding the family's past are uncovered.

The Farrells love the Neighborhood and attempt to keep the family together through the empty ritual of Sunday dinner at the grandmother's house; she married her boyfriend, Burke Kennedy, after her husband's untimely death. Noele, who dates a congressman's son, is able to secure the "Company's" assistance in locating and freeing her long lost Uncle Danny, pilot and adventurer who lives for living, not for revenge. After twenty years of exile in a Chinese commune, Danny returns to become a novelist and to rekindle his old love for Irene, now married to brother Roger.

Uncle Monsignor John Farrell turns out to be the one the family has been protecting all along, since he apparently caused Grandfather Clancy's death. He had come to the justifiable defense of his mother, who was being beaten; but his career as a priest would have been ruined, and thus the cover-up.

Noele, the Christmas child, begins to receive threatening calls because of her family research which touches on some mob involvement; she is finally abducted, raped, and thrown naked on the basketball courts at Saint Praxides. Despite an additional attack, her spirit is not broken. Father Ace McNamara reminds everyone that "Christmas is the surprise of light coming back, Easter the surprise of spring returning. Our faith is the ability to be open to surprises (311).

The lesson Noele learns is "to live with suffering and tragedy (356). Inspired by the song "Lord of the Dance" sung by Mary O'Hara, Noele leads not only the congregation of Saint Praxides but also the Farrell family to light and love. As she is riding in a car, Noele, too, experiences the Presence: "Then Noele saw a broad beam of sunlight move lazily down Jefferson Avenue, like a sophomore girl slouching home from the Ninety-fifth Street bus on a warm, Indian summer afternoon, daydreaming about a senior boy to whom she has never spoken a word in her life (378). Noele's true parents, Danny and Irene, were married the day after Easter and she was born on Christmas Day, three weeks early. The scene of Noele going to O'Hare Airport to "rescue" her Uncle Danny is striking:

> And then suddenly there she was, striding purposefully down the length of the ticket line with the Holy Saturday sunlight burning bright in her long red hair, piled high on her head like a flaming strawberry ice cream cone. (394)

So ends Andrew Greeley's Passover Trilogy about the modern Church, in love and grace and hope and light and life. Greeley's informative introduction to the single edition of the three novels leaves no confusion about the purpose he intended these modern parables to serve or their meaning:

> I conceived "The Passover Trilogy" as a meditation in story form on these three different themes of the Catholic Passover. The feast of the unleavened bread is a feast of commitment, of covenant— between God and people, and among the people of God and to one another. *Thy Brother's Wife* is a story of commitment, of a covenant renewed in the Holy Thursday liturgy between God and people, between priests and God, and between priests and people.
>
> The feast of the paschal lamb is a feast of sacrifice, of one creature taking on the sins of the whole community. My Good Friday meditation, *Ascent into Hell*, is the story of a man who spent much of his life in the misguided crucifixion of himself, a man who discovers at last that the Lord of the Passover is not a God of rules but a God of love, a God whose forgiveness cannot be earned since it is already given. Holy Saturday, the festival of fire and water, is a feast of rebirth, of coming back from the dead, of beginning once again, themes found in *Lord of the Dance*. "Resurrection," to quote Noele Marie Brigid Farrell, the novel's heroine, "isn't supposed to be easy." (ix)

These modern parables cry out to be looked at not solely within the historical literary tradition, but as gripping, fanciful stories— contemporary romances of the soul. They move from darkness to light, from maleness to femaleness, from separateness to unity—of society, of the universe, of the supernatural.

WORKS CITED

Greeley, Andrew M. *Ascent into Hell*. New York: Warner, 1983.

——. *Lord of the Dance*. New York: Warner, 1984.

——. "The Making of a Storyteller." *Thought* 59 (Dec. 1984): 391–401.

——. "The Muse: Handmaiden or Partner." Commencement address presented at Bowling Green State University. Bowling Green, Ohio, 20 Dec. 1986.

——. *The Passover Trilogy*. New York: Avenel, 1987.

——. *Religion: A Secular Theory*. New York: Free Press, 1982.

——. *Thy Brother's Wife*. 1982. New York: Warner, 1983.

Shafer, Ingrid H. *Eros and the Womanliness of God: Andrew Greeley's Romances of Renewal*. Chicago: Loyola University Press, 1986.

18

ALLIENNE R. BECKER

Virgin and Martyr: A Story of God?

$\mathcal{A}$lthough Andrew M. Greeley says that he tells "stories of God," his novel *Virgin and Martyr* is a tale of lust, murder, and the breaking of vows in which priests and nuns make a greater commitment to self-seeking of radical political activism than they do to Christ. When the drunken Father Tierney tries to rape Catherine Collins, the protagonist of the story, she foils his attempt and, as he writhes on the floor in pain, tells him, "If you ever try that again, I won't just knee your balls, I'll cut them off" (257). Shocking behavior for those committed to following Christ in a special way.

To be sure, Catherine is a very complex person of profound contradiction and paradox. As her story begins, Father Ed Carny, who sold her for money to a band that raped and sodomized her, proclaims: "She died an unspeakable death because of our sins. She's a modern St. Catherine, her body broken on the wheel of American imperialism" (3). This statement refers to the belief that Saint Catherine of Alexandria's body was broken on a wheel. To which Father Blackie Ryan, a *persona* for the author, comments, "psychoanalysts said that of course St. Catherine's wheel represented female sex organs" (4). Soon the reader learns that our heroine is in fact not virginal: in addition to having been raped many times, she has had other sexual encounters.

Reprinted, with minor revisions, from the *Journal of Popular Literature* 4 (Spring/Summer 1988): 49–58.

Still later one learns that Catherine is not a dead martyr, but a woman who is very much alive. Who and what is this enigmatic woman who captures the readers' attention and keeps them in suspense until the very last page of the novel? How is her story a "story of God"?

Although Andrew Greeley is not a consistent symbolist, he uses symbolism in a rich and varied manner. To find who and what Catherine is, one must search her story for the clues the author gives about her. Ironically, her patron saint, Catherine of Alexandria, was eliminated from the Church's calendar of saints, because scholars claim that she was merely a legend and never existed. Catherine Collins is as enigmatic and as legendary as the saint whose name she bears. Although she is neither virgin nor martyr, the acts of Catherine Collins are described in detail as in the affidavits that Father Ed Carny produces when he tries to claim the wealth of her vast estate:

> The testimony was quite spectacular: long weeks of humiliation, torture and rape. Although she was beaten, suspended from the ceiling, burned with cigarette butts, violated many times, and tied to a table with electrodes attached to her genitals, Cathy refused to reveal the names of the revolutionaries she had helped. Nor did she once curse her tormentors or cry out for mercy. Her fingers were broken and then her arms and legs. Her face was slashed, nailed were pulled from her fingers and toes, but still our brave martyr would not surrender.
>
> Finally, on a lovely spring morning in 1975, she was dragged into the courtyard of the Esmeralda Barracks, and while the two witnesses, Paola and Isabella, were forced to watch, she was executed. (8)

According to Father Ed Carny, her longtime mentor and ill-chosen spiritual advisor, they take off her clothes and rape her many times before they bayonet her and cut off her breasts, arms, and legs with a chain saw. Father Carny had sold her to the military police in the Latin American banana republic of Costaguana, because he wanted money and a martyr for his cause. Although she was completely untrained and unprepared for the Latin American project of Carny, he had persuaded her to join him there. When she prepared to leave, he decided to cash in on her vast fortune, which he knew she had willed to his work. The ghoulish *commandante* Don Felipé Gould, head of the military police, and his cohorts were determined to enjoy their prey before killing her.

The first night they raped and sodomized her about twenty times. Before she finally escaped sometime later, they had raped her, in her own words, a "couple of hundred times" (494).

Can such a horrible tale possibly be a "story of God"? Before answering this question, let's consider Catherine. Was she a saint as those people claimed who built a shrine complete with statue in her honor and led prayers to her?

Her childhood and adolescence were exemplary. She went to Mass every day and was prefect of the Sodality of Our Lady. Although outwardly she was a chaste young girl, her cousin Mary Kate Murphy, the psychiatrist, describes her as "a ticking sexual bomb" waiting to explode (55). Darkness lurks in the depths of her wonderful brown eyes (39). Since she constantly denigrates everything she does and calls herself "flaky," the reader concludes that she has an incurable inferiority complex and a desire to be a martyr.

Catherine's parents, Erin and Larry Collins, bear a large part of the guilt for what happened to their daughter. Her mother, "clad always in black and looking like a poster for Lady Macbeth—or maybe one of the witches," is a religious fanatic who had a taste for sensationalism (37). Because her father, occupied with financial affairs, has no time for her, she spends most of her life searching for a father's love and approval from surrogates.

One of the greatest paradoxes of Cathy's life is that she becomes a nun but admits to Mary Kate just how much she wants a man. "I mean, I REALLY want one," she confesses with embarrassment (57). If Cathy's ill-chosen spiritual director, Father Ed Carny, had not pressured her into entering the convent, she probably would have followed her strong womanly instincts and married her childhood sweetheart, Nick Curran, and been the mother of a large family. When she embraces the religious life, her parents completely reject and disown her, causing her greater disorientation.

Throughout the novel Cathy takes counsel with people whom she considers competent to advise her. At each turning point of her life, she receives both good and bad advice. Unfortunately, she refuses to hear what the sound people say, but rather opts to follow the counsel of those who are part of the lunatic fringe. She will not even heed the good advice of Pope John XXIII, with whom she has an audience while in Rome. When she blurts out to him that maybe she will be a martyr like her patron saint, he replies, "St. Caterina was a verra wisa woman, philosopher, teacher. You be a wisa woman, Caterina. Teacha others. Is harda to die, but isa much harda to be a wisa teacher. You be a wisa teacher, eh?" (102).

Others also give her good advice. Frequently, Blackie Ryan, her cousin, encourages her to marry Nick Curran and enjoy her life. A confused Cathy replies, "But I can't believe we were created merely to enjoy life. Oh, I don't say that you and Father Lyons are wrong and the nuns and Father Ed are right. I'm simply all mixed up" (111). In his efforts to manipulate her, Father Ed makes her feel guilty that she is a rich American and gradually leads her into communism. Father Lyons tells her that she can serve God just as well as a wife and mother as she can a nun (121). But Cathy can't convince herself of this despite the great love she shared with Nick Curran. "I wonder if that's true," she asks. "The nuns don't think so. And neither does Father Ed" (121). She capitulates, follows Father Ed's advice, and finds the approval she has been seeking from her own father from this evil priest. She passes out radical leaflets for him and takes part in public protests in the streets until she finally becomes the victim of a brutal beating by the police.

When Roy Tuohy appears on the scene, he vies with Father Carny for the control of her life. Carny wants her to join his group of religious radicals in Latin America; Tuohy wants her to help him write a book. To Blackie, Tuohy is a cheap hack peddling other people's ideas as his own and a "pure fraud" (226). Blackie imagines him as

> an Irish Dracula, lean, sallow, bloodlessly handsome, with a high forehead and slightly receding hairline, which seemed to give him small horns on the top of his head. He wore a tailor-made black suit and dark tie and lacked only the cape and the fangs to give Bela Lugosi a run for his money. Moreover, his voice was a nasal whine, the sort one would expect in a creature returned from the grave. And he treated students like his life depended on sucking their blood and draining away their vitality. (229)

When her religious congregation refuses to let her take her vows at the customary time because of her involvement in political activism, Cathy also becomes his victim, by becoming the wife of this priest who does not even bother to request a dispensation from his promise of celibacy. Father Tuohy, a homosexual with a black lover, marries Catherine, in a ceremony in which no mention of God is made and during which he preaches a forty-five-minute homily on revolution. Dressed in a red monastic robe belted with a gold cord, he outshines his bride, who wears a simple shapeless brown sack of a dress. Their marriage is in the words of Cathy "more or less" consummated (359). As Dr. Mary Kate Ryan Murphy, psychiatrist and cousin to Cathy, explains, "Power is more important to him than sex. Dominating a woman is more pleasurable than fucking her" (346). When Cathy finally realizes that Tuohy is destroying her by using her abusively, she leaves him, making the proverbial leap from the frying pan into the fire by joining Father Ed Carny in Latin America, despite the fact that she still is very much in love with Nick, who is waiting for her to come to her senses and marry him.

The Cathy who goes to Costaguana is no saint. She is proud, self-willed, uncharitable, and unkind. One can see this from what she told her cousin Blackie when he asked her to reconsider before marrying Tuohy: "Goddamn you to hell, you miserable fucking asshole" (342).

The way she treats the other members of her religious congregation is further evidence of her spiritual state. When Mother Martina reproves her for bringing procommunist propaganda into the classrooms, she loses her temper and says "the most terrible things" (251). Words like "bitch," "asshole," and "fart" fall easily from her tongue. When Nicholas tries to comfort her after she has been brutally beaten by the police, she spits in his face and shouts at him, "Fucking pig" (311).

When, because of her radical views, her congregation refuses to let his make her final vows at the appointed time, Cathy, impatient with the idea of waiting, with her usual impulsiveness sends a one-sentence reply to her superior, Sister John Jerome: "Fuck you and the whole order" (338). In a similar vein, when her cousin Blackie invites her to his ordination and first Mass, she reproves him for accepting celibacy and blasts him with the following: "You miserable son of a bitch, how dare you invite me to your ordination and first Mass?" (350). Obviously, charity, obedience, and humility are not her virtues.

As she continues on her downward spin into communism, Cathy experiences despair, anger, and bitterness (293). Under the tutelage of Father Roy Tuohy, she comes to believe that the resurrection of Christ is irrelevant (325). "It all seems so irrelevant to the suffering of the poor people with whom we must identify" (327). This statement reveals how completely Cathy is deceived, for Christ's glorious resurrection is the keystone of Christian life. Human life is in vain without Christ and His triumph over sin, death, disease, sickness. Yet, even though she does not identify with Christ, she tells Father Blackie that she believes she is called to be a priest (327). In the same letter she reports to Blackie that she has no time for prayer. "Roy says our best prayers, our only valid prayers, are the prayers of our life in revolutionary meetings and on the streets" (329). She no longer goes to Mass because she "can't participate in the liturgy performed by an all-male priesthood." Instead, on Sundays she attends "a Eucharistic banquet conducted by one of the other sisters at Assembly. We permit only women to participate and it is a celebration of joy and love and anticipation" (329).

In Costaguana Cathy comes to advocate terrorism and even receives "the Lenin prize for the best revolutionary sharpshooter" (380). When the San Tome silver mine is blown up and a large number of miners, perhaps as many as three hundred, are killed, Cathy comments that these men were "martyrs for the revolution" and that "their lives were not much better than death, anyway" (381). To justify her involvement with those who murdered these innocent miners, she explains, "We kill when we have to, not out of hatred, but out of love and with a sense of repentance" (382). To which Blackie responds, "Where did a sweet young woman who made Indians laugh learn the drivel about murdering with love and repentance?" (383). Can this tale of murder and vulgarity be a "story of God"?

When she is sold to the military police of Costaguana, Cathy hopes to be "brave as Joan of Arc at the stake" (465). However, since she has lost the spirit of prayer and her sense of union wih God, all that she can pray for is death. Completely undone and distraught, she accepts her degradation. She is most obviously no saint. She even contemplates suicide, but as she places a gun to her head the thought occurs to her, "It's a mortal sin." Then she immediately adds, "God would understand. He loves me" (470). Despite everything, Cathy still has faith that God loves her. Instead of killing herself, she uses the gun to kill her captors. "She reached her hand up to heaven partly in defiance and partly in plea. 'Get me out of this and I promise you I'll put my life back in order. I promise. I promise!'" (473). Although she is unable to pray, she clings to her rosary. After killing García and López, she decides that she will also, if she has the chance, kill Don Felipé Gould, who had dunked her head into a latrine bucket full of excrement. "That would be her final service to humankind, eliminating Don Felipé" (477). Cathy is not Christ-like in her attitudes or her behavior.

The story ends with Cathy finally escaping from Costaguana, returning home, forgiving Ed Carny for what he had done, and marrying Nick. Catherine Collins virgin and martyr will become Catherine Collins mother and witness, witness to the mercy of God's love which never ceased pursuing her no matter how far from him she strayed.

Catherine Collins' story is indeed very much a "story of God." Catherine symbolizes the Church, the bride of Christ, which often falters and fails, but never completely abandons him. Throughout the centuries the story of the Church resembles in many points the story of Catherine. Heresies, financial dishonesty, sexual scandals, murders, and every other imaginable sin has afflicted the Church of Christ. No matter how grave the situation, the gates of hell have never prevailed against her and never will. For in time she always turns to Christ, as Catherine does to Nick, who is a Christ-figure in the story.

Even Cathy comes to realize that Nick is Christ to her. He never gives up on her, just as Christ never abandons his Church. In a Christ-like manner Nick is constantly ready to forgive and make a new beginning of their relationship. Greeley indicates the role that Nick plays by naming him after the legendary Christmas saint. Throughout the story Nick pursues Catherine but never forces her to come to him, although everyone, including Cathy, admits that he could have spared her much suffering and error if he had only used force on her. Similarly, Christ never compels the Church to love him.

Those who want their stories of God to be filled with pious platitudes and people who never sin, at least not sexually, find it hard to accept Cathy Collins as a correlative of the Church. Should not stories of God, they ask, be beautiful, chaste, loving, and holy? How can the love that Christ has for his Church be depicted by the love of a man like Nicholas Curran for Catherine Colins? Yet, Saint Paul in his Epistle to the Ephesians compares the relationship of Christ and his Church with marriage. In so doing he was following in the tradition of Old Testament Scriptures in which Israel, a type of the Church, is likened to an unfaithful wife. Passages in the Bible are far more explicit that those in *Virgin and Martyr.* Compare the novel with the word of the Lord which came to the prophet Ezekiel in the form of a story about His beloved people, whom he regarded as His spouse.

The word of Yahweh was addressed to me as follows, "Son of man, there were once two women, daughters of the same mother.

They became prostitutes in Egypt, when they were girls. There their nipples were handled and their virgin breasts were first fondled. Their names were: Oholah the elder, Oholibah her sister. They belonged to me and bore sons and daughters. As regards their names, Samaria is Oholah, Jerusalem is Oholibah. Now Oholah played the whore, although she belonged to me, she lusted for her lovers, her neighbors the Assyrians, dressed in purple, governors and nobles, all of them young and desirable, and skillful horsemen. She granted them her favors . . . and she defiled herself with all the idols of all those she lusted for. She did not denounce the whoring begun in Egypt, where men had slept with her from her girlhood, fondling her virgin breasts, debauching her. . . . Though her sister Oholibah saw all this, her own lust and whorings were even more shameful than her sister's. . . . She flaunted her whoring, she stripped naked; then I turned away from her as I had turned away from her sister. She began whoring worse than ever, remembering her girlhoood, when she had played the whore in the land of Egypt, when she had been infatuated by profligates big-membered as donkeys, ejaculating as violently as stallions." (Ezekiel 23:1–20)

Again in the Old Testament God compares the infidelity of his people with that of a sinning woman in his dealings with the prophet Hosea, whom He instructs: "Go, marry a whore, and get children with a whore, for the country itself has become nothing but a whore by abandoning Yahweh" (Hosea 1:2). In the Bible the people of God are repeatedly likened to a woman who abandons him. In using this same kind of symbolism, Andrew Greeley depicts Catherine Collins, a correlative of the Church, as abandoning Christ, suffering, repenting, and emerging stronger, wiser, and more faithful because of her experiences. He thereby demonstrates that all things do indeed work for good for those who love God and are called according to his purposes.

"I will never be the same," she [Catherine] said uncertainly, wanting our reassurance that she would.
"It will always be a part of your life," I [Blackie] said. "The issue is whether you emerge a better or worse woman because of it." (401)

When the novel ends, the reader is convinced that Cathy has indeed become a better woman, that she will never again abandon Nick, and that for the rest of her life she will be a witness of God's forgiving and providential love. The reader knows that, if because of some weakness, Cathy fails again, Nick will be patient and forgiving with her. The reader also realizes that if God can forgive Catherine her sins of hatred, murder, faithlessness, adultery, disobedience, selfishness, and pride, He will also show mercy and compassion to all his other erring children. Finally, as the reader finishes the novel, he leaves it on the shelf but takes with him in his soul an increase in faith, hope, and love. He knows that no matter how bad the scandals of wrongdoing are, Christ will not abandon his Church. He forgets the evil deeds that have transpired between the covers of the book and in the Church and only remembers that God loves and forgives sinners. *Virgin and Martyr* is most definitely a story of God. His love is abundantly evident in all the faithful people in the story, like Blackie, Mary Kate, and Nick.

WORKS CITED

Greeley, Andrew M. *Virgin and Martyr*. 1985. New York: Warner, 1986.
The Jerusalem Bible. New York: Doubleday, 1966.

19

BERNARD J. GALLAGHER

Lord of the Dance: *A Parable for Modern Catholics*

$\mathcal{A}$t first glance, Andrew Greeley's novel *Lord of the Dance* appears to have all of the necessary ingredients for a successful television soap opera. For instance, it offers us a multitude of love interests. There is Irene, the beautiful wife, mother, and temptress who has one secret marriage to her credit, a second marriage currently disintegrating and an attraction to her husband's clerical brother. There is the boyishly handsome Roger, a professor who dabbles in politics and extramarital affairs with equal élan. There is Brigid, once married to a drunken and brutal husband, now married and in love with Burke, the man forced upon her by the very same drunken and brutal husband. The novel, in addition to these love interests, offers us elements of mystery and violence. Both Clancy, Brigid's first husband, and Florence, Clancy's sister-in-law, have died mysteriously. There is Rocco Marsallo, the villain who enjoys brutalizing others, especially beautiful young women. There is the mysterious disappearance and apparent death of Danny and his equally mysterious reappearance. There is Noele, the adolescent on the verge of womanhood and love. In short, *Lord of the Dance* is a novel filled to overflowing with sexual tensions, murder, deceit,

An earlier version of this essay was presented during the third of four sessions dealing with Andrew Greeley's fiction at the Popular Culture Association Meeting in New Orleans, Louisiana, 26 Mar. 1988.

betrayals, anger, power struggles, and ill-gotten gain. But in spite of this plentitude of seemingly attractive frills, the novel (especially to the modern Catholic) has much more to offer than entertainment (though it thankfully has plenty of that). I would, in fact, argue that *Lord of the Dance* is a parable which, in the fashion of the New Testament parables, calls a community to self-examination and in so doing criticizes both the Roman Catholic hierarchy and the way in which that hierarchy has been slow to reassess the traditional and institutional symbols of its Church.

Lord of the Dance is a parable, for it shares in what Robert Funk identifies as the basic character types, episodic pattern, and dual vision of the New Testament parable. It has, for instance, the three essential groupings of character endemic to the New Testament parable (Parables 47–59). It has a "determiner," or one of those characters who function as authority figures and who "dominate the denouement" (50). It has justified respondents, or those characters who usually act "in accordance with contemporary standards . . . of expected behavior" (47). And it has unjustified respondents, or those characters who, because of their laziness, indolence, or wastefulness, are considered sinners (59).

Lord of the Dance, besides sharing in character types common to the New Testament parable, also shares in the episodic pattern associated with "parables of grace" (*Parables* 59). It builds to a *peripeteia* in which those who act in accordance with convention are unrewarded and in which those who do not act in accordance with convention are rewarded (59). In other words, those who appear on the surface to be morally acceptable (devoid of serious and apparently irredeemable flaws) miss entering into the kingdom.

Although I am not willing to argue that Funk's groupings of character and his analysis of plot completely fit the characterizations and plot of *Lord of the Dance*, I am more than willing to argue that a more than coincidental similarity may be found between the plot and characters of Greeley's novel and Funk's analytical view of the plots and characters found in New Testament parables. Furthermore, I am also willing to argue that neither the number of characters found in the novel nor the length of the novel itself invalidates the comparison which I am attempting to draw. In addition to all of this, Greeley himself at least intimates that a connection exists between the parables of the New Testament and his storytelling; in an interview published in the 1985 Fall/Winter issue of the *Journal of Popular Literature*, he establishes a connection between his storytelling and storytelling as the "principle mode of transmitting religion through human history," and he explains that he writes "seriously" insofar as he wrestles with serious theological issues in his fiction (Marsden and Marsden 103, 104). On the basis of both Funk's analysis of the New Testament parable and Greeley's sense of the role of storytelling in the transmission of religion through history, it seems reasonable to look for and evaluate the kinds of connections that may exist between *Lord of the Dance* and the parables of the New Testament.

The easiest place to begin is with the character Funk defines as the determiner; and Mary Noele or Noele Marie is the one character who clearly functions as the determiner in *Lord of the Dance*. All the lines on the chart (her map of the truth) she constructs converge on her (454). It is she who inspires Irene to take herself seriously and to insist on her own self-worth (418). It is she who parents her father and advises him "to sit up straight" in both a literal and a moral sense (372). It is she who tells her Uncle John in which direction to direct his love when she invokes her "mother superior tone" and says, "Uncle Monsignor has his parish to love" (391). And it is she who presides over the basketball court (360).

Moreover, other characters in the novel respond to Mary Noele accordingly, almost as if they intuit that she is somehow beyond herself. Ace McNamara wonders how "a family of self-preoccupied cowards could have produced a Noele" (287); Burke finds Noele "scary" and Brigid acknowledges that Noele is at least "very smart and very tough" (221).

Furthermore, a series of pentecostal images, which include "swamp fire" (299), "fire and water" (501), "cyclone" (64), and "Flame," the car (361), clearly aligns Mary Noele with the power of the Holy Spirit. In fact, Noele's confident and enthusiastic pursuit of the truth about herself and her family also establishes her as a representative of the Holy Spirit, because She, through Mary Noele, "calls us forth with His dazzling fire" and "reassures us when we are discouraged and frightened" (Greeley, *Great Mysteries* 29). The novel further calls extraordinary attention to this pentecostal imagery when Mary Noele passionately invokes the presence of Holy Spirit as she speaks about the "Lord of the Dance" (100), the very same Lord of the Dance that Andrew Greeley in his book *The Great Mysteries: An Essential Catechism* explicitly identifies with the Holy Spirit (29).

The majority of the remaining characters in the novel belongs to Funk's third category, the category of unjustified respondents or sinners. To begin with, virtually the entire Farrell family has closed itself off from grace, since they have chosen to "turn away stubbornly from the possibilities life offered them" and elected instead to seek meaning and substance in the "dull terms of respectability and social approval" (288). On a psychological level the preceding statement describes that state of mind with which many are familiar; the Farrells have closed themselves off in order to protect that portion of the ego which fears and trembles at the prospects of uncertainty, change, death, and loss of identity. On a spiritual level, though, this passage suggests that the Farrells are sinners because they have closed themselves off to life or grace. In other words, the Farrells generally choose to ignore what Greeley calls the graciousness of reality (*New Agenda* 294).

And if the observations about the refusal of the Farrell family to remain open to life are not enough to identify them as members of that larger family of people we call sinners and whom Funk calls the unjustified respondents, virtually all family members (in their deepest thoughts) identify themselves as sinners. Roger, for instance, thinks that

he was a fine one to talk about the Ten Commandments. Another
hour—he glanced at his watch—well, another forty-five minutes,
he'd violate the sixth commandment, commit adultery once again
with Martha Clay. And in the pleasure of bizarre fantasies, he
would forget the family past. (202)

John Farrell, while reviewing his conversation with Monsignor Mortimer,
realizes that Mortimer and the cardinal threaten him only because he is
subject to vanity and only because he likes being recognized when he walks
down Michigan Avenue or when he buys "something from a shop" (24).
Irene hates herself for her "envy" of Noele's "confidence, popularity, and
grace" (27) and she "despairs" because she believes her life to be "an utter
waste" (239). Brigid Farrell not only knows that she is a sinner, she also
"knows" that she is "damned" and that "From the day of her arrival in
America . . . her life had been nothing but sinful—lust, deceit, adultery,
even murder" (86). Danny cannot seem to make a commitment; instead, he
seems always ready to withdraw at the time he is most needed. He says to
Noele that he has been a "runner" all of his life, that he has been "running
from responsibility" for his mother's death and that he's not much good at
"loving or hating any longer than a week" (374). Even the amoral Burke
does not fall outside of Funk's third category of unjustified respondents, for
Burke's vision of life, though not as guilt-ridden, is as dead as that of the
Farrell family's. He, however, is a hard-bitten existentialist who confronts
the absurdity of the everyday with absolute loyalty to Brigid and with no
regrets for the choices he has made (329). Consequently, he differs from the
Farrell family insofar as he feels no guilt for what he has done and he is
similar to them insofar as he cannot accept such a wonderful absurdity as a
forgiving and redemptive God.

    For the most part, the clergy occupy Funk's category of justified respond-
ents. Clerics tend to constitute the majority of those characters who fall into
this second category of Funk's, because they are the only characters in the
novel who are expected to take public moral stands with any degree of
regularity and because so much of the drama in the novel revolves around
the secret sins and private anguish of the Farrell family.

    There is, however, another and more compelling reason for the dominat-
ing presence of the clergy in this second category. Because of their positions
of authority within the Catholic Church, they have a vested interest in
preserving the laws and symbols of the traditional and institutional Church;
for by preserving the institution, they assure themselves of a secure
existence, an existence of an institution. Consequently, they most often
choose to play it safe rather than to confront an irrational universe and
make a leap of faith based on a wonderful but absurdly hopeful vision of a
God who is so forgiving that by human standards He seems crazy (*Great
Mysteries* 69). Since the clergy in the novel are so generally caught up in the
problems of the institutional and traditional Church, their focus and

behavior are similar to those of the priests, scribes, and Pharisees in the New Testament. In fact, both groups place themselves outside of God's grace as they turn traditions and institutions into idols. Funk himself makes essentially the same point about institutionalized religions in general when he claims that parables explain "why IRS officials and prostitutes understand the kingdom, whereas theologians, Bible scholars, and professional pietists do not" (*Parables* 65).

The cardinal, of course, is foremost among the tribe of justified respondents. He is embarrassed by John's talk show program because, according to Monsignor Jim Mortimer, the cardinal objects to answering questions from other bishops about a priest whose talk show incorporates "actresses and feminists and homosexuals and radicals and even heretics like Hans Kung" (21). Ironically, the cardinal and his spokesperson seem upset because John Farrell extends the good news to those who are not, at least in the eyes of the established Church, justified, indeed to those with whom Christ more than likely would have associated (*Parables* 65). The real reason for the cardinal's outrage, though, is his unwillingness to share the spotlight with John.

Lower-level clerics, of course, follow on the heels of the cardinal and his pet monsignor. Dads Fogarty, a fellow priest and a representative of what we might call the self-righteous right, seems to find John's talk show program unacceptable because it addresses, among other things, "the androgyny of God" (112). But like the cardinal, his reasons for disliking John are personal (112). The intellectual and the political left of the clergy are also included in this group of justified respondents. An unnamed priest and social activist who appears on John's talk show seems to be convinced that his solution to the problems of the nuclear arms race is The Only Viable Solution. Such self-righteous condemnation of those who differ intellectually and politically from him, of course, clearly identifies him as a character who considers himself to be among the elect or justified. It also means, paradoxically, that he has perhaps unwittingly moved outside the realm of the Holy Spirit and the real Church (*Catechism* 79; *Great Mysteries* 26).

People other than clerics, however, also fall into Funk's second category. Larry Rieves, a secular columnist, criticizes John Farrell for being on an "ego trip" (167), for "shallow posturing" (167), and for being insensitive to the needs of the parishioners of Saint Praxides (168). Geraldine Leopold and Martina O'Rourke, two vigorous women members of the parish council, also succumb to their pride and antipodal ideologies as they seek to assert both themselves and the fact of their righteousness or justification (166). There are also the Mrs. Riordans and the bitchy members of the "hospital volunteers' governing board" (236) who seek to establish themselves as members of the socially and spiritually justified (189).

Let me digress briefly to soften what may appear to be the anticlerical tenor of my remarks. *Lord of the Dance* places all of the clergy, except Ace

McNamara and John Farrell, on the periphery of the action. As a result, we have little sense of their internal struggles and we tend to see them as examples of those people who have elected to "build up massive walls of protection around . . . [their] bodies and spirits" so that they "need never feel shame" (*Great Mysteries* 26). The irony, of course, is that they have used the Roman Catholic Church and the symbols associated with it to reinforce rather than tear down those massive walls that isolate them from their fellows. Ace McNamara is the one noticeable exception to this sort of clerical behavior in the novel; he very carefully nurtures growth and guides the Farrells on their various spiritual pilgrimages. Furthermore, he is smart enough to know that those he counsels must make their own decisions; and he is also loving enough to understand that even seemingly sinful decisions (John's attraction to Irene or Irene's desire for John) generally are the symptomatic expressions of deep feelings of anguish, shame, and fear. Indeed, his degree in psychology introduces a new element into the Roman Catholic concept of sin. Sin, from the viewpoint of the psychologist, is not simply a matter of will and knowledge, for the psyche often confounds the will. I do not, however, mean to say that Ace McNamara approves of any and all actions or that he allows people to think that they can escape the consequences of their actions. I simply mean to say that Ace McNamara, unlike the rest of the clergy in the novel, seems to possess a great compassion and understanding for human beings, a compassion and an understanding that dissolve the rather simplistic and legalistic visions of people and sin espoused in the once popular *Baltimore Catechism*. Now, with your indulgence (no pun intended), I'll resume where I left off.

In spite of the fact that the novel introduces many more characters and offers us a much more extended story than any of the parables (or gospels for that matter), it groups its characters in the same pattern that Funk finds in Christ's "parables of grace" (Parables 59). Moreover, the novel follows essentially the same episodic pattern employed by the parables of grace:

> It [the parable] is not . . . an old story of our own to be recovered, but a new story that opens up into a new world, where things run the other way around: the poor and the destitute are surprised by their good fortune, while the established and the comfortable are shaken from their lethargy. If the parable is a threat to the habituated . . . crystallized world, it is full of promise for those who are ready to greet the world. (17)

Now, of course, no one in his right mind will argue that the Farrells are poor and destitute in any conventional sense. Indeed, they are a rich and influential Chicago family. However, their wealth neither assuages their pain nor provides them with the courage to embrace openly the world with all of its pain and all of its glory. In fact, their wealth is only another meaningless exterior behind which they hide (not that I personally would mind such an exterior). I would argue, therefore, that because the Farrells are deprived of dignity and meaning, they are, in the truest sense of the word, destitute. I would also argue, then, that the Farrells' reemergence from behind both the facade of their wealth and the many barriers their lies and secrets have erected constitutes a *peripeteia* that is essentially identical to the *peripeteia* described by Funk in the passage quoted above. In short, the Farrells discover that the world "is full of promise for those who are ready to greet [it]," as the novel ironically subverts the self-righteous and self-assured vision of complacent and defensive clergy (Funk's justified respondents) rather than the vision of the sinful Farrells.

The novel, *Lord of the Dance*, and the parables of Christ achieve their respective *peripeteia* because both, in the words of Funk, bring two logics, the literal logic of the everyday and the imaginative logic of the metaphorical, into juxtaposition (*Language Hermeneutics* 227). In other words, the speaker omits "romance, idealization, false mysticism, escapism, fantasy, and sentimentality" in order to create a sense of the mundane nature of the world which threatens our faith (153). I of course would be exaggerating if I claimed that *Lord of the Dance* omits any "romance, idealization, false mysticism"; the Farrells are clearly larger than life and their passions may be more wide-sweeping and involved than ours. However, what imprisons them or keeps them from the Easter vision and the second chance at a beginning is the world of the everyday. In other words, the Farrells are everyday enough to be subject to the same sufferings which plague all of our lives. They

> invent defense mechanisms to keep others at bay.... [They] are silent and reserved so that [we] will think ... [them] strong.... [They] must always have... [their] way.... [They] turn to neuroses, to compulsions and obsessions, to erratic and unpredictable behavior, to paralyzing fears... to focus attention away from who and what... [they] truly are.... [They] kill... [themselves] slowly in order to protect... [themselves] from sudden death by shame of being for what... [they] truly are. (*Great Mysteries* 26)

The most obvious way in which the Farrells flee from themselves and seek refuge in the world of the everyday may be found in their commitment (if I may be permitted such a word) to what Ace McNamara calls the "dull terms of respectability and social approval" (288). Few of us, if any, have had to experience the degradation that Brigid felt when her husband ordered her into the arms of Burke or when her husband beat her; and yet she is as bound by convention as the Mrs. Riordans of the world. She believes herself condemned to a "vast black pit" (127) and she is forever a "Muggins permitted to peer at the window of the great house and amuse those who really belonged" (262). Insecurity, the need for affection, lust, and greed all motivate her; in spite of her great wealth and power, then, she is subject to the world of everyday, for that is the world of money, power, fear, and sex.

And what is true of Brigid is essentially true for all of the Farrells, with the exception, of course, of Noele. John relies on others to validate his being; even though he is the host of a semipopular talk show, he finds himself almost incapable of confronting a passive-aggressive assistant who is using John's sense of fairness to unseat Noele and send the Sunday folk mass spinning off in a pre-Vatican II direction (137). That someone whom we might normally regard as so powerful and noteworthy cannot take even the simplest action without the urging of another demonstrates how entrapped he is in the world of everyday; indeed, he seems to be little else than a mirror trying to reflect back at the viewer whatever reflection that viewer would prefer to see. John Farrell, then, is trapped by the world of the mundane, because he wants to do nothing that will disrupt the illusions of those who surround him and because he wants to do whatever he can to keep everyone happy.

Roger, though "besotted with Martha" Clay (161), never loses sight of what is socially respectable. Although he doesn't want Martha to visit her former husband, he does not want to appear to be condoning the double standard of the male chauvinist; consequently, he makes no special plea with Martha when she indicates she is returning to Boston during Christmas break in order to see her former husband (203). Moreover, Roger builds his candidacy for the governorship of Illinois on his apparent respectability; consequently, he finds himself concerned not with issues and truths, but with family scandals (246). Indeed, the possibility of a scandal is so unnerving that a young college student named Kramer seems to hold Roger's entire future in his hands. However, it is the issue of his own sexuality that Roger seems to find most disturbing. He finds that his wife is "terrifying in bed" and that his "mistress [is] reassuring" (271); he toys with the fantasy of "Martha as a young man" and counsels himself that "a little bisexuality never hurt anyone" (155, 159); he later worries that he may be gay and wonders about his infatuation with Danny (297); and, most important, I think, Roger looks for master-slave relationships in which he can easily play the role of the dominant member, not so much out of an intrinsic dislike or fear of women, but because he, like John, relies totally on the external world to validate his being (52). In other words, Roger needs to be esteemed by others, in particular women, in order to establish a sense of security and identity; and his reliance upon external validation, then, is nothing less than a reliance on the everyday world for identity and meaning.

Irene, despite a wealth of resources which include beauty and creativity, lives in constant fear of the following two questions: "Who do you think you are?" and "What will people say?" (31). In fact, her parents so frequently put these two questions to her that she, as an adult, realizes that she is "not stupid" and that she is "afraid" (31). It is, of course, her fear which leads her to hide her stories in a carefully locked desk drawer, marry Danny in secret, and then give up her baby.

Danny may not be quite so directly reliant upon the external world for validation. The other Farrells seem to believe that they will be happy so long as the external world approves of them; Danny, on the other hand, defines himself by way of contrast. He establishes his identity or his being in the world as he directs anger toward the external world and hides behind his claim that he is someone who runs rather than someone who commits. Naturally enough, Danny experiences anger because of his capture and imprisonment by the Red Chinese. However, a good deal of his anger results from the guilt he feels because he realizes that his mother died to protect him (474). And in fact, the CIA's psychological profile of Danny clearly establishes the possibility that a good deal of Danny's humor masks the anger he feels:

> "They tell me that he's a shrewd, flexible guy and that the comedy act is one of the masks he hides behind to survive, a life-long defense mechanism that happened to be very useful for the last eighteen years. . . . But there is anger and fear at the core. It's the personality he went to China with and the one he came out with, and everything is intensified because of the China experience." (312–13)

In spite of the personal strength which permitted Danny to survive eighteen years of internment in Red China, he, like the rest of the Farrells, resists the disclosure of genuine feelings and the possibility of true human relationships as he defines himself in opposition to the everyday.

Even the hard-bitten Burke defines himself by externals. However, he is not concerned with the approval of society in general. He is, instead, more concerned about the approval and love of Brigid. Indeed, on several occasions Burke will end a quiet moment's or an evening's reflections with a statement that reveals the extent to which he has created an idol out of Brigid: "If anyone threatened Brigid again, he would stop at nothing to protect her. God—if there was one—should expect nothing else from him" (89). Funk's statement that "things as they are" (*Language Hermeneutics* 153) form the base from which the speaker builds his parable seems true, then; Brigid, John, Roger, Irene, Danny, and Burke all locate their identities in the world of the external or in the world of the "dull terms of respectability and social approval" (288). In addition to this, each of these characters makes the painful discovery that respectability and social approval are never capable of providing him with either the hope or the happiness sought. The Farrells, then, are limited and unhappy for the simple reason that their senses of identity are simply "constituted . . . by reflecting or mirroring the world, and . . . by reflecting on its reflecting" (*Language Hermeneutics* 227).

Of course, the New Testament parable does not extol or vindicate the virtues of everydayness and practicality. Instead, it is a story which "cracks the shell of mundane temporality" (*Language Hermeneutics* 156) in order to trace the "incursion of the divine into history" (154) and to "raise the potential for the new meaning" (138). Likewise, *Lord of the Dance* establishes itself in the everyday world only to show the inadequacy of that everydayness and to raise the possibility of another newer and better vision. In the parable of grace the determiner is the one who in some way cracks open the world of everydayness and exposes the presence of the divine in the world. And in *Lord of the Dance* it is Noele, the one character whose enthusiasm, passionate commitment, and desire for truth (all qualities of the Holy Spirit) introduce the element of imaginative logic into the everyday, who brings down the edifices and barriers of the everyday world which the Farrells have erected. In short, Noele is the one whose energy and actions introduce the possibility of a *peripeteia* in Greeley's *Lord of the Dance*.

Two obstacles other than everydayness play a large role in the resistance the Farrells put up to Noele's pursuit of the truth and to the incursion of the divine into their everyday world. The first obstacle which stands between the Farrells and Noele's truth or Funk's imaginative logic of the metaphorical is unfortunately a rigid and tradition-bound Church which cannot speak to the suffering of the Farrells.

I do not mean to say that *Lord of the Dance* disputes the claim of the Roman Catholic Church as to who constitutes its membership and as to its special connection with the Holy Spirit. However, the novel clearly does dispute the idea that the Holy Spirit empowers the hierarchy to function as absolute dictators within the Church, and it attacks the ease with which those in power choose to mix dogma with personal interests. The "psychopathic" cardinal (112) is, of course, the most notable example of such abuses of authority. He uses his position as the "representative of the Pope, the vicar of Christ" (399) in an effort to force John Farrell to resign from his position as a talk show host; he also uses that same authority to establish a reign in which he is "the sole policymaker in the archdiocese" (20) and to insist on absolute obedience in matters not pertaining to faith (349).

Although the cardinal may only be a hypothetical example of the hierarchy gone awry, Greeley, in his books *The American Catholic: A Social Portrait* and *The Great Mysteries: An Essential Catechism* makes it clear that the cardinal has his basis in fact. Greeley writes:

> The striking differences in attitudes and values between bishops and their priests is not a function of their ages; bishops are more conservative than priests of their own age groups. . . . The priests, by and large, reflect the difficulties, aspirations, and problems of their people, but these insights are not reflected upward to the bishops. . . . In the absence of research . . . or shared values with their clergy and laity, the bishops will report to Rome not what is happening but what they think is happening. . . . And given the way they [bishops] are selected, there is no reason why one would expect bishops to reflect the feelings of their clergy or their people. . . . Cautious, conservative, safe, men . . . [are] usually

> appointed to the largest, most influential cities in the country.
> These men... [can] be counted on to do nothing creative or
> imaginative.... (*American Catholic* 158)

That Greeley levels such a charge against the bishops is particularly
damning when we realize that he also thinks of the Holy Spirit as the
inducer of creativity, generosity, vulnerability, and intimacy and as the
guiding spirit of the Roman Catholic Church (*Great Mysteries* 35; *Catechism*
79). Greeley, however, is not attacking the authority of the Church per se.
Instead, he is warning us not to confuse traditions of authority rooted in a
monolithic system and ritual with the indwelling of the Holy Spirit. His
condemnation of the hierarchy of the Church is much more direct and
scathing in his book *The Great Mysteries:*

> ... a certain authoritarianism and dictatorial style has crept in
> from the world outside and has affected the behavior of some
> Church leaders. They have acted more like secular princes ... rather
> than like servants of God's people. (97)

In short, both Greeley's novel *Lord of the Dance* and his scholarly writings
indicate that the world of the everyday has crept into the institution
charged with providing a vehicle for the very thing the parable and the
novel both invite: the incursion of the divine into the everyday. And it is
this failure of the hierarchy to separate their interests from the interests of
the Holy Spirit and the Church that makes the institutional Church,
especially in the case of John Farrell, an obstacle in the way of achieving the
Easter Vision.

Paradoxically, the disturbing portrayal of both the cardinal and the
institutional Church serves as yet another strong indicator that *Lord of the
Dance* is a parable. For according to Funk, it is precisely the "distortion of
everydayness" in the parable (*Language Hermeneutics* 158) or the calling of
attention to the deformity of the cardinal and the institutionalized Church
that wakes us to the realization that everydayness requires us to abandon
the possibility of hope and growth, a growth which transcends the concerns
of the everyday. In short, the novel works in a fashion similar to the
parables of Christ, because it destroys our comfortable illusions about the
established order.

The second major obstacle (other than everydayness itself) that cuts the
Farrells off from the Holy Spirit and the graciousness of reality is ideology
or symbol.

Allow me to digress once again. I equate ideology and symbol because
ideologies are essentially collections or systems of symbols which provide
their practitioners (or believers) with a hermeneutics whereby they may
read the text of the world and locate themselves and their experiences
within that text. Greeley, in his book *The New Agenda: A Proposal for a New*

Approach to Fundamental Religious Issues in Contemporary Times, seems to suggest the same sort of definition. Indeed, the main thrust of the book is that Yahwistic symbology best meets all of the needs of human nature. The argument itself is elegantly simple: Greeley first suggests that modern Catholics must abandon what he calls "apologetic Catholicism" for a "hermeneutic" approach to Catholicism (54–55). He next reinterprets a number of Yahwistic symbols, being very careful to see how well these symbols align with the values we find embedded in history, culture, and psychology. Then, in order to demonstrate the need for the hermeneutical approach to Catholicism and the efficacy of the Yahwistic system of symbols, he compares these Yahwistic symbols with other systems or collections of symbols. The point of this digression, then, is twofold: Greeley seems to equate ideology with symbol and he seems to believe that our ability to leave behind the everyday and enter into the world of the imaginative, creative, and spiritual depends on what our symbols will allow us to see or anticipate as being there.

Indeed, symbols prevent us from looking upon experience

> as the passive submission of the subject to the impressions coming to it from the outside. Rather man opens himself to the world through the symbols of the imagination that sift, select, and organize these impressions and constitute his living experience. Symbols are co-constitutive of man's experience. They represent his own creative contribution to the experience of the world. (New quoted Baum 25)

Symbols, then, allow us to take the raw material of our lives and to place it into a context which will provide us with meaning of some sort. However, as we manipulate symbols, they, in turn, manipulate us into a particular vision. The net result of what we might wish to call this "mutual dependence" upon interpreter, hermeneutics, and text is that the symbols we choose determine our ability to be liberated and creative.

Moreover, symbols are not free-floating. Institutions fasten upon them with great ease for a variety of reasons. First and foremost, a set of symbols provides the institution with a system or hermeneutics for interpreting the nature of the world and of life. Second and less obvious, the institution usually appropriates symbols friendly to its aims, and provides itself with a hermeneutics which will eventually be used to justify its existence. And once symbols become encrusted with this "protective body of interpretation" (*Language Hermeneutics* 162), they become part of the institution and part of the tradition surrounding that institution. Consequently, symbols which once were liberating become barriers which preserve a meaning and prevent a life. The upshot of all this is rather simple. The Yahwistic symbols on which the Catholic Church was built eventually became trapped in protective layers of interpretation. As these symbols fell within the scope of tradition, they began to lose their efficacy. And as they diminished in their capacity to aid people in their engagement with the world, they increased in their capacity to protect the institutional Church. Consequently, symbols which once were meaningful and helpful began to serve not as a means of interpreting the world, but as a means of both shutting it out and controlling the faithful.

Now to return to the main thrust of the argument: Since the creativity and liberation of the person depend upon how well that individual's set of symbols corresponds to his nature (which is there but cannot be directly disclosed) and the nature of his experience, we can conclude that symbols chosen by the Farrells are not particularly efficacious. For one thing, we already know that the Farrells are prisoners of themselves and of their fears of rejection, pain, and vulnerability, because the world of the everyday figures so prominently in shaping the symbols upon which they rely.

However, the values and symbols of the everyday are not the only symbolic systems that prevent the Farrells from finding an Easter Vision. In fact, at least two more sets of symbols bind them to the earth and prevent them from recognizing the imaginative incursion of the Holy Spirit into the world. With the exception of Burke, all of the Farrells are bound or restricted by their limited and apologetic sense of Catholicism. Brigid, Roger, John, and Irene, for instance, seem well acquainted with the apologetic notion of sin. Brigid thinks of herself in terms of "lust, deceit, adultery...[and] murder" (86); Roger thinks of himself in terms of the adultery (202); John thinks of himself in terms of adultery and pride (24); and Irene thinks of herself in terms of adultery and covetousness (27).

Moreover, all of these characters seem well acquainted with the teachings of the Church on sin found in the *Baltimore Catechism*. They, at least by implication, seem to know that "sin is any willful thought, desire, word, action, or omission forbidden by the law of God" and that mortal sins are "grievous" offenses "against the law of God" which deprive "the sinner of sanctifying grace, the supernatural life of the soul" (*Catechism* 48). They all, as they assess themselves, are convinced that their desires and anxieties lead them into willful commission of acts of wrongdoing, and that their choices threaten their spiritual well-being. Unfortunately, this knowledge of how they define a sin and of what sorts of punishment a particular sin may bring does not enable them to place their actions into a context that allows God to enter their lives. God remains for them a rational construct found within the pages of the *Baltimore Catechism*, not an actuality found in the lovemaking of a husband and wife, or in the integrity and courage of a priest who believes more in the mission of the Church than he believes in the hierarchy, or in the boundless energy, passion, and enthusiasm of a teenage girl.

In fact, the Farrells only understand their actions in a most limited sense; they do have an idea that they have done wrong, but they have no idea of why they have done wrong or of how their willingness to expose themselves to risk in their everyday lives will invite the presence of God. Consequently, the Farrells also fail to go beyond their lists of wrongdoings and examine the etiology of their sins. And because they know they do wrong without knowing why, they condemn themselves to the existence of Sisuphus; they hate the wrongs they do, but they cannot find a way to break out of their pattern of sin and guilt.

In short, the Farrells are prisoners of the "apologetic Catholicism" of the *Baltimore Catechism*: their senses of themselves, their God, their Church, and their sins are "devoid of cultural, psychological, and historical perspectives" (*New Agenda* 63). Indeed, their senses of themselves, in spite of all their wealth and sophistication, presuppose the existence of a well- and rationally ordered world, a world in which God can be circumscribed by language and understood (in part) by reason. Consequently, they become lost souls when they discover that they live in a world which defies logic and which, given their nineteenth-century rationalistic bias, leaves them only their self-doubt and self-loathing.

In fact, the Farrells' reliance upon the kind of vision that we associate with the *Baltimore Catechism* keeps them from clearly appreciating and understanding the presence of the Holy Spirit, the grace of God, and the resurrection of Christ in their daily lives. Given their penchant for guilt and for conceiving of God in rational and abstract terms, it is more than likely that their conception of the Holy Spirit parallels that of the *Baltimore Catechism*: the Holy Spirit proceeds "from the Father and the Son. . . . He is called the Gift of Love of the Father and the Son" (25) and He provides us with both "the three theological virtues" of faith, hope, and charity and the "seven gifts" of "wisdom, understanding, counsel, fortitude, knowledge, piety, and fear of the Lord" (87–95). The function of the three virtues, ideally speaking, is that they "help us to follow the guidance of our reason and faith"; and the function of the gifts, on the other hand, is to "help us to follow readily the inspirations of the Holy Spirit" (96). Moreover, the Holy Spirit, when listened to, also brings the twelve fruits of "charity, joy, peace, patience, benignity, goodness, long-suffering, mildness, faith, modesty, continency, and chastity" (96).

This is the bloodless, spiritless, rational, and dogmatically accurate definition of the Holy Spirit on which every Catholic over thirty cut his teeth. Unfortunately, this definition makes no contact with the problems and anxieties of real life. As a result, the Farrells do not recognize that their refusal to tell Noele the truth about her origins and their interest in "dull . . . respectability and social approval" (288) shuts them off from each other, from the possibility of mature and intimate relationships, and ultimately from the Holy Spirit.

Indeed, the very point of *Lord of the Dance* seems to be the necessity of risking vulnerability, openness, and honesty in order to allow meaning, hope, and the Holy Spirit into our lives. The novel teaches us that it is human to want to avoid pain, failure, rejection, and ridicule (*Mysteries* 30) and that it is usually human to desire intimacy and, therefore, to trust. Furthermore, it also demonstrates that the battle fought by the Holy Spirit for our souls occurs in our everyday lives and that the Holy Spirit, the One who brings us light or truth, fire or passionate commitment, and wind or enthusiasm, "calls us forth" from behind the barriers we have erected into a fuller but more dangerous life (*Great Mysteries* 28–29). In fact, Greeley himself seems to describe the very point of *Lord of the Dance* when, in *The Great Mysteries*, he writes, "The mystery of the Holy Spirit . . . [both] reveals to us that the pains, the failures, the rejections, the ridicule, the shame we risk in the open life are not permanent" (30) "and liberates the authentic self" (33).

Not only do the Farrells miss seeing the potential for the Holy Spirit to enter into their lives, they also miss seeing the potential for grace and resurrection in their lives. And once again the factor which limits their vision is a sense of both grace and resurrection that is abstract and seemingly irrelevant to everyday existence. Grace, for the Farrells, is a familiar but meaningless concept. They, as products of Catholic schools, know that

> There are two kinds of grace . . . sanctifying . . . and actual. . . .
> Sanctifying grace . . . is a sharing in the life of God himself. . . . Actual grace is a supernatural help of God which enlightens our mind and strengthens our will to do good and avoid evil. (*Catechism* 81–83)

Consequently, Irene does not appreciate the fact that Noele's "confidence . . . and grace" may stem from something more than the joyful exuberance of adolescence (27) and Roger can't understand how Maryjane sees "grace" in him (393). In the case of Noele, her "gracefulness" manifests largely because her openness and vulnerability have made her a receptive vessel of the Holy Spirit. In Roger's case, his gracefulness manifests itself only after he has begun attempting to restore some level of integrity to his life (i.e., he is honest with Irene and himself about their relationship).

In short, the novel demonstrates that both Noele and Roger unwittingly receive God's love or *charis* because their honesty and openness permit them to accept God's "unrestrained gift" of Himself and to give themselves back in return (*Great Mysteries* 70–77). And Roger, in particular, experiences the presence of grace because his attempt to restore his personal integrity, his willingness to tough out the possibility of a scandal in his political campaign, and his willingness to start forgiving himself and begin focusing on the problems of his wife and daughter all allow him to experience the forgiveness he has so desperately sought from the beginning of the novel. Grace, then, finally begins to have real significance in real life.

The symbol of resurrection is perhaps the one symbol which the Farrells find the most difficult to understand in conjunction with their own lives.

Obviously, the resurrection, at least as it is defined in the *Baltimore Catechism*, has little to do with the everyday lives of the Farrells. It is an event which occurred long ago and which is proof positive that Christ is "true God and . . . [that] we . . . shall rise from the dead" (72).

And although the story of Christ's resurrection appeals to "our best dreams" and demonstrates that "evil is not ultimate and good is" (*Great Mysteries* 44, 47), it also serves as a call to authentic being, to a personal identity founded on openness, vulnerability, and honesty. And once we realize that the story of the resurrection is not just a story about what happens at the end of the world but instead a story about what happens every day, we can begin to see that Danny's return from China, Noele's recoveries from being brutalized by Marsallo's henchmen, and Roger's, John's, and Brigid's recovery from their lies are all instances in which the story of the resurrection is pertinent; for in each case, the particular character must arise from psychic death and return to the world and human relationships without sacrificing openness, vulnerability, and honesty.

Lord of the Dance, then, criticizes the obvious problems within the institutional Church; it also criticizes the reluctance of modern Catholics and the institutional Church to reexamine their symbols and the impact of those symbols in the daily life of the Catholic. In other words, the Farrells, and Catholics like them, fail to grow spiritually and psychologically because the hierarchy is unwilling to redefine either the power relationships within the institutional Church or the symbols by which the members of the Church interpret their lives.

However, the limited and rationalistic thinking behind the apologetics of the *Baltimore Catechism* is not the only obstacle that stands between the Farrells and the Easter Vision. They must not only go beyond the world of the *Baltimore Catechism*, they must also go beyond the limited realm of a number of worldly ideologies as well. For instance, Roger must recognize that the scientific approach to the study of human behavior (sociology) will not provide him with an eschatological vision. Science is a discipline of the everyday and not of the ultimate, and, therefore, when it asks why, it only asks why in the most limited sense, the sense of physical causation. The radicalism of the unnamed priest who is both a guest on John's talk show and a social activist provides us with another example of the limitations of an ideology rooted in the everyday; good, for this individual, is apparently defined exclusively in terms of the here and now. And although the Roman Catholic Church advocates working to eliminate the nuclear arms race, it does not allow our sense of ultimate meaning and purpose to rest solely on the basis of achieving a temporal good. In short, the symbology by which the social activist operates is far too limited to admit God. Irene must recognize that drinking, bathing, dieting, and eating, the ideology of the hedonist, will not assuage her pain or heal the emptiness and hurt she feels. The ideology of pleasure, which makes pleasure an end in itself rather than a celebration of God (I'm not suggesting that we all start fasting or don hair shirts), offers no relief, no answers for the questions and doubts which so bedevil her. There are, of course, a host of other ideologies out there waiting to bedevil the Farrells and others like them. But, as Greeley points out in his book *The New Agenda*, Freudianism, Marxism, Communitarianism, Behaviorism, and a host of other isms promise us salvation through rebirth, but also close off the possibility of the incursion of the divine into the everyday (188).

When considering the impact of symbol systems upon the lives of each of us, Greeley himself recommends that each of us

> be critical about his own symbols . . . and also about the fantastic array of modern insights that the various modern symbol systems convey . . . [and that each of us not seek] . . . a shallow, superficial harmony in which everything is integrated in some artificial new synthesis. . . . (*New Agenda* 295)

Lord of the Dance, then, demonstrates not only how our attachment to the everyday and our desire for security can keep us from authentic being; it also demonstrates how the ideology of "apologetic Catholicism" and a host of other ideologies stand in the way of the Farrells and their desire for intimacy and love. Furthermore, *Lord of the Dance* invites modern Catholics to self-examination and an examination of their Church and its symbols in order to demonstrate that authentic being is not bestowed upon us by the hierarchy of the Church or the well-ordered and rational world of "Apologetic Catholicism."

That the Chicago literary critics dislike much of Greeley's fiction should not be surprising (Marsden and Marsden 111). Parables are supposed to upset and redefine the established order. That "in one week" Greeley was "viciously denounced" by both *The National Catholic Quarterly* and *The National Catholic Register* for writing fiction "devoid of serious theological content" (Marsden and Marsden 116) should not be surprising either. Parables speak not to the justified and powerful, but to the disenfranchised and outcast, Matthew Arnold's Philistines and the Catholic Church's sinners. It should not, therefore, be surprising that Greeley's fiction instructs and delights a large audience as it insists again and again that even they, the unjustified, have several chances to begin their lives as they seek to find themselves.

WORKS CITED

A Catechism of Christian Doctrine: Revised Edition of the Baltimore Catechism. Patterson, N. J.: St. Anthony Guild, 1949.

Funk, Robert W. *Language Hermeneutics and Word of God: The Problem of Language in the New Testament and Contemporary Theology*. New York: Harper & Row, 1966.

————. *Parables and Presence: Forms of the New Testament Tradition*. Philadelphia: Fortress, 1982.

Greeley, Andrew M. *The American Catholic: A Social Portrait*. New York: Basic, 1977.

————. *The Great Mysteries: An Essential Catechism*. New York: Seabury, 1976.

————. *Lord of the Dance*. 1984. New York: Warner, 1985.

————. *The New Agenda: A Proposal for a New Approach to Fundamental Religious Issues in Contemporary Times*. New York: Doubleday, 1973.

Marsden, Michael T., and Marsden, Madonna P. "A Conversation with Father Andrew Greeley, Bestselling Storyteller." *Journal of Popular Literature* 1, no. 2 (Fall/Winter 1985): 101–26.

20

MARY ANN LOWRY

Parables of Love:
The Fiction of
Andrew M. Greeley

"Romance is the structural core of all fiction," claims Northrop Frye. "It brings us closer than any other aspect of literature to the sense of fiction . . . man's vision of his own life as a quest" (*Secular, Scripture* 15). Andrew Greeley's novels are recognized as quests, but there is considerable disagreement about the nature of each quest. For those who see only lust, let them. For those of us who find love, we need to delve more deeply into it. Each novel does, indeed, present some explicitly sexual scenes, but from them emerges the fulfillment of love. And from the lovers' joys, their fragile delight in spiritual communion, further emerge the traditional literary forms of comedy and romance with which Greeley accomplishes his "comedies of grace," his "parables of love." Representative stories—two of the Time Between the Stars novels and the Passover Trilogy—serve to illustrate the superimposition of various patterns, including comedy and romance, employed to create these modern parables.

The related patterns of comedy and romance share a visit to a natural world, a descent into romantic confusion, interference of the supernatural,

Reprinted, with minor revisions, from the *Journal of Popular Literature* 4 (Spring/Summer 1988): 25–36. An earlier version of this essay was presented in a session on living authors chaired by Allienne R. Becker at the Northeast Modern Language Association Convention, Boston, 2 Apr. 1987.

and a return to the mundane world with promises of marriage and a new life. The quest is confused at first. The pattern, however, is eventually clear, and the end is a celebration of symmetry. According to Frye, "The mythical or primitive basis of comedy is a movement toward the rebirth and renewal of the powers of nature" (*Natural Perspective* 119). Since the symmetry of nature is the coupling of the sexes and the promise of creation, this means the coming together of male and female. The traditional end of comedy is, therefore, the celebration of marriage. This is similar to Greeley's position before he began writing novels and is an integral part of the story line he incorporates in them. More than a decade ago, he wrote that when Christian lovers unite,

> there is "a revelation, a sacrament, the Eucharist, a participation in the basic life forces of the universe." Their union should bring to mind the festivals of the ancients, celebrations that fused religion and sex in sheer exuberance over the fact of life. . . . Believe in the import of Scripture: "life for all its tragedy, is still ultimately a comedy, indeed a comic, playful dance with a passionately loving God" (Kotre 219–20, paraphrasing and quoting Greeley's *Love and Play*)

Citing the mystical experience that changed the pagan Saul of Tarsus into the Christian Saint Paul seems apt. Saint Paul came upon the truth as he traveled the road to Damascus, where suddenly he surrendered hate for love. Sometime later, he wrote eloquently of the old and new, the moral and resurrected selves: "What is sown in the earth is subject to decay, what rises is incorruptible. What is sown is ignoble, what rises is glorious. Weakness is sown, strength rises up" (1 Cor. 16: 42–43).

In *Lord of the Dance* the Farrell martriarch corresponds to Saint Paul in her conversion from hate to love. As a young woman, Brigid Farrell's husband sent her to Burke for the express purpose of yielding to him in exchange for political favors. "The first night with Burke Kennedy began in shame, fury, and terror and ended in mind-numbing pleasure" (84), and they have been reaching out to each other in love ever since that night. Further, Greeley emphasizes in his fiction the correspondence between spiritual and physical love with the symbolism of fire and water:

> The fire and water service [the high point of the Christian Passover Triduum] was adapted from Roman pagan spring rites of the fourth century. The union between the male (fire) and the female (water) was interpreted by the early Christians to mean that when Jesus rose from the dead, his marriage to his spouse, the church, was consummated, and that those who are baptized in the waters of Easter are the first fruits of this union. It is therefore the Christian conviction that the fire and water ceremony of Easter Eve tells the story of human love that is a correlation and continuation of divine love. ("The Passover")

Compounding these mythical, spiritual, and physical positions is the Irish Grail quest. Ireland's "era in transition from paganism to Christianity" (*Magic Cup* 288) is the late sixth-century historical setting of Greeley's Grail novel. *The Magic Cup* presents the prototype of the quest that, with changes correlating to the twentieth century, appears throughout his novels. The elements of the legend include:

> vengeance by blood, after some action that . . . has led to the infertility of the kingdom; the impotence of the king . . . ; ritual sacrifice . . . , tasks inflicted . . . [upon the Quester(s)]; and the queen, princess, or empress who controls the drink of power and sovereignty. . . . (*Magic Cup* (286)

Most important of all is the fact that "The Quest for the Grail is inextricable from the quest for woman" (286), and this appears in each of the contemporary novels.

As Shafer points out in *Eros and the Womanliness of God*, echoes of names from this early novel link those following. The author's own sense of the comedic, a not unimportant element in these modern parables, is also clear. Liam, the Scottish lord husband of Marge, sister of protagonist Hugh Donlon, is "the friendly local Irish wolfhound" (*Ascent into Hell* 476), echoing Podraig, the Irish wolfhound, who is "the sacred vessel . . . the Hound of Heaven" (*Magic Cup* 287) in the prototypic novel. In addition, Brigid, the original magic princess, who is equated with the cup, appears in all the novels, with the new characters sometimes carrying her name, sometimes only her attributes, especially as the young King Cormac observed with regard to Biddy in particular and women in general: "Their bodies are traps; their tongues weapons" (*Magic Cup* 57). And so, indeed, it is with the women in Greeley's novels who bring the promise of grace to their men.

In *Thy Brother's Wife* Nora Riley, foster sister to the two Cronin sons, was taken out of an orphanage and into the family when she was only ten years old. She marries older brother Paul, a politician with aspirations to the presidency, has three daughters by him, learns that her husband is a profligate, with his father's weakness for women, plus some of his own, and few of his strengths. Paul escapes from a hotel fire, after a dalliance with the teenage daughter of longtime friends of the family, only to drown in Lake Michigan soon thereafter. He had taken out the family boat, named after his mother, long thought dead, but really confined to a mental institution, by their now aging father. With Paul dead, Sean's decision involves whether or not to leave the priesthood and marry Nora, the woman he had loved for years and who loved him in return. Their one interlude together resulted in the birth of a son, a golden boy, who died in a few short years, a victim of leukemia. After more than a quarter of a century, Sean seems destined to marry his Nora, but she has other plans.

She will continue the commitment to her marriage and her own life, replacing Paul in the Senate, while Sean will continue his commitment to the Church, which he does during Easter week, a time of rebirth, on Holy Thursday, the day of recommitment. "You damn fool," he wrote to himself in the journal he had kept for years, "you missed God's sign for thirty years" (493). It required Nora, his personal "angel," to reveal it.

In *Ascent into Hell* Maria Manfredy, temporarily adopted by the Donlon family to spend a summer at their beach cabin with their high-school-age daughter, looks like a "countess," is the daughter of a "shoe repairman," and can make "a simple thing like swimming a sacrament, a revelation of God's grace" (16, 26). A quarter of a century later, she is destined to become the "Sacred Love" of the Donlon son. Like Sean Cronin, Hugh Donlon was promised to the priesthood by his parents when they were young. Unlike Sean Cronin, he left the priesthood, married an ex-nun, was miserable, entered the Board of Trade, and was reasonably contented there, until he was arrested, convicted, and imprisoned for his brother's fraud. Only after Hugh's wife and children die in a fiery plane crash while she is running away to Mexico with his brother Tim does Maria, also widowed, come to Hugh's rescue, clearing his name, making love to him, and claiming "she's God's will" for him (479). Even Cardinal Cronin must admit that she "may be right" (479). She is, and Hugh, returning to her, not the Church, after Good Friday services of Easter week, admits to himself that "he loved her with the certain knowledge that she was the love of his life" (482).

Cathy Collins of *Virgin and Martyr* thinks she is destined to become a nun; instead, she will marry lawyer Nick Curran, a fact that takes her years and untold suffering, including a wrong marriage and divorce, to learn. Inheritor of seven million dollars when her parental home, with her parents in it, is blown apart by a leaky gas main, she disregards the money and gives herself to helping the people of Costaguana, Conrad's imaginary Latin American country in *Nostromo*. There, betrayed for money by Father Ed Carny, a hero to her since childhood, she is tortured, raped, and almost killed by a political sadist. She escapes, healing her burned body in the ocean and any other water she can find and donning a disguise that even Nora Cronin, the bishop's gorgeous and talented sister-in-law, does not recognize when they travel on the same plane; makes a new life for herself in Florida teaching the art of painting; and is discovered there by Father Blackie Ryan and Nick Curran. Narrator Blackie, who recognizes in retrospect that Catherine was "a magic young woman," makes clear to her the nature of her personal quest: "I suggest that now you realize that you have sought for remarkability outside yourself when it was in fact always lurking within you, unformed, nascent but ready to blossom" (73, 499). The road back is not easy, but she makes it, and her wedding to Nick is planned for "the day after Christmas" (532).

In *Angels of September* Anne Marie O'Brien Reilly, now in her fifties, is a "woman in an Irish myth, a faerie queen perhaps," with "magic gray eyes"

(65). There were seven in her family, but all—her parents, her brothers, her sisters—are dead. Her first love, Dick Murray, was killed in World War II. Her two marriages failed; her first son is still listed as missing in action in Vietnam; her daughter-in-law dislikes her and will probably keep her grandson away from her; and her own daughter doesn't seem to like her very much either. Her life has been a long series of good-byes, except for her youngest son, Mark, and his wife, who adore her, and Father Blackie Ryan's cousin Mike Casey the Cop, widowed after twenty-eight years of marriage to someone else, with whom she went to grammar school. Her art gallery, even if it doesn't fulfill her, will keep her busy. It seems to serve as a meeting place for other questers: Cardinal Cronin and his evidently remarried sister-in-law, Nora Hurley; Marie and Peggy Donlon, Hugh's wife and mother; Cathy and Nick Curran and their two children. "The other kind of loneliness could be filled only by a man who loved her. Or a God who loved her" (49). After psychiatric counseling, she can accept that God freely loves her; after investigation by Father Ryan and Superintendent Casey, she knows that she did not start the school fire that killed her sisters; and after the strange white fire in her gallery and with the help of Michael Casey, she casts out the demon that had plagued her, arising Phoenix-like on the Feast Day of Saint Michael, the wager of war against the minions of evil, once again the two persons fused into one, "Michael/Anne Marie or Anne Marie/Michael . . . wrapped up together like two infants in a thick winter blanket, a warm protective envelope of peace and then joy" (42). No date is set for the wedding, but it will come, and she will show his paintings in December.

Although comedy is close to romance, with a similar pattern of descent and return, there are some important differences, and *Lord of the Dance* fulfills these, as does the Irish legend before it. Romance places greater emphasis on the relationship of fathers and daughters, more concentration on the power of evil, and directs more attention to the shaping of a new world. According to Frye, "the descent theme" in romance "is the discovery of the real relation between the chief characters and their parents" (*Secular Scripture* 122).

Noele Farrell's history term paper about her family turns into a mystery about Navy pilot Danny Farrell, missing in action over China since 1963. Soon-to-be-eighteen Noele turns up all sorts of frightening and fascinating information about the Farrell family, but she does not learn that Danny is her father until, largely due to her efforts, he is released by the Chinese after eighteen years of imprisonment. Her term paper assignment thus becomes a search for the missing father and his significance as she rummages through old photographs, asks questions that others would rather leave unanswered, and accidentally finds a short story written by her mother that raises even more questions in her "Celtic goddess," "changeling," "fey" mind that knows what people are thinking whether or not they speak their thoughts.

What began as the innocent research for a high school assignment and Noele's quest for identity became for her an encounter with the evil of the murder of Danny's mother in 1944 and his probably planned death or disappearance in 1963. She emerged from unconsciousness, hurt and humiliated, but worrying more about others than herself (*Lord of the Dance* 434–35). She accepts from Father Ace that "suffering goes with being human," exclaims, "I never lose fights," and continues, "And I won't lose this one" (436–7). Knowing full well that the demons could still hurt her but that she would prevail against them, she opts for truth, thereby clearing up the lies of years and making a second chance possible for the Farrell family. The fact that "All the Farrells had been reborn, one way or another" (504) completes the final vision of a brave new world in romance, which is profoundly more optimistic than comedy. In both there is the implied celebration of marriage. If Irene and Danny are not a princess and prince, they are married and the natural parents of Noele, their very special daughter conceived at Eastertime and born on Christmas Day, who insists upon their reuniting for the rest of their lives.

Danny's "wandering days are over" (503), his quest finished; but what does the future hold for the eighteen-year-old with the Christmas carol, Virgin Mary, ancient Irish, modern Irish name of Noele Marie Brigid Farrell? Her trinity of given names underscores her qualities and offers hints about her future. The first, Noele, highlights her red and green, Christmas/Easter image, as well as her position as leader of the teenage guitar folk Masses at Church. She leads the congregation in two hymns. The initial one, early in the novel, is her favorite—"Lord of the Dance" —which she introduces with exegetic comments:

> "Our lives are a dance, and our friends and families are our dancing partners, and God is the head of the dance. He calls the tunes, and directs the music, and invites us all to dance. Sometimes He even interrupts our normal dances so that He can dance just with us. Lets all sing it like we were dancing so that God will know that we are ready to dance with Him whenever He wants." (99–100)

The last one, at novel's end, concludes with "Alleluia!" an exclamation of praise to God. Combined, they form an integral part of Noele's character and a summation of the story's moral. The second name, Marie, suggests her "little mother" attributes evidenced by her concern for others. Like the namesakes of her third name, Brigid, she has the resiliency of the Irish princess of old and the toughness of her modern grandmother, so she looks forward to playing "basketball or volleyball" after Easter on the courts where her attackers dumped her, a sort of resurrection (478). She has gained her father's knowledge of evil and death, survived with a renewed ability to love, and will not give up her Corvette Flame or her boy/man Jaimie Burns. She knows that the Noele/Jaimie person will, with time, take form again.

She has hope. Her visionary ability to recognize the harmony of a world where even the fish seem "to dance in the water" (*Magic Cup* 207), what Frye calls "the green world," Tillyard refers to as "the cosmic dance," and Greeley titles "Lord of the Dance" affirms her positive view of life, both at the beginning and at the conclusion of *Lord of the Dance*, before and after brutalization:

> The trees on the curving streets of the Neighborhood, which Noele thought was the most totally cool place in the world, were turning red, reminding her of the vestments the priests wore at Mass on Pentecost. And the big oaks around the Courts were pure gold, making the sun-drenched asphalt look like a grove. Noele . . . insisted that the Courts were sacred. (15–16)

> . . . Noele saw a broad beam of sunlight move lazily down Jefferson Avenue, like a sophomore girl slouching home from the Ninety-fifth Street bus on a warm, Indian summer afternoon, daydreaming about a senior boy to whom she had never spoken a word in her life. Dark clouds moved ahead of the sun as though running from it, and Jefferson Avenue was bright all the way to Ninety-fifth Street. . . . She . . . imagined the little Irish kids dancing on the Courts with the Lord of the Dance. (479)

A worthy descendant of the prototypic Brigid, Noele Marie Brigid Farrell opts for the comedian-leprechaun's forgiving attitude of her long-lost father. She sees the combinatorial value of Yeats' "dancer and the dance," where no one thing is separate and all are part of the whole. She combines the old and the new religions in her seer's view of the annual rebirth of the natural world to the promise of spring, followed by the fulfillment of summer, and of the Risen Christ, who offers His joyous dance of life and love to all who will partake of it.

Every protagonist does not have Noele's all-encompassing view of the Lord's dance of life, but some come close, each experiences an epiphany, and all find fulfillment. In Nora, his foster sister and his brother's wife, Sean Cronin sees "an angel of love," recognizes the "twisted lines of God," and accepts the archbishopric of Chicago (*Thy Brother's Wife* 492–93). Hugh Donlon, ex-priest and widower, feels "a burst of light and warmth engulf him. . . . It was an implacable and impulsive Love, one that forgave without being asked, never turned away from the beloved, and wanted only that the beloved surrender to Love and be happy. A Love like Maria" (*Ascent into Hell* 485). His life was changed, his decision made. For Cathy Collins, it is narrator Father Blackie Ryan who sees the "quicksilver mists" following her, but she considers "that Nick might be Christ for her" (*Virgin and Martyr* 519). For Anne Reilly, even though it took the "One in Charge a long time to work things out," it is "the wild dance" of natural phenomena exorcising a demon, whether real or imaginary, so she and Casey the Cop could be "together again, the way they were in the snowdrift [when they were children] and the way henceforth they would always be" (*Angels of September* 336, 435, 451).

Greeley's layering of patterns to tell his parables seems akin to Flaubert's tiers and layers of symbolism in the famous fair scene of *Madame Bovary*. Understanding requires a deal of deciphering. Yet, still another pattern emerges in human responses to the acceptance of the multidimensions of love. It is harmony, expressed by the dance; anticipation, revealed by hope; fulfillment, manifested by a smile; and joy, which makes itself known by an occasional wink.

When young King Cormac was close to broken by pirates' torture, his Brigid revealed herself to him as the princess he had so long sought. A tiny light began to shine, "a pinpoint of hope," although he "did not want the extra suffering," and he smiled. He continues to smile at Brigid's words and antics when she becomes his bride, while his wink is the outward sign of the inwardly happy man indulging his wife or acknowledging when she is right and he is wrong (*Magic Cup* 226, 270). If Hugh Donlon had decided to return to the priesthood, Cardinal Cronin says that the Pope would have accepted him and winked "a frosty blue eye" while doing so (*Ascent into Hell* 479). Cathy Collins grins and winks at her cousin Father Blackie Ryan, acknowledging that her "resurrection has been fun" (*Virgin and Martyr* 532), before she testifies that she is very much alive and claims Nick Curran for her husband. Grandmother Brigid Farrell winks at Burke, her lover for thirty years before their marriage, as he undresses her while she carries on a telephone conversation with her son. Finally, resurrected Danny Farrell winks "like a mischievous leprechaun" as he brings those two old lovers together again after a seemingly unmendable breach. Their future is the "pain and delight of beginning again" (*Lord of the Dance* 493), and, in an encapsulated form, their future embodies Greeley's parables. Pain is the suffering that comes with living; the delight is in loving.

WORKS CITED

Frye, Northrop. *A Natural Perspective: The Development of Shakespearean Comedy and Romance*. New York: Columbia University Press, 1965.

———. *The Secular Scripture: A Study of the Structure of Romance*. Cambridge: Harvard University Press, 1976.

Greeley, Andrew M. *Angels of September*. New York: Warner, 1986.

———. *Ascent into Hell*. 1983. New York: Warner, 1984.

———. *Lord of the Dance*. 1984. New York: Warner, 1985.

———. *The Magic Cup: An Irish Legend*. 1979. New York: Warner, 1985.

———. *Thy Brother's Wife*. 1982. New York: Warner, 1983.

———. *Virgin and Martyr*. 1985. New York: Warner, 1986.

Kotre, John N. *The Best of Times, the Worst of Times: Andrew Greeley and American Catholicism, 1950–1975*. Chicago: Nelson-Hall, 1978.

Shafer, Ingrid H. *Eros and the Womanliness of God: Andrew Greeley's Romances of Renewal*. Chicago: Loyola University Press, 1986.

Tillyard, E. M. W. *The Elizabethan World Picture*. New York: Random House, 1942.

Yeats, William Butler. "Among School Children," stanza 8. In *Selected Poems and Two Plays of William Butler Yeats*. Edited by M. L. Rosenthal. New York: Macmillan, 1965.

21

MICHAEL T. MARSDEN

Andrew Greeley's Time Between the Stars Series and the Religious Imagination

Grace builds on nature.
> —SAINT THOMAS AQUINAS, quoted in *God Game*

"*. . . theologians don't deliver precincts.*"
> —NICK CURRAN in *Virgin and Martyr*

*I*n an earlier study of Andrew Greeley's fiction which focused on his Passover Trilogy ("The Feminine Divine: A Search for Unity in Andrew Greeley's Passover Triology," pp. 175–184 in this volume), I argued that his fiction was necessarily "felt sociology," that is, a humanized storytelling process in which the sociological truths about the human condition are presented in story form so that we can better deal with them and absorb them. I would further argue in this essay that Greeley's fiction is "felt theology," that is, humanized theology presented in the narrative tradition utilized by all good religious storytellers.

As much as Greeley chooses to evade the title "theologian," he is, as his friend John Shea so clearly points out, a theologian pure and simple. I would only add that this latter-day Thomas Aquinas' *Summa Theologiae* is contained in the *corpus* of his ever-expanding fiction where he presents, examines, and caresses theological point after theological point. In short, Greeley's fiction is a best-selling catechism for the literate who respond most positively to his theological tales, because he speaks directly and with the authority of the particular experience which becomes universalized in the telling of the tale.

An earlier version of this essay was presented during the second of four sessions dealing with Andrew Greeley's fiction at the Popular Culture Association Meeting in New Orleans, Louisiana, 25 Mar. 1988.

At the very beginning of *The Religious Imagination*, Greeley outlines the "highlights" of the religious imagination as it operates in our lives:

1. Religious imagination is an essential key to understanding human religious behavior.

2. Religion is a meaning system expressed in "symbols"—images that are prior to and perhaps more powerful than propositions. They and the meaning we give them constitute the religious imagination.

3. All religious symbols are implicitly narrative and merge with our own stories to give them meaning and purpose.

4. Human beings have a built-in propensity to hope and the capacity for experiences which renew their hope.

5. Certain realities are especially likely to trigger experiences of hope. These experiences are recorded first of all in the imagination.

6. Religion is an activity of that dimension of the human personality which may be called pre-conscious, poetic, or creative.

7. Religion becomes a communal event where persons are able to link their own grace experiences with the grace experiences of their religious tradition.

8. Our religious stories are basically stories of relationships. (1)

It would seem to be a given that Andrew Greeley carefully and thoughtfully works through these various points about the religious imagination in story after story, all the while weaving his garment of contemporary theology in which readers finally find themselves clothed without even being fully conscious of the transformation.

The focus of this study of the religious imagination in Greeley's fiction is on the series of novels referred to as the "Time Between the Stars." Although he has written at least six of these stories concerning three Chicago families, only three of them have been published to date— *Virgin and Martyr, Angels of September,* and *Patience of a Saint.*

The actual time frame of these stories is between the 1933–34 and 1992 World's Fairs, which as Greeley notes in his *Confessions of a Parish Priest* are "represented by the fourth and eventual fifth star in the Chicago Flag" (454). He goes on to note that "the neopuritans who dominate the Chicago elites have sunk the 1992 fair" (454). Greeley describes the world of these novels and the families which inhabit them this way:

> These families, the Ryans, the Collinses and the Caseys, represent the social and religious evolution of Chicago Catholics over the last half century. In particular it is the story of the Ryan family—Ned

Ryan, the patiarch, a naval hero in World War II, a shrewd, gentle, kindly man, and his mercurial, passionate, splendid first wife, Kate Collins Ryan, and then, and especially, their children, Mary Kate Murphy, the psychiatrist, Eileen Ryan Kane, the lawyer and eventual federal judge, and John Blackwood Ryan, Ph.D., eventually a monsignor and rector of the Cathedral of the Holy Name.

Blackie holds all the stories together and, while never the protagonist in any of the books, is nonetheless the central figure in the saga. Blackie Ryan is a character who has lurked in my imagination for a long, long time. While sometimes he speaks in my voice, he has an identity and integrity of his own. He is younger than I am, physically different, and has a degree in philosophy (albeit empirical philosophy) instead of sociology. Moreover, he is in much better stead with ecclesiastical authorities. Blackie has some of the characteristics of Chesterton's Father Brown, deliberately and consciously cultivated, according to the adolescent nieces and nephews in his family. His sister Mary Kate puts it a little better, perhaps: "The Punk was born with the persona; he developed the personality to fit it." . . .

As the various characters in the Ryan clan and their entourage of relatives and friends emerge from my imagination, I learn more about their world and about the years between the thirties and nineties which I share with them. The Ryans have become a matrix for my imagination, producing not only major novels but mystery novels and short stories. My editors have often pushed me to prepare a family tree, but I am not quite yet prepared to do that because I don't think I yet know all the Ryans well enough. Eventually, perhaps. (454–55)

Greeley's first novel in this series, *Virgin and Martyr*, has been read far too literally by a number of the critics. It is, as Greeley clearly states, "about the dangers of religious enthusiasm, about the critically traumatic times of the late sixties in the Church and about God's grace . . ." (455). It should be read not as a literal tale about a confused, tormented young woman who becomes in turn a nun, a chauvinist's slave, and a revolutionary, but a parable about the stages of change and disintegration the Catholic Church experienced during the 1960s and 1970s and which, like the main character, is saved only by the infusion of grace into its life. In his note at the beginning of the novel, Greeley refers to the tale as one about "temptation." I would only further suggest that it is a story about the Church's temptation as it struggled during its darkest days in modern times to retain its dignity in a confusion of directions.

Catherine Collins is only acceptable as a character if she is perceived as a composite of forces in the modern Church which have striven to tear it apart. The other major characters include Nick Curran, a successful lawyer who has always loved Cathy, and Blackie Ryan, who has been her major confidant as they grew up together and matured into different representations of the Church's several directions. Blackie Ryan is the intelligent, perceptive, sturdy standard-bearer who, while open to reasonable change, harbors a deep respect for the essential truths of the Church. Cathy, however, is seduced by causes, most dramatically by the "Movement For a Just World" led by an unbalanced Father Ed Carny. Unloved by her parents, Cathy tries to find her salvation through a series of causes which carry her into the major movements which marked the unstable exterior of the Catholic Church in the 1960s and 1970s. From traditionalist to charismatic to disciple to revolutionary, Cathy's life story becomes a map of these fads inside and outside of the Church which characterized that period of time.

Assumed a martyr, Cathy becomes a statue on the grounds of her alma mater before Nick and Blackie establish that she is really alive and living under an assumed identity. Part artist, part idealist, and part outcast, Cathy Collins finally succumbs to being a currency courier for the mob until she is betrayed by Father Ed Carny into the hands of the diabolical Felipé Gould. Escaping from her torturers, she is able to assume a whole new identity until she is located by Blackie Ryan and Nick Curran and brought back into the warmth of the family circle in Chicago to become the fated wife of Nick.

The theme of the novel is stated more clearly in the beginning pages as Nick receives his theological training under the direction of Blackie:

> "No one resists grace, Nick. It's a combination of mist and quicksilver. It sneaks through the cracks and the crannies, fills up the interstices that our plans and programs and personalities leave empty, takes possession of the random openings we give it and then, when we least expect it, when we've done everything in our power to stop it, BANG! there's the big surprise." (13)

Although shunned by her parents, Cathy is adopted by the Ryans, especially Joe and Mary Kate Murphy, who become her surrogate parents just as Blackie Ryan becomes her surrogate brother. The actual transformation Cathy undergoes in her several stages of development is effectively chronicled through a series of letters to Blackie. She is taken from the traditional Church of the early 1960s to the brink of her own destruction and back again into a state of grace.

Unlike her patron saint, Catherine of Alexandria, Cathy is neither a virgin nor a martyr, though she is presumed to be both by others. In actuality, she is propelled toward a sexually and spiritually fulfilling union with Nick, something both have always desired but which both have failed to acknowledge. The warm image of an Indian summer day, the cool images of lake beaches and ice-cream cones, and the comforting image of the promise of Easter ceremonies form the matrix into which grace enters.

Catherine Collins' stardom comes as she assumes the role of media symbol for the anti–Vietnam War movement in the late sixties. As a nun of the new world, she represents the change in the Church that takes it from the sanctuary and into the streets seeking redress of wrongs. On the way to her "martyrdom" in the country of Costaguana, she marries an arrogant ex-priest and fails at everything, including being true to herself. Always running from herself and grace, she flees to the distorted and convoluted revolutionary ideology of Father Ed Carny in Latin America and learns to embrace violent solutions for social ills.

As Cathy begins to question the tactics of the revolutionaries, she and Nick, on the pretext of handling some legal matters, arrange a reunion in Latin America which results in an awkward, animal-like coupling. But the workings of grace have been inititated and will develop, despite external circumstances such as Cathy's arrest and torture and eventual escape. Nick Curran says of the final moments of the holiday: "And so we were kind and good to each other for the only completely honest minutes of the holiday, healing with now infinitely sensitive bodies the pain of our common uncertainty and fear" (339).

Assuming the identity of Angela Carson, former nun and revolutionary Cathy Collins disappears until she is discovered by her clever cousin, Blackie Ryan, and her lover, Nick Curran. She is rescued from the darkness and brought, together with her sunburst paintings, into a life of love. She and Nick enjoy a happy existence in Greeley's later novels, proving that resurrection is possible even in this life. But the message of the novel is not one of an individual who survived the times of radical change, but of a congregation unable to stop grace from working its magic in their lives.

The second novel in the Time Between the Stars series, *Angels of September*, continues the exploration of the religious theme of grace's insistence on being a part of our lives, no matter how we would try to refuse her entry because of selfishness or guilt. Set in the Indian summer days of early autumn and against the breezy freshness of Lake Michigan, this novel is rooted in the horror of a Catholic school fire which haunts the dreams of the novel's protagonist, Anne O'Brien Reilly. It is also rooted in the urban landscape of Chicago, which in the novel becomes the true earth for its characters. Thus the novel cleverly and insistently weaves a tale around the four essential elements: earth, air, fire, and water.

Anne Reilly, in her mid-fifties and the owner of a fashionable downtown Chicago art gallery, reigns as the beautiful, intelligent, and haunted inheritor of telekinetic power. Her personal life has never been fulfilled, in large part because of a childhood guilt about her role in the school fire and her anguish over having confessed that imagined guilt to a crazed parish priest, Desmond Kenny, who forced her to pose for his bizarre paintings. As the novel opens, she is hosting a show of Father Kenny's paintings as a sense of real and imagined catastrophe plagues her daily life and drives her to the brink of insanity. It is only through her mature love for a childhood

soulmate, Mike Casey, now deputy superintendent of police, that she is
saved. He offers her a combination of physical and spiritual love which
allows her to accept the message of God's love she has so steadfastly refused
for several decades: "In her heart she did not see how she could be forgiven,
not even by a God who, if Father Ryan was to be believed, cheated on His
own rules to capture those He loved" (8–9).

As a child Anne knew that Mike Casey *knew*, that he shared the same
sensibilities. In a lyrical moment in the early part of the novel, Anne Marie
and Mike are walking home from school on a snowy afternoon after he had
bettered her in the spelling contest. She leads other boys in pelting him
with snowballs and rubbing his face in the snow. Finally, Mike fights back
and hits her. They roll in the snow until they have a special experience:

> Then in the faint light of the street lamp, he looked into her
> flaming gray eyes and saw himself.
> His pain and loneliness and misery in her eyes. How could that
> be? What was she doing with his feelings? Why would she feel
> that no one liked her either?
> Such terrible pain, much worse than his, Why? (42)

Later the sexual implications of that experience would become clear to
Anne and Mike as they struggle to make sense of their graceless world.

Anne's first marriage was to an immature man who beat his children and
wife and who was unable to deal positively with the intellectual challenge
his art historian wife provided. Her second marriage was to a "supposedly"
ex-priest, Matthew Sweeney, who is shallow and conceited and turns
charismatic before he can do Anne any more harm. Her life has been a
searching for love in all the wrong places.

The novel strikes a clear tension between the force of retribution,
effectively represented by "Divine Justice," Father Kenny's perverted painting, and the wise words of Blackie Ryan, who reminds us that "Hell is not
responding to God's love" (73). The essence of the novel is a frightening
tour through the hell we create for ourselves because we cannot become free
of guilt and accept God's grace. Unlike Dante's Inferno, this modern-day
hell is as near as our workplace or living space and has an unnerving
resemblance to a botched Catholic upbringing. It is only through the
"foreplay of religious storytelling," to borrow and transform a phrase from
Greeley, that like Anne Reilly we are able to return from the land of the
dead and live fully in the knowledge of the presence of grace in this world.

Part, but certainly not all, of Anne's hell is created by an unfeeling
Church which lacks the compassion to deal effectively with her bad
marriage to a brutal husband. She raises her children outside of the
comforting circle of the Church, alone and dependent upon the kindnesses
of others, which are few and far between. Of her three children, the oldest
son joins a commune and calls her only when he or the commune needs
money; her daughter becomes a social radical and is embarrassed by her

talented, sensuous mother; but her youngest son, a successful broker on the
Board of Trade, becomes her one loving support in an otherwise harsh
world.

While she succeeds in the eyes of the world, earning her doctorate and
the respect consistent with her talents, she fails in her own eyes because she
cannot confess the past and be freed from it. The prelude to her freedom
comes through her intense, physical love with Mickey Casey:

> Under the hazy sky and with the wind caressing them, their love
> was at first leisurely and relaxed. Then it changed as though
> enormous currents of energy had been unleashed in their bodies.
> They struggled and rolled and twisted and shouted and yielded
> completely to the power of their joint energy. Sweaty body
> pressed furiously against sweaty body, both struggling to give
> totally and absorb totally. She was even more wanton than she'd
> been in the morning, a source of mind-shattering, rib-bursting,
> life-draining pleasure, ecstasy that Mike Casey had never known
> before and of whose existence he had never dreamed. (292)

Anne and Mickey's union has been foreordained since their first conscious meeting in that grammar school classroom, because, as Mike succinctly
states, "... we have the same kind of sympathies, that we live on the same
emotional wavelength, maybe? We are both supersensitive, passionately
eager to help, and very easily hurt" (301). Despite the failings of the
Church, both remain stubbornly Catholic as they seek to sort out their lives
and begin again. As Mike tells Blackie, "... it's the same Church that's
tormented her that's also helped her become who she is" (446).

Despite the fact that Anne and Mickey alternate their tender sexual
interludes with attendance together at Mass, Anne remains obsessed by the
ghost of Desmond Kenny and her self-imposed guilt for the school fire. It is
only through the extraordinary efforts of Blackie Ryan, his sister, psychiatrist Mary Kate Murphy, and Mike Casey, the cop, her three angels of
September, that Anne is pulled out of her mental state of living hell.

The time frame for the novel is nicely articulated through a remark
offered by Blackie Ryan that Mickey and Anne actually met for the first
time as small children at the World's Fair at the Century of Progress in
1934. This memory of a long-forgotten chance meeting points the way
toward the human solution to Anne's suffering. When Anne confesses her
guilt to God and humankind, the only response she receives is a visit from
her three angels. Finally, armed only with determination and prayer, Anne
and Mike storm and exorcise the demons in her gallery, driving them from
their lives forever. On the feast day of Saint Michael they are given a
glimpse of the future:

> There would be love and champagne and more love and then
> many sunny private beaches. They could all wait, however. Now

he and Anne were together again, the way they were in the
snowdrift and the way henceforth they would always be. (451)

So ends the second story in the Time Between the Stars series as grace is
once more allowed to enter and work its magic in the lives of Greeley's
characters. If his stories offer a theology, and I certainly would argue they
do, it is a theology which is love-centered and which offers salvation
through guardian angels, not through a fear of demons and Divine Judgment. This theology is a healing theology of joy and transformation and
fulfillment.

Greeley's theological conversation continues in an effective fashion in the
third novel in the series, *Patience of a Saint*. This captivating tale of a
hard-boiled Chicago newspaper columnist, Red Kane, who is struck down
like Saint Paul while walking on Chicago's version of the Road to Damascus,
Wacker Drive, explores the implication of sainthood in the modern world.
The message of the novel is clearly set forth in "A Theological Note" at the
end of the novel:

> This story is about falling in love again with your spouse, in its
> mixture of familiarity and mystery perhaps the most intense erotic
> experience that can occur in the human condition. Indeed it would
> seem that the evolutionary process has developed a uniquely
> human sexuality (as compared to that of the other primates)
> precisely to facilitate such intense eroticism. It might be argued
> that the rediscovery of mind-bending and body-wrenching mys-
> tery in the midst of everyday familiarity is what, specifically,
> human sexuality is all about. (442)

Red Kane, two-time winner of the Pulitzer Prize in journalism, has been
leading an increasingly empty existence since his journalistic hero, Paul
O'Meara, disappeared one evening twenty years ago in a snowstorm outside
the *Herald Gazette* offices. He is irascible, lonely, drinks more than he
should, ignores his wife of twenty years and his children, and has a mistress
(several of them in succession, to be precise). But on the Feast of All Saints
he has a mystical experience in front of the green tower at 333 Wacker
Drive where he experiences "The Holy Ghost... with warm breast and
with ah! bright wings" (13). The actual experience is described by Greeley
in these terms:

> Then time stood still, the whole of eternity filling a single second
> and a single second filling the whole of eternity. He was opened
> up like a lock on the Chicago River and everything flowed into
> him, the 333 Wacker Building, the city, the blue sky, the lake, the
> world, the cosmos. With them there was a love so enormous that
> his own puny identity was submerged in it like a piece of
> driftwood in the ocean. The invading love was searing, dazzling,
> overwhelming. It filled him with heat and light, fire that tore at

his existence and seemed about to destroy him with pleasure and joy. (13)

Red Kane's archenemy is Harv Gunther, one of the last of the Chicago robber barons turned philanthropist and civic leader. When Red comes across evidence linking Harv to the snuff murder of a young teenage prostitute, he sets out to trap the most elusive prey of his career and capture another Pulitzer Prize. Under the influence of the Bat Wielder of Wacker Drive, who has sandbagged him, Red Kane focuses on the difficult task of becoming a saint.

He becomes kindly to his co-workers and superiors at the newspaper, falls in love again with his wife and engages in the most intense sexual exchanges of his life, learns to be accepting of his in-laws, the Ryans, makes giant steps toward being an understanding and effective father for his son and two daughters, and generally becomes a model for all those who come into contact with him. Eschewing the "creature" and smoking, he once again turns his energies to completing the novel for which he received an advance and which he never finished.

His columns lose their cynical edge and become oriented toward new crusades, as the earlier idealistic Red Kane is resurrected and appears daily in the *Herald Gazette*. He decides to gamble all on an exposé of Harv Gunther but awaits the proper moment.

The heart of the novel focuses on his rekindled love affair with his lawyer wife. The Wacker Drive Raider takes possession of Saint Redmond of Lincoln Park as he begins to equate his wife with God. There is for Red a feeling that the Bat Wielder of Wacker Drive is "womanly in its affection and tenderness" (46). In his drive toward perfection, Red develops a deep and extended longing for sexual contact with his wife, which is presented in sacramental terms. The coupling of Red and Eileen on Thanksgiving evening is described in this manner: ". . . his wife was a particularly compliant and luminous lover—like a sanctuary lamp in a darkened church" (292). The union with grace can only occur after the self has been dissolved into the other and become one. Then grace can enter and sexuality leads to selflessness and oneness.

This sacramentality of sex is pursued more explicity in Red's "blasphemous fantasy that when he screwed Eileen he was screwing God. . . . Now sexual roles were confused and so were God and Eileen. When she would squirm under him or over him, her wet body straining for release, grunting and moaning in a desperate lunge for pleasure, he would be obsessed by the imagination that he was now invading god" (293).

At the height of his obsession with Eileen and her sexuality, Red delivers a sermonlike statement to Eileen on the nature of God:

> "God is a tender, passionate lover, like me at my very rare best. . . . Or even more when you heal me like you did today.

God's a chocolate malted milk, with two squirts of whipped
cream. He's not waiting to zap us. Rather He's standing around
patiently biding his time until we are ready to return His love."
(313)

This religious awareness and his saintly progress turn sour on Red when
his long-awaited attack on Harv Gunther backfires, his novel is rejected by
the publisher, his family turns on him, and he is misunderstood by a
psychiatrist. Only Blackie Ryan keeps a rational head in the midst of all of
Red's problems and shows him the way out. After defining sainthood for
Red as "excelling in the demands of everyday life" (410), and reminding Red
that "Husband and wife are sacraments of God for another, the best
hint each will ever have in this world of what God is like" (412), Blackie
sends Red on his way with perhaps the best advice in the history of popular
fiction: "Never, Redmond Peter Kane, I repeat, NEVER fuck with the
Lord God" (414).

But Red Kane is insistent in his attempts to resurrect the "old Red
Kane," the cynical, drinking, smoking, nasty columnist/father/nonlover. He
proceeds to try and wreck the Christmas holiday barely two months after
his radical conversion to the "new Red Kane," The novel ends with the
Kane family at Christmas Midnight Mass in their neighborhood parish
church as Red Kane senses the presence of the Bat Wielder behind him. We
are never left to doubt that the Hound of Heaven will catch her prey.

While it may be true that theologians do not deliver precincts and that
the city of Chicago will not earn its fifth star by hosting the World's Fair in
1992, it is also true that through Andrew Greeley's storytelling millions of
readers are being prepared for an eventual coupling with Grace. There
should be no question about the ability of best-selling fiction to serve as a
vehicle for theology via the imagination of such a contemporary Thomas
Aquinas as Father Andrew Greeley.

WORKS CITED

Greeley, Andrew M. *Angels of September.* New York: Warner, 1986.

——.*Confessions of a Parish Priest: An Autobiography.* New York: Simon & Schuster,
1986.

——.*Patience of a Saint.* New York: Warner, 1987.

——.*The Religious Imagination.* New York: Sadlier, 1981.

——.*Virgin and Martyr.* New York: Warner, 1985.

22

ANNE K. KALER

The *Legenda Aurea* Lives Again: Andrew Greeley's Use of the Saints' Lives in His Novels

In *The Life of Saint Anne* Frances Parkinson Keyes quotes a friend of hers as saying that "Catholics have two priceless treasures . . . a treasure of gold and a treasure of silver. Our treasure of gold lies in the Scriptures and Divine Tradition . . . our silver lies in the popular traditions which we may accept or not as we choose, but we are nearly always happier for having done so" (32). While the Church retains the golden treasure in the stories from the Gospel and the lives of the saints, a concurrent stream of popular literature provides a silver treasure which authors employ as storytelling devices, as plot structures, and as models or archetypes. One of these writers is Andrew Greeley.

While martyrs were granted immediate sainthood, saints developed when the popular *cultus* was recognized by the local Church authorities and eventually by Rome, so that the majority of saints' days in the calendar of the Roman Church commemorate saints who had no other canonization than general approval. Because of the haphazard Christianization of former pagan deities, places, and feasts, the Roman Church about A.D. 1000 began to impose stricter criteria for sainthood. Since the middle of the nineteenth century, the Bollandist Society, a group of Jesuits working out of the

Reprinted, with minor revisions, from the *Journal of Popular Literature* 4 (Spring/Summer 1988): 77–106.

post-Enlightenment preoccupation with separating imaginative reality from factual reality, have in their volumes of *Analecta Bollandiana* methodically investigated each early saint's credentials. Unfortunately, the Bollandists are better known for their iconoclastic removal of the saints from the calendar than for preservation: Saint George, Christopher, Catherine of Alexandria, and Philomena have all been remartyred because their *cultus* can be traced back to a pre-Christian celebration of natural phemonena such as the change of seasons.

For centuries before this, the major source for the saints' lives was a massive work by Jacobus de Voragine (1228–98), first entitled by its author *Legenda Sanctorum* but soon elevated to *Legenda Aurea*, or *The Golden Legend*, because of its popularity; over five hundred copies exist in manuscript form alone; over one hundred and fifty editions and translations were printed. In 1483 William Caxton's foreword commented that "as gold is the moste noble above al metalles, in lyke wyse is thys legende holden moost noble above all other werkys" (v). Divided into four volumes, roughly approximating the liturgical year, this latest translation from the Latin was intended as a "layman's lectionary... a 'lesson' or 'reading'... an account to be read as their [the saints'] feasts recurred during the year" (viii).

While the coming of the Renaissance and the Reformation allowed the *Legenda Aurea* to fall into disuse, the tradition of the saints' lives was not completely abandoned as a method of teaching morality through good stories: Alban Butler, an eighteenth-century priest and scholar, compiled a more modern version of the *Legenda*, familiarly called *Butler's Lives of the Saints*, heavily detailing the lives of some fifteen hundred saints with footnotes, bibliographies, corrections, and exhortations. This 1756–59 edition was updated by the Jesuit Herbert Thurston from 1926 to 1938 and further expanded and updated by Donald Attwater in 1956 to include twenty-five hundred or more saints. Since the Jesuit president of the Bollandist Society acknowledged that the revised Butler "nearly always bears a relation, direct or indirect, on our... studies (Butler viii), the latest edition of Butler is probably as correct a version of the saints' lives as the layman is likely to get.

But a new hagiographer is popularizing the ancient legends in so subtle a way that most of his readers are unaware of it. Andrew M. Greeley in his many novels consistently uses the saints' lives—from de Voragine, from Butler, and from the "silver treasure" of popular tradition—to provide recognizable archetypes for his characters and his readers, to bolster his plot structures with familiar story lines, and to create a new interpretation of what it means to be a saint. As Ingrid Shafer states in *Eros and the Womanliness of God*, "it is the task of the Christian not to repudiate the symbols of the past but to reinterpret them, to discern their meaning in and for a new age, to make them the key for understanding the present" (15). So also do Greeley's saints' lives, as natural extensions of Church tradition and Jungian archetypes of "pre-conscious chaos of amorphous drives, needs, and wants that constitute our instinctual heritage," serve as the "myths and rituals [which] integrate the individual into the larger patterns of society" (Shafer 13). Like the medieval writer who did not try for originality for it's own sake, Greeley tries to present the old archetypes in a new form. Although just how he does this is a valid study for the scholar, such emphasis is not new to Greeley; in an early work on mysticism, *Ecstasy: A Way of Knowing*, Greeley says that mythopoeic knowledge "seeks to embody human experience in forms that appeal not only to the intellect but to the whole person . . . In both its style and language it uses symbols rather than prose. . . . There is a strain toward concern for the ultimate. . . . Every poem, every novel, tries to say something basic about the human condition" (60).

If Greeley adopts the role of the Celtic bard who records historical events composing folk songs, then given his background, stepping from the role of priest and sociologist into the role of storyteller is not contradictory for him. Indeed, he is quite outspoken on this latter role. Discussing Saint Catherine of Alexandria in *Virgin and Martyr*, he mourns that "it is a shame to lose her. That's what happens when you let scholars take over from story tellers" (65). He snaps that Saint Nicholas' story as a "wonder worker . . . representing God's love for little children all over the world . . . [was spoiled because] the damn fools in Rome have to demythologize him just when the story was getting good" (369).

When Greeley chooses the saints' lives for inclusion in his novels, he chooses those stories for which he feels empathy—familiar, mystical, incredible, and complex—finding in them those archetypes that make them serve as symbols of the larger pattern and avoiding saints whose lives are too factually detailed. He chooses those almost exclusively early saints whose prior existence symbolizes natural phenomena, which he then embroiders with complicating detail by weaving them into his text so cleverly that they become, at once, archetypes, symbols, and characterizing devices for his characters, like the knotting devices in Celtic manuscripts. So convoluted is Greeley's generous mix of his major sources—de Voragine and Butler, as well as modern popular tradition—that to achieve his characterization he will, as Ingrid Shafer states, "use *any* expression, *any* image, *any* story which might conceivably serve to break through the safe categories of conventionally dead piety and spread the 'Good News' of the implacably loving, passionately pursuing androgynous Deity" (231). Thus, the role of storyteller is a godly one or, as the narrator of *God Game* claims, "every story teller is a theologian and every story is about God, one way or another" (16). And, as any good storyteller will, Greeley picks and chooses those elements which will suit his stories: specifically, those elements are the solar calendar as a complement to the liturgical one, the use of fire and water imagery, the differing methods of martyrdom, the question of virginity and sexuality, and, finally, the problem of how to become a saint.

Greeley's novels are consistently based on the liturgical year's coincidence with the solar calendar and natural phenomena: his first work, *The Magic Cup*, is a retelling of the Celtic legend of the hero's quest for the Grail and the Grail Maiden Brigid, an emanation of the Celtic goddess of nature. In his Passover Trilogy—in which *Thy Brother's Wife* exemplifies Holy Thursday, *Ascent into Hell* demonstrates Good Friday, and *Lord of the Dance* centers on Easter Sunday and the Resurrection theme—Greeley employs the major events of Christianity as paradigms for his character formation. His *Death in April* takes place from January until Pentecost, with the concentration on Holy Week and the fifty days following it. *Angels of September* ends on September 29–30, the feast day of Saint Michael the Archangel and all the other angels; *Patience of a Saint* starts on the Feast of All Saints and ends on Christmas; *Happy Are the Clean of Heart* has the hero pursue the heroine from Twelfth Night to Candlemas, and she is brought back from the dead on the feast of the dead, the Feast of All Hallows or Saints—Halloween. *God Game* and *The Final Planet* both have climaxes centered on the seasonal festivals in their futuristic worlds.

Greeley uses especially those saints whose lives coincide with the changes of seasons, especially of the winter solstice, often naming his characters to agree with the natural/liturgical calendar. In *Patience of a Saint* the major character is Redmond Patrick Kane. This name suggests the Saturnalian aspect of the winter solstice, for the "redman" of Irish lore is an itinerant seller of red dye whose name, like that of the gypsies, was used as a threat to bring children into line. The dark mark of the biblical outcast Cain disappears in the visible change in Kane's life as he becomes the Christianized form of the sun returning in his nickname "Red." Kane's second mystical experience takes place at the Church of Saint Clement, whose feast is November 23 and who is the patron of blacksmiths, who themselves were outcast for their profession's suspicion of magic and who were often tattooed on the forehead, like Cain, in honor of their pagan sun god. So, when Blackie Ryan, the narrator of *Virgin and Martyr*, states that Saint Catherine of Alexandria is "one of those great winter saints who prepare us for Christmas and promise us spring—Andrew and your man [Nicholas] being the others" (65), Greeley's choice of names for his heroine (Cathy) and for his hero (Nick) is a reminder of this solstice convention, since Saint Catherine's day is November 25 and Saint Nicholas' day is December 6. Even Greeley's inclusion of Saint Andrew as a solstice saint—his feast is November 30—is made more convincing by the fact that the Saint Andrew's cross, which is in the shape of a distended X superimposed on a cross as it appears on the British flag, makes it a sun sign.

Greeley's use of the legend of Saint Catherine of Alexandria as the basis for Cathy Collins in *Virgin and Martyr* is deliberate; Blackie Ryan comments to Nick that, despite the Bollandist findings that there is "no record of any such saint," the similarities between the two women "will not escape you—talent, noble family, torture, death, disappearing body, miracles" (65) and tersely summarizes the legend from Jacobus de Voragine: "a young woman of noble family, vowed to chastity and brilliant in philosophy, who refutes all the pagan philosophers, is tortured to death by being strapped to a wheel of an oxcart at the order of the cruel Emperor Maxentius—who had propositioned her, by the way—and then beheaded. Her body disappears because some passing angels steal it away from the wretched pagans" (64).

While many other early saints' lives follow the same formula, no other one fits in so many particulars. Cathy and Catherine are the same age when their story starts—eighteen—but Cathy's eighteen is so far removed from the maturity needed for Catherine's swift martyrdom that Cathy's growth is in itself a slow and painful martyrdom of the integration of her personality. According to their authors, both women are beautiful and gracious as befits heroines; both are abandoned by parents, "left alone in a palace filled with riches and servants" (de Voragine 709) or, in the case of Cathy, left to her own devices by her parents, who are more concerned with money-making and false piety; both reject money in favor of heavenly reward, although Cathy eventually claims her inheritance to resurrect herself to a lifetime of responsibility instead of a swift and glorious death. In Cathy's favor is her bold and outspoken manner against injustice, real or otherwise; Catherine goes "boldly [to] a long disputation with the Caesar" (709), which ends in her death. Both are threatened to die by a wheel which is ineffectual, both are sexually harassed by their captors, both are beheaded in the legend, and both have bodies which mysteriously disappear.

Yet Cathy is given a choice of patron saints to follow; as a teenager Cathy visited Pope John XXIII, who asked her which of the great Catherines—of Siena, of Genoa, or of Alexandria—she took as patron. Catherine of Siena (1347–80), a Dominican tertiary and mystic, contracted a "marriage" with Christ, complete with a diamond and jeweled wedding ring visible only to her, just as Cathy fulfills the nun's concept of "marriage" with the Divine Bridegroom. If Catherine of Siena is not the saint for Cathy, neither is the second Catherine mentioned—Catherine of Genoa, a fifteenth-century woman who wanted to be a nun but who was married at fifteen to a dissolute husband and spent ten years in depressed melancholy before turning to the frivolities of society. A Lenten conversion led to mysticism, after which she gave herself to the service of the poor, reformed her husband, cared for his illegitimate child, ran a hospital, and died so far in the odor of sanctity that her body remains to this day incorruptible in a glass casket in Genoa (Cruz 160). Cathy, too, followed this path: she wanted to be a nun and was unable to do so; she married briefly a dissolute and impotent husband who bankrupted her mentally and monetarily just as Catherine of Genoa's husband bankrupted her completely before he became a Franciscan tertiary and took a vow of chastity; Cathy "ran a hospital" in the sense that, like the Genoese Catherine, who began her service to the poor in the lowest form of hospital work, she served the poor as an unskilled nurse's aide in the Costaguanan clinic. In the penitential spirit of the times, both medieval Catherines fasted continuously without harming their health, existing for long periods on the Eucharistic Bread alone. Cathy, as a novice, achieved malnutrition and anemia by her overly strict fasting against the direct orders of her superiors; this "disobedience" is balanced when she loses weight in prison and cannot regain it.

Like most mystics, both medieval Catherines gained fame through their writings: Catherine of Genoa for her works on Purgatory, Catherine of Siena for her many letters of admonition to the clergy which led her to be proclaimed a Doctor of the Church in 1970 by Pope Paul VI. According to de Voragine, the mythical Catherine of Alexandria (the site of the famous library) was so well "educated in all the liberal arts" (709) that she refuted fifty philosophers in a lengthy theological debate, converted them, and led them to martyrdom. She also "taught" Christianity to the wife and steward of the emperor, both of whom were subsequently martyred. If Cathy does not exactly defeat fifty philosophers, she does embrace fifty different theories as radical to her society as Christianity was to the Roman one; it is she who is writing the philosophical book attributed to her husband, Roy, a fact which another Catherine, Mary Kate, exposes as a farce. Cathy in her own right is an educated woman and a teacher; as a nun, she obtains a college degree in elementary education and is eventually offered graduate study as a "sop" for her rough treatment in grade school. She later spurns that opportunity, complaining that the need for Ph. D.'s is irrelevant.

The phrasing of Blackie's initial introduction of her as "Saint Catherine of Chicago, virgin and martyr—my cousin Cathy" (*Virgin and Martyr* 3) consciously parallels the addressing of the saints—first name plus the city primarily connected with them (e. g., Catherine of Genoa.) Neither of the medieval Catherines was a martyr and only one was a virgin, but both were essentially teachers in the sense that their mystical writings have continued beyond their death. So also, Catherine of Alexandria's legend qualifies her as a learned woman and teacher; yet Cathy ignores this aspect, insisting on that Catherine as her patron solely because she is a virgin and martyr, despite Pope John's reference to her as "a wisa woman, philosopher, teacher" and his admonition that it "is harda to die but isa much harda to be a wisa teacher" (86). The phrase also sets up the ironic and misleading comparison, for Cathy turns out to be neither virgin nor martyr, although the wise woman of Greeley's canon, his sister, psychiatrist Mary Kate, notes Cathy's "martyr complex" (302).

So, having rejected two possible candidates for Cathy's patron, Greeley settles on the winter solstice saint Catherine of Alexandria, whose flaming Catherine wheel of the returning sun serves as the sacramental symbol of the feminine power over the sun. While in imagery woman is usually water and man fire, paradoxically in pagan practices, she was often accompanied by her complement—fire to her water—an image that Greeley has used before in his Passover Trilogy with the immersion of the Easter candle into the newly blessed Easter water. Most frequent in Greeley's theogony is the Celtic myth of Brigid and her Beltane fires, heralding the return of the sun as seasonal beacons. An interesting corollary Greeley draws upon, is that Alexandria, the seaport home of his Cathy's saint in Egypt, was known for its lighthouse, which served as a beacon for incoming ships, just as the gilded lamp of the Statue of Liberty—rechristened Lady Liberty to deify her as an emanation of female power with the sun or light—welcomes ships to America in the New York harbor.

The author has precedent for his belief in the popular tradition of the spinning or flamingly acrobatic sun: the declaration of Mary's Assumption into heaven, celebrated on August 15, Christianizes the pagan celebration on August 13 of Diana, the goddess of the August skies, which in its turn was the pagan explanation of the shower of shooting stars and the aurora borealis, which occur the first two weeks of August. The same time period contains the feast of Saint Clare of Assisi, whose symbol is a monstrance, a sacred vessel to hold the round eucharistic Host for exposition. The monstrance is usually cast with rays emanating from it like a sunburst. The most recent precedent in popular tradition is the dancing sun which accompanied visitations of Mary, the mother of Christ, at Fatima in 1917 and Medogorje most recently.

Specifically, Greeley adopts Catherine of Alexandria's flaming or spiked wheel, which has its foundation in the solar calendar as a symbol of woman's power over natural phenomena. As such, it is the image of the wheel that most persists. When the misguided priest who betrays her to her torturers eulogizes Cathy as a "modern St. Catherine, her body broken on the wheel of American imperialism," Blackie counters ironically with the modern Freudian view that "the St. Catherine's wheel represented the female organs" (3). This minor exchange in itself shows Greeley's intent to characterize the villain by his dependence on the older discredited version of Catherine and her wheel while Blackie, Greeley's *persona*, has the correct and corrected version.

While the "fiery revolving sword" of death appears as early as Genesis 3:24, while the sun-wheel wings of cherubim circle the Godhead, and while the wheel of Dame Fortune predicts men's destinies, de Voragine embellishes this ancient sun design by describing the Catherine wheel as "a horrible device... an engine [with] four wheels, studded with iron saws and sharp nails [and] two of the wheels should revolve in one direction, and two be driven in the opposite direction, so that grinding and drawing her at once, they might crush and devour her" (713). Derived from these four wheels, the four-wheeled Ford used to transport Cathy to Don Felipé's mountain camp from which no one escapes becomes her threatened instrument of death, and the helicopter which searches for the escaping Cathy is a spinning death wheel in the sky.

Where de Voragine likens his saint's name to a "*catenula,* a chain" (708) to heaven, Butler, who calls the entire tale a "completely worthless *acta*" (4:420), has no reference to chains, yet in iconography as recent as 1965 in Christina Hole's *Saints in Folklore,* the saint is shown chained with a crown on her head (68). So also is Cathy "chained" by ropes which she must loosen by "sawing" them against the metalwork of the Ford, her death machine. In the Catherine legend the exploding wheel became the death machine to overly curious bystanders; just as Cathy kills Don Felipé's henchmen with the "rounds" of ammunition she inserts into the "cannon" (381) or gun, so also, by implication, Cathy's wheel kills Don Felipé himself by another "round" machine of death, the machine gun. Even Cathy's parents are killed in a flaming gas explosion.

Greeley's masterful adaptation of the legend to his story appears in his use of the chain saw to allegedly murder Cathy: "Had not her still living body been torn apart by a chain saw in the courtyard of a South American military barracks?" (3). As a storyteller and sociologist, Greeley had to be sufficiently aware of the current American stream of "chain saw massacre murder" films to know the extent of horror such an image suggests; yet what a practical way he invents to cut off someone's head in this modern day when swords and axes are improbable weapons; surely, the machete, a common tool in a Central American country like Costaguana, where the chain saw would seem to be relatively rare, would have been a more logical choice, except for the fact that as an author he wanted to find the closest physical weapon to the Catherine wheel. And he did so in the chain saw, which combines the persistent image of the chain and the saw with that of the spinning sun image of the wheel, transmuting the death instrument of the Catherine legend into an engine powering a chain with spiked or sawed edges rotating in an elliptical orbit. Even the motion used in chopping with a chain saw is in itself a partial circle as the wielder starts at the top of an arc and proceeds to the bottom, much like a golf swing that needs a follow-through.

Despite its Eastern Church origins and probable pagan influences, the Catherine wheel has been a popular image in European culture in its recognized form of the spinning wheel in both fairy tales and *chansons de toile*. While tradition makes Saint Catherine patron of all those engaged with wheels, it was the spinsters who used their spinning wheels to twist tightly worsted thread who honored her on her feast day, November 25, by declaring a holiday and by chasing young men on the street, much in the manner of Al Capp's Sadie Hawkins Day; lace makers in England dressed in men's clothes went begging for "Cattern-cakes or 'wigs' because of their wig-like shapes" (Hole 76); women over twenty-five were said to "do St. Catherine's hair" (76). Thus, Saint Catherine became the natural patron of unmarried women in the textile industry and her sponsorship extended to lacemakers because they formed patterns, often circles, with threaded bobbins. Ditties imploring her help (and that of Lucy and Agnes), as well as practices of foretelling the future by mirrors, crosses cut in willow branches, peelings from apples and oranges tossed over the shoulder, were all popular appeals to virgin saints to secure a husband. It is not surprising that Cathy paints sunbursts, and teenage Noele of *Lord of the Dance* plays "roundball" sports like basketball while her mother weaves stories.

Cathy's connections with the Catherine wheel as the flaming or spiked sun are many. When Blackie and Nick discover her paintings at the college, they are "gold and silver sunburst[s] . . . explosions of color, most of them light and ethereal . . . a few were more somber, a sun rising over industrial smoke stacks" (*Virgin and Martyr* 371–72); the polarized gold (male) and silver (female) conventions of the colors of the sun appear even in the door of the room which is decorated with "gold and silver Gothic letters" (371). The gold and silver image persists: when Cathy flees her captors, she exists on oranges, bitter oranges, which symbolize her power as a controller of the sun—in the bright globe of the orange—and her lack of power, in the bitter orange. Her torture consists of the application of electrical charges, a modern form of fire; she is tortured with cigarette burns, in themselves round hot objects; she saves herself through the modern firepower of gunpowder when she guns down her assailants.

The legendary Catherine's prayer to the Lord that the "machine might fall to pieces" is answered when "instantly an angel of the Lord struck the monstrous mill and it broke apart with such violence that four thousand pagans were killed in its collapse" (De Voragine 713). Cathy's "rage and the anger that were still inside her exploded" (*Virgin and Martyr* 381) when she could not break the strap holding her prisoner in the Ford. This breaking or explosion outward represents the convention of the stylized sun and its rays; in the virgin-martyrs' case, it represents a concentration of their power over the sun so much that, while a purifying test by fire is common to such martyrs, it seldom kills them. Where Catherine of Alexandria encourages the fifty converted philosophers to persevere in their fiery martyrdom, Cathy is surrounded by inflammatory revolutionaries who revile the government forces who "blew up our mines and bridges" (350) and killed three hundred miners in San Tome. This has a double meaning; silver to a Christian is always reminiscent of the betrayal of Christ by Judas for thirty pieces of silver; Greeley increases the number a tenfold to three hundred silver miners and puts them in the mine dedicated to Saint Thomas, another solstice saint who is known best for coming to earth on his feast day, December 21, on his fiery chariot to summon up the souls of the dead Thomases to pray with him in front of a red glowing cross in the graveyard.

All this flame imagery is foreshadowed early in the plot line when Erin Collins, Cathy's overly pious mother, warns the merry party of teenagers to enjoy the New Year's celebration of 1960 because the world is going to end in catastrophe before 1961. Citing the Fatima letter which supposedly foretold the end of the world by fire, Erin unwittingly introduces the larger solar nineteen-year cycle of the conjunction of the sun and the moon. This larger pattern, which led to the ritual killing of the king of the wood every nineteen or twenty years, according to mythologists, represents the changing of generations in a primitive society; Odysseus takes nineteen years to return home, and tradition has it that a president elected every twentieth year will not survive his term, as Kennedy, cited by Erin, did not. This use of foreshadowing is a helpful device for the author to demonstrate the twenty years' difference between a child of the sixties, Cathy, and the mature woman, Angela-Cathy of the eighties.

Thus, Cathy's choosing of Catherine of Alexandria places her right in the middle of solar change, for Catherine's feast is November 25, a day close enough to the astrological sun sign of Scorpio to warrant attention. Female Scorpios are allegedly sexually promiscuous despite their being a water sign. Just as Cathy is beaten in prison, Catherine, in an inexplicable phrase in de Voragine, is "beaten with scorpions" (713), perhaps a whip shaped like scorpions' tails or perhaps an echo of her sun sign, or perhaps the recalling of the Lord's protection of the Israelites from the "burning serpent . . . and the scorpion and the *dipsas*" (Deut. 8:15). The latter is a serpent which causes thirst, another water sign, as Cathy is plagued by thirst in her escape and seeks solace in the sea. In addition, the unfounded tradition that scorpions when surrounded by a ring of fire will sometimes sting themselves to death appears when Cathy considers suicide when surrounded by her assailants.

Not all flaming sun images are in this one novel. In *Lord of the Dance* Noele's red Chevy is named Flame and has all the characteristics of a guardian angel. Genesis 3:24 suggests the popular tradition that the unnamed cherubim with "the fiery revolving sword" who drove Adam and Eve from the Garden of Eden was actually Michael, the protector of Israel. In iconography he is shown in full medieval battle armor (excluding wings) with a long spear rather than a sword, stabbing to death a writhing fire-breathing dragon, the physical form of the devil who preys on helpless maidens: this last image extends to the secondary saint—Saint George, himself the sun god Perseus—who also saved a maiden from the dragon by his sword and/or his spear. The fire image combines with water when the warrior angel who took over the thunder-and-lightening aspects of pagan storm gods fought against the fire in Anne Reilly's art gallery amidst a thunderstorm, only to have Anne defeat the flaming picture with a waste basket, decorated with Monet's water lilies because only a woman can control the power of flame.

Other saints' lives contribute to Greeley's linking of the flaming or fiery sun with his heroes' and heroines' seasonal changes. Most notably, the virgin and martyr Saint Lucy, whose day is celebrated on December 13, which falls on the old calendar's winter solstice, is represented by a young daughter of each household who becomes the Lucia Bride or Queen, wearing a wreath of lighted candles and dressed in white with a red sash— for light and fire, virginity and martyrdom, a color combination irresistible even to Hardy in his creation of his pagan Tess in her fateful Maywalk. In this same custom, the town selects a Lucia Queen to parade and to bless the houses in the ancient mumming tradition, accompanied by young men dressed as old men with red beards—the old year and the young year with the red flame of the sun—and masked demons and trolls as the captured winter forces defeated by the returning sun of Lucia. In *Patience of a Saint* the naming of Red Kane's dog Luciano, a form of Lucy or perhaps after the gangster of the same name, neatly contrasts the irony of the coal-black Labrador, the epitome of the old dead year, with the "Red" of the hero's name.

Often accompanied by a male complement of the proto-martyr Saint Stephen, whose feast day follows Christmas and ends the changing period of the sun, Lucy's images include a burning lamp, because she "controlled" the fire and escaped being burned to death. As the saint of blindness, Lucy is shown with her eyes on a plate, the symbol of the discredited legend of her plucking her eyes out to mar her beauty to preserve her virginity but, more possibly, a symbol of her control of the source of light. In her transformation into Angela Carson, Cathy changes her eye color with contact lenses to protect her new identity as an integrated Jungian whole.

The first week of February when the lengthening days provide more light is held sacred by liturgical calendars. Wicce celebrated a major feast of light; Druids worshipped Brigid, and the Christianized Celts honored Saint Brigid, Saint Mary of the Gael, at this time; Christian churches celebrate Candlemas Day, the day that Mary, following the Jewish custom, went to the Temple forty days after the birth of her son to be cleansed of the stain of childbirth, a ceremony of "churching" for new mothers that some Christian churches preserve by having a woman approach the altar with an unlighted candle to receive the light from the priest. The feast of Saint Blaise on February 2 celebrates the blessing of the throats of the pious in commemoration of his having saved a child who swallowed a fishbone; while this seems to have no connection, most of the virgin-martyrs, who could not be harmed by fire, were killed by a sword thrust into the throat or by beheading, as was Saint Blaise. An exception is Saint Agatha, whose feast is on February 5, Greeley's own birthday, and who is the patroness against fire, because she was rolled naked over a bed of hot coals; de Voragine's account does not state this as the cause of her death; rather, an earthquake forced her torturers to flee and she simply expired. Another springtime connection, albeit slight, appears in de Voragine's account of a Nicholas in the tale of Saint Patrick who entered Purgatory where one punishment was a "gigantic wheel, with men bound to each of its spokes and the wheel spun so swiftly that it seemed to form a circle of fire" (194).

If fire seems to predominate in Greeley's imagery, it is followed closely by water as a salvation theme, embedded in the Celtic belief that wells, fountains, and water sources have resident spirits which sanctify them. The major saint in Greeley's canon to exemplify this is Saint Nicholas, a fourth-century bishop of Myra, known in the East as a saint for sailors and in the West for children and prisoners, whose December 6 feast makes his association with Catherine of Alexandria and Cathy Collins of vital importance.

Because he is from the seaport of Myra, Nicholas is a water saint "in charge of working wonders at sea. Since a fair number of sailors do survive bad storms, it was natural that he would receive credit for it" (*Virgin and Martyr* 367). When he is tracking Cathy down on December 5, Blackie decides to "wait until the Feast of Saint Nicholas, which is also the feast of Poseidon" (368). When Nick jokingly wants credit for "the storm missing Mobile," Blackie assures him he might "make an appropriate Poseidon" (369). Nick is imbued with water imagery: the rainstorm with its "heavy drapes of humidity" (29–30) off Lake Michigan when he first courts Cathy; Blackie's turning to the wall the picture of the Battle of Mobile Bay; the corridor at Saint Peter's College being "moist with humid atmosphere" (371).

In *Death in April* Greeley blatantly makes his heroine's name Evalina Brigid, a combination of the diminutive of the first mother's name, Eve, and that of Celtic goddess. His hero, Jim, calls her Lyn or Lynnie and insists on identifying her with the lake: "Lynnie and the lake. The girl is the lake is the grail is God" (64), because for him she merges with the "dark brown woman dressed in white who so often came to him in his dreams and always by the lake of his childhood" (239); repeatedly, he sees both the lake and Lyn as a necessary death of self for him: "the lake looked sinister under the quiet April sky. . . the lake is evil" (64), and he prefers the "waters of the Mediterranean [which] would be cool, not numbing cold like the great silent lake which stirred listlessly beyond the park" (243). The connection of the lake and the woman is a consistent one in the Celtic lore; Arthur's Lady of the Lake gives him Excalibur and receives it back; the Arthurian knights search for the Celtic Grail as Jim searches for his impetus to write his novels. When he is finally convinced that Lyn will help him solve his drinking problem, he regrets that it will "mean the end of gin and Scotch, and a lot less wine and brandy too" (254). Lyn, however, is not seen in water colors but in the warm colors of the sun goddess—peach, beige, or apricot, none of which would complement her violet or April eyes.

While the association of saints with specific places (Genoa, Alexandria, Siena) was an early form of identification, its purpose serves a modern author well in his use of topical or symbolically meaningful names. The actual title of Greeley's novel should be *Saint Catherine of Chicago: Virgin and Martyr,* since this is the most familiar listing in Butler's *Lives,* but the omission of the first part suggests Cathy's identification with the city of Chicago. Such was the case with Catherine of Alexandria, whose legend was brought to the west by the Crusaders (a fact noted by Blackie) and who is connected with the Egyptian seaport. One discredited version renders her a princess (hence her crown), daughter of a Cypriot king who was made governor of Egypt, King Costus, a possible source for Greeley's imaginary Costaguana. She even traveled after her death when her body was carried to a monastery on Mount Sinai, allegedly by "some passing angels" (64), according to Greeley, but more probably by Eastern monks who were commonly called "angels" because of their holy lives.

While Cathy travels from her secure Chicago area to the Midwest school to a New York ghetto to Costaguana, it is her final travel that makes the story of Cathy Collins into the legend of Saint Catherine of Chicago. Her martyrdom in a foreign country and her unfound body enable her to be used as a martyr for the cause; a statue commemorating her sacrifice is installed on a high hillside at Our Lady of the Hill (Mount Sinai) by "angels" of the overly pious Catholics like Rosie O'Gorman, who acts like a rich backer of a theatrical enterprise, and "angel," in her role as a "Charismatic matron, married to a fabulously wealthy Silicon Valley president [who] could do anything you want with the feast of an excommunicated saint" (15). Thus, the two Catherines are "thrown out" of the calendar: Catherine by the Bollandists exposing her as a legend, Cathy as a discredited saint. Cathy as a courier transporting money is an "angel," since that is the origin of the word "angel"; when she reappears at Saint Peter's College, named after Simon-renamed-Peter, she is Angela Carson; the last name "Carson" is a pun on Catherine's wheel again—the "son" (or daughter) of the cart, since Greeley is the only hagiographer to refer to the wheel as an "ox cart" (64).

Place names continue to have significance. When Blackie and Nick trace Cathy, it is to the city of Mobile, a clear indication of her nature as a "wandering Thamaturge" like Saint Nicholas in Blackie's description of him (368). Like most saints whose bodies were considered movable even if their feasts were not, Saint Nicholas also shifts from the city of Myra to Bari to "Northern Europe, particularly Holland and the Germanic states. From Holland he journeyed to New Amsterdam" (369) and then to the entire world as Santa Claus, in which role he most fully uses his power of bilocation.

As the city of God and the city of man have long been in opposition, so also does Greeley find in cities a sense of polarity which his characters must reconcile. In *Death in April* the hero, Jim, finds that Chicago with all its memories "disarms" (244) him while Paris does not; rather, it becomes the ultimate muse for a midwestern writer. Lyn, whose life overflows with the noise of children, does not provide the hothouse "environment a writer needs" (247), but, like the city itself, she captivates him in an odd mixture of Chicago and Camelot, "the city and Lynnie... elegant, outrageous, crude... Chicago as Camelot, Lynnie as Guinevere" (244). Greeley doubles his meaning here because the patron saint of Paris is Saint Geneviève, the origin of the name Guinevere. In essence, any city which contains Lyn is Paris or Paradise and therefore the city of God to Jim, and, indeed, that is where the characters are headed at the end of the book. Chicago plays the same role to Red Kane, who cannot be lured from it by the glamour of eastern newspapers; it provides solace and danger to Lisa Malone in *Happy Are the Clean of Heart*; it is home to most of Greeley's characters.

Such name playing merely reinforces Greeley's strong addiction to Jungian archetypes in the choices of names and places for Jim's women: his daughter, Clare, in Italy is associated with Clare of Assisi in her virginal brilliance; his mother, Laura, also has an Italian connection with Petrarch's Laura, a name which is given to a group of Eastern houses clustered around a central church for a community of nuns or priests; Monique is French for Monica and her motherly role to Jim in advising him to pursue his old love reminds the reader of Monica's constant prayers for her wayward son, Augustine. These women, along with Lyn, provide him with the goddess myth of mother, daughter, sister, and lover.

In *Lord of the Dance* Greeley plays with the name of Daniel Xavier Farrell in connection with place. Daniel, the prophet of the Old Testament, was imprisoned in the lion's den, where he was visited by angels; Daniel Farrell, as a flier or as one with wings, is imprisoned in China for eighteen years, visited only by memories; one of his patrons, Francis Xavier, convert of Ignatius of Loyola and first Jesuit missionary, died, like Moses, before he reached his goal, China. Both "return" to their birthplace, the saint as a relic, Daniel as a released prisoner.

Even in minor items, Greeley suggests more symbolism in his use of saints' names. Saint Jarlath, an inoffensive fifth-century Irish monk, does not deserve to have his name given to the infamous inner-city school in many of the novels. Neither does Saint Ignatius of Loyola, hardly a minor-league saint, deserve to be relegated to the name of a girls' school. Saint Brigid and Saint Brendan lend their Celtic names and reputations for wandering to the order of space explorers (American, of course) in *The Final Planet*, the modern version of the Irish *peregrini*. Saint Columban, that greatest and most controversial of seventh-century Irish wandering monks, may have given a form of his name to Saint Columbanus, the shoddy college Cathy attends, especially since his feast is celebrated on November 23 in Ireland and November 21 in Italy, where he settled; the fact that the feast of the sixth-century poet and bard Saint Colman is on November 24, further reinforces the solstice convention. The most complex of Greeley's uses of minor saints is in the parish of Saint Praxides or Praxedes; according to Butler, she was a Roman maiden who protected Christians during the persecutions, even to burying them, and it was at her tomb that Saint Agnes was going when she encountered her martyrdom. In *Lord of the Dance* Greeley refers to Saint Praxides' window as showing her with some kind of a "farm implement over her shoulder... Prax's ax, the parishioners called it" (320), perhaps a reference to her habit of burying ubiquitous martyrs.

Along with obscure references to saints, Greeley uses several modern saints in a way that satirizes the pious "legends" about them. In particular, the story of Saint Thérèse of Lisieux sending a rose as a sign of her favor to a devotee evolves into a farcical episode: when Noele needs such a favor, the van in front of her car Flame suddenly opens and "a bundle fell onto Flame's waiting hood... it was only when her fingers were about to touch the package that she knew what would be in it... 'Totally excessive,' she said hotly. 'I asked for one, not a bouquet!'" (114).

If Greeley can cite his litany of saints, his characters also have their favorite "saints" from popular literature. Blackie is not unwilling to be described in several novels as being like G. K. Chesterton's detective Father Brown—"short, pudgy, cherubic with curly brown hair, apple cheeks, and an expression of impenetrable composure. He is the kind of utterly unimportant-appearing person that you wouldn't even notice... the brightest man I know, ruthlessly loyal" (64). Noele, who is herself a detective, seeking her father like Oedipus, is compared by her family condescendingly with Agatha Christie's Miss Marple and the teenage Nancy Drew; she sees herself, however, as "Roderick Alleyn, Hercule Poirot, and Lew Archer, all rolled into one" (87), a nice combination of male detectives all known for their cool logic. The archetype of the hero searching for his own or her own destiny is a pervasive one in Greeley's novels, usually ending with the hero or heroine being pursued by the Hound of Heaven or the androgynous loving Deity who strikes Red Kane with a "cosmic baseball bat" (*Patience of a Saint* 3).

Greeley concentrates on the martyrdom of his characters—whether it is by physical, psychic, or psychological torture—since not all solstice saints were martyrs in the truest sense of the word. Nick makes the mistake of assuming that Nicholas' red robes are those of a martyr, only to be corrected by Blackie that "those are bishop's robes that the good Claus wears. He was a martyr in the sense that he was tortured for his faith but apparently was too stubborn to renounce it and too stubborn to die" (*Virgin and Martyr* 368), just as Cathy will prove to be "too stubborn to die" later in the story. Greeley ties other characteristics of Nicholas to his Nick: his love of children, which comes from a misinterpretation of the size of small figures in iconography used to show inferiority to the larger saint, and his care for unmarried women, shown in his using his wealth to provide dowries for them. Nicholas is, however, the spirit of Christmas that Greeley favors, shown in his description as "a wonder worker with bishop's robes and a beard and an American accent representing God's love for little children all over the world. And the damn fools in Rome have to demythologize him just when the story was getting good" (369). Greeley reinforces this care of Nicholas for unmarried women in his care of Cathy and, even in a minor way, when he has Nick comment that an art student's plaster statue of Santa Claus is built like a "heavyweight boxer" (371)—that is, one who could defend a maiden, as Nick can and does—rather than like the paternal portly figure of Santa Claus.

The means of martyrdom are an important linking device that Greeley uses. Catherine's martyrdom follows the familiar virgin-martyr path: the ordinary tortures do not kill her or the other early spurious martyrs; they must be beheaded or jugulated.

The origin of her name, Catherine, in Jacobus de Voragine's account, does offer some concepts that Greeley repeats: "Catherine comes from *catha* 'total' and *ruina* 'ruin'; for the edifice of the Devil was wholly destroyed in her" (708). Cathy sees herself as a "nasty little rich bitch with terrible guilt feelings about the way I was raised" (*Virgin and Martyr* 403) but one who is finally reduced by physical suffering to someone with "little will or personhood left in her. She had been broken" (379). Greeley follows his theory on sainthood as Jungian integration of disparate elements—of struggle not against the physical devil, but against the inward demon. Thus the alleged dismemberment and disfigurement of Cathy is a dual device used by Greeley as a recalling of the martyrs and as a Jungian disintegration, because only after complete disintegration of self can the new self synthesize itself, just as only by separation of body and soul can the saint achieve heaven. Where Catherine of Alexandria in her role as sun goddess accepts her death by the phallic sword, she is fulfilling her integration which separated the head (reason) from the body (emotion) to form a greater union of soul with its natural end (the Godhead) or, in sexual terms, to form the marital union exemplified by the voice of Christ inviting her to "Come, My Beloved, My Spouse" (de Voragine 714).

Other facets of martyrdom are suffered by Cathy in alignment with the female martyrs, most of whom are subjected to sexual harassment in the legends. Many had their breasts ripped off as Cathy has her breasts cut off; many like Cecilia and Lucy are put into brothels to destroy their virtue, but miracles prevent their being harmed. Stripped, their hair grows to cover their nakedness; approached, they are made so heavy that they cannot be moved; tempted, they find their would-be seducers blinded or killed. Greeley, in his own way, is as delicate as early hagiographers—he gives no particulars about Cathy's frequent rapes by her captors. Why does he not protect his heroine(s) from such violation? In Cathy's case, the humiliation caused by her imprisonment and rapes is a necessary step in her spiritual journey. She needs to suffer in one way but she needs more to learn the value of trusting in God and in others. For instance, when she is being taken to Don Felipé's mountain house from which she may never escape, she is forced to kiss him; only after this act of obedience, the subjugation of her own will to the will of another, albeit an evil person, can she begin to fight back to her personhood. Because she had consistently refused the love of God through his envoy Nick, she has fallen subject to wrong loves—Roy, Ed Carny, her espoused and beloved social justice causes, and finally Don Felipé, whose misplaced "love" is sadistic.

Greeley's view toward rape is that, while it is a physical violation, it is more importantly a violation of a woman's integrity or freedom of action and choice; hell, he implies, is a woman's constant fear of being invaded. He dismisses Cathy's lack of virginity with the casual assertion that "a couple of orgasms in this day and age could hardly be held against you" (*Virgin and Martyr* 3). So also when Noele is raped in front of her boyfriend Jaimie, she is emotionally secure in herself because she is the child conceived at Easter and born on Christmas Day, as her name indicates; the legend associated with this is that anyone born on Christmas Day cannot lose his soul to the devil, so that Noele has her worst battle won and her only role is to straighten out the rest of the family's problems. Her violent loss of virginity is represented by the smashing of Saint Praxides' window; her martyrdom is in her frustrating search for self and family. Essentially, the modern martyr is one who suffers psychic tortures, like Greeley's heroes and heroines do, and the modern virgin is one who preserves his or her integrity, even if it means losing virginity or innocence in the pursuit of self-knowledge.

The ancient methods of torturing female martyrs does provide a wealth of inventive devices for a novelist like Greeley, especially since the threat of fire neatly ties in with his concept of the martyrs as atavistic sun goddesses. Quite a few, like Saint Catherine of Alexandria, could not be harmed by fire, just as Cathy cannot be burned by the sun, according to the Ryan family, because she "never burns, just tans" (39). Like the three men in the fiery furnace in the Book of Daniel and like early Roman Christians required to burn incense before a statue, most martyrs were tortured with that which was at hand—heat. Agatha had her breasts crushed and cut off before being tossed on hot coals, Saint Cecilia was partially beheaded in a suffocating bath, Saint Lucy was threatened with burning before being jugulated.

Most of these methods are used by Greeley in his martyred heroines: Lisa Malone of *Happy Are the Clean of Heart* is paralyzed and burned with cigarettes; Cathy is tortured with beatings, attempted drowning in excrement, rape, and electrical charges, the modern version of fire over which she has no control because she is not yet an integrated person. On the other hand, Noele is so tortured mentally by the specific telephone threats—to "cut off your tits" (*Lord of the Dance* 318) being the mildest of them—Greeley likens it to the modern torture by electricity so that "the shock waves of terror raced through her nervous system, as if she had touched a live electrical wire" (288). Anne Reilly of *Angels of September* is tortured by the double symbol of fire in her life—the tragic school fire and the diabolic painting.

The earliest Roman martyrs, like Felicitas and Perpetua, were killed by beasts in the Colosseum; the attempted rape, mutilation, beating, and burning methods came later. Other assaults on his heroines combine both the early Colosseum martyrdom by beasts and the sun image. Noele's relationship with her car is so strong that she names it Flame, a guardian angel that tries to defend her when she is assaulted by the van, which is Greeley's version of the beasts: "she barely saw the van before it hit her. A huge monster, like a giant bull elephant, smashed into Flame, turned him over, and extinguished all the lights in Noele's head" (*Lord of the Dance* 298). Cathy in her escape is "paralyzed . . . hypnotized by the gigantic eye of the train, like a one-eyed monster [whose] horn screeched" (*Virgin and Martyr*

387). Most of the martyrs suffer decapitation or jugulation: "the most painless death...frequently used for women...the sword, with one blow, cut the great blood vessel at the base of the neck and a massive hemmorhage brought death rapidly." (Andre-Delastre 70).

When the persecutions ended, the medieval saints "martyred" or mortified their flesh to achieve its subjugation, like Catherine of Genoa or Catherine of Siena; when modern saints mortify their flesh with misguided observances, such as Cathy does with her extreme fasting, they are rightly reprimanded that the way to become a saint is to excel "in the demands of everyday living" (*Patience of a Saint* 410).

The description of the torturers is fairly stable: in the saints' lives they are always men with governmental authority, who seem to enjoy their work or who give in to their anger at a woman defying their authority. Jaimie, Noele's faithful young knight, describes Rocco Marsallo, Noele's torturer, as a man who "enjoys beating other people to death with a baseball bat...and burning women with cigarette butts" (*Lord of the Dance*) 164), just as Cathy suffers from Don Felipé's cigarette burns and Lisa Malone suffers her beating from her attacker. Naturally, the hagiographers give them little sympathy; Greeley, on the other hand, while he sees them from the perspective of mentally ill beings who have recognizable psychotic problems, nonetheless lets his characters punish them and rejoice in it.

Despite their sufferings, the martyrs manage to reverse the order of nature on their torturers. While Ed Carny's first words to Nick are "Look at your hands, Nick. They're dripping with her blood" (*Virgin and Martyr* 3), when the martyrs' breasts or heads were cut off, milk not blood often flowed from the body. This substitution of the natural nourishing fluid for normal human blood reinforces the saint's role as supranatural beings whose laws transcend the natural. Other fluids issue from the bodies of the martyrs and saints: the oil which comes from Saint Catherine's body on Mount Sinai turns up "all over France, healing the sick and restoring sexual potency to both men and women...[with its] marvelous curative powers" (64), according to Blackie. Saint Nicholas' body also has a steady flow of miraculous oil and water flowing from it.

One minor connection is that during torture Cathy's fingers are supposed to have been broken off; answering the prayer of a monk for a relic, Catherine's legend in de Voragine makes "one of the fingers [which] broke from her hand" go to him. Another time, when a man had become lax in his devotion to her, Catherine passes him by disguised "with a veiled face, as a stranger" (715); Cathy in her disguise—"wig, glasses, and blue contact lenses, a simple disguise which could fool a lover" (*Virgin and Martyr* 387)—is not recognized by Nick until she reveals herself.

Greeley employs other particulars to link the saints' lives with those of his characters. Saint Nicholas of Myra, as described by de Voragine, was a rich young man who used his wealth "to promote God's glory" (12). The most familiar story is of Nicholas' tossing three bags of gold into the window of a destitute father's home to provide him with dowries so that he would not have to sell his daughters into prostitution. Greeley's Nick is not rich himself but he performs the same duty when he protects Cathy's money from Ed Carny, the one who has "sold" her into the prostitution of her prison. As a lawyer, Nick is an advocate for Cathy's rights, just as Nicholas is described as being "persuasive in speech, forceful in counsel" (de Voragine 18). Greeley's Nick even imitates his patron's "gravity of mien . . . [and] humility" (18); so close is this association in Blackie's mind that he describes Nick as a monk, like the Nicholas of Chaucer's "Miller's Tale," who would have been "in another and more rational age . . . a cleric, a studious responsible scholar of canon law with an even-tempered disposition that would fit well into community life" (*Virgin and Martyr* 5). Although Saint Nicholas was never a monk, Nick himself sees the similarity in his "mostly monkish life" (5) and in his timorous treatment of women.

Nick's upbringing is nothing like the saint's. He is not of parents who "having brought him into the world, abstained from all contacts of the flesh and lived in godly love (de Voragine 17). Nick's parents are seldom mentioned; his mother is a "land-grubbing, penny-pinching, perpetually whining mother" and his sisters are so "bitchy [that] Nick was defenseless when it came to women (*Virgin and Martyr* 11). With Cathy he is able to practice Nicholas' virtue of being "severe in reprimand" (de Voragine 18). Nick's one advantage is the ability to restore life to the dead like Saint Nicholas, for he brings Cathy back to life with the help of Blackie.

Greeley's casual list of categories under the patronage of Saint Nicholas provides a clue to Nick's characteristics. The sheer number and illogical relationships between the groups (bankers next to thieves, small children next to scholars) with New York City tacked on the end, throws the reader off the author's intent. While such heterogeneous grouping has no value and serves only to prove that Saint Nicholas was a panacea for lost causes, a more careful inspection shows that Greeley uses most elements in an elemental plot way—Nick is a banker, a moneyman not above "thieving" Cathy's estate from its claimants; Cathy is always with small children; she lives in New York with Roy as an essentially unmarried woman because her marriage is invalid and Roy is impotent; she is a scholar. That leaves "sailor," and Nick is certainly attached to Lake Michigan, as are most of Greeley's heroes.

On what level do the saints' lives as described above merge into Greeley's characters? He himself says that "characters do not emerge as the *tabula rasa* which liberal social science likes to think is the human personality at the beginning of life. Characters spring into existence . . . fully grown and with biases and prejudices. . . . The story teller . . . has to make do with what his preconscious has given him in the way of character fragments" (*God Game* 15). In the author's pre-conscious, with his Catholic background enhanced by his priesthood studies, the golden tradition of the Scriptures and the saints' lives are so woven into the fabric of his novels that he cannot provide an unhappy ending, because his sources see the only ending in salvation as stated in their sainthood. Yet Greeley sees that "none of my novels has a conventional happy ending [because] no one should have any illusions that life with their lovers will be simple or easy or, much less free of daily conflict... humankind is born of two incurable diseases: life, of which we all die, and hope, which says maybe death is not the end" ("In Defense" 31). Believing as he does that "religion is man's attempt to provide ultimate explanations of life... a primordial criterion for identifying with others... a strain toward the ecstatic and the transcendent" (*Religion in the Year 2000*, 99), Greeley creates his characters' lives after those models of the saints who serve as archetypal patterns of larger concepts, as familiar guides toward sainthood for the uninitiated, and as sensual living examples of those who come to realize that while "tragedy may leave the protagonist dead... it leaves us very much alive and challenged to continue" ("In Defense" 31).

WORKS CITED

Andre-Delastre, Louise. *St. Agnes*. New York: Macmillan, 1962.

Berger, Peter L. *A Rumor of Angels: Modern Society and the Rediscovery of the Supernatural*. Garden City, N.Y.: Doubleday, 1969.

Butler, Alban. *The Lives of the Saints*. Edited by Donald Attwater. New York: P. J. Kenedy, 1956.

Cruz, Joan Carroll. *The Incorruptibles: A Study of the Incorruption of the Bodies of Various Catholic Saints and Beati*. Rockford, Ill.: Tan, 1977.

de Voragine, Jacobus. *The Golden Legend*. Translated by Granger Ryan and Helmut Ripperger. New York: Longman, Green, 1941.

Greeley, Andrew M. *Angels of September*. New York: Warner, 1986.

———. *Ascent into Hell*. 1983. New York: Warner, 1984.

———. *Death in April*. 1980. New York: Dell, 1984.

———. *Ecstasy: A Way of Knowing*. Englewood Cliffs, N. J.: Prentice-Hall, 1974.

———. *The Final Planet*. New York: Warner, 1987.

———. *God Game*. New York: Warner, 1987.

———. *Happy Are the Clean of Heart*. New York: Warner, 1986.

———. "In Defense of Hopeful Endings." *Writer's Digest*, Jan. 1987, 31–34.

———. *Lord of the Dance*. New York: Warner, 1984.

———. *The Magic Cup*. New York: McGraw-Hill, 1979.

———. *The Mary Myth: On the Femininity of God*. New York: Seabury, 1977.

———. *Patience of a Saint*. New York, Warner, 1987.

———. *Religion in the Year 2000*. New York: Sheed & Ward, 1969.

———. *Thy Brother's Wife*. New York, Warner, 1982.

———. *Virgin and Martyr*. New York: Warner, 1985.

Hole, Christina. *Saints in Folklore*. New York: M. Barrows, 1965.

Keyes, Frances Parkinson. *The Life of St. Anne*. New York: Hawthorn, 1955.

Shafer, Ingrid H. *Eros and the Womanliness of God: Andrew Greeley's Romances of Renewal*. Chicago: Loyola University Press, 1986.

23

INGRID SHAFER

The Dance of Creation and Incarnation: God, Woman, and Sex in the Novels of Andrew Greeley

In his fiction Andrew Greeley spins a dazzling array of tales around the new/old double helix of the sacramental potential of human beings (most specifically women) and erotic passion. Greeley's theology flows from the nondualistic stream (separated by Thomas Aquinas from its world-denouncing Gnostic/Manichaean/Augustinian tributary) of the Catholic tradition which considers the natural world of matter and senses analogous to (and participating in) the Really Real. In this perspective, nonjudgmental maternal love and ecstatic sexual union (in a committed, caring relationship) emerge as the symbols *par excellence* for the way God relates to us.

All human beings have mothers, half the population is sexually attracted to women, and the other half generally looks for tenderness in a man. Christians believe that humanity was created male *and* female in the divine image. Thus, Greeley's focus on the neglected feminine dimensions of the divine has both a sound empirical and a sound scriptural basis. The time has definitely come, Greeley insists, for humanity to grow up, to pass from infancy to maturity and recover beyond the rod-wielding paternal God of

Reprinted, with minor revisions, from the *Journal of Popular Literature* 4 (Spring/Summer 1988): 107–124. An earlier version of this essay was presented under the title "God, Woman, and Sex in Greeley's Fiction" in a session on living authors chaired by Allienne R. Becker at the Northeast Modern Language Association Convention, Boston, 2 Apr. 1987.

proscription the maternal God of unconditional acceptance and the androgynous God of fiercely tender passion.

While feminist women theologians have been in the forefront of the struggle to transcend patriarchal stereotypes of divinity, they are certainly not alone. Among twentieth-century popes, God was seen as Mother by Angelo Roncalli (Pope John XXIII), who (like the medieval mystics Dame Julian of Norwich and Saint Bernard) employed the image of "mother" for a *caring* God, and Pope John Paul I, who perplexed theologians writing for Italian papers by casually referring to God as "Father, but, especially, Mother" (quipping, when challenged, that he had merely quoted the prophet Isaiah). Karl Rahner felt called upon to justify the use of the expression "God, our Father" as intending *not* the "hard and inhumane" paternalism of tradition, but "tender," "forgiving and merciful" grace, popularly linked with the term "mother" (*Gnade als Freiheit*). Other (male) theologians, such as Teilhard de Chardin, Edward Schillebeeckx, Henri de Lubac, and—most recently—Leonardo Boff, have eloquently addressed the issue. Even in the culturally conditioned androcentric context of first-century Judaism, Jesus compared his Father with a wealthy woman rejoicing over having found the one piece of lost silver, and himself to a brood hen and nursing mother. In 1977, shortly before he began writing novels, Andrew Greeley himself explored the question of divine androgyny in *The Mary Myth: On the Femininity of God.*

As early as 1970 (*A Future to Hope In*) Greeley had insisted that "the ideal human personality is androgynous; that is to say a complex and balanced blending of the so-called masculine and so-called feminine traits. . . . To be fully human, man needs submissiveness and woman needs assertiveness" (33–34). What makes intimate male-female relationships vital, terrifying, joyous, and sacramental is precisely the ebb and flow, challenge and response, of what Greeley calls "intimacy transformation" (*New Agenda* 139). Investing in the other is a risk, a "limit experience." We wonder what will happen to us "in the complex interchange of giving and taking, surrendering and conquering, yielding and demanding . . ." (139). Still, in the end, marriage and sexual intimacy call "forth the best of faith and hope and love within us, while simultaneously reassuring us that as we stumble out of the prison of our fears and insecurities to give ourselves in loving service to the other, we are valuable, worthwhile, and need not feel shame or inadequacy" (225).

Lovemaking (always contrasted to sex without love) between *equals* can be the closest thing to knowing how God feels about us. In *Sexual Intimacy* Greeley observes that he doubts that most married couples think of sexual intercourse as a reflection of Yahweh's passion, because "nobody has ever suggested to them that the quality of their love of which sexual intercourse is, of course, at the very center is the most effective way they have of revealing God's love . . ." (187). Now, fourteen years later, he can point to a series of novels which for his readers do precisely that, present committed sexual passion in scriptural imagery.

In *The Bottom Line Catechism* Greeley notes that "our nature as sexual persons reveals to us a dependence on the love of others, and hence, ultimately, the love that created us" (128). Sexuality is God's way of forcing or luring us (not through fear but through the promise of supreme pleasure) to acknowledge that the I-atom finds no fulfillment apart from the We-communion. Greeley continues, "The power of sexual hunger breaks us out of the hard shell of selfishness and tips the balance of the scales ever so slightly in the direction of selflessness. Our sexuality forces us to live not only for ourselves but to live for others" (128).

Ideally, sexual love allows us to receive as we give, to give as we receive; it is an invitation to radical intimacy involving perfect mutuality, a *physical* manifestation of the bipolar structure of the Cosmic Life Force, the oscillating dance of creation. "The nerves and muscles of the human body, and particularly of the human sex organs, were made to be played with by a member of the opposite sex" (*Sexual Intimacy* 100). It is in this sense that men *and* women have the right, the obligation, to expect their partners to use their bodies the way they were "intended to be used" (159). In the context of *mutual* pleasuring grounded in respect, commitment, and love, the term "using" simply denotes that we should not allow our own and the other's talents to be buried. To "use" another becomes abuse only when the motive is selfish, when the ultimate end does not involve *joint* fulfillment of a common goal. Of all human activities, lovemaking at its best is the *only* one which involves complete physical *and* spiritual "communion" (humans are the only animals who routinely have sex *face-to-face*); it is the most mutual and also the most cooperative.

Precisely for these reasons, sexuality (if severed from love) can lead to the most terrible instances of exploiting and violating another. Rape, as Greeley insists again and again, is a form of crucifixion, a Good Friday, seen, however, not only in its isolated horror but also in relation to Easter Sunday. The human tragedy becomes the divine comedy as the victim emerges as the victor. Cathy, Anne (*POS*), Noele (*LOD*), and Greeley's other rape and torture victims ultimately fight their way back from the very "gates of hell" and "rise from the dead." Thus, instances of brutalization of women in Greeley's stories are the direct result of his emphasis on the womanliness of God and represent the demonic shadow cast by the sacramental potential of sexuality. "God the Father gave His only Beloved Son" is transformed into "God the Mother gave Her only Beloved Daughter."

Greeley's "sacramentality of sexuality" is inexorably linked to his conviction that human beings are most supremely themselves when they relate lovingly, intimately, and trustingly to an other, both "The Other" (God) and "the other" (a member of the opposite sex). In *A Future to Hope In* he notes that "friendship between a man and a woman, reinforced by the throbbing

union of their bodies and preserved and enriched by the sensitive tenderness of their common life, is the model on which all human relationships
must be based." While all human friendships are potentially sacramental,
the grace experience is purest and most powerful in heterosexual union
within a committed and caring relationship. Greeley might claim empirical
validation for this assumption by pointing to the association between mystic
interludes and true *love*-making which serves as a common triggering
mechanism for such experiences (*Ecstasy* 92; *POS* passim). If we go one step
further and admit (in keeping with Incarnational theology) that we "know
God in and through our human relationships (and particularly the most
powerful of those human relationships, erotic love), it is perfectly consistent
(albeit anathema to hard-core feminists) for (heterosexual) men to imagine
God as a Woman and for (heterosexual) women to imagine God as a Man.
Nongenital friendship (particularly between members of the same sex),
while surely potentially grace-conferring, is not the occasion of ecstasy, nor
does it fully satisfy the human yearning to escape atomistic isolation and be
joined to the mysterious "other."

While the themes of the sacramental power of sex and women are
implicitly part of the Judeo-Christian heritage (surviving in the Song of
Songs, nuptial imagery and rituals, as well as some aspects of the veneration of Mary), they have been largely repressed and distorted by official
teachings. They live in popular myths, legends, plays, and stories—such as
the traditional romance, so aptly called "secular scripture" by Northrop
Frye, and most particularly the Grail cycle. (This connection is particularly
striking in Wolfram von Eschenbach's *Parzival*. See my "The Virgin and
the Grail: Archetypes in Andrew Greeley's Fiction" in this volume, especially pp. 65–67.) They are also found encoded in two millennia of artistic
conventions which link, for example, as art historian Leo Steinberg noted, a
Hellenistic bronze statue of Cupid and Psyche with numerous chastely
incestuous versions of the Madonna and Child, and dazzle us in such works
as Rubens' allegorical hymn to conjugal passion, the "Garden of Love."

Within church walls, they lurk beneath such ancient liturgical practices
as the traditional Easter vigil of plunging the phallic candle into the
archetypally feminine baptismal waters (noted by Greeley in *DIA* and
LOD), and the celebration of the Annunciation (impregnation), Christmas
(birth), and the Circumcision of the Lord (January 1). They provide the
symbolic substructure for the central Catholic mystery of transubstantiation, the moment of the consecration of bread and wine, which evokes the
instant of the Incarnation, the merging of the infinite and the finite, the
"enfleshment" of God, fertilization within a woman's ovarian duct and
descent into her womb, signified by the eucharistic cup. This most sacred
of all human actions (in the Catholic perspective) is ultimately a symbolic
reenactment of the procreative event, just as communion is a baptized form
of the pagan ritual of the eating of the god.

Leo Steinberg follows historian John O'Malley in arguing that early

Western medieval and Byzantine artists were concerned primarily with symbolically affirming the absolute Godhood of Christ, while theologians of that same period emphasized Christ's suffering, death, and resurrection. In the High Middle Ages (as my above-stated "Wolfram thesis" would support) and most emphatically during the Renaissance, Western Catholicism shifted toward a more "incarnational theology" which celebrated what Steinberg calls the "humanation" (German: *Menschwerdung*) of God and implicitly prepared the way for such twentieth-century concepts as Karl Rahner's "sacramentality of the world." One of the main manifestations of this new perspective in Catholic art was a delightful crop of very naked Christ infants, their genitalia prominently displayed, and a number of paintings of the adult Christ, seemingly tumescent beneath token loincloths, to symbolize an erection-resurrection equation (turned by Boccaccio into an explicit pun in one of his bawdier tales). Titian's portrayal of sacred love as a gloriously naked female (which a similarly "attired" Maria cites in Greeley's *AIH*) seems like another example of this insight. An additional bit of evidence for Steinberg's humanation hypothesis (not mentioned by him) is the emergence and veneration during the fourteenth and fifteenth centuries of the *vierge ouvrante*, a carved Madonna (and baptized Great Mother) whose body literally opened up, triptychlike, to reveal within her belly images of the trinity.

There are several ways in which this ideological shift can be interpreted. The generally accepted model (hailed by most "liberal" academics and decried by religious fundamentalists) depicts the post-Renaissance West in the grip of progressive secularization, citing such observable phenomena as the separation of Church and State, the declining role of the Church in education, the adoption of the scientific method to ascertain facticity, the demythologizing of scripture, "situation ethics," the rise of secular humanism. This paradigm is tacitly grounded in one of two presuppositions. The first involves an essentially non-Incarnational view of God as radically "other" and by definition separate from the world, revealed exclusively through a small canon of officially sanctioned Scripture and represented only by established churches whose dogmas and moral dicta must be accepted by believers blindly and *in toto*. The second either denies God's existence or considers the question of divine existence or nonexistence irrelevant to the human business of living in the world.

This is a view which confronts the contemporary situation through dualistic ideological spectacles directly the obverse of those worn by second-century ascetics seeking to escape what they considered an intrinsically evil and ultimately illusory material world for the only true reality of spiritual purity. It might be considered a modern-day upside-down gnosis which like its ancient counterpart splits the ontological whole into two radically opposed hemispheres and promises salvation (in the modern case *from* the "lie" of religion) through special knowledge. In sharp contrast to their Hellenistic precursors, however, contemporary "gnostics" consider the empirically quantifiable realm as the sole (albeit only provisionally "true") reality, and label the quest for transcendence and ultimate meaning an infantile delusion.

In both his sociological studies and his stories, Andrew Greeley demonstrates, argues for, and imaginatively presents an alternate paradigm, a "steady state" model of religiosity which allows for shifting modes of relating to the Really Real without insisting that our age (or any age in history) is in the final analysis less (or more) "religious" than any other. Greeley refuses to grant the contemporary gnostic's premises. God for him is neither nonexistent nor irrelevant. Furthermore, God is *both* transcendent *and* immanent; *both* totally other *and* totally familiar ("homely," as the great mystic Julian of Norwich put it). As immanent, God dwells in the world and is revealed precisely in and through the ways human beings relate to one another, and most specifically the ways they love one another, spiritually *and* physically.

As a priest Greeley posits the presence of a living, gracious, personal God who is "in love" with each and every one of us. As a sociologist he finds this God in neighborhood communities. As a man he envisions this God as a woman, his anima, his muse, a cross between Saint Brigid (Mary of the Gael), Jessica Lange of *All That Jazz,* and the proverbial "girl next door," the "Daughter of Jerusalem" turned "Mother from Sligo" (*POS* 80). Greeley's "shocking" use of erotic imagery to symbolize divine passion is not only true to the nuptial and erotic language of the Old Testament (not yet bowdlerized by Hellenistic life- and world-negation), it is also directly connected to Catholic Incarnationalism and points toward Jesus' self-identification as the "Son of Man" who dwells incognito among us (Matt. 25: 31–46).

Leo Steinberg considers Christ's Renaissance sexuality not the beginning of a profaning, demythicizing naturalism, but a sophisticated artistic code for expressing the early modern emergent consciousness of the humanation of God, a humanation which, implicit in the Christ event, had taken fourteen hundred years to become explicit, and which with Rubens would explode in a riot of color and light, angel-winged cupids and pagan deities gathered together to celebrate fruitful nuptial passion, allowing nature and all of history to serve as the "bread and wine" in a cosmic eucharistic consecration. When challenged by the harsh Protestant (particularly Calvinist) iconoclastic call to turn away from this earth and its enticing lure, Catholic artists responded with works reflecting a world so confident of being divinely grounded that neither the celebration of sensuality nor the presence of pagan conventions could in any way detract from this state of blessedness.

Seen in this perspective, and despite post-Reformation magisterial Catholic withdrawal into fearful siege rigidity and reactionary authoritarianism (or the Deists' distant God of impersonal philosophic abstraction), the modern period can be interpreted not as one of creeping secularization, but as one of progressive and universal "divinization" (of God present, though largely unrecognized, in the world), a position without which Georg Wilhelm Friedrich Hegel's _Phenomenology of Spirit_ is opaque to the reader and the Romantic movement makes no sense. Even Ludwig Feuerbach's radical humanism and denial of the transcendent God can be interpreted in this manner if joined to his enthusiastic endorsement of the _human_ potential for holiness and goodness. Our age allows us to discover God in and through nature, science, scholarship, the arts, literature, and human relationships, through intuition _and_ reason—_if_ post-Cartesian anthropocentrism is linked with Incarnational theology. It is in this spirit that the Jesuit Father Richard Blake noted in a review of the controversial film _Hail Mary_ that as he watched the film "the Word . . . was made flesh" for him, "not an idea, but wondrously and beautifully through the cells and fluids of a woman's body" (_America_ Nov. 1985).

Truly, the time has come to transcend (not deny but fulfill or complete) the Transcendent "Father/Judge/King" God (whose absolutization split the world into two antithetical realms and severed Her/His primordial androgyny) and appropriate for the present and future the Incarnation in the second naiveté (Paul Ricoeur); to look for God once again in the world of the senses and recover divine _fullness_ by exploring His long-neglected femininity (as essential as Her traditional masculinity).

Who is this feminine dimension of the divine, largely absent in the dominant conventional Judeo-Christian God-image of the elite: this Woman God, this Lady Wisdom, this Cosmic Nymphomaniac, this Divine Comedienne, who lurks in the popular tales and symbols of the Judeo-Christian tradition and leaps out of Greeley's stories?

First of all, let us look at Greeley's Woman God in terms of human categories like those we might apply to a summer love or fiancé or spouse. A note of caution is in order at this point: the vivid descriptive detail in Greeley's fiction might tempt us to judge his stories by the standards of realistic fiction and forget that those tales are not literary videotapes of human interaction, but consciously crafted parables designed to illustrate the workings of grace in and through the elements of human experience. It is not Greeley's primary intention to imitate the external world, but to render that world transparent to the mystery within and beyond; to express the ineffable in humanly accessible universal images; to fascinate and illuminate. Since his real subject, the one ever-present protagonist of his fiction, is God Herself, his paradigmatic sacramental woman (though of course occasionally both deaf and blind to God's love and her own strength and goodness) is in many ways "super woman"—at once dream, beacon, horizon, and inspiration.

Herself is young and old, tall and short; a blonde, a redhead, a brunette; both countess and waitress, both water waif and Lady Wisdom; a cool glass of lemonade on a hot day, a warm refuge in a blizzard. She is at ease with computers, children, and most of all herself; a professional artist, banker, writer, lawyer, psychiatrist, business executive, *and* passionate lover. She likes being a woman, knows how to play, and enjoys sailing, waterskiing, and designer clothes. She is generally a chocolate addict who is crazy about raspberries and not averse to an occasional sip of Bailey's Irish Cream. Sometimes She is even a man—like Father Blackie, Nick Curran, or Mike Casey, all of whom manifest the archetypally feminine traits of nurturance and tenderness. Her eyes are often green or blue. She is never fat and never flat (unless She is male), always intelligent, and generally Irish.

Precisely because of Greeley's fondness for sacramental Celtic females, it is highly significant that his most spectacular Woman God (and luminous prototype for all the others) is not Irish, but one hundred percent Italian: Maria Manfredy of *Ascent into Hell*, who saves the Irish priest Hugh Donlon from the psychological equivalent of Dante's frozen pit of hell. Since there is a close association between Woman God and the Church as nonjudgmental, passionately tender, maternal presence, Maria represents a latter-day caring complement to Roman self-righteous imperiousness (exemplified as early as A.D. 663 by Latin claims upon the Irish Church at the Synod of Whitby). Maria's role in Hugh's life constitutes Greeley's veiled affirmation that it is his intense loyalty to the Real Roman Church of Communal Love which inspires his unrelenting struggle against her authoritarian and inflexibly legalistic perversion.

Next, let us focus on the God aspect of Woman God by weaving appropriate passages from Greeley's fiction into a composite analogical portrait arranged by four categories.

MYSTERIUM FASCINANS ET TREMENDUM

She is the one who makes us want to run and whom we can't escape—though we are never quite sure whether to run toward Her or away from Her (*VAM* 337). Both supremely fascinating and utterly terrifying (*LOD* 212), She lures us into the depth of Her Selfhood (*FP* 126; *DIA* 83), which might also be our very own self, filled with joy and life . . . and love (*AIH* 44). Does Her radiance spell Life or Death? Is Her beauty the end of all our yearning or a trap, a dangerous garden with deadly flowers, a cold, slimy cave in disguise (*FP* 193), a sailboat in the clouds bound to capsize and drop us straight into the fire-belching crater of a volcano (*AIH* 158)? Are we but gnats with a fatal attraction for Her consuming flame (*DIA* 79, 83; *TBW* 167)? Are Her waters those of birth and baptism, or eternal damnation (*TBW* 167)?

MADONNA ET MATER ALMA
(Great and Nourishing Mother)

Our head against the softness of Her breast, we fall, fall back into childhood and beyond into the primal waters whence we came (FP 127; AIH 356). Her milk is sweet and warm, Her breast a communion chalice, a sacrament, generously offered to the tormented archbishop (CS 235), the passing stranger in a foreign land (ROS 139), Her husband (AIH 7). She is the One who mothers all of us according to our needs; an enveloping, caressing, encouraging, reassuring Presence which absorbs, bathes, and soothes us, dissolving all our night terrors in gentle laughter (TBW 276, 302; LOD 378). She is the One who has always loved us and always will no matter how much we hide from Her, forever waiting to snatch us out of the very jaws of hell (AIH 456). She is peace, joy, forgiveness; She is what is most gentle in all the women in the world, nursing, healing, loving us; pure radiance which cleanses and renews (CS 30).

THE PARACLETE: LIGHT, FIRE, PETER PAN

She is the Holy Spirit, the Paraclete, the spirit of courage which translates hope into action, a cosmic Tinker Bell flitting about the universe in ever-new manifestations (ROS 267–68). She appears, Lady Cardinal Deirdre, like Moses' burning bush in a cloud of smoke, a female Zeus, hurtling lightning bolts from her Brigid crozier (FP 284–85). Her long red hair piled high like a flaming strawberry ice-cream cone (LOD 396), She rescues us from a burning boat (DIA 42) or Lucifer's burning house (HAM 241), dragging all of us into heaven by the skin of our teeth (or other available parts of our anatomy) (AOS 2). She leaps out at us from our wife's green eyes and the gracefully curved green glass tower in a modern city, halting time, opening us up to the universe, dissolving our identity in the fires of ecstatic love, destroying, transforming us in the crucible of pleasure and joy (POS 13–14).

LOVE AGAINST DEATH

She is the one who dissolves pain and death into laughter and resurrection. Her love is stronger than death, and it is ours whether we want it or not. We have absolutely no choice (though, of course, we are free to reject the gift, thus in a sense creating our personal hells) (CS 306). She is the power of springtime renewal who cracks and melts our winter glacier (AIH 356) and covers the rolling fields with flowers (AIH 352). She is irresistible Grace which sneaks through the cracks and crannies of our personalities, takes possession of the random openings we give it, and then, when we least expect it, when we have done everything in our power to stop it, BANG! there's the big surprise (*VAM* 13). She loves us, and we wonder what She sees in us (*POS* 81–82). She is an implacable and impulsive Love, one that forgives without being asked, never turns away from the beloved, and wants only that the beloved surrender to Love and be happy. We cannot hide from Her, escape from Her, turn away from Her. There is no exit (*AIH* 366). Unlike Sartre's, Her motto is not "Hell is Other People," but "Heaven is Other People."

Here you have Her, seen not under the aspects of Magic Princess and Holy Grail as the present writer describes Her in *Eros and the Womanliness of God*, but portrayed as the Eternal Feminine at once our mother, our childhood sweetheart, the most passionate flesh-and-blood lover we can embrace, and a magnificent divine spider who dances across the cosmos spinning her invisible web of grace to trap and save each and every one of Her wayward children. Fascinating and terrifying, all-nourishing and all-consuming, the water of baptism and the fire of the crucible, She is that Love, that divine *hesed* which conjoined to *zedek* (righteousness) created the universe; that Love, to quote Dante, "that moves the sun in heaven and all the stars." In honored Celtic tradition She pursues Her chosen with a vengeance, entwining them in silver threads and pulling them, kicking and screaming, through and beyond darkness and death toward the upper regions of joyous ecstasy and eternal life. In Her, with Her, and through Her "we shall be young once more, we shall laugh again" (*Confessions* 77).

WORKS CITED

Texts

Greeley, Andrew M. *Death in April*. 1980. New York: Dell, 1984.   [*DIA*]

———. *The Cardinal Sins*. New York: Warner, 1981.   [*CS*]

———. *Thy Brother's Wife*. New York: Warner, 1982.   [*TBW*]

———. *Ascent into Hell*. New York: Warner, 1983.   [*AIH*]

———. *Lord of the Dance*. New York: Warner, 1984.   [*LOD*]

———. *Virgin and Martyr.* New York: Warner, 1985.   [*VAM*]

———. *Happy Are the Meek*. New York: Warner, 1985.   [*HAM*]

———. *Angels of September.* New York: Warner, 1986.   [*AOS*]

———. *Patience of a Saint*. New York: Warner, 1987.   [*POS*]

———. *The Final Planet*. New York: Warner, 1987.   [*FP*]

———. *The Rite of Spring*. New York: Warner, 1987.   [*ROS*]

Other Sources

Greeley, Andrew M. *A Future to Hope In*. New York: Image, 1970.

———. *Sexual Intimacy*. Chicago: Thomas More, 1973.

———. *Ecstasy: A Way of Knowing*. Englewood Cliffs, N.J.: Prentice-Hall, 1974.

———. *The New Agenda*. New York: Image, 1975.

———. *The Mary Myth: On the Femininity of God*. New York: Seabury, 1977.

———. *The Bottom Line Catechism*. Chicago: Thomas More, 1982.

———. *Confessions of a Parish Priest: An Autobiography*. New York: Simon & Schuster, 1986.

Shafer, Ingrid H. *Eros and the Womanliness of God: Andrew Greeley's Romances of Renewal*. Chicago: Loyola University Press, 1986.

Steinberg, Leo. *The Sexuality of Christ in Renaissance Art and in Modern Oblivion*. New York: Pantheon, 1983.

TABULATION OF SOURCE TEXTS

MYSTERIUM FASCINANS ET TREMENDUM

ROLE

BOOK	GOD	HUMAN	PAGE						
DIA	*Lynnie*	*Jim*	33	49	79	83	87	99	247
CS	*Ellen*	*Kevin*	211						
TBW	*Nora*	*Paul*	74	169					
	Angèlica	*Sean*	137						
	Nora	*Sean*	167						
AIH	*Maria*	*Hugh*	44	47	121	158	268	357	358	364
LOD	*Irene*	*Roger*	212						
	Irene	*Danny*	287	317	392				
VAM	*Nick*	*Cathy*	255–56	397	428				
	Cathy	*Roy*	281						
AOS	*Anne*	*Mike*	26	37	42	43	67		
	Mike	*Ann*	42	60	126	288			
POS	*Eileen*	*Red*	12	154	312	343			
	Red	*Eileen*	312						
	Red	*Helga*	161						
FP	*Sammy*	*Seamus*	126						
	Margie	*Seamus*	165	168	193				

MADONNA ET MATER ALMA

ROLE

BOOK	GOD	HUMAN	PAGE					
DIA	Lynnie	Jim	21	64				
CS	Ellen	Kevin	18					
	Ellen	Patrick	30	251				
	Maureen	Patrick	235					
TBW	Mary Jane	Sean	17					
	Nora	Sean	31	60	276	302		
	Nora	Paul	105	107	169	276		
	Sean	Sandra	98					
AIH	Peggy	Tom	6	7				
	Liz	Hugh	180					
	Maria	Hugh	355	356	357	367		
LOD	Irene	Danny	322					
	Noele		378					
VAM	Nick	Cathy	346	420				
	Cathy	Kids	63					
AOS	Anne	Mike	99	101				
POS	Eileen	Red	73	79	80	161	166	341	343
	Red	Daughters	226					
	Red	Eileen	73	80	313	341	426	
FP	Sammy	Seamus	127					
ROS	Marie	Brendan	139					

THE PARACLETE: LIGHT, FIRE, PETER PAN

ROLE

BOOK	GOD	HUMAN	PAGE						
DIA	Lynnie	Jim	13	42	57	79	84	244	
CS	Ellen	Kevin	280						
TBW	Nora	Sean	28	30					
	Nora		42						
AIH	Maria	Hugh	15	24	29	31	257	277	336	365
LOD	Noele	Family	79	286	395				
	Noele	Danny	252	394	396				
VAM	Cathy		326	401-2		437			
AOS	Anne		2						
	Mike	Anne	101	217					

BOOK	GOD	HUMAN	PAGE
POS	Red		3 13 14 39 46 49 65 75–76
			166 178 279 312 334 408 412
			440–41
	Eileen	Red	66 73 83 151 250 252 343 440–41
	Red	Eileen	81 82 250
FP	Deirdre	Seamus	284–85

LOVE AGAINST DEATH

ROLE

BOOK	GOD	HUMAN	PAGE
DIA	Lynnie	Jim	52 57 99 124
	Jim		100
CS	Ellen	Kevin	17 280 306
	Kevin	Maureen	306
	Ellen	Maureen	306
	Maureen	Children	62
TBW	Sean	Paul	12
	Nora	Sean	60
	Nora		246
AIH	Maria	Hugh	18 45 257 334 341 352 356
			366–67
	Liam	Marge	100
	Hugh		155
LOD	Irene	Danny	185
	Noele	Rapists	344
	Noele	Family	378
	Noele		378
VAM	Cathy		13 401–2 415 437
	Cathy	Indians	307
	Cathy		393 396
	Nick	Cathy	422 430 438
AOS	Anne		27 48–49 61 217 343
	Dick	Anne	144–45
	Anne	Mike	272
	Mike	Anne	293 417
	Mary Kate	Anne	409 411
POS	Eileen	Red	23 75 81–82 133 151 154 183
			184 191 344
	Red	Eileen	154 191 306 327
	Red		146

V

Exploring the Labyrinth: Mysteries and Speculative Fiction

24

RAY B. BROWNE

Expanding Parameters of Crime Fiction: George C. Chesbro and Andrew Greeley

The detective story as a literary genre began and developed in its early years as a formulaic way of approaching its subject. The subject was the disruption of society by an act of violence. The guilty party needed to be found, and through this act the pieces of society were restored and the feeling of safety and security in society reinstated. Conventional wisdom was that the detective story by definition was limited in its scope and approach. John Cawelti represented this point of view quite well when he stated: "The angle of vision enforced by the conventions of the classical detective story is inevitably a limited one, because its basic assumptions are bound to the social and ideological patterns of Western bourgeois democracies in the 19th and 20th centuries."

However, genres of literature have a way of developing with a life of their own, and of therefore breaking out of the assumptions and strictures of the past and developing new purposes and means of attaining them. Such has been the case of the detective story. Partially because of the decline of the Western novel in the United States and for other reasons which are primarily philosophical, social, aesthetic, and financial, the detective story has broken its bounds and developed into the broader crime fiction, and

Reprinted, with minor revisions, from the *Journal of Popular Literature* 4 (Spring/Summer 1988): 59–76.

with this development a whole new set of parameters has developed. Crime fiction is now vigorously spreading out in all directions and including virtually all aspects of life and society within its bounds. As it develops, more people are getting into the act, thus bringing in many people whose primary purpose is not merely to show society threatened and reassured but, although they are using crime fiction as a medium, to develop many new ideas and areas not hitherto thought to be within the province of detective fiction.

For example, more academics are writing about crime in academia; more clerics are writing about crime in the Church; firemen have laid down the fire hose and taken up the fountain pen; housewives have put aside the vacuum cleaner for the typewriter; lawyers are pleading their cases between book covers rather than before the bench. These writers—and many other kinds—are democratizing and ventilating areas of civilization and culture which in the past were considered sacrosanct—or uninteresting. Professional writers like the two English authors Ruth Rendell and P. D. James are exploring the psychology of crime victims and criminals. John D. MacDonald expanded his subjects to include ecology and environment, Ross Macdonald enriched his excellent stories with Freudian needs and substitutions. Many Americans, especially new ones like Joan Hess and Teri White, are searching for the humanistic impulses between individuals and in society.

Two of the leading authors of this new kind of crime fiction are George C. Chesbro, author of half a dozen books, and especially noteworthy in his latest two books, *Two Songs the Archangel Sings* and *Veil*, and Father Andrew Greeley, best-selling author of what he likes to think of as modern parables or novels of grace. Together these two authors bring significant new dimensions into the genre of crime fiction.

Chesbro in his earlier books had involved an unusual person, a four-foot-six-inch dwarf who is a Ph.D. professor at an uptown New York City university, who is also a black-belt karate expert and an ex-performer in the circus. But in these two latest books, this individual, given the heroic name of simply Mongo, is much more than conventional hero or trickster. He serves the societal purpose that both hero and trickster serve, but also much more.

In one of the earlier books, *City of Whispering Stone*, Chesbro has Garth, Mongo's normal brother, who is a member of the NYPD, kill the woman he loves in order to save Mongo. The woman, named Neptune, is evil, and thus deserved to die. But after the death, Garth asks his brother: "Do you suppose this is what they mean by 'male bonding'?" and Mongo says he thinks so, that is, the negative side of "bonding."

In *An Affair of Sorcerers* Chesbro makes his statement more comprehensively, effectively, and affirmatively. One villainess has been destroyed, while another female—named April to symbolize spring and a new beginning of life for Mongo—has saved Mongo both physically and spiritually by giving of herself freely and willingly. Having been denuded of all humanhood and will through torture and deprivation, Mongo had tried to isolate himself from all humanity, especially from April, the symbol. But she, wanting to have Mongo rejoin society, ritualistically begins to cleanse him of his past and to reintroduce him into the brotherhood of man. She does this through the age-old ritual of bathing the individual, then of going to bed with him. But the sex she employed in her ritual was far more than mere intercourse. As Mongo said of the encounter, in his "exhausted state sex was the farthest thing from my mind. April was offering me her wholeness, her *self*. Lying in her arms, my face pressed against the soft flesh of her breasts, I could hear her heart beating; I felt safe." To Mongo, "Offering me her body was an *act* of love, not making love."

April is Mother Earth, ritualistically joining herself with mankind in order to have from the union a glorious transformation develop. What develops is love which includes more than sex. It is brotherhood and sisterhood and wholeness which bonds people and society together. This bonding is made spiritual in addition to mythological when Chesbro has Mongo reenact a scene reminiscent of Herman Melville's famed sequence in *Moby Dick*, when the Puritan minister ascends to his pulpit to preach and pulls the rope ladder up behind him, thus isolating himself from humanity, only to discover that the true meaning of humanity is love and brotherhood. Mongo serves as both a mythological and a quasi-religious individual who symbolizes the bond that binds mankind together.

This bonding takes new development in Chesbro's two latest books, *Two Songs the Archangel Sings* and *Veil* (both 1986). These books not only develop Chesbro's older themes but blaze new trails into the nature of reality and reflection in, or control of, art. Art, perhaps because of its potential for violence, is increasingly coming into crime fiction as a subject or background for development. One of the oldest American painters of this type is John Jericho, six-foot six-inch giant created by Hugh Pentecost (Judson Philips), a violent painter who "paints what he sees and feels in vivid colors" and who is "a sucker for the helpless, for the lost causes of individuals and groups." Various other writers use the crime story genre because it allows them probings that other genres, they think, does not tolerate. For example, Peter Clother, art critic, poet, and novelist turned to crime fiction, in a novel like *Dirty-Down*, to explore the workings of modern art. The art world introduces not only a new background for crime stories but also new dimensions in the workings of the human soul and hand.

No one really investigates the fields more dramatically or searchingly than Chesbro in his two latest novels. Although both develop through and around the conventional characters Garth and Mongo, actually they center on a new character named Veil Kendry who is the cause of the action in one book, *Two Songs the Archangel Sings*, and the center of action in the other, *Veil*. Since it is impossible to tell externally which book Chesbro wrote first, we can more easily begin with *Two Songs*, which involves our familiar dwarf, Mongo, and his policeman brother, Garth.

In this book Mongo drops by the Greenwich Village loft of his artist friend Veil Kendry to see how he is getting along. Mongo has known his friend for some ten years, and recognizes that he is a most unusual and violent person. His background Mongo does not know. What were his antecedents before he came to New York Mongo has never inquired into because he feels that to ask would be an invasion of privacy. Mongo knows only that Veil Kendry is a most unusual painter. He paints large mosaics that cover an entire wall, then he cuts the large picture into smaller squares, frames them, and sells them as successful and meaningful pictures. He does not paint portraits; all of his works are mystical landscapes, ethereal and wispy, best seen through the corner of one's eye, and with the assumption that another world, another reality, is trying to intrude into human consciousness.

When he drops in to see his friend, Mongo discovers that Kendry has gone, leaving all the lights burning in the apartment, and has left Mongo a hard-to-find note that says in its oblique way that Kendry has been frightened out of his normal life-style and gone underground to achieve some purpose. The message is in the form of a painting that some powerful people want who are willing to kill many times for it. Mongo starts out to find his friend and assist him. He is beaten up, nearly killed, persecuted by an unknown individual. The trail to find the evil ones leads to upstate New York and the Catskills and finally back to Washington, D.C. Throughout the attacks on him and his brother, Mongo and Garth are saved in the nick of time by an unseen individual who can slink through woods, fences, locked doors, and use his immense power as a karate expert to rescue his friends from any danger.

The story climaxes in Washington, D.C., before a Senate committee that is investigating the appointment of an individual, Orville Madison, who has been nominated to be Secretary of State. Members of the committee are all obviously in favor of the nomination no matter what dirt might be raised about Madison's past and the necessity of blocking such a madman from the position. The ending of the novel is a fanciful one. In the locked-door room of the committee's meeting, while Mongo and Garth testify, Kendry appears from nowhere and threatens the senators; Garth, who throughout the book has been suffering some kind of mental imbalance which seems to indicate that he is going mad, shoots Madison twice before he is carted off to the insane asylum for observation and probable death. The cause of the whole affair was that Madison, the nominee for Secretary of State, has a dirty past, created when he was head of the CIA and stationed in Southeast Asia, where he headed every possible kind of dirty-trick operation, including child prostitution, murder, and massacres, and then imported his Southeast Asian puppets and allies into the United States to further his lust for power. All this information was contained in the symbolism of the picture that Kendry had painted and turned over to Mongo and which the forces of evil were trying to find. The ending of the book is fanciful—

as the whole book is—and just a bit incredible. But it contains a message and probing that are carried further in the other book of the pair. That message is male bonding and the need for compassion and assistance for other individuals. The need covers both of Mongo's companions.

Garth has been carted off to an insane asylum, probably to die there. Mongo recognized that he must continue to serve his brother. As he said: "From now on, I thought, my life belonged to my brother." So he would serve his brother. But he also had another to serve, Veil, for, Mongo realized, "Veil, with his injured arm, would certainly need help." And need it Veil does, for no sooner does Mongo stake himself out so he can see Veil's apartment with him working in it than the lights go out, and Mongo rushes over, Beretta in hand, to see who has attacked his friend this time. In this world people always need help.

Veil, Chesbro's second book in this series, is the story of the years Veil Kendry spent before coming to New York City and taking up painting as a way of making a living and releasing all the pent-up passion and hate that he had accumulated working for the CIA and for himself as private investigator in Southeast Asia.

In this book Veil is invited to a mysterious institute on the West Coast of the United States, where he is supposed to mix with other geniuses while the director and his staff try to find out what makes geniuses work, what drives and directs them. It soon becomes apparent, however, that there is more afoot in this institute than meets the printed announcement, or that somebody is out to eliminate Veil. His first day there, a blond giant emerges from the swimming pool where Veil is working out and tries to murder him. Though tired and somewhat confused, Veil manages to kill his assailant. Then he goes on a search to find out who is out to kill him. What he finds out ties in directly with what is going on at the institute, and this reveals very well Chesbro's expansion of the parameters of crime fiction.

The institute is interested in what they call the Lazarus People—that is, people who are clinically but not biologically dead and therefore have passed on into a state of experience which is extrasensory and extra-experiential.

In this state the Lazarus People find complete happiness, suspended, as it were, from care, from pain, from everything except a longing to remain forever in the bower of bliss. But being biologically alive, they can return to consciousness and life, often trailing clouds of regret and looking forward to returning to the state of suspended pain and life.

Kendry, it turns out, has been invited to the institute because through his paintings the director of the institute has seen that Kendry, although he does not know it, is one of the Lazarus People. He was once clinically dead, at the age of three, and his artwork reflects that state in a language which he intuitively and unconsciously employs and which communicates to other people who have made the same trip. Again, the secrets of the paintings are to be viewed and understood only obliquely, when the eye sees the painting without the restrictions of cold logic and reality.

Veil is one of the most violent persons in crime fiction, more violent than John Jericho; Veil's use of violence is almost pathological. Despite or because of his violent past, Kendry is attracted to and becomes fast friends with the director of the institute, Jonathan Pilgrim. He also falls in love with Sharon Solow, Pilgrim's beautiful associate, who is in charge of the Lazarus People research.

The degree of Chesbro's interest in the subject of the transitional state between life and death may be revealed in the degree to which he pushes the development in this book. Pilgrim—obviously symbolically named—has been to the "Lazarus Gate," loved it there, and wants to go back. His research at the institute is something of a symbolic way of staying at the Gate. According to psychiatrist Dr. Solow, Pilgrim is in love with Lady Death and wants to embrace her forever. Pilgrim approaches death and because of his unwillingness to fight for life is about to cross the threshold at the Lazarus Gate and die biologically. He could return to life if he willed it, but he does not.

Because he can approach the Lazarus Gate and return if he so wills, Kendry goes to it to try to talk Pilgrim into the desire to return to real life. But he finds Pilgrim happy where he is and with no wish to come back to a life which is stale, dry, and painful in comparison with that in the Lazarus Country. Kendry knows that in approaching the Gate he is jeopardizing his life, because he may or may not be able to return to regular life. But he is willing to take the risk because he admires and likes Pilgrim—a continuation of the Chesbro theme of sacrifice that one individual is willing to make for another, the bonding that makes life bearable and useful.

The plot thickens. Kendry is having a hard time at the Lazarus Gate convincing Pilgrim to return to this world. Sharon, back in the everyday world, is lonesome for the man she loves, Kendry, and the man she admires, Pilgrim. So she decides to try to join them at the Gate and either stay there with them or convince them to return. When she joins them, she complicates matters because apparently she is having more difficulty than they in returning. But so deep is her love and respect that she is willing to take the risk. And she is in great jeopardy. She keeps disintegrating in Kendry's arms, with him fighting all the time to make her corporeal and return her to life.

Obviously this material is the stuff dreams are made of. Chesbro recognizes that, and develops his novel through twin thrusts of reality and dreams. Since he has been to the Lazarus Gate, Kendry is able to dream—just as he is able to make dream paintings which are real truth only to other dreamers. Chesbro has spent much of the novel *Veil* investigating the power, direction, and secrets of dreaming. Often the chapters in the novel alternate, with Kendry dreaming in one and back in the wide-awake world in the next.

As the final seconds of *Veil* tick off, Chesbro sets about explaining his concept of dreams. He talks about Veil Kendry and his gift: "Vivid dreaming is his gift and affliction, the lash of memory and a guide to justice, a mystery and sometimes the key to mystery, prod to violence and maker of peace, an invitation to madness and the fountainhead of his power as an artist."

But through dreams, apparently, Kendry achieves the highest form of statement of human beings, that of transcendental love, of the bonding of one person to another. Together, in the land beyond reality that is the world of dream, Kendry and Sharon "reaffirm the truth that love and courage, while not antidotes to death, are the heart and spine of hope. They meet and talk many times—of their love, of the near death experience, and of dreaming and escaping from dreams. Then in one dream, when all the mechanical things have been disconnected from her body, Sharon is able to allow Veil gently to lift her in the arms of his mind and roll her away with him. . . ."

The two novels, especially the second, which is used to explain much of the first, are experimental probings. They are studies in the psychology and reality of dreams. As such they are extraordinary. Both books are also reaffirmations of Chesbro's larger message about the indispensable value of love and friendship, of the bonding and power of community. Without love and friendship, all things disintegrate. *With* them, disintegration does not matter.

Father Andrew Greeley is another writer of crime fiction who expands the horizons, techniques, purposes, and accomplishments of crime fiction. Of all writers of crime fiction he surely is one of the more "serious" and "high-minded," in that in this fiction, as in his other forms of writing, he says he wants to win the souls of men and women to God. His fiction carries the freight of a philosophy more characteristic of the pulpit than of the "mean streets" of much crime fiction.

Whatever genre Greeley is writing in—his well-known novels of divine love and grace, or science fiction or crime fiction—he usually is suggesting a sermon, trying to demonstrate that God loves everybody and that every-body should come back to Her. In crime fiction Greeley thus preaches an ecumenical catholic philosophy which includes everyone and which results in novels that are quite unusual and that broaden and enrich the genre, making it more religious and more humanistic. The result is a kind of religious humanism which resonates in the genre with a different tone and message. To achieve his purpose, Greeley has designed his book on crime fiction to take up different Beatitudes from Christ's Sermon on the Mount, to give each a modern and up-to-date interpretation and then to see how they fare in present-day society.

The first in the series, *Happy are the Meek* (1985), develops a complicated plot. The object of the crime is a mean and sadistic man who has been killed in a double-locked room: so the mystery is a locked-room within a locked-room mystery. Each character is passionate, lustful, especially the men. Often the women appear to be mere female bodies—with no brains—

but as the story develops they become strong and well-developed individuals and personalities. Greeley's style of presenting the story is potentially
confusing. Each character speaks in the first person, in separate chapters; so
the novel is a series of first-person accounts developed in concurrently
unfolding chapters. But Greeley is an accomplished novelist; so he carries
off the potentially confusing parallel tales with clarity and character development. Leading unrelentingly toward an obvious conclusion, the novel
ends with a surprise, and a surprising attitude on the part of the author.

The leading character is the Reverend Monsignor John Blackwood Ryan,
S.T.L., Ph.D., called Blackie, a very effective Reverend Eye. In the hands
of the veteran author, Blackie hits the boards walking at full speed, of
course. But he is not quite yet the full and multi-appealing character that he
will become in later books. Blackie is, Greeley has said, most like himself of
all the characters he has developed. Blackie is at least a part-memory of G.
K. Chesterton's Father Brown, as Greeley constantly reminds the reader.
But Blackie is less Brown than Brown is, is more Blackie than Greeley
sometimes seems to want to admit. Blackie is a little absentminded, a little
diffident, somewhat given to mysterious twinkles in the eyes, and to
presenting the side rather than the front of his character. He is somewhat
literary, as indeed the whole book is; Greeley obviously likes to have echoes
of other literary works in his ears. But Blackie rises far above the literary
ghosts. He has a very sane view of life, and takes himself with an ironic
grain of salt. For example, he says at the beginning of *Happy are the Meek*,
vis-à-vis the work he can do in the Church and confessional: "You'd be
surprised at how many bleeding statues stop bleeding in my office in Holy
Name Cathedral Rectory." Called the Punk by those who know him best,
Blackie is the Catholic Church's Everyman, and as such he is a useful
instrument in pushing Greeley's belief that he and his fiction are solid and
useful instruments of the Church.

For Greeley has a purpose which transcends the limits of the crime novel.
In these novels he is concerned with mankind's relationship with God.
Greeley feels that man tries to work out a contract with God which is
binding especially on Her part; we pay the price and God is duty-bound to
fulfill Her part of the contract. Greeley feels that God's love, far from being
contractual, is freely given, not subject to rules, and therefore mankind
should interpret the Scriptures freely, especially the Beatitudes, which
represent an important part of God's words to mankind through Jesus
Christ.

Greeley retranslates the Beatitudes. Thus the King James Version of
"Blessed are the meek, for they shall inherit the earth," should be modern-
ized into the meek being "those who are in harmony with the present
processes of life, not those who try to suppress the processes with sweetness
or compulsive responsibility." So biblical Beatitudes and other messages are
in Greeley's mind positive rather than negative and inhibiting forces.

In the second of his three crime fiction books, *Happy Are the Clean of Heart* (1986), Greeley makes his question very clear. He wants to know whether the "pure in heart," as announced in the eighth verse of Saint Matthew's recording of Christ's Sermon on the Mount, are really blessed and what does "pure in heart" really mean, in new and contemporary translations. Greeley himself believes that, despite what the Church has taught in the past, purity of heart does not mean "immunity to erotic images or longings." That kind of negation, he believes, "belongs, perhaps, to angels, and, perhaps, to us after we are dead." Moreover, he adds, "it is not at all clear that very many people would opt for such purity of heart. Life without erotic longings might be easier, but it would certainly be much more dull." "Cleanliness of heart" (King James Version: "Blessed are the pure in heart"), in Saint Matthew's Gospel, Greeley insists, "Means integrity of motivation, clear-headedness about the reasons for our behavior, honesty to ourselves about the purposes of our actions, a vigorous resistance to self-deception and, especially, refusal to succumb to the insidious, demoralizing, and pervasive vice of envy to be intimidated by those who have succumbed to that vice." This book tests the virility of love over envy.

Happy Are the Clean of Heart has a clear-cut case of the desire of personal growth to the limit of one's individual ability, especially in the enjoyment of erotic beauty, and the counterweight of envy. Lisa Malone, a famous singer who may have passed her prime, precipitates a crisis in her world, as well as in the world at large, by making a movie in which she appears in what seems to be but is not complete nudity and sings and acts in sexually suggestive ways. In deciding to make the move, she, at least in her own words and justification, had far more than lust and greed as her motivations: "When I decided to try to turn *The Friendship Factor* to a film and at the same time demonstrate to everybody that the erotic attractiveness of a woman's body could be an integral part of a great film performance, for the first time in my life I was responding to God's call. It took a lot of nerve. I was afraid I'd fail and be humiliated. I was even more afraid that I would succeed and maybe be destroyed completely because I had succeeded." In other words, for her to succeed in showing God's grace in the erotic attractiveness of the female body, she would fail, because her motivation and accomplishment would be misunderstood, and tarnished by envy.

In fact, in attempting the movie, Lisa Malone chanced the fate that she feared even more than success—that of being false to God's wish that people be true to those they love and owe loyalty to, and of therefore being forced to be alone, cut off from friendship.

The Friendship Factor, Lisa was afraid, would in fact become the murder factor, for she felt that although she had finally done what God wanted her to do, people were going to read the message differently, and out of envy murder her physically or spiritually. Thus the tie that should bind everybody together in friendship and love would in effect become divisive and separate everybody one from another, through envy, since envy is an isolating and separating disease. This is one symbol that plays throughout the book. And it is clear and pervasive.

Lisa had begun as a precocious and envied kid, remained so through public school, and then went off to realize her ambitions in the eyes of the public. Success cannot go unenvied by the persons with whom she grew up. And one, as the book begins, determines to murder Lisa because of all the "evil" this worldly successful woman has achieved. Of course, in the book, everybody connected in any way with Lisa is suspected of the murder, especially her sometimes-estranged husband. Everybody envies Lisa, apparently, as capsulized in the words of one: "You're an evil woman. You act in dirty films, you wear filthy clothes. You flaunt your vulgar body. You lead a scandalous life. You sing obscene songs. You're a drug addict. You killed your own father. . . .You were always a spoiled, stuck-up brat." So much for that all-inclusive envy.

The other symbol that energizes the book is that of togetherness, voiced here in Lisa's word "both." This word reveals Lisa's real character and desires. She does not want to be alone; as a singer and entertainer she has always tried to be a member of some group. Now she wants to make the movie *The Friendship Factor* in order to strengthen her bonds of friendship. She wants to make the movie because she feels God wants her to, and she wants the love—not hate—of the people who see it and know her. She wants to love and be the good wife to George, her husband, not to slip from him, to lose him. In other words, she wants the happiness that God wants everybody to have, not the hate and fear and alienation that usually result when an individual achieves her or his potential. Apparently, despite all her troubles, Lisa does achieve her goal, for in the end of this book, there is an epiphany which coalesces all disparate elements into a thrust toward the sky.

The detecting agent who gets involved in the mystery of the book, as in the mysteries of the human heart and spleen, is Monsignor John Blackwood Ryan, the axle on which the book spins, though by no means the only important character. Blackie as he insists on being called, is a diffident, laid-back, bumbling-stumbling stubby priest whose instincts concerning the motivations and actions of the human animal, though they sometimes wander, always come back to the center and drive home. In a whole stable of Irish and Catholic characters, Blackie stands out as the kindest, most perceptive, and most humanistic.

Greeley's third crime novel, *Happy Are Those Who Thirst for Justice* (1987), which also revolves around Blackie Ryan as problem-solver, is considerably more complex than the earlier ones. This book takes up the teaching of the Beatitude which many people think of as essentially having to do with the concept of justice but which, according to Greeley, was intended by Christ to mean much more (King James Version: "Blessed are they which do hunger and thirst after righteousness: for they shall be filled"): "The justice of which Jesus preaches in the Sermon on the Mount," Greeley says, "includes political and social justice but it is not limited to it. Rather those who hunger for justice are those who hunger for what God wishes in all aspects of personal and social life. In the individual's personal life it is passion to do that which one does best and in which one finds the greatest challenge and excitement, because they are clearly what God wants and expects."

Happy Are Those Who Thirst for Justice is a story of the squelching of the individuality of the weak by the strong. In this case a domineering woman, Violet Elizabeth Sullivan Enright, is a matriarch who rules with an iron and heavy hand over all she touches. She denies self-fulfillment to all people she knows. This "invasion of the human heart," as American novelist Nathaniel Hawthorne called it in the nineteenth century, is her mortal sin. In committing it, Enright invites destruction from others. Everybody wants her dead, and nearly everybody has said so many times. Thus when she turns up dead, there must be some sorting out of people who might be suspected. Through various tangled webs, Blackie conducts his indirect and oblique inquiry and discovers, of course, the villain in the clothes of the least suspected of all the possible culprits.

This book, like its predecessors, builds on the beauty of erotic truth and physical passion because they are, in Greeley's words, "clearly what God wants and expects" from people who mature in personal growth and responsibility. Passion does not lower man's position in his and God's eyes. On the contrary, it raises him. Passion makes people better citizens—in this world and in the next. As Greeley says, through passion "are depressive Irish nerds (and presumably nerds of all nationalities) civilized. And humanized." In addition to the free expression of honorable passion, *Happy Are Those Who Thirst for Justice* also preaches democracy. Autocrats are pretentious and evil; all Irish have burned the same peat, eaten the same potatoes, and cursed the same adversaries. All human beings are the same under the skin of pretense.

That democracy is important in Greeley's novels. Most of his characters are Irish Catholics. And as characters they stand out, individualized and each a person in his/or her own right. Greeley, although a superb Catholic Irish storyteller and very much interested in telling stories, as Christ told parables to make his points in little sermonettes, is still very much interested in giving sharp, clearly defined pictures of people who act in the stories. His novels thus become animations of characters, who stand out in the story like mountaintops above a mist under which the life of the story is enacted. But the characters are not as giantlike and heroic as they seem when their heads stand above the clouds, for just beneath the clouds lie the plains of humanity, of which the Irish characters are very much a part, inescapably and irretrievably, of the whole of humanity.

So where do these three books place Greeley in the development of new areas in the world of crime fiction? In the forefront, in at least two areas. In the first place no other author surpasses Greeley in the forthrightness of his message of the need for both physical and spiritual love and the inseparability of the two in the eyes and plans of God. In a genre which is characterized by sex, violence, pornography, Greeley brings a new meaning to the words *erotic love*. There is no masochism, no sadomasochism, no violence for its own sake, no ugly passion and sex. Instead there is a straightforward, clean, one almost says "pure" sex, beautiful and uplifting, that inspires and enriches. It is something like the purity of the love Sir Galahad had in his Quest. In Greeley the sex grows in a love of self, of companion, of community, and of a proper role in God's plan. Sex is a sacrament, a way of achieving grace and godliness when used in its proper, fullest human sense.

There is also a new dimension in the degree to which religion—or Christianity—is injected into crime fiction. Through the years Catholic writers like G. K. Chesterton, Leonard Holton, Ralph McInerny, William X. Kienzle, and Lawrence Saunders have used the Catholic Church and its teachings and practices as background, even foreground, for their novels. But their purposes have been different from Greeley's, at least in degree. They are novelists, who happen to write about Catholicism because they know it. Greeley, on the other hand, is a Catholic writer who is still serving the desires of his heart and of his Church. He is preaching. He is saving souls. In Greeley's books there is a love—a Catholic God's love for Catholics, to be sure, but also a nondenominational God's love for mankind and womankind in general. This love expands into something more than mere erotic love of man for woman or for God or of God for mankind. It is a religious humanism which reaches out and has all people love all people and through that love reach up to God. It is a comprehensiveness and fullness not seen in other writers of crime fiction. It is really a remarkable attempt and achievement when a crime story glosses one of the Beatitudes of the Sermon on the Mount.

The crime novel in the hands of George C. Chesbro and Andrew Greeley has indeed come a long way from the greatly restricted, asocial, at times rather trivial and silly puzzles in which people seem to live in hermetically sealed societies where nothing counts but the people involved in trying to find the parts of a puzzle. In Chesbro and, especially, Greeley, the subject is society and culture and the people living in it. In such writers of this new school of crime fiction as Ruth Rendell, P. D. James, John D. MacDonald, and Ross Macdonald, and dozens of others, there is a new interest in humanity and humanism which shows the importance and complexity of democracy and people. In Chesbro and Greeley the thrust is carried out in new ways and to new limits.

In Chesbro we see one thrust of love and companionability—of "bonding" —which ties people together into meaningful entities with strength and a future. In Greeley this "bonding" is energized by a spirituality which makes love fly from earth into a new union with God. In many ways,

Greeley seems like William Blake's paintings translated into crime fiction. The thrust is ever spiritual and ever upward.

In both these authors, then, new thrusts and new dimensions are being introduced into crime fiction. Crime fiction is opening up widely enough to enfold all such approaches. Perhaps what we are witnessing in this development is the growth of a conventional and somewhat restricted genre of literature into a, perhaps *the*, general novel form of the last decades of the twentieth century.

25

JUDITH J. KOLLMANN

Father Brown, Father Blackie: The Priest as Detective

*I*n the beginning, there was Father Brown, who so dominated the field of the Catholic detective story that for nearly fifty years only a half dozen minor writers used the clerical sleuth. In the past decade, however, the priest as detective has become popular once again, and several extensive series have been published. Among these priest detectives are William Kienzle's Father Robert Koesler; Ralph McInerny's Father Roger Dowling; and Father Andrew Greeley's Father Blackie.

The current popularity of the character is due to at least two factors. For one, the detective story is tremendously popular and so many varieties of detectives have been exploited that in desperation writers have had to turn even to the clergy for fresh possibilities, and, of course, a certain rabbi has flashed, meteorlike, across the skies of detective fiction, illuminating fresh woods and pastures new in clerical sleuthing. In addition, Catholicism itself has obligingly become a controversial topic—so it is worth writing a novel featuring a priest sleuth just to discover why the chap is still in the priesthood.

The present paper explores the relationship, or the lack of it, between the archetype (Father Brown) and his progeny. While there may have been

An earlier version of this essay was presented during the last of four sessions dealing with Andrew Greeley's fiction at the Popular Culture Association Meeting in New Orleans, Louisiana, 26 Mar. 1988.

other writers of priestly detective stories, for the purpose of this study
Kienzle, McInerny, and, in particular, Greeley are not only sufficient but
very apt. All three authors come from a similar cultural milieu—of approximately the same age, they are strongly affiliated with Catholicism (Greeley
is a priest; Kienzle is a laicized priest; McInerny attended seminary and is
Professor of Philosophy at the University of Notre Dame). Moreover, they
are all midwesterners. Kienzle lives in the Detroit area, while McInerny
and Greeley reside in Chicago. And all three are currently active writers in
the field. Thus they offer a splendid opportunity for a study in the degrees
and variety of literary indebtedness.

Anyone who chooses a priest as his detective must perforce be conscious
of Father Brown, and either reject him as a model or imitate him. In
Fathers Koesler and Dowling we have instances of, mainly, rejection of the
prototype. In Father Blackie we have a character who explicitly points out
the similarity between himself and Father Brown, thereby inviting us to
perceive simultaneously both the debt and the differences. The first question, then, is why McInerny and Kienzle have rejected Brown; and the
second is why Greeley not only imitates him but reshapes the archetype to
his own ends.

The reasons that lie behind a decision to imitate or not to imitate Father
Brown are undoubtedly multiple, but they include how the writer intends
to achieve verisimilitude and the purpose to which the sleuth and the
subject of Catholicism will be put. Recently I met Professor McInerny, and
in the course of our discussion asked him about Father Dowling's relationship to Father Brown. The gist of McInerny's response was that there was
very little, because, as the creator of contemporary tales of detection, he
could not accept as realistic Chesterton's rationale for Brown's crime-solving
method. He referred specifically to the following passage:

> "You see, I had murdered them all myself," explained Father
> Brown patiently. "So, of course, I knew how it was done. . . .
> "I had thought out exactly how a thing like that could be done,
> and in what style or state of mind a man could really do it. And
> when I was quite sure that I felt exactly like the murderer myself,
> of course I knew who he was. . . .
> "I mean that I thought and thought about how a man might
> come to be like that, until I realized that I really *was* like that, in
> everything except actual final consent to the action. It was once
> suggested to me by a friend of mine, as a sort of religious
> exercise." ("The Secret of Father Brown," *Secret* 11-12)

McInerny suggested that as a basic procedural premise a religious exercise
of this nature is irrational and therefore contradictory to fundamental laws
of detective fiction. In fact, the textual evidence of the stories themselves
refute McInerny's specific charge while sustaining his point in other ways,

for despite Brown's claims in the passage above, he actually proceeds in a more logical manner. While other characters allow themselves to be deceived because of their preconceptions, it is always he who observes the plain facts, and who, eliminating the sleight of hand, deduces the solution by means of common sense.[1] However, from the beginning (a good example is the early story "The Blue Cross") there is indeed a strong streak of the flamboyantly irrational in the tales, as, for example, the glorious coincidences in "The Blue Cross" that are airily explained with the statement that "The most incredible thing about miracles is that they happen . . . there is in life an element of elfin coincidence which people reckoning on the prosaic may perpetually miss" (*Innocence* 11). With this introduction, Chesterton defends the professional policeman, Valentin, in his absurdly irrational procedure. Chesterton needs Valentin's behavior for thematic reasons, but McInerny is correct: modern readers cannot accept any professional who acts as Valentin does, Frenchman or not. Besides the illogical element in the Father Brown stories, there are other somewhat dated features, as, perhaps, the priest's role as a Hound of Heaven.

Then there is the question of purpose. If one has a Catholic priest as detective, one must of necessity also write a story about Roman Catholicism—and therefore one must have something to say about this topic. There are many detective tales containing interesting backgrounds devoid of thematic content, but Roman Catholicism does not, on the face of the evidence, appear to be one of these. This is not to say that the purpose must be primarily theological, or even that it must be didactic; in fact, both McInerny and Kienzle use Catholicism mainly because the profession of the detective opens the door to unusual murders (priests and nuns killed according to the rosary, or a decapitated head wearing a cardinal's hat, for instance)[2] and to the rich background potential of customs and liturgies. But a significant thematic issue develops from Kienzle and McInerny's mutual interest in describing what it is like to be a priest, especially an older priest, who has elected to remain in a radically changed Church. The picture which emerges is one of a lonely and somewhat isolated life that nevertheless has its delights, satisfactions, and, even, peace.

Kienzle has observed the affinity between himself and McInerny, whose work he admires, and in *Kill and Tell* Father Koesler compares himself with Father Dowling:

> Both were in their mid-fifties; neither cared for canon law; both got along ably in the modern Church, but both thought the good old days really were the good old days more than less, and neither understood the very young new Roman Catholic clergy. (174)

In their development of their priestly characters, both writers generate sympathy and understanding for clergy who are caught between their own dedication on the one hand and the developments within the new Church on the other (by "Church" I mean both the ministers and the ministered), and, in the process, theological concepts invariably emerge from the moral cruxes. But Kienzle and McInerny's interests lie *primarily* in describing what it is like to be a priest, and theological issues emerge in the wake of the description.

Chesterton and Father Greeley invert this. Neither is particularly interested in the daily routines of a priest's life and both Father Brown and Father Blackie are as disassociated from their parish assignments as it is possible for parish priests to be. Kienzle, for example, takes extensive time and space not only to describe the routine of confession but to recount amusing anecdotes, such as the series of penitents who once described a sin as "playing the fiddle." At first, the confessor "decided not to inquire too deeply into the exact nature of this crime. One tended not to inquire too deeply into such matters in direct proportion to the number of years one had been hearing confessions," but eventually,

> the priest lost the battle with his curiosity and asked, "Just what do you mean by 'playing the fiddle'?"
> "Fornication," responded the young man.
> Considering the mild penances he'd been handing out for one of Catholicism's traditionally most grievous sins, the priest leaned out of the confessional door and called out, "Will the first violin section please come back in here?" (*Kill and Tell* 68)

In contrast, Father Brown is a traveler, a visitor; he appears in London, in South America, Mexico, and North America; in Norfolk, in Scotland, along English rivers, the Champs Elysées, and in a pass through the Italian Alps. He is in virtually a different place for each story, and, if sedentary, it is only for an evening, or long enough to watch a charade (during which three diamonds are stolen), or to listen to a set of footsteps. Similarly, Father Blackie is rector of the Cathedral of the Holy Name in Chicago. He even has a Dickensian suite in the rectory. But rarely does he celebrate a Sunday Mass in his cathedral; never, so far in the series of murder mysteries, has he sat in the confessional. His routine duties are always preempted by his staff so he can be free to sleuth at his cardinal archbishop's orders.

Like Father Brown, this freedom from sacerdotal routine allows Blackie to be free to center on *his* investigation—unlike Fathers Koesler and Dowling, who are far more peripheral to the investigative process. Normally, Koesler and Dowling solve a crime by happening upon a final piece of evidence or making a deduction that they, from their vantage point as priests, are best equipped to make, such as realizing that a series of murders is based upon the Fridays of Lent and the rosary (Kienzle, *Rosary Murders*). They are dependent upon close friends in the police forces to do most of the actual investigation for them. Brown and Blackie (Blackie within more curtailed limits) are less dependent upon the professionals. However, this freedom to investigate is more than a narrative technique; it also affects the nature of the ministry of both priests. Koesler and Dowling are parish priests who, dedicated to their vocations, stick to their parishes. Brown and Blackie, equally dedicated, are (to use Father Greeley's descriptive term for Blackie) "street priests" who take Christianity to the people as well as having people come to them. This is a reflection of thematic purpose, for, insofar as it is compatible with the nature of the form, Chesterton's and Greeley's detective fiction is emphatically theological, even metaphysical, often demonstrating the presence, and exploring the nature, of the supernatural as it manifests itself in the natural world.

For if daily routine and background color are largely ignored, then the writer of the Catholic mystery appears to be left with virtually one purpose: the narrative has to be theologically oriented. In Chesterton's case this meant being didactic. Each story is an exemplum, since Father Brown is a member of the traditional teaching Church as well as (in his pursuit of the criminal) a Hound of Heaven—a Christ-figure who pursues the sinner in the hope of bringing him to repentance. His major theological premise is made most explicit in one of his earliest stories, "The Blue Cross," in which he asserts that the universe is rational because it was created by a God who bound Himself to reason, and that, "Alone on earth, the Church makes reason really supreme. Alone on earth, the Church affirms that God Himself is bound by reason" (*Innocence* 24).

His stories, judging from textual evidence, were written first to combat English anti-Catholicism which considered not only that "those popish priests were deucedly sly" ("The Hammer of God," *Innocence* 185), but that Catholicism was replete with superstition. However, the tales were also arguments against pseudo-science. Repeatedly, the alleged scientists (or other modern professionals) in the stories, when confronted with a baffling crime, leap to the conclusion that a supernatural agency is involved. The implication is obvious. When man turns away from true religion, he makes himself vulnerable to false ones. Father Brown delivers a short homiletic on this topic in "The Oracle of the Dog":

> "It's the first effect of not believing in God that you lose your common sense and can't see things as they are. . . . a dog is an omen, and a cat is a mystery, and a pig is a mascot, and a beetle is a scarab, calling up all the old menagerie of polytheism from Egypt and old India. . . . and all because you are frightened of four words: 'He was made Man.'" (*Incredulity* 70–71)

And finally, in later works such as "The Secret of Father Brown," Chesterton voiced another objection to pseudo-science: namely, that it dealt with the exterior of man, making a friend a stranger and dealing only with the superficial. His argument, predictably, was that Catholicism dealt with the interior person and that, therefore, Catholicism humanized mankind rather then objectifying it.

Father Brown is primarily an allegorical figure—a traveler whose real home is not in this world; his function is that of guide, pursuer, and, above all, instructor. One reason (among several) why Chesterton made him physically into such an awkward nondescript is that spiritually and intellectually the little sleuth was so much the superman that *something* had to be done to keep him human. Fundamentally, the Father Brown we read about in the early stories is the same unchanged person we read about in the last tales. His character has not modified or developed because there was no need: like Aphrodite, but for different reasons, he was born complete, the perfect embodiment of the ideal Catholic priest of the early twentieth century. A successful practitioner of all the human virtues, he teaches, and there is nothing that he needs to be taught.

Upon this paradigm is Father Blackie based, and, to be certain his readers do not overlook this, or remain in doubt, Father Greeley explicitly points out the relationship in every novel in which Blackie appears. For example, in *Happy Are the Meek* Blackie states:

> My siblings' offspring claim that I deliberately cultivate the appearance of G. K. Chesterton's Father Brown. One of their parents, my sister Mary Kate (the distinguished psychoanalyst, of whom you've doubtless heard), comes closer to the truth when she says, "The Punk [a normally affectionate diminutive to which she is addicted] was born with the persona and cultivated the personality to fit it." (2)

The most obvious points of similarity between the two characters are, of course, physical appearance. Father Brown is short, round, dumpy, and so nondescript as to be readily overlooked, discounted, or underestimated. In "The Blue Cross," Valentin, that great detective, is searching for the tall, disguised figure of the jewel thief, Flambeau. He sees

> a very short Roman Catholic priest going up from a small Essex village.... Valentin gave it up and almost laughed. The little priest was so much the essence of those Eastern flats: he had a face as round and dull as a Norfolk dumpling; he had eyes as empty as the North Sea; he had several brown-paper parcels which he was quite incapable of collecting. The Eucharistic Congress had doubtless sucked out of their local stagnation many such creatures, blind and helpless, like moles disinterred. (*Innocence* 9)

His clothes are the traditional black suit, Roman collar, and "a hat like a black halo" ("The Mirror of the Magistrate," *Secret* 20). One of his few hobbies is the study of the philosopher-theologian Saint Thomas Aquinas.

Blackie is short, plump, "a metabolic freak" (*Clean of Heart* 65), who describes himself as the most innocuous and least romantic of men. You could enter an elevator I was riding and not even notice I was there. Indeed, often I am the little man who wasn't there. Occasionally even I manage to be not there again today. (*Meek* 2)

Blackie's clothes are reminiscent of Brown's frumpiness, although they are more trendy, ranging from a collection of items that include a Chicago Cubs jacket as well as an antique maroon smoking jacket and a World War II aviator's jacket. He also sports a well-worn and rarely cleaned Aran sweater, and "a fake navy commander's cap, which has 'BOSS' emblazoned on it in gold letters" (*Clean of Heart* 88). Rather than parcels and an umbrella, he manifests manual incoordination by being incapable of cleaning his own eyeglasses. He has several hobbies, but notable among them is his interest in the philosopher-theologians William James and Alfred North Whitehead.

But even in these personal details, even where there is similarity, there are at times notable differences. Their names, for instance, are similar in that they are both names of dark colors. But Father Brown is "Brown" because, probably, of the name's classless anonymity within the tight English class system. Most readers may consider black a more dramatic color than brown, but of more importance, Father Greeley has not named his sleuth "Father Black"; he is Blackie, which, like "The Punk," is an affectionate diminutive, and, like "The Punk," "Blackie" implies a completely different personality than "Father Brown." Would we, after all, feel the same about Chesterton's sleuth if he were "Brownie"? Moreover, an affectionate diminutive means Blackie has at least one person who feels affectionate *toward* him. He is unique among the four priest detectives under discussion because he is the only one who is not lonely and who possesses an identity beyond his priesthood. Blackie has a family, and therefore a history, a social class in addition to that given by his profession, and a community which manifests itself as at least one neighborhood in Chicago's South Side (*Clean of Heart* 27) as well as the greater urban environment of Chicago as a whole. Blackie is John Blackwood Ryan, S.T.L., Ph.D., whereas Brown is always a visitor who exists in the present moment and who has only one recurring friend in Flambeau. It is a significant point of separation between the two sleuths, suggestive of points of departure in the theological interests of their creators.

G. K. Chesterton invented Father Brown for propaganda reasons, to defend that "popish nonsense," Roman Catholicism, as a bastion of reason and compassion. Father Greeley created Blackie for public relations—not to defend the Church, but to explain what the Church ought to be: namely, the entire body of believers, both laity and clergy, functioning sacramentally toward each other. This is merely what Father Greeley, in his as-yet-unpublished "A Catholic Theology of Popular Culture" maintains is the function of the best popular communications media; for, in his words, "a sacrament is nothing more than a sign of the presence of God" (87), and is

"everything that has the potentiality of revealing the source of our hopeful-
ness" (62). As a result, Blackie is very human. Unlike Father Brown, he is
highly imperfect, and, although as a priest he is a teacher and as a detective
he is a "savior" (210), like the rest of mankind his is a deprived world and an
incomplete personality. Therefore he, too, is a student, who learns from his
parishioners and, at least to some degree, matures. Therefore it is a
give-and-take situation. Furthermore, Blackie is an imperfect savior and but
moderately successful as a hero. Yet he remains a formidable detective,
who, incidentally, detects with a suspiciously Brownian flair, discounting
the occult flimflam, spotting the elusive bit of hard evidence, and basing his
conclusions on reason and common sense.

Father Blackie is, incidentally, a character found in a number of Greeley's
novels, and although he exhibits sleuthlike characteristics in several, I will
restrict my observations and conclusions to those works in which he is most
clearly the classic detective. These are the three murder mysteries in the
Beatitudes series: *Happy Are the Meek, Happy Are the Clean of Heart,* and
Happy Are Those who Thirst for Justice. In *Happy Are the Meek* Blackie's
imperfect self is evident when he is revealed as possessing the major flaw of
prejudice. As a result, he completely misevaluates Susan Wade Quinlan,
the wife of the deceased Wolfe Quinlan, as "one of the memorable fluffheads
of our era. Not totally unattractive, mind you, until she opens her mouth.
Pink cotton candy at a circus" (2). A few pages later he calls her one of the
"pseudomeek" (12), which means a person who "blunder[s] through life
convinced that if you do the right thing, nothing wrong will happen" (12).
Blackie has judged her based on his own irritability; his memories of her in
the eighth grade; and on hearsay coupled with the casual interpretation of
another's idiom: "Eileen says she's a poor dear woman. It means the same
thing" (14), that is, as being a "fluffhead." Thus Father Blackie has
demonstrated that he is as capable as anyone else of being superficially
prejudgmental, of generalizing ahead of his data, and of a callow, patronizing wit. In short, he succeeds in making a fool of himself. Later, however,
when Sue tells her own story, and he finds out what lay behind her
apparent "fluffheadedness," he is reduced to tears. By the end of the novel
he recognizes her for what she has always been: never a fluffhead, always
one of the genuinely meek. Blackie has a good deal to learn in this novel,
and, to his credit, learns it.

Still, Blackie *is* a teacher. One of a priest's functions is to explicate
theology, and therefore it is always he who explains what the governing
beatitude of each novel really means. So when his cousin Annie asks,
"Won't the meek inherit the earth?" (13), Blackie responds,

> "Not that kind of meek. Saint Matthew meant those who are in
> harmony with the processes of life, not those who try to suppress
> the processes with sweetness or compulsive responsibility. The
> French translate the word *débonnaire.* I suppose teenagers like The

Cat of Packy Jack would say 'cool.' Debonair or cool Suzie Quinlan and Larry Burke are not." (13)

The theology is correct, the evaluation wrong. It is interesting that Father Greeley is, like Chesterton, fond of paradoxes, for Sue Quinlan, beatified through her living the virtue of meekness, is, according to canon law, an adulteress. Yet she is closer to being a saint than anyone else in the novel.

In regard to Blackie's role as detective, Father Greeley gives an interesting, if indirect, insight in "A Catholic Theology of Popular Culture." He discusses Ellis Peters' Brother Cadfael series, describing a comment Mircea Eliade made to him

about the "soteriology of the mystery story." He meant that the detective in the mystery plays a savior role, he is the one who by solving the puzzle "makes things right again"—restores the proper balance of the cosmos and reasserts the triumph (always tenuous) of cosmos over chaos. . . .

I have no doubt he is right. . . . The extent to which grace is present in the mystery depends on the skill of the story telling and the suspense of the battle between cosmos and chaos. Just as there are villains in the world, so there are saviors, men and women who, if they don't make everything right again, at least devote themselves decisively to the cause of cosmos over chaos. They are not infrequently men and women who have many of the characteristics of Brother Cadfael—patience, wisdom, sensitivity, humor. (210–11)

Father Greeley may agree with Eliade, but in his novels it is significant that the detective is *not* the only savior; nor can he, single-handedly, make things right again. This is especially clear in *Happy Are the Meek*, although the other novels demonstrate it as well. While Blackie does much to solve the mystery and definitely accomplishes what he was instructed to do by Archbishop Cronin—to solve the riddle of Wolfe Quinlan's death and, if suicide, to find evidence of Quinlan's remorse—he fails to rescue the innocent damsels from physical danger: no Travis McGee he. Susan Wade rescues both herself and her daughter. The best Blackie can do at this juncture—and, to be fair, it is better than anyone else connected with the investigation—is to realize what is happening and to bring the gendarmes. His essential role, however, is that, having discovered the truth of Quinlan's death, he can clear at least one person's life (the killer's) of festering guilt and lay to rest the doubts and suspicions the rest of the individuals involved would continue to harbor, poisoning all relationships. Thus, Blackie is a spiritual savior of both Susan and Laurel Wade.

In *Happy Are the Clean of Heart* Blackie discovers the would-be murderer and, having set a trap, catches her in the act of attempted murder. His sense of timing has improved. However, the victim of the attack, Lisa, had been aware that her life would be threatened if she chose to make a film of real genius, and, regardless, elected to make it. And other equally important issues have been resolved ably by the characters before Blackie arrives on the scene to untangle the threads of the whodunit.

The crimes function as catalysts that force characters to resolve at least a few long-pending difficulties in their lives, and on the whole they are remarkably successful. Blackie's role is as the facilitator of the final truths, but he remains one among several "men and women who, if they don't make everything right again, at least devote themselves decisively to the cause of cosmos over chaos," all of whom share Brother Cadfael's patience, wisdom, sensitivity, and humor, and all of whom demonstrate a major tenet of Father Greeley's main theological thesis regarding popular culture: "God speaks through the people to the institutional church just as He/She speaks to the people through the leaders of the institutional church. Both the learning church and the teaching church represent the voices of God" ("Catholic Theology" 11). Thus, in Father Blackie, Greeley presents his readers with the democratization of the contemporary Church: Blackie speaks to his people, but his people also speak to him. And miracle of miracles, he listens.

NOTES

1. For an excellent discussion of Father Brown's use of reason, see Lynette Hunter, *G. K. Chesterton: Explorations in Allegory* (London: Macmillan, 1979), 140–58.

2. Kienzle's *The Rosary Murders* (1979; New York: Bantam, 1985) and *Death Wears a Red Hat* (1980; New York: Bantam, 1981).

WORKS CITED

Chesterton, G. K. *The Innocence of Father Brown*. 1910. New York: Penguin, 1975.
———. *The Incredulity of Father Brown*. 1926. New York: Penguin, 1975.
———. *The Scandal of Father Brown*. 1935. New York: Penguin, 1982.
———. *The Secret of Father Brown*. 1927. New York: Penguin, 1975.
———. *The Wisdom of Father Brown*. 1913. New York: Penguin, 1975.
Greeley, Andrew M. "A Catholic Theology of Popular Culture." Unpublished manuscript.
———. *Happy Are the Clean of Heart*. New York: Warner, 1986.
———. *Happy Are the Meek*. New York: Warner, 1985.
———. *Happy Are Those Who Thirst for Justice*. New York: Warner, 1987.
Holquist, Michael. "Whodunit and Other Questions: Metaphysical Detective Stories in Post-War Fiction." *New Literary History* 3 (1971): 135–56.

Hunter, Lynette. *G. K. Chesterton: Explorations in Allegory.* London: MacMillan, 1979.

Kienzle, William. *Death Wears a Red Hat.* 1980. New York: Bantam, 1981.

———. *Kill and Tell.* 1984. New York: Ballantine, 1985.

———. *The Rosary Murders.* 1979. New York: Bantam, 1985.

Kroetsch, Judy A. "Father Brown and Miss Marple: Similar Yet Unlike." *The Chesterton Review* 12 (1986): 345–53.

Reinsdorf, Walter. "The Perception of Father Brown." *The Chesterton Review* 10 (1984): 265–74.

26

MARY ANN LOWRY

Death Under a Beatitudinal Umbrella: The Mysteries of Andrew Greeley

*A*ndrew Greeley's mysteries furnish readers with puzzles to solve involving a death that looks like murder in *Happy Are the Meek*, an attempted murder in *Happy Are the Clean of Heart*, and murder in *Happy Are Those Who Thirst for Justice*. He employs the three classic elements in crime detection: means, motive (including fear of discovery, that most powerful of motives), and opportunity. While revealing the frequently bewildering, sometimes predatory, and always violent struggle going on in a given time and place beneath the veneer of civilization, he also communicates the immediacy of the message of the Beatitudes in his intellectual-quest-for-truth stories.

Although Blackie Ryan, the understanding priest who suggests solutions to problems, fires barrages of solving shots throughout most of Greeley's fictional canon, it is in the three classical English puzzle mysteries that Blackie becomes one of the family of compelling fictional sleuths. As such, he has a long line of literary ancestors, including Dame Agatha Christie's Hercule Poirot. Both Poirot and Ryan are small of stature, unassuming, and brilliant, a disconcerting combination to those who commit crimes, and both disguise their brilliance behind their diminutive stature and feigned bumbling. Even their names reinforce the impression. Poirot's name comes

An earlier version of this essay was presented during the last of four sessions dealing with Andrew Greeley's fiction at the Popular Culture Association Meeting in New Orleans, Louisiana, 26 Mar. 1988.

from *poireau*, the leek, which also means "wart" in French, while Father Ryan, frequently referred to as a type of G. K. Chesterton's Father Brown, insists upon being addressed simply as Blackie. Of himself, Blackie says, "You could enter an elevator I was riding and not even notice I was there." His sister Mary Kate (the distinguished psychiatrist) comes closer to the truth when she said, "The Punk . . . was born with the persona and cultivated the personality to fit it" (*Meek* 2). Their antagonists treat both with amusement, tolerance, or even contempt—until the time comes for revelation, when their prior attitudes are replaced with awe and fear as they are revealed despite their often careful planning and apparent ability.

By the time Blackie appears on the scene, the killing (as distinguished from murder), the attempted murder, or the murder has been committed. "See to it" are the words spoken to him by My Lord Cronin, cardinal archbishop of Chicago which begin the leprechaun-looking priest's involvement in a case. He conducts his investigations through a series of interviews, each one followed by his retrospective musings over what each suspect said to him. To clarify the physical aspects, he devises a chart of who supposedly was where and when. To help with his searches of lives, homes, and habits, he has Mike Casey the Cop, retired Chicago superintendent of police, to consult. His methods may be different, but they produce results; rigid police methodology sometimes is similar to the *alazon* of classical comedy, for it can block recognition of the criminal. Most important, he introspectively thinks about the Beatitudes, from which the series derives its titles, as a means of understanding the mental and emotional states of suspects.

One of the special appeals of a Greeley priest-as-detective novel is the pleasure the reader derives from the tone of the book. The attitude toward life expressed in the style frequently becomes more important than the puzzle. Although the police are involved, the story line avoids an immersion in their methodology. Instead, it involves Blackie's musings about the Beatitudes and their lessons for living our lives, and that tone, in my opinion, is splendid. One small indication of this quality of tone is Blackie's correction of himself early in the first novel of the series when he changes his word choice from "suspects" to "people" in considering those who might have done the deed.

While Blackie searches for the key to each puzzle, readers feel the caring tone as they discover societal settings of Chicago neighborhood and Ryan family. Even when the setting spans half the North American continent, as it does in *Happy Are Those Who Thirst for Justice*, moving back and forth between California and Chicago, the tone is the same. It is those with mixed motives, outsiders to neighborhood and clan, who provide a world of pettiness, scheming, lies, jealousy, crossed ambitions, greed, and murder. The key or clue to solution does not simply unlock the door to the room where the crime occurred; it also reveals character. The criminal types are those people with mixed motives, while those who truly belong to neighborhood and clan are the single-minded people, those who live by the beatitudinal purity of purpose that is visible to all who will recognize it. Emphasizing this theme of mixed versus pure motives are pseudo-servants-of-God. In *Happy Are the Meek* Father Armande theatricalizes himself to prey on lonely people for money, property, and power. In *Happy Are the Clean of Heart* Sister Winifred parasitically attaches herself to star Lisa Malone for money "to buy guns for revolutionaries in Central America" (145). In *Happy Are Those Who Thirst for Justice*, Padre Adolpho, who looks "like a malign Friar Tuck," is an "illegal alien" and a Franciscan hit man (235–6).

Living in accordance with the lessons of Christ's Sermon on the Mount, Blackie respects women, and the hungry, the clean of heart, and the meek respect him in return. His personality analysis is usually correct, but his initial "fluffhead" evaluation of Sue Quinlan (*Meek*), with whom he went to school in the neighborhood, is wrong. Later, he changes his evaluation to "survivor" with "a sufficient amount of biblical meekness to survive twenty-four years of hell" (204–5) in her marriage to Wolfe Quinlan, who died in a locked-room freak accident with a medieval broadsword through his ribs. Wolfish in his greed for worldly things that money could buy, in his lust for another man's wife, and in his brutal treatment of friends and family, Wolfe died as he had lived, alone, and was mourned by few or none. His death gives Sue her chance for life, and Larry Burke, an honest, handsomely muscled, and brainy Chicago investment manager who had loved her for years, is waiting to cherish and fulfill her.

There was no murder, but there was a crime. In his lonely drunkenness, Wolfe made sexual advances toward his daughter, Laurel, so it was with attempted incest that his life ended. Sue begins her harmonious life without Wolfe in the light of Burke's love and by demonstrating that biblical meekness is not weakness. She is strength personified in defense of Laurel against the false Father Armande, who tries to sacrifice both mother and daughter as brides of Christ in a warped ritual of sex and fire for his devil worship cult. After Armande's death, Sue, stark naked, leads Laurel to safety, and she displays no false modesty about her nakedness, no false meekness, in her relief at their escape into the protective custody of firemen. In a mother's righteous defense of her daughter, she is strong, thus displaying in a human manner the Christ-like strength that is true meekness. In her concern for Laurel, she forgot about her own safety, thereby gaining the mastery over her human nature that is the essence of biblical meekness.

Lisa Malone, a Hollywood singer and actress (*Clean of Heart*), also went to school with Blackie in the old neighborhood. She is one of the two women that Blackie admits to loving, without, of course, breaking his priestly vows, so the person who viciously attacked her, putting her in a deathlike coma for most of the story, must be found. To five of the people he interviews, she is different persons:

> For Kerry, she was a beloved, if naive rival; for George, a
> magical, mysterious, ultimately frustrating wife; for Ken Woods,
> the star he had created who had turned on him; for Blackie
> Ryan . . . well, a memory that proved he did have other choices
> besides the priesthood. To Sister Winnie the Pooh, she was the
> faithless student who refused to respond to God's call time after
> time. (157)

Rather than all these different portraits, Lisa is what she is: "One of the
clean of heart, the purely motivated, the single-minded" (228), a human
being of luminosity, the star quality. As an adult, when she warned Tad
Thomas "off her marriage," that was the real Lisa. As a teenager, when she
dragged Blackie, "not protesting very loudly, to her senior prom and
assaulted . . . [him] with kisses and caresses in the Forest Preserve parking
lot" (181), that was the real Lisa. She is transparent. She is the same age as
Blackie, approaching her fortieth birthday, and is still reaching for the stars
in *The Friendship Factor*, a film she stars in and produces. She is sweet, kind,
considerate, generous, loving, and she knows with the certainty that only
the pure in heart can know that her vocation is "from God" (242). How
could anyone hurt such a person?

Although murder after mutilation was intended, it was interrupted by
the arrival of Lisa's husband, George, the accountant, whom the police, not
Blackie, consider a prime suspect. And Blackie, of course, is right. George,
the Bean Counter, may not have understood why his beautiful and successful wife loved him, but love him she did, with the devotion that only the
clean of heart can give. She very clearly defines her husband's relationship
with her in her private letter to Blackie, wherein she writes of George: "He
has been my epiphany, firm and loyal and generous and tough, with enough
flair and wit to be always a surprise, like I imagine God to be" (248). And
George loves her in return. How could he not?

The clue to solution lies in Lisa's consideration of others. She remembers
the favorite drink of every visitor to her home. Whether the individual had
been a guest only once previously or multiple times, on succeeding visits
she has that person's favorite drink prepared and waiting. Although the
favorite drink key appears in every person's interview, Blackie searches for it
throughout the story, almost has it several times, but it continues to elude
him. When finally revealed, vodka unlocks the door to the successful
torturer and attempted murderer's mind. Kerry Randall, Lisa's friendly
rival in school back in the Neighborhood, who insistently professes love for
the star in public but harbors hatred for her in her heart, is the one who
drinks vodka, the guilty person. She is not one of the biblical single-minded
clean of heart. She cannot tolerate the success that *The Friendship Factor*, a
film depicting a message of death and rebirth (253) that will probably win
an Academy Award, is bound to be; she is Salieri to Lisa's Mozart (263);
Kerry's motivation is envy, a mixture of love and hatred.

Blackie hopes big for Lisa's recovery with five pounds of dark chocolate (her favorite), not two, and his hope and prayers are answered. She revives from her coma, confused, but correcting her speech, on Halloween, All Saints' Day. It is symbolically Christmas, though, the time for joy in giving, and the Lady/Lord God has given Lisa a second chance to continue her service in films and her love with her Bean Counter accountant husband, George.

Working from intuition, involvement, and feeling, Blackie continues his investigations in the third mystery, wherein murder does, in fact, take place. His interest continues in both those suspected of the crime and those who were victims, and his interest in the victims seems to become a theme of the guilty victim. Wolfe Quinlan was too greedy for materialistic things of the world and almost completely inconsiderate of people, making himself a prime target for murder, although his death was accidental. Lisa Malone, in her single-minded pursuit of love with her husband and for their children, involvement with her profession, and concern for her friends and acquaintances, seemed too good for an imperfect world peopled with imperfect human beings, and it was just such an imperfect being who tried to kill her. Most members of the family of Mrs. Sullivan Enright, guilty of being "an angry lioness . . . devouring matriarch" (*Thirst for Justice* 44–45) type, had reason to murder her with the single shot through the head that killed her.

Mrs. Enright makes her first appearance when she initiates a verbal battle with Mary Kate, Blackie's psychiatrist sister. Joe Murphy, Mary Kate's psychiatrist husband, decides that, if he were a betting man, he would put his money on his wife. Although the outcome of that altercation is unclear, it becomes unimportant in the afternoon of that same August day in Monroe Harbor when Violet Enright does, indeed, lose her life to a small bullet from "a small automatic—a 9mm Beretta . . ." in a securely locked stateroom (64) of her huge yacht, the *Violetta*.

An encapsulated account of the people on board describes the personalities of Violet's family:

> A hippie ex-priest with a jewel-crazy wife, a discredited bishop, a bisexual surgeon whose wife was a nympho, a lonely and beaten woman, a feisty granddaughter with a threatened lover, a somewhat sinister banker, and a mysterious visitor from the County Galway. . . . (59)

Fionna Downs, the "feisty granddaughter," an only child who is also Mary Kate's patient, finds the body, and thus becomes the prime suspect of the police, not Blackie. The dignified "mysterious visitor" with a good figure is Mary Feehan, Eugene Enright's nurse when he was dying and his beloved during World War II while he was serving in England. Out of that love match was born Rita Downs, Fionna's mother, who is separated from her husband in California and currently living with Violet, her purported mother.

As if that cat's cradle of interpersonal relationships were not enough, the "sinister banker" is the father of Fionna's fiancé and is ultimately revealed as Violet's sadistic lover and the biological father of her two "nerd" sons. Further, he has one of those sons, Dan, as well as his wife, killed by drug hit men in an unsuccessful attempt to cover up his misappropriation of Violet's money. His biggest mistake, though, was in having those hit men attack Mary Kate. Irish Amazon that she is, Mary Kate, soon to earn her black belt in karate, suffers a gash but injures both attackers seriously enough for them to require hospital treatment. Nevertheless, an attack on any member of the Ryan clan is totally unacceptable to all of them, so Blackie had to become involved. This was the beginning of the end for banker Vinney Nelligan, who, when unmasked, howls like the "raving madman . . . he had become" (290). Hate, greed, love, lust, ambition, fear—the list of Vinney Nelligan's mixed motives seems endless.

Vinney was hungry but not in the biblical sense. He lusted, but he did not love, and it is love that makes human beings hunger and thirst. Righteousness, joy, and peace come first in the hearts of those who yearn for these qualities, which are manifestations of love. With them, they bring a life of generosity and justice to one's fellow beings, with justice triumphing in the life of the world. This could form the basis for a fitting escutcheon for Blackie and his family, who are generous in giving of themselves, their money, their time, and their talents to others.

The world of Ryan clan and Chicago neighborhood may be circumscribed, but it serves as microcosm to the larger world, and this is how it should be in mystery stories, where the happy ending reigns supreme. Despite the concern with "crime, violence, and murder," plots are neatly closed. "The criminal is always caught. Justice is always done. Crime never pays" (Mandel 47–48). Everyone is revealed, only those people with mixed motives to their detriment. Order is restored, and there is hope in the world—another instance of the Lady God's scheme of "drawing straight with crooked lines" (*Clean of Heart* 157; *Thirst for Justice* 231; and every other Greeley novel).

As Blackie Ryan prepared to solve Violet Enright's murder, he says, "There was a lot of love in this mystery" (265), but there is a lot of love in all three of the mysteries; there is, in fact, a lot of love in all of Greeley's novels, embracing the spiritual love of *agape* and the sexual love of *eros*. Both are expressed in the symbol of the loving man and woman. Whether or not the couple is married, their love is an affair, a *ménage à trois* with the Lady/Lord God: "God's delight is infinitely greater than the orgasms of the two lovers, who may understand dimly at the fringes of their consciousness that they have been trapped by the Great Voyeur" (*Meek* 206). Ironically, it is in the third, most complicated of the mysteries that the notion of the second chance is made most clear, underscored by duality in the second gun, the second grandmother, the second secret. Drs. Mary Kate and Joe Murphy have the second quarter of their lives together to look forward to;

Lisa Malone, awakening from her coma, marks the second chance for love with her husband, George, to continue; and Larry Burke's love for Sue Quinlan, a survivor of twenty-four years of miserable marriage, is her second chance for life. In Blackie Ryan's words:

> What else are priests for except to preach about the second-chance-bestowing goodness which lurks in the sun and the stars and the lake and the sky and the Hubert Humphrey Metrodome and in the body of the passionate lover? (*Thirst for Justice* 302)

Thus, love is hope in Greeley's fictional world, just as the union of one man and one woman throughout his canon becomes the persistent symbol for all the love that should exist in the world, for loving is living.

WORKS CITED

Greeley, Andrew M. *Happy Are the Clean of Heart*. New York: Warner, 1986.

———. *Happy Are the Meek*. New York: Warner, 1985.

———. *Happy Are Those Who Thirst for Justice*. New York: Warner, 1987.

Mandel, Ernest. *Delightful Murder: A Social History of the Crime Story*. Minneapolis: University of Minnesota Press, 1984.

27

ANNE K. KALER

Seraph Fire and Science Fiction: Andrew Greeley's Use of Angels in His Novels

*W*hen asked if Catholics still have to believe in angels, Sean, the hero of Andrew Greeley's *Angel Fire*, responds, "Only if they're science fiction writers" (47).

Such banishing of angels to a science fiction/fantasy setting provides the priest author and his characters with a fantastic dimension where they accept the reality of spiritual beings—angels or demons—as plot participants. Such freedom allows him both to debate traditional angelology and to create new functions for angels as messengers, as guardians, as creatures of light or dark, as patterns of energy, and, eventually in the case of seraphs, as fireballs of love.

When man assigned the wings of birds to the human form to represent the swiftness of the intuitive thought process, wings became integral to angels. Originally in Hebraic angelology, only two groups of angels had wings—the seraphim had six, to shield the Godhead from human view; the cherubim had two, to support the Ark of the Covenant. Stemming from the winged bird-spirits of Hindu and Persian mythology, the "karibu," the Hebraic cherubim's wings surrounding a human head provided artists with the innocent-faced cherubim representing pure thought in their role as

---

An earlier version of this essay was presented during the third of four sessions dealing with Andrew Greeley's fiction at the Popular Culture Association Meeting in New Orleans, Louisiana, 26 Mar. 1988.

messengers, which were later transformed into erotic Renaissance *putti*.

Seraphs derived from the Syrian six-winged serpent-demons of wisdom and eternity, represented by the snake's biting its own tail and the annual shedding of its skin. The word "seraph" means "child of an adder" (Hahn 19); the Druids called themselves the Adders; the Gaelic goddess Cerridwen's cart was drawn by dragon-serpents; the cobra's hood formed the Eye of Wisdom in the tiara of Isis. Greek myth has the healing spirit of Gaia's son Python enter the single serpent twined around Asclepius' staff at Delphi; Hebrew myth has Hezekiah stop the Jews from worshipping a crucified winged serpent; Isaiah has a seraph cleanse his lips with a burning coal. As "supernatural serpents with fiery bites [which] might be explained as ardent zeal and love of God" (Hahn 19), seraphs fit Greeley's use as symbols of God's fiercely burning love for His/Her creatures.

Once mankind caught on to angels, they multiplied more rapidly than the saints. Over ten thousand were recorded—ones like Tzadiquel who governed Jupiter every Thursday—so many, in fact, that the Church in 745 had to limit devotion to angels to the three major ones: Michael, Gabriel, and Raphael. Nevertheless, the number expanded into the nine choirs of angels in medieval days to complement the theory of correspondences.

In *Angel Fire* Greeley provides possible theories for the existence of angels based on scientific principles rather than on Christian tradition. The hero, Sean, is given a girlfriend, Stacey, who tapes nocturnal noise to search for hidden messages from extraterrestrials whose communication patterns, she assumes, "will be essentially binary and therefore understandable to humans" (16). Her narrow scientific view blinds her to the possibility of spiritual beings; the neo-Nazis of Project Archangel, the plot which attempts to imprison Gaby as a hostage in their negotiations with other extraterrestrials, suffer the same shortsightedness.

However, even though he is an empiric scientist about to win the Nobel Prize for his contributions to the "punctuation point" theory of evolution, Sean's mind is less narrow. To him Stacey's white noise, "the functional equivalent of white light—waves that occupy all the spectrum" (13), sounds like the "harmonious conversations of choirs of angels" (15). Adopting the medieval theory that the concentric orbits of the heavenly bodies which were controlled by angels produced the musical scale, Sean easily "sees" the angels as sound patterns—songs, if you will, which are an integral function of angels—just as he "sees" Gabriella's body as a pattern of light energy. When she finally consents to sing for him, it is the first sign of her love: "a pure and lonely voice . . . then a mighty choir of eight parts" (112). She plays on the harp of Brian Boru; she avoids direct questions as to whether she sang at Bethlehem or whether she will blow the last trumpet. Later, she dances him up to the sky and down where "they may have passed a cemetery on the way down with an open tomb. Open and empty" (203), the final proof of her angelic obedience to Christ.

Even before he meets Gabriella, Sean comes to hint at angels' existence as "another 'punctuation'" (3–4) point in his theory of evolution which supports Gabriella's description of angels as "products of a different evolutionary process, which happens to be in a more mature state of development" (4). He can even affirm that "good spirits were problematic. Evil spirits were a given" (4). But it is not until he accepts Gabriella as an angel that the scientific proof of angels and the emotional proof of their songs balance to make his early haiku come true:

> *sound snow white and dirty*
> *fell from the sky one day*
> *angel fire angel song (13)*

Thus is the name of the novel derived.

The theory of guardian angels was integrated into Christian belief from the Egyptian concept of the *Ka*, the double spirit which stayed with a person throughout his life. While angels are occasionally mentioned as guardians by Greeley's *persona* Father Blackie Ryan, in *Angel Fire* they are more often specified as natural phenomena, "a function rather than a person" (34). Still, they lurk on the fringes of doctrine as "passionate light, fireballs of love" (34).

It can be argued that the word "angel" comes from the root *ang*, from *angaros*, courier or messenger in Persian mythology, and from *angiras*, or divine spirit, in Sanskrit, combined with the *el* ending from Hebrew, meaning "of God." Even the spelling of the names of Greeley's heroes and heroines incorporates the *el* of angels: to show up her Christmas angel motif, Noele of *Lord of the Dance* uses a single *l* rather than the more familiar double *ll*; Michele of *God Game* opts for the single *l* rather than the conventional *elle*; Maria Angelica is the heroine of *Ascent into Hell*; Eileen Kane of *Patience of a Saint* hints at the *el*; Michael Casey of *Angels of September* is called Michael only when he is acting as Saint Michael. On the whole, Greeley uses nicknames and names interchangeably.

In *God Game* the angel is called an "ilel," a word which Greeley admits he made up. While any Hebrew species of angel with the root of *el* means "of God," the word not only has possible cognates in C. S. Lewis' use of "eldil" for the inhabitants of his Perelandra series but also has an interior alliterative connection with that of "Tinker Bell . . . and Ariel" (62) and Michele. The names of the author's angels are mostly standard—Michael, Gabriel— but his character Ranora's name seems to have no basis in discernable angel or saint names; in private correspondence, Greeley admits that the name may be a "mixture" of Nora as a Celtic diminutive of Eleanor or El-Nora (Nora of God) and of the Egyptian sun god Ra, but avers that "I don't know why that mixture seemed appropriate" (Letter, 8 Aug. 1987). His narrator shortens Ranora's name to "Nora, a name the author has used repeatedly, and which becomes significant in *Angel Fire* when Gabriella manipulates Sean to fall in love with a real Irish woman named Nora.

Gabriella of *Angel Fire* is a form of Gabriel. Gabriella defines her own name as coming from the Hebrew word *gabor* (strength) and meaning "Strong One of God" (27). Actually, she claims it is only one of her names, a "name for phenomena that your species has come to associate with my presence" (28). Her nickname is "Gaby," Greeley's commentary on the woman angel's ability to charm the man with her words.

As a priest Greeley could be expected to use angels as messengers or guardians in his novels; however, as an author of science fiction and fantasy he goes far beyond the popular and pious tradition of angels by portraying them as distinct fellow beings with personalities, tempers, and temptations, much as Roberta McAvoy does in her Damiano trilogy.

For example, he claims that the character of Podraig, the Irish wolfhound in his early novel *The Magic Cup*, was "intended to be more than a simple canine, a first cousin or rather an ancestor of Don Bosco's [dog] Grigio" (Letter, 8 Aug. 1987). In *Lord of the Dance* Noele's car, the red Chevy Flame (named perhaps for a seraph), which takes the brunt of her attack by the villain's van, has all the characteristics of a guardian angel. Sean Desmond in *Angel Fire* has the distinction of having a seraph as a guardian angel and as a lover. Anne Reilly in *Angels of September* has actual people acting as protectors—"three guardian angels [and] St. Michael, the archangel" (343–4).

In *Virgin and Martyr*, when Cathy Collins transports the money for an underground terrorist organization, she is actually called a courier—a term used by the Mafia for such a messenger. To avoid detection, she adopts the name Angela Carson because as an "angel" she is invisible, yet her only "angel" (or demon) is the sheet which wraps around her in her escape (390), making her "invisible." But Greeley pushes the image further when he makes Saint Catherine of Alexandria the patron saint of Cathy, because, according to Jacobus de Voragine's *Golden Legend* account, Saint Catherine had angels who "stood by her and admonished her to constancy, . . . salved her wounds, . . . destroyed the wheel [the death machine of the flaming wheel]," just as Cathy Collins evades the killing helicopter of her captors. "Angels" is a term used both for the Eastern monks who preserved the saint's relics and for the beings that "bore her body. . . to Mt. Sinai" (707–13), just as the alias of Angela Carson preserves Cathy's identity.

In addition to their role as guardians of mankind, the angels in pre-Newtonian physics moved the heavenly bodies in their circles; with this astrological origin, the Persian theogony developed angels to cover any inexplicable mystical experience—dream, vision, visitation, or hallucination, a device which Greeley uses heavily in *God Game* when the characters from his alternate cosmos "flit" and "frolic" (49) through the port created by his computer.

One aspect of angels as guardians is explained by Gabriella in *Angel Fire* when she accompanies Sean to his Nobel Prize speech and defends him from Project Archangel foes, occasional assassins, and random evil forces. She admits that "the story of Tobias and Raphael is a folk tale with spiritual theme. . . . Angels are God's companions for humans on their journeys, hence the Hebrew name for us can mean 'companion'" (234); in contrast, the Nazi-like villains in the novel refer to angels as "socialist aliens" (243). She acts as Raphael by guiding the stubborn Sean toward his destined love, the Irish Nora; she acts as Gabriel by controlling electronic media; she acts as Michael by defending Sean, even taking a madman's bullets into her own body to save his. Dismissing most of Sean's questions as "superstitious folklore," she evades the question as to whether she will be the angel who blows the trumpet on Judgment Day, admitting, however, that as a musician she "could wake up all the dead in the cosmos" (29).

In *God Game* both Michele, the teenage neighbor of the narrator who plays the flute, and Ranora, "blond pixie wrapped in peppermint candy with snapping eyes and a determined little jaw" (304) who conquers her world by playing seductive melodies on a hornpipe, are connected with music. While Ranora has most of the angelic attributes, she most resembles a guardian angel, "a conscience, a sister, a daughter, a mother, and a haughty archangel. She was also pure hell when she was displeased" (62). Within the fictionally real world of the computer novel, she is an analogue of the narrator's adopted "niece" Michele, who is, in her turn, a namesake and a protégée of Michael, the archangel, mainly because she makes the mysterious telephone call that precipitates the solution. Michele is just one aspect of the angel as messenger in this complex novel.

In *God Game* the computer becomes an "angel" insofar as it is activated by "crackling lightning and booming thunder" (19) hitting the narrator's inexpertly rigged satellite-dish computer system. The interactive computer game allows the narrator to issue commands to the inhabitants of an alternate world through his computer, which becomes the voice of God. While the archangel Michael does not overtly cause the computer to malfunction, it is his "sign" or lightning that causes the computer to have an angelic voice as a messenger to the alternate world. Michael's name is repeated in the choice of Michele for the narrator's teenage friend's name. And the "creatures of light," the "ilel," or angel, and mystics may ignore Planck's wall and slip through such slits in time to "transcend physical barriers [and] may flit across these physically impenetrable boundaries" (49).

While the plural unnamed cherubim of Genesis 3:24 with "the fiery revolving sword" who drove Adam and Eve from the Garden of Eden were condensed down to one archangel—Michael—popular tradition multiplies the evil spirits for the lone hero/angel to defeat. In his medieval treatise on saints' lives, Jacobus de Voragine's Michael, the warrior angel who will defeat Lucifer and his rebellious angels, is so powerful a protector of the elect that de Voragine insists that as "often as there is a work of wondrous power to be wrought, Michael is sent to perform it" (578).

That the devil is never singular comes from the popular tradition that the fallen angels were the two hundred "Watchers" or "Those Who Sleep Not" who were vulnerable enough to human passion to marry human women.

According to other myths, devils are lesser gods demoted by monotheism. In prefatory passages to *Angels of September* Greeley quotes the prayer after Low Mass from the pre-Vatican Council Liturgy. Saint Michael is implored to "defend us in battle [and] be our protection from the malice and snares of the Devil . . . and the other evil spirits." In Revelation 12:7–8, quoted on the same page, Michael and his angels are waging "war upon the dragon and his angels [which] fought but they had not the strength to win." When in *God Game* the author laments the lack of a dragon in his interactive fiction game, he also recognizes that it is easier to battle a bevy of devils than just one, especially since many of those evil spirits are buried in the human psyche as shadows.

As a police officer under the protection of Saint Michael, who was named patron of the police in 1950, the hero, Mike Casey, in *Angels of September* has to subdue the plural forces of evil and, more correctly, keep the peace in his role of defender of the elect. If, as is suggested by Blackie, the mischief in Anne Reilly's art gallery was caused by the Celtic belief in the lost souls in purgatory, the emphasis is on lost *souls*, not a singular soul. Yet it is the soul of the tortured painter Desmond Kenny which must be laid to rest, a responsibility of Michael the Archangel whose job it is to transport the souls of the dead to heaven. If the demons are at the bottom of the painting's pursuit of Anne's sanity, Michael does defeat them and, by implication, the Antichrist. Just as Michael the Archangel is the only angel to have seen hell as he escorted the devils into it, Mike Casey is the only one other than Anne to see the painting change into a hell about to absorb Anne, and it is he who exorcises the demon of Anne's guilt caused by her delusion that she started the tragic school fire.

Greeley heightens his use of more than one angel by the date of the climax—September 29, the liturgical feast of Saint Michael and all of the angels noted in Blackie's phrase that includes Michael "with Raphael and Gabriel and the rest of that crowd" (344). Greeley's *persona* Blackie Ryan claims that "the whole dumb crowd" of Mike's helpers are "not nearly as swift as they ought to be" (345); yet, Mike is backed up with this hastily called host of "angelic" helpers by Blackie with his holy water and stole, Mary Kate Ryan with the Irish pike (perhaps a form of sword), and Deirdre Lopez, the patrol officer with her gun (a modern fiery sword), from whom Greeley derives his title, calling them in his concluding note, the "four principal 'angels' of September—priest, lover, psychiatrist, and patrol officer— [who] represent the Church at its most effective caring best" (452). In the same note, he acknowledges his indebtedness to the tragic 1958 fire in a Chicago school—a fire in the school of Our Lady of the Angels.

Medieval iconography developed Michael's warlike qualities until he emerged as a full-fledged warrior angel complete with Roman armor (excluding wings) with a long spear rather than a sword, stabbing to death a writhing fire-breathing dragon, the physical form of the devil who preys on helpless souls, embodied as ubiquitous maidens needing rescue. The origin of such myths in Greeley's writings can be substantiated in his incorporation of the search for Jungian integrity among the three divisions of human nature—the male warrior or animus, the feminine anima, and the dark shadow energies of the dragon. This last image extends to the myth of the early sun god Perseus—who also saved a chained maiden from the sea-dragon by his sword and/or his spear and who defeated the snake-headed Medusa by using the sun sign of his mirrored shield. A later variant of the story occurs in that of Saint George, discredited by the Bollandists in their cleansing of the Calendar of Saints of such pagan elements.

The image of Saint Michael as a warrior angel wielding his fiery sword also became blurred with the Scandinavian myth of Odin as the god of storms, hurling thunderbolts, like his Greek and Roman counterparts of Zeus and Jupiter, on the heads of malefactors. Thus, the culminating scene in the art gallery is complicated by a vicious thunderstorm (which Greeley acknowledges is based on actual meteorological phenomena of September 1983) which helps to put out the fire but prevents help from reaching those inside.

Fire and water are both characteristics of Michael; de Voragine recounts that Michael divided the Red Sea for the Israelites and saved a pregnant woman from the sea "so that she brought forth her son in the midst of the deep . . . and came ashore rejoicing" (580). In *God Game* both Michele as a water-skier and Ranora as a swimmer and dunker are connected with water.

Greeley sets up a water and fire imagery early in *Angels of September* when the cardinal, visiting the art gallery to see Kenny's painting, comments that the artist makes "Hieronymus Bosch's hell look like an idyllic scene in Monet's garden" (1). Here, for other imagistic and symbolic purposes, Greeley switches roles—Mike Casey cannot control the diabolic fire with his fire extinguishers, since he is human, but Anne, as the water and fire image, is able to battle the flaming picture with a wastebasket decorated with Monet's water lilies because only a woman can control the power of flame. Until she incorporates the angelic power of flame, borrowed from Michael's flaming sword, into her own being, she cannot "defeat" the flaming picture or her own guilt over the school fire.

Fire images are all angel-connected as signs of angelic wrath or powers; Michael wields a flaming sword, Gabriel is the angel of light—the light of knowledge. Thus he appears to Mary in the Annunciation; de Voragine interprets the scriptural phrase, "the power of the most High shall overshadow thee" as "a shadow is formed by light falling upon a body" (206). In *Angel Fire* Gabriella's name is Light, an appropriate name for a seraph whose heavenly duties include shielding the light of the Godhead from human view, a sort of asbestos angel. As such, Gabriella, like all the other angels, is connected with unusual meteorological occurrences; the host of singing angels at Bethlehem (Luke 2:8–18) proclaimed the birth of Jesus from the heavens, and in the second chapter of Matthew, the star of Bethlehem guided the wise men to the Christ Child. And just as Michael's protégé Mike Casey defeats his demons during a thunderstorm, Gabriella destroys the nefarious Project Archangel with her pillar of fire during a snowstorm, and summons up a "gigantic waterspout" (225) to defeat the pursuing trawler.

In this fanciful tale of a man whose guardian angel, the seraph Gabriella, accompanies him in the form of a silver-haired strikingly beautiful mature woman, Greeley gives the reader a fairly standard rendition of the history of angels from the mouth of Blackie himself and a biased one from Gabriella: "we do not act as messengers for Anyone, at least not regularly. Although there are times when there are special missions which we feel that we must take on, we are as ultimately uncertain about the existence of Anyone as you are" (60). When the reluctant hero demonstrates his academic curiosity about Gabriella's angelhood, Greeley likens her answers to those familiar ones given by his Irish Female God—irrelevant and distracting but fascinating: "We are compelled to go forth . . . [as] messengers, secret agents, overseers . . . because it is in our nature to do so. . . . We are . . . companions on pilgrimage . . . [who] enjoy observing and sustaining patterns of beauty and goodness" (222).

The concept of angels as energy sources or patterns of energy seen in color and form neatly fits into both the science fiction mode and the traditional concept of seraphs as flaming angels. Gabriella's specialty is protecting Sean by managing his dealings with the electronic media—a role to which the archangel Gabriel was assigned in 1951 when he was upgraded from patron of telephones and telegraphs to patron of all means of electronic communication. As a seraph acting as a guardian angel, she incorporates all of these elements of messenger with her control over the electronic media—Sean's press conferences, his speeches, and his telephone calls to his daughters and to Blackie.

Greeley uses the same angelic terms for the intensity of the power of light in this novel: "Gaby's fire ball penetrating the sky. Angel Fire! . . . Laced with gold and silver . . . raging blast furnace, an out-of-control inferno" (256). Explaining carefully that the seraphim are patterns of creative energy, Greeley prevents his mortal from seeing the exact size, shape, and power of Gabriella until she is forced to exert energy to destroy the lab of the nefarious Project Archangel. As all descendants of the nuclear holocaust of 1945 must, the author uses images of nuclear destruction but without harmful radioactivity: "a vast pole of bubbling light . . . terrible red heat and light . . . then the brightest, cleanest, most terrible white light . . . Angel Fire! Seraph Fire! . . . a fusion reaction . . . a seraph, a being on fire with love, and now with love driven by anger" (249). Love equals light and heat.

As a seraph Gabriella controls heat so efficiently that her version of sexual foreplay nearly kills her mortal lover and charge, Sean, much as the hero in *Cocoon* is nearly killed by the laser beam dance of love of his alien lover or, more classically, like Semele being consumed by Zeus' splendor. This concept of the love of creatures for one another as a reflection of the

Divine Love for creatures is a repeated theme in the author's works and is, indeed, the reason for his writing. "Erotic love, insists Greeley... actually constitutes *the* symbol of divine passion," according to his critic Ingrid Shafer in her work *Eros and the Womanliness of God* (152).

Whenever creatures of light are postulated, adversarial creatures of darkness are suggested. To avoid simplistic polarities of good and evil, Greeley maintains steadily that demons are creatures—not creators—of evil, that random evil seems to exist, that most evil comes from human weakness which prevents humans from understanding and complying with the Divine Love shown them:

> There are, I think, powers of evil on the loose in the universe.... Whence come these powers of evil I don't know and whether they are in some sense personified I don't know either. Like Blackie Ryan and Gabriella I am inclined to believe not but I think we deceive ourselves completely if we do not understand that, as the Scripture says, we are wrestling with principalities and powers. (Letter, 28 Jan. 1988)

Here he uses traditional angelology but skirts assigning individuality to evil. Rather, he finds evil in the nonintegration of the Jungian components in the human personality; the animus, anima, and shadow, transforming the ancient concept of demons into a modern explanation of the shadow forces of the human personality.

For example, the fragmentation of the self as evil, random or otherwise, appears in *War in Heaven* in the hero's name, Jeremiah Thomas Keenan. Jeremiah was the prophet of doom who "wrestled with an explanation of why the people of Israel were faithless to their God. Thomas was the apostle who needed scientific proof of Christ's death and resurrection. The name "Keenan" suggests the Irish practice of "keening" or wailing over the dead. Because Greeley only writes "comedies of Grace," his hero describes the Jungian birth struggle of the integrated self in the following words:

> From the depths of my being... something powerful, indeed indomitable began to struggle free... a magic sword [Michael's weapon], a massive pike [Irish war weapon], a deadly lance [Saint George], an eighteenth inch gun from Yamoto? An Fh-1, the jet I had flown.... It was the memory of my experience of unity [with Andrea], the merging of my selfhood with her selfhood. (195–96)

When this psychomachy, this full-scale war for Andrea's soul, almost forces him to surrender her, a "blond winged giant in navy dress whites and five stars of a Fleet Admiral [carrying] a Browning Automatic Rifle" (198) shows up—Saint Michael again defeats the forces of evil.

While angels are evolving along with the rest of the universe, the lesser spirits, like leprechauns and other faerie folk, seem frozen like mammoths in some alternate evolutionary process. The computer in *God Game* with its randomizer gives perhaps the best explanation any of Greeley's heroes can come up with. In *Rite of Spring* Blackie rejects the Greek philosophy that "everything that happens in the world is directly attributable to God" (197). Some things, he implies, must be evil and, although God would like to prevent them, He can't because of our free will which we hold in common with the angels. Greeley resorts to the storyteller image often that "God is the great improviser, the great player-by-ear. When bad things happen, or we do bad things to one another, He simply adjusts His game plan and achieves His goals by an alternative path" (197).

The yet-unpublished novel *War in Heaven* deals with random evil as self-inflicted horror in two ways: the mental attack on the hero's memory by the souls of the men the hero killed in the war and the mental attack on the heroine by her memory of the deaths of her husband and child. The physical attack on both by the unnatural elements of the thunderstorm in the Arizona mountains only strengthens the randomness of evil forces. At the appropriate times, an angelic presence, usually a policeman or a military figure, routs the demons; in the final confrontation, the hero's brother, a seminarian, notes that he did not help his brother because at that time "he wasn't my brother. He was Michael, Seraph. Specialist in wars in heaven" (401).

This same unspecified randomness occurs in his lengthy list of reasons for the attacks by the demonic painting in Anne Reilly's art gallery. Thus, Greeley's version of Saint Michael the archangel, Mike Casey, does not fight a singular demon—the Devil or Satan—but rather a plural host of demons inhabiting Desmond Kenny's painting of "Divine Justice," demons which in Blackie's summary are the result of "two psychic fields [coming] into proximity with each other [which] merge and create transiently a highly destructive reality, a temporary being . . . a dense, convoluted and extremely evil if only temporary network of psychic energies" (440–41). "Psychic" is the operative word here; within the realistic world of that novel, the perception of evil as evil often lies in the minds of the characters and not in the real world—that is, Anne's mistaken belief that she has set the fatal school fire.

Just as Gabriella cannot know with certainty the existence of Anyone or of God, so also are Greeley's demons reduced to patterns of energies "not personalized like your Satan," as Gabriella reminds Sean (70). Greeley gives the devil even less credence in *Virgin and Martyr* where the hero Nick sees an apparition of "a visage of pure horror, maniacal, evil" (59) in the mirror at the home of "Little Angelica," the pseudo-saint who has caught Cathy Collins' enthusiasm, but the vision has little effect and no foreshadowing in the plot.

Being scared of unexplainable things or our own projected fears seems a reasonable approach, if balanced with the "impulse in the human personality that it will all still work out for the best . . . [that] all of these defiances of evil can be subsumed under one label: Hope'" *(Catholic Theology* 181). Such an outlook prevents Greeley from participating in tales of horror as such; rather he writes fantasy because "if Fantasy Romance is written out of the world of our dreams, Horror Romance is written out of our nightmares . . . as the story tellers try to explain the existence of evil which cannot be attributed to human evil alone" (174).

This distinction lodges him solidly on the borders of the created fantastic world, for, whereas fantasy intrudes into the real world, angels and demons have a separate and real existence, not dependent upon fantasy. For example, in *God Game* the narrator never "goes" into a fantasy world or creates one; however, he does manipulate characters in it by using the computer as an "angel" to deliver thought messages by typing words which are understood by the good characters—those who pray to their God. The computer can locate the forces of evil with no difficulty, since they are scattered in characters who do not pray and they are not centered in one adversarial being.

In *A Catholic Theology of Popular Culture* Greeley suggests that "our ancestors postulated a devil as an explanation for the cosmic evil" (179) but rejects that "the cosmic evil energies need to be personified [because] once you have personified them, you are no closer to an explanation of why God tolerates such energies" (180). While Greeley admits Lucifer into the realm of the angels, he gives him little attention, dismissing him as an active agent in the diabolic happenings in the Reilly art gallery in favor of unnamed and unspecified demons.

In his *Angel Fire* Greeley puts forth an interesting speculation on the fate of Lucifer: his heroine Gabriella Light's name clues Sean into her role as "complement" or mate of Lucifer [the light bearer]. He was, she insists, "Yahweh's jester . . . not a bad angel . . . he was a good spirit, he never defied the Most High" (70) and she still mourns for him. He is gone from angelic existence, "mortal too, like all energy patterns" (65), but she defends his "going" as "an absurd misunderstanding . . . a silly folk tale which the author of Revelation uses to illustrate the problem of good and evil . . . . We are such terrible arguers . . . That's where the story started" (220–21).

Thus, the role of Greeley's angels hovers between somewhat realistic works in which the hero is bemused by angelic or demonic intervention (*Angels of September* and *War in Heaven*) and science fiction and fantasy works (*Angel Fire* and *God Game*) where the angel or "ilel" is a creature whose powers supersede even her creator's.

As Ingrid Shafer notes in her seminal work on Greeley, he makes a "conscious attempt to tease the Christian comedy of grace out of the new-old symbols" (5). Where science fiction writers attribute good spirits as defenders or teachers of the hero on his journey and create evil spirits to entrap the hero, they usually envision the good spirits as pre- or anti-Christian forces of nature, while the evil ones reside in organized religion itself. Greeley, as a priest who criticizes his Church openly, as he would criticize any family member privately, still comes to her defense by using the "given" of angelic and demonic forces as structuring elements in his novels. In this way, his belief in the other world's influences dovetails neatly with his needs as the science fiction writer whose imagination, like that of the androgynous and loving God he professes, does not limit His/Her creation.

Since Greeley groups his novels into general categories like the Passover Trilogy and the Beatitude mysteries and since two of his recent novels were about the archangels Michael (*Angels of September*) and Gabriel(la) (*Angel Fire*), logic would seem to demand that his next novel about angels be about Raphael in his role as a companion on a journey with Tobias or as a guide for young lovers, and *War in Heaven* does indeed depict an angel who is necessarily named Michael to agree with the "war" of the title but who acts as a companion on the hero's journey and as a guide for young lovers.

One final angel remains. In various works, Greeley has claimed that over half of the population has had experiences with the "otherworld." Many times those experiences are "near-death" happenings in which a figure of light questions the person. In Hebrew myth Michael is the Angel of Death who escorts the souls to Paradise, although Christian tradition claims that role for Christ. In *The Religious Imagination* Greeley reiterates that any manifestation of a "grace experience" often involves the person's realization of his closeness to the other world in such an angelic experience. He quotes Bob Fosse's *All That Jazz* as the "'particular judgment' in which Fosse reviews his life with the Angel of Death . . . runs down the long corridor toward the light [where] 'Angelique,' the Angel of Death, dressed in filmy bridal clothes . . . welcomes him into their nuptial chamber" (19). In *Angel Fire* Gabriella almost causes Sean's death through the ardor of her lovemaking; she admits that "it is impossible for our two species to unite without destruction. Our love is too terrible" (257).

While he has yet to deal with the Angel of Death as a character, Greeley has maintained a determinedly optimistic and hopeful view of his fictional worlds—that, eventually, in the words of Christ to Julian of Norwich, "All manner of things will be well." To aid humans—fictional and real—Greeley ends *Angel Fire* with an old nun's dictum: "Your guardian angel watches over you and protects you all your life. Whether you like it or not" (301).

WORKS CITED

de Voragine, Jacobus. *The Golden Legend*. Translated by Granger Ryan and Helmut Ripperger. New York: Longman, Green, 1941.

Greeley, Andrew M. *Angel Fire*. New York: Warner, 1988.

———. *Angels of September*. New York: Warner, 1986.

———. *Ascent into Hell*. New York: Warner, 1983.

————. *A Catholic Theology of Popular Culture*. Prepublication copy, courtesy of Andrew Greeley.

————. *God Game*. New York: Warner, 1987.

————. "In Defense of Hopeful Endings." *Writer's Digest*, Jan. 1987, 31–34.

————. *Lord of the Dance*. New York: Warner, 1984.

————. *The Magic Cup*. New York: Warner, 1979.

————. *The Religious Imagination*. New York: Sadlier, 1981.

————. *Rite of Spring*. New York: Warner, 1987.

————. *Virgin and Martyr*. New York: Warner, 1985.

————. *War in Heaven*. Prepublication copy, courtesy of Andrew Greeley.

Hahn, Emily. *Breath of God: A Book About Angels, Demons, Familiars, Elementals, and Spirits*. Garden City, N.Y.: Doubleday, 1971.

Shafer, Ingrid H. *Eros and the Womanliness of God: Andrew Greeley's Romances of Renewal*. Chicago: Loyola University Press, 1986.

28

ANNE K. KALER

God, Greeley, and the Computer: Andrew Greeley's New Narrative Trinity in God Game

*A*uthors have played God almost as often as God has played Author. But where God may speak "in diverse ways," the human authors justify their compulsion to play god by inventing one or more personae to mask the author's voice. So when the narrator-hero of Andrew Greeley's *God Game* stumbles into a fantasy world within a computer game where the computer becomes the voice of God, Greeley as an author has to extend his narrative technique to seven differing levels of narration.

Just as a program is the guiding pattern for a computer, Greeley uses a software package of an interactive fiction game to strengthen and reiterate his insistence that grace is the guiding pattern of life. Such interpenetrations of Greeley's religious beliefs and computer realities into the world of fantasy (and vice versa) make the book a multidimensional work of seven separate levels. Each level is rampant with storytelling, computer instructions, medieval battles, futuristic telepathy, romantic themes, human doubts, pixie angels, personal commentary, and intriguing twists—literary, theological, romantic, and humorous. Like the Ptolemaic universe, each sphere of narration circles back to Greeley's avowed purpose: "Thus are we all storytellers, narrating the story of our own lives and finding in our religion,

---

An earlier version of this essay was presented during the last of four sessions dealing with Andrew Greeley's fiction at the Popular Culture Association Meeting in New Orleans, Louisiana, 26 Mar. 1988.

whatever its over-arching symbols, the cosmos-making themes that give final purpose to our existence" (11).

The narrative structure in *God Game* differs from Greeley's earlier "comedies of grace" and from his Blackie Ryan mysteries where the demands of the plot dictate the tale-telling style. Even when he creates a single point of view with a single narrator, his vision is consistently that of the creator/author, controlling with his single set of eyes all worlds he sees; for instance, in novels like *Virgin and Martyr* the narrative is split among several narrators using epistolary and journalistic chapters.

In this later novel of *God Game*, however, Greeley juggles at least seven separate levels of narration; no longer is he satisfied with the simple telling of a tale, since the nature of the game-playing itself seems to dictate a chronological order. "God draws straight with crooked lines," Greeley warns before the story begins, and this fantasy world which he creates has the complexity of narrative voices complemented by the foreshadowing and recriminations, comments and complaints, injections and interruptions, typical of Greeley's style.

Like a Chinese ivory ball in which each smaller ball is carved from and entrapped within the ball immediately larger than itself, Greeley layers seven separate narrative worlds in this novel. While such sleight of hand shows his growing control of narrative form, his real reason is, as always, to present a completed circle or pattern or Chinese ball in literature that will bring the reader to an appreciation of the larger pattern of God and His Universe. Thus, when he claims that "religion in its raw and elemental manifestation plays a "momma" function, he means that "it tells stories which suggest that there is order in the confusion, meaning in the terror, cosmos in the chaos" (8). Traditionally, the imposition of order on chaos is a masculine one—the rational and patriarchal order subjugates the fantastic and feminine disorder. The combined effects of Freud, Jung, Fraser, Eliade, Campbell, and Matthew Fox have restored the respectability of Goethe's Eternal Feminine as the balancing element to scientific and empiric studies. And that storytelling circular pattern of religion is as ultimately feminine a muse as Dante's Beatrice or Joyce's girl-in-the-Liffey or Graves' White Goddess or Greeley's Celtic mother-muse.

Superficially, *God Game* is a science fiction/fantasy novel where the real world intrudes on a created world; the masculine or rational world "creates" the feminine or fantasy world. Specifically, this incorporation of the Jungian masculine outward quest of the hero for self-identification with the Father, and the feminine inward journey of awakening or acceptance of the Mother's creative ability within all of us, needs the complexity of narration which Greeley gives it. The basis for his complexity of approach lies in his belief, quoted from Northrop Frye's *The Secular Scripture*, that "identity and self-recognition begin when we realize that this is not an either-or question, when the great twins of divine creation and human re-creation have merged into one, and we can see that the same shape is upon both" (vii). That same shape is the story told by the mother, the muse, the matter or *mater* of the act of creation, fertilized by the rational brain, but embedded in the maternal and material womb of words.

Greeley's "human re-creation" of the "divine creation" leads to his choice of seven significant and separate levels of narration, necessary to suspend the story in its fantasy web. The first level is that of Greeley the author who controls the other levels as creator. The second level is that of the narrator or storyteller in the novel; the third is the game-player; the fourth, the land itself; the fifth, the land's inhabitants; the sixth, the angelic dimension; and the seventh returns to the Godhead. All these levels interact with each other, and all are present at any given time within the novel, just as the ivory balls are "trapped" each within the other.

Why seven? The use of seven is a common theological and numerological one. Seven is a prime number, divisible only by itself; it is the number of theological virtues and vices seen from medieval morality plays to Laurence Sanders' works; its origin may stem from the seven openings of a man's body versus the eight of a woman's; it is the number of candles of the Menorah (which is lit by the lesser, feminine servant eighth candle).

But seven is the sum of three and four, the first one a prime in itself and the basis of the Christian concept of Trinity—Father, Son, and Holy Spirit. These three "divisions" of the Godhead appear as an overriding structure of the seven levels of narration. For example, God the Father is Greeley as author—integral, controlling, ultimately omniscient. God the Son, the Christ, is the active participant, the Doer in the novel—he is Greeley as the narrator/storyteller and game-player. God the Holy Spirit is the action played out—Greeley's creation of the land, the inhabitants, the angels/computer. In this Trinity of narrative levels, the last, seventh level—that of the Godhead itself—is essentially Greeley's version of the Godhead. But, as happens in every Jungian trinity or triad suggested, a fourth element appears to become the fourth corner of the triangle—to square the triangle so that it can be incorporated again into the circle. And that element is always the feminine one. So also in *God Game* is the overriding element of the feminine creative force the major focus within the novel, a prime theme in most of Greeley's works. This novel shows a writer analyzing his own writing into its component parts and synthesizing it into a readable tale, a man who has used the rational masculine force joined with the feminine creative force to make a new creation.

So strong is this feminine element that not only is the resolution brought about by the action of Ranora/Michele, the twin teenage messenger angels, but the final touch is provided by the Jewish skeptic Nathan's wife, who assures the reader that the characters the narrator seemingly abandoned are not all forgotten. "They're being watched over" (303). Her name is the complement to that of her Jewish husband, whose name, Nathan, means

Grace; she is Elisa, the modern form of Elizabeth, the mother of John the Baptist, the precursor of Christ, as Nathan as a Jew is the precursor of the Christian priest/narrator.

But how does he achieve his first level—that of Greeley as author?

With as minor a detail as the fact that his narrator—a priest-writer-sociologist—is never named, Greeley underscores the narrator's role as the Old Testament God, the One whose name cannot be uttered or written. Early on in the novel, Greeley deals with the "uneasy relationship between author and narrator," a tension he considers "inevitable given the propensity of narrators to take stories away from the author" (53). He then warns his readers against "the narrator's sly hints that he is me" (54). In the author's note at the end, he reaffirms the separation of the two beings—Greeley as author and as narrator: "he (and I with his uninspired cooperation) has created a world in which there are solid grounds for hope. . . . justifiable arguments for an Other Person who loves" (307), a fictional cosmos, admittedly considerably less complex and problematic than the world in which we live (307).

To do so, he must first distance himself as the author Greeley from the narrator *persona* of *God Game*—that pseudo-autobiographical operator-narrator *persona* of an unnamed priest located in the Chicago area near Lake Michigan where he water-skis, uses a computer, and tells stories. But even Greeley's Blackie Ryan pales in comparison to intricacies of this *persona*, because Greeley has extended the authority of his narrative voice from that of the simple storyteller into an attempted new literary format of multiple levels of narration. Although every author develops a *persona* through whom he speaks, Greeley is criticized because he tries to present the world of the Irish Catholics around Chicago; he is criticized because he does so in his sociological texts and surveys, in his teachings, in his religious writings, in his romantic "comedies of grace," in his short stories, in his poems, in his science fiction and fantasy writings. Can he be faulted because he attempts to do the same thing many ways, because he is creative in many areas, because as a storyteller he must tell the same story of salvation again and again? And if he grows in his craft, who should criticize him for trying to tell a better story?

An author imitating the Author plays the Puppet Master role—controlling the puppets' strings and shutting them up in the toybox when the game is finished, but never constructing or "creating" them. Rather than being such an unfeeling manipulator, Greeley's narrator suffers as much as his creatures do, not an unlikely happening from a priest concerned with expounding the message that God did indeed suffer for the sins of man.

As a non-God creator who must create from the matter of his own mind, Greeley uses the previous pool of prose fiction modes of the journal, the autobiography, and the tale: as a journal, it is reflective of the narrator's changing attitudes toward himself and his world(s); as a pseudo-autobiography the novel imitates the heritage of Defoe's *Robinson Crusoe* and his use of immediacy as a narrative technique; as a tale it selects only those elements which will tell the story best.

The journal technique is informal, as if Greeley were a genial storyteller retelling a tale. But if the story is totally autobiographical, then the truth is seen from the narrator's perspective only and the work becomes a journal of life experiences, reflected on in tranquillity or scribbled immediately after the event. To prevent this, Greeley's use of the computer as omniscient *voyeur* allows the narrator to adopt the attitude of a bemused traveler to a far realm, an early prose fiction ploy to show the faults of a society. In this way the computer is like the archangel Raphael in disguise, since it is one of Raphael's duties to guide the traveler.

The sense of immediacy Greeley attains by jumping from level to level is designed to convince the reader of the versimilitude of the story as an immediately recorded story. When the narrator tries to explain why every-thing in the alternate world seems somehow inaccurate, he muses that it may be a "problem of translation. Perhaps our receiving mechanism has to adjust to signals, electronic or spiritual . . . Or perhaps there is a mecha-nism, a censor—make the 'c' a capital if you wish—that filters out informa-tion that we don't need or shouldn't have . . . an author" (36). He thus reinforces the possible truth of his world and rejects responsibility for the world as a created being of an "author."

The ingenious first-person narrator is no naive recorder of events. He insists he is not the author Greeley and that the novel is not "Speculative Fiction" but rather a "sober" report by a social scientist of what happened when he began to play an interactive fiction game (46). To support this, he calls upon another early prose fiction device of versimilitude by detailing computer terms and by keeping "every move of the game recorded . . . on the Alpha 10 [disk] on my shelf in my office at Grand Beach" (305). His calling in of scientists to attest to the veracity of the tapes heightens belief, especially when the narrator even offers to send out the names of several scientists.

Specific realistic details about the computer's capacity, including its "sophisticated parser [with] a slow game for those with a PCxt or a clone and a fast game for those who have a machine with an Intel 286 chip like your Compaq" (3), provide versimilitude to sustain the reality of the narrator's world; however, this is not as easy a task on the printed page. Here the author uses different fonts to indicate who is speaking: the narrator "talks" in a thinner typeface; the computer in darker caps of that same face, for angels' voices are not the same as either God's or man's voice.

While a tale has simple plot line and simple characters, the telling of it may invite a canon of techniques; the author may digress into subplot or moral wanderings, such as Fielding did in *Tom Jones*; he may comment upon writing as process of individuation, such as Sterne did in *Tristam Shandy;* he may embellish the plot with complications from another world, such as Dickens did in *The Christmas Carol*. No two people tell the same tale.

For that reason, some distancing has to take place between the creator of the first level, the narrator of the second level, and the game-player of the third level. For example, despite the power he grants him as a storyteller, Greeley never makes his narrator think that he has created the world (the "land" as he calls it); the narrator knows that he can use the computer voice as a message sender to interfere, suggest, and rearrange, but he cannot create or destroy the "land." To reinforce the narrator's role as an author of fiction and not a creator of worlds, Greeley's narrator comments that the name of the game is deficient: "A Medieval/Futuristic Fantasy Romance" covers all popular fiction demands, save for "mystery" (17).

The second level of narration, that of the storyteller, Greeley claims, is "a kid's . . . desperate plea for meaning . . . [for] Momma's story [to put] some order into the confusion, some cosmos into the chaos" (8). Following his often used premise that "every storyteller is a theologian and every story is about God, one way or another" (16), Greeley insists that the computer program of interactive fiction is only a series of "gimmicks to teach students. . . the craft of storytelling" (15). He consistently calls the action his narrator performs a " 'story' not a 'game' "(18). This insistence on authorial control reinforces the role of divine interference into human actions and negates the Deistic idea of God as whimsical, vacillating, and sometimes irresponsible game-player.

Greeley's novel refines the leisurely pace of the storyteller to suit the weaving of his tale from smaller components of interjections and asides—a collage effect where the synergistic impact outweighs the individual comments. Greeley is frequently accused of writing his works in haste with multiple personalities and personal intrusions thrown in to amuse (or distract) the reader. In this novel, however, the intrusions or flittings from level to level provide an opportunity to see the integration of his levels and the breadth of his literary control. Yes, there are personal references but they are the product of the overstimulated mind of the author in a creative and playful mood. For storytelling is play.

Bruno Bettelheim in his article "The Importance of Play" sees that

> although the words play and game may seem synonymous, [play is] characterized by freedom from all but personally imposed rules (which are changed at will), by free-wheeling fantasy involvement, and by the absence of any goals outside the activity itself. Games, however, are usually competitive and are characterized by agreed-upon, often externally imposed rules . . . and frequently by a goal or purpose . . . such as winning the game. . . . Children recognize early on that play is an opportunity for pure enjoyment, whereas games may involve considerable stress. (44–46)

Greeley's narrator wants to play, to tell the story in his own manner, on the second level of narration; the limitations of the computer game cause him stress, throwing him into the third level of narration—that of the game-player, where Greeley is always conscious of the limitation of preset characters implicit in the "game."

This third distinct level, differing from the narrator who tells of one side of the narrator's personality—that of the adventurer or hero on his quest for the perfect ending. The conflict necessary to any fictional action is provided by the author for the reader—mystery writers depend on the unexpected murder, horror writers on the unexpected attack, romance writers on the unexpected lover—but none is as familiar as that of the interactive fiction game. The natural way of expressing human conflict lies in the concept of the game, often mock battles between the heroes of cities with their sports teams or the video computer games of the young. Because games provide a simplistic model where evil forces can be defeated by the forces of good, the operator who is in control of the game acts as the hero.

Greeley uses Bettelheim's concept that a game may have rules but play is unstructured to show that a story may be a playful event because it is unstructured but that a game—as the computer program shows—must have rules and requires a game-player who recognizes the rules of the game. His third level of creation, then, is such a game-player who is forced to abide by the limitations of the program while being a hero.

Although the game-player narrator claims to be "electronically illiterate" (16), he is capable of hooking up his computer with the satellite dish, of programming the system to save the game on disk, of loading and executing the program, of distinguishing between commands and utilities. Through-out the novel he gives instructions in computerese—just enough to be explicit and not enough to confuse a computer illiterate. While he makes the typical response to ill-written manuals, he provides an anatomy, in Northrop Frye's terms, of how to become too involved with computer games.

He does make one major mistake that a computer literate would not—he starts up his program in the midst of a thunderstorm. He connects the computer to his wide-screen TV and runs the hookup through the satellite linking it to a "massive green mesh disk . . . listening (as [he] used to tell people jokingly) for communications from outer space or from God" (17). Soon he would discover that the satellite dish and its receiver box were the distant "cause, or maybe only the occasion, of my God problem" (17).

The proximate cause is lightning striking the satellite box which acts as agent to propel his computer capacity into the alternative universe by turning the screen "black, then blank" (19). When the power comes back on, a movie with real-life characters appears on the TV screen in place of the prior animated blips of graphic design: the configurations of the Duchess, the "blob of blue on a beige background," and the Duke, "red on black," have been transformed into a "slender and elegant, a brown-eyed, brown-skinned, long-haired, dark lady . . . in a blue gown" and a "medium sized man, with broad shoulders and fair hair, wearing some sort of weird red armor" (19–20).

The short-circuiting somehow opened a "port" or "gate" or slit in the fabric of time and dimension. Greeley intensifies this image by deprecating his own definition of how these "gates" work: "elaborate and complex interpretations of intricate and unpredictable patterns of spiritual influences . . . [which create] a reverse flow" (155) between the two worlds. The term "port" for portal that Greeley uses is partially explained by the sign he sees for LaPorte County, "the gate to the prairies and the world beyond," but he concludes that it was "an accidental juxtaposition of names. Two utterly different kinds of gates" (156), that is, the "portals to the west" and the "gates" of a computer's binary system.

The third set of implied gates jumps into the sixth level of narration—angels guarding gates or the unnamed "cherubim with the fiery revolving sword" of Genesis 3:24; perhaps the modern revolving satellite dish struck by lightning is an afterimage of this flaming solar wheel of popular hagiography. Traditionally, the gates of Paradise were guarded to prevent the reentrance of the unworthy Adam and Eve by Saint Michael the Archangel. His propensity as a thunder-and-lightning archangel stems from the "fiery revolving sword" or lightning; his posture as a warrior angel led to his being the patron of those engaged in warfare—policemen, in particular.

The land in which the game is played—the fourth level of narration—is suggested by the computer program but created as an alternate universe by the lightning stroke. While the narrator ponders on his entrance into a fantasy world in a "different dimension of reality" (23), he also wonders about the actual source or existence of his game world: he doubts that he is "in touch with another planet"; he opts for "another cosmos, one 'adjacent' to ours but on different dimensions of time and space" (30). He sums up his speculations in a six-part hypothesis that "neighboring cosmoi [which operate] with a different set of elementary forces [are now] impenetrable [except to] love . . . and mind and spirit [which may] flit across these physically impenetrable boundaries . . . and frolic . . . with considerable and mostly benign effect" (48–49). Those beings who "frolic" across the boundaries between the cosmoi are "virgin potential bearers of life [who have] freedom of movement which makes Planck's Wall look like a beaded curtain" (50). The references to the theories of Max Planck are a consistent element in Greeley's novels; Planck's Wall is, he notes in a letter (10 Sept. 1987), "that time in the first tiny fraction of the universe when there was a unified force—that is to say, when gravity and electromagnetism were the same force," the One Force of God. Thus, any exchange of beings across cosmoi violates the laws of nature as we know them, and the propensity of atoms or angels to slip through impenetrable "walls" aligns itself with the Jungian concept of dreams as guides on the inner journey, in this case as using the "port" created by the computer and lightning stroke.

The idea is not new. It is the stock explanation for otherworld experiences as short circuits or cracks in the computer or, perhaps in Greeley's priestly view, even the way some of us get into heaven. But what makes this book different from other science fiction and fantasy novels is that the computer is only a means of communication for the program of interactive fiction; it is only a series of "gimmicks to teach students... the craft of storytelling" (15). He consistently calls the action his narrator performs a "'story' not a 'game'" (18); yet, as the novel develops, so also does the character of the computer as a separate entity which spans three levels—as tool for the game-player, as voice of God for the land, and as God for the land's inhabitants.

The computer never becomes a sentient rational being who creates or alters the land without the explicit commands of the narrator, any more than angels create or alter the messages to the worlds they visit. At no point does the computer force obedience by suppressing free will. To those beings in that other world, the voice of the computer is a being called "The Lord Our God," because their prayers are answered in dialogue with this being. The narrator is never able to convince them that he and his computer are creatures also, nor does he try; it is enough that the computer voice of the narrator is the controlling force in their nontechnological universe.

Sometimes the role of the narrator as an unbiased observer is shattered by the emerging personality of the computer, which, when it does not understand a direction, "flashes back impatiently" (25), and snaps back, "DON'T TALK THAT WAY TO ME" (277) to the narrator's cursing. This interaction of tool and master is a reflection of the responses of creatures to a narrator God mirrored in the rest of the novel. It also provides Greeley with an arena for his fast comebacks and serves to lessen the God-like quality of the narrator.

Because the narrator's computer is based on the binary system of toggle switches—it is either zero or one, on or off, right or left, male or female, saved or damned—Greeley is able to show how his narrator is forced to extend his view of the "land" from a simplistic one where good and evil polarities abound to one of complex realities similar to the one in which the narrator lives. So when Greeley protests the lack of a dragon in the game, he is protesting the lack of a visible evil to combat, such as appears in myth and video games. Thus, in such an interactive fiction game which overlooks complexity or human emotions, Greeley's hero tries his best to see his "land" in terms of right and wrong, only to find that reaction does not follow action, that his best intentions often lead to further complications, and that the computer develops into a prickly character in itself with as much free will and opinion as other Greeley characters.

Although the computer is a tool and technological reality for the narrator, it appears as the interior voice of God or angelic intuition to the characters in the fantasy world. There, the computer acts like a messenger or angel delivering the word of the narrator "God," just as Saint Gabriel "announced" the coming of the Messiah in the New Testament or as the host of angels "announced" the birth of Christ at Bethlehem.

The fourth layer of narration, the "land" itself, which can be called into existence or dismissed by the computer program, embodies the very essence or purpose of fiction by providing the reader with a controllable universe. Patterns in literature reinforce larger patterns in life because they are manageable in size—we can understand a simplified pattern. As Greeley says, "fiction doesn't imitate life. Life imitates fiction. Sometimes life imitates fiction imitating life . . . sometimes fiction can take control of life" (11). When it does so it provides an observable pattern such as Greeley's creation of his "land."

Greeley's "land" is both medieval and futuristic, an alternate Garden of Eden and a partial Utopia; it is not a glorified Paradise. For example, the scientists called in to examine the taped document find that the otherworld was a "nice imitation" (35) of our world's landscape but that the oak tree has leaves with different ribs, the branches are at angles that could not support weight, the bark is "wrong." Even the inventor Nathan comments that "nothing is quite right, color, shapes, angles, perspectives. But at first you are dazzled by the dramatic colors and hardly notice" (36). This testing device supports Greeley's use of versimilitude to heighten his narrator's credibility.

The land summoned up by the computer program contains elements of both a science fiction and a fantasy world: since the intrusion of the computer-god into the otherworld is accomplished by technological means, it qualifies as science fiction. As a fantasy world, it has a medieval/futuristic setting. As do most fantasy worlds, its medievalism with its simplified feudal structure resembles those "petty fiefdoms in early modern Italy" (35) with two city-states with "stolid burghers . . . , [a] nobility who had larger farms in the countryside" (35), and farmers. The medieval flavor is heightened by primitive weaponry for the hand-to-hand single combat needed to prove the bravery of the characters.

Blended into this land, then, is a utopian futurism with its indestructible fabrics and improved communications systems such as mental telepathy. This enables informal communication with their God to seem normal, although in their formal communication with God, the inhabitants of the "land" are "not quite like us" (33); their "Lord Our God was worshipped privately with almost no formal ritual. He was addressed much like a passionately loving and indulgent parent or even a sexual lover" (34). To readers of Greeley and students of the great mystics, this concept of God as an implacable lover connects aspects of spirituality with fantasy. Whereas most fantasies have a matriarchal triad of Earth Mother goddesses opposed to a patriarchal set of gods, Greeley, as a Catholic priest who insists on an androgynous god with the Celtic name of Herself/Himself, uses the narrator as an androgynous Self in opposition to the weak and scheming patriarchal clerical structure of formal religion in the "land." Thus, the "God" in the land is a melding of the rational aspect of the narrator with his feminine or creative side, while Ranora, the angelic sprite, and G'Ranne, the mystic, and the other characters in lesser degree dialogue with their Lord God on an informal nonsexist basis. In such a land, G'Ranne (a version of the Celtic heroine Grainne) can pursue her God with a "tearstained, joyous face . . . radiant in the light . . . Teresa emerging in the light of Mount Carmel after the Dark Night of the Soul" (302), and Ranora can scamper about as a "wonderful imp child . . . to remind us how to laugh" (304).

Stripped of technological confusion, the land's only problems are those of fantasy worlds—simple patterns of good and evil which allow the characters to achieve actualization of the Jungian search for self-identity, that is, to be most fully oneself, which, according to Greeley, is to be the most unified with God, as is G'Ranne, who is just one of several mystics in the book. So strong is their passion between lovers that it is "more fearsome than their hatred" (29); so violent and honest are their emotions, which are not "toned down the way we tone down raw human emotion when we depict it artistically" (28), that the tapes must be repressed; so potent are their passions that the tapes must be "locked up in another country . . . because the biologists and social scientists who came to our seminars unanimously agreed that we couldn't show the tapes outside the controlled environment of a university" (28–29).

Complexity of plot actions may exist, but complexity of intent, of human desire for the good as he or she sees it, does not exist here. Even when characters err, their intentions are never menial. While the inhabitants of the land—the fifth level of Greeley's narration—do not worry about material things for survival, they do struggle with human emotions, free will, and random evil, which are common to all cosmoi.

Evil as lodged in the cardinal, for instance, or in the three stooges, is cartoonlike. For example, while the computer complies with the narrator's request to spot the villains by accessing UNREST, the visible evil he does find lies in the priestly clan who seek to overthrow the rule of the Duke and Duchess with their own theogony. Less evil descendants of the minor devils of medieval theater, are the warrior clowns who keep trying to make bombs to destroy the forces of good. Appropriately named after the Three Stooges—Larry, Curly, and Moe—the three devils resemble the triad of Lucifer, Beelzebub, and Mephistopheles in Marlowe's *Dr. Faustus*. Here the computer in its role as the avenging archangel Saint Michael responds to the narrator's command to ZAP the minor devils by becoming "ingenious in its destructive techniques" (187), without ever actually hurting anything but the egos of the clowns, just as Saint Michael will defeat but not destroy the fallen angels in the final battle in the Bible. Certainly, Greeley's compassionate God can forgive fallen angels as readily as He can forgive fallen men.

As Greeley the author, he has his characters arising from the genetic pool of his preconscious. On the one hand, he admits that "characters do not emerge as the *tabula rasa* [but rather] spring into existence . . . fully grown . . . . The story teller . . . has to make do with what his preconscious had given him in the way of character fragments" (15); on the other hand, he suggests specific methods "to permit his authors to build their own character/personality program . . . through 'pre-characterization' " (15–16). The solution he finds is that "the people I had to deal with . . . were persons I might have created . . . characters who lurk in ready made, 'off the shelf' bits and pieces in my own preconscious" (16). From these characters, the storyteller molds the lives that "are stories that God tells. We write them together with God. Coauthors . . . . Maybe God has a program like ours in which he does His coauthoring with keystrokes" (6).

The sixth level of narration provides a familiar medium for the supernatural forces—angels and those acting as angels. While the narrator "plays" at the game until it becomes "work" then "life or death" to his sanity, his mind, first intrigued by the rational parameters of the "double decision-tree algorithm" (7) and "N options for beginnings and endings" (5), soon must draw on the Jungian forces of the anima for compassion and the shadow for energies to make difficult decisions. Into these areas—the anima and the shadow—fall those inexplicable creatures and events not comprehensible to human reason. Thus, not until all three Jungian elements work together is he able to solve the problems of the "land" but only with angelic intervention of Ranora in the form of Michele and her telephone call. The inspiration, which originated from Ranora to Michele, was beyond the narrator's control, since he could not control Ranora. This suggests the author's belief in angels who, as messengers of God Herself, can "inspire" human actions.

In *Angle Fire* Greeley has angels identified as "patterns of energy" searching for the beauty in other patterns of energy, such as human beings, so that his use of the computer—the extension of the human brain, so to speak—as a messenger angel is not so farfetched. But, as priest-narrator, he is conscious of his preconscious working so that the computer's capabilities must be altered, he avers, to accommodate free will—of author as God. In order to do this he makes use of the familiar concept of angels as messengers, delivering messages of explanation or direct orders to his creatures. In this novel the message sender is a computer, who, like an angel, does not alter the message.

What makes this book different from other science fiction and fantasy novels is that, while the computer merely activates a programmed game in the narrator's real world, to those beings in that alternate universe the computer is the voice of God as perceived by intuitive thought, a process usually attributed only to angelic intelligence. The computer operator—the narrator—as the controlling force in the life pattern of the land's inhabitants experiences an un-God-like horror and fervor when he undertakes his task to act as a good God to "his people." It is this same horror that prevents the hero from becoming God.

The infusion of knowledge into the consciousness of the otherworld people is immediate and intuitive, a characteristic of angelic messages. Often these messages appear within dreams in the narrator's world, as they have done before in the Bible as prophetic dreams. But, in the "land," the messages are immediately perceived by the awake inhabitants as interior voices different from our Jungian concept of subconscious inner "voices."

Once Planck's wall has been penetrated, the narrator's world can be visited by angels from the "land." As the novel progresses, the two worlds do affect each other through dreams for benign effect; the characters from the land visit the narrator and others in dreams; they drink his Bailey's Irish Cream; they influence the "real" people in the narrator's world to make important decisions, never being mistaken for the angels of the narrator's own world. Thus, the narrator's friend Michele is the "Precinct captain in charge of waterskiing" (5), especially on one ski, because Saint Michael, the patron of policemen and "precinct captains," is often pictured with a spear (or ski) to defeat the devil; it is Michele's mysterious telephone call which leads the narrator to the final solution to the problems in the "land." As Ranora is a complement to Gabriel, Michele admits to having played the flute as a child, the closest musical instrument to Ranora's pipe and the Irish tin whistles the protagonist's daughters in *Angel Fire* covet.

If angels exist in the narrator's world, angels other than the computer can also exist in the "land"; in fact, they can become main characters as Ranora is in Greeley's own version of an angelic protective spirit of the "land." He coins the world "ilel," and describes her as a combination of "Tinker Bell and Ariel . . . and a haughty archangel" (62). "Ilel" seems analogous to C. S. Lewis' "eldil." (Greeley admits in private correspondence that the word is manufactured but may have been influenced by these two sources.) "Ranora" as a name may be an echo of his many strong female characters named Nora, combined with the Egyptian word for the sun god Ra, since she shields the Duke from the sun with her red and white peppermint striped dress.

Ranora, as a "sprite spirit," in Greeley's own words (Letter, 8 Aug. 1987), is a combination of the major angels with a dash of teenage girlish Irish whimsy, "an imp, a pixie . . . a female leprechaun, a trickster, a wise woman, a conscience, a sister, a daughter, a mother, and a haughty archangel" (62). As a counterpart of Saint Gabriel with his trumpet which will awaken the dead, Ranora's joyous piping of individual leitmotifs casts a spell or a charm over inhabitants of both worlds, just as the storyteller "charms" by his words. As Saint Raphael, the guide of young lovers and a companion on a journey in the scriptural story of Tobias, Ranora herself manipulates the love affair of the Duke and the Duchess by leading them to their bridal bed on the houseboat; she revives the marriage of N'Rasia and Malvau, the older lovers, by her piping. The narrator even refers to her as his "messenger" (291) when, as Saint Michael, she defends the helplessly bound Duke against his murderers with the wrath of her pointing finger until the lightning and thunder, usually associated with Saint Michael, save the day; in fact, Greeley slips a pun in about his "ilel": "giant blue sparks, a thousand el cars' third rails, leaped in every direction" (295) as the lightning scares the murderous crowd.

At every turn, however, Ranora obeys the commands of the voice of the computer, albeit with some challenging, just as her counterpart Michele acts as the angelic sprite who solves the puzzle of the game with her telephone call.

Outwitting a computer in a game imitates real-life confrontation of good and evil while avoiding the usual bloodshed such a confrontation brings about. However, ever since the computer Hal's artificial intelligence outmaneuvered that of his master in *2001*, the computer as malevolent force itself has replaced the evil scientist who created it. But Greeley has precedent for a loving computer; in his earlier book *The Final Planet* the computer Podraig, which runs the ship, is a beneficient one named after Saint Patrick; it is just flippant enough to give it a feasible, realistic feel as a person, just as the computer in *God Game* is feisty.

The computer's artificial intelligence also provides Greeley with a trickster/ straight man outlet for his personal comments, so typical of Greeley's fiction. When ordered to execute an orgy, it responds dryly, "ONLY TWO CHARACTERS PRESENT," providing the narrator with the chance to comment that the programmer's "hobbits had interesting minds." When further ordered to execute again, it answers, "DEFAULT. EXECUTING" and the narrator responds with "a default orgy? Only in the digital world of computers" (130-31). When the computer runs out of energy, it improvises by commenting: "ZAP TEMPORARILY EXHAUSTED. EXECUTING RAIN" (296).

This leads into the seventh level of narration with a Supreme Being as the energy source of the narrator's world and of the "land." As the narrator says, "Authors need characters, God needs people" (305). It is at this point that the narrator and the author are both most separate and most close. When Nathan asks what will happen to "all those people now that you have deserted them?" the author replies, "Nothing more than what happens to my characters when I finish a story. I still worry about them, but I'm not responsible for them. My grace doesn't have to war with their free will." Nathan persists that the narrator has "abandoned them" and it is his wife who puts the men's minds to rest with the comment that "they're being watched over" (303). To Greeley's women, God's in His (or equally Her) heaven and all's right with the world.

Communication into the fantasy world of the narrator depends on the computer-angel-messenger and, as such, is limited to a computer language of short direct commands without explanation. Often these commands are more prophetic than angelic. If the author seems to reduce the narrator to a frenetic zealousness, he has examples from Scripture where the prophets, who delivered unpopular messages in the same way the computer does— terse and obtuse—obtained as little satisfaction in acting as agents of God. So also are the narrator's computer messages simple suggestions in the beginning—a gentle word, a hint—but, as the story goes on, the narrator suggests more and more strongly as his patience wears thin until he becomes the angry Old Testament God of "fury and wrath [who] would zap them all . . . just for the pure hell of it. Their malice called to heaven, that is to me, for vengeance. I'd delete the lot of them" (290). This descent from the mild-tempered God to the raving maniacal tyrant shouting orders at the end of the game imitates the frustration of any game and, indeed, of any perplexing computer program. When a computer, which is the epitome of logic, appears to perform illogically, man's systems overload and he cannot cope with it. Thus the narrator's frustrations with his "people," who consistently exert their free will as he tries to guide them toward a happy ending, is pitted against the cool computer logic which does not comprehend qualifying adjectives. Angels as messengers do not qualify or comment on their messages in Scripture; they simply deliver them to characters who find them easy to misunderstand.

A similar theme occurs in John Updike's *Roger's Version* where the hero, Roger Lambert, confronts his opponent, Dale Kohler, who tries and fails to prove that God is demonstrable by computer based on the random occurrences of 24 or "basic physical constants . . . the terms of Creation" (228–29). When Dale

> began to punch commands at random, in the middle of the garbage I was getting on the screen, there flashed suddenly this beautiful number: one point zero zero zero zero zero zero zero zero, I don't know how many zeros, maybe ten and then a one. Now nowhere in nature is a calculation going to yield such an odd amount [yet] when I tried to go back to it and take a printout, the computation was gone." (230).

Roger counters with the defense that "a God Who let Himself be proven . . . [would] be too submissive, too passive and beholden to human ingenuity, a helpless and contingent God" (235). Dale's activities, he argues, represent "a kind of obscene cosmological prying that has little to do with religion" (219). The same issue—two different storytellers.

"I don't have the imagination to do Speculative Fiction" (46), Greeley the narrator protests. Yet Greeley does and has—his first attempt, although not his first book published, *The Final Planet*, is speculative fiction, as is *Angel Fire*. If they are not fully in the realm of science fiction, they certainly are fantasy. The *persona* that Greeley adopts as the narrator, then, is that of the fool in the old adage "Fools rush in where angels fear to tread." If the narrator is the fool, then the computer in its role of angel has worn the wings off its disk drive in guiding the many levels of narration in this novel.

Greeley starts the novel by indicating that it is sometimes "hell to be God" (1). He concludes by saying that while "it's hell to be God . . . it's also fun to be God [because] you are loved by a lot of wonderful people; which is why God, the Other Person that is, doesn't quit" (305). Even here, he has circled back to the first level of narration from the last level so that the narrator *persona* judges "the Other Person" with anthropomorphic wryness. As author, as narrator, as game-player, Andrew Greeley extends the Jungian triad of self-individuation to a seven-leveled circular pattern worthy of the Irish knotted design in the book of Kells. As tale teller, he has freed the entrapped story levels in the Chinese carved balls, using the cool logic of a computer as a laser and the intense involvement of a master storyteller as a pattern.

WORKS CITED

Bettelheim, Bruno. "The Importance of Play," *The Atlantic Monthly*, Mar. 1987, 35–46.

Greeley, Andrew M. *God Game*. New York: Warner, 1986.

Updike, John. *Roger's Version. 1986*. New York: Fawcett Crest, 1987.

29

NICK ROSSI

Once Upon a Time

$\mathcal{T}$he silent church repeats my whispered invocation of the Trinity as I kneel before the altar. I clutch the pencil tightly and look around to make sure I am alone. I realize that I am probably not supposed to be here. Or am I...? I back out of the oasis of light that separates the altar from the black church. Looking down the aisle toward the door, I remember the lines which end Joyce's "Araby": "Gazing up into the darkness I saw myself as a creature driven and derided by vanity; and my eyes burned with anguished anger" (*Dubliners* 158). I feel compelled to stay. Who's writing this story anyway?!? In *God Game* Andrew Greeley postulates that "our lives are stories that God tells. We write them together with God. Coauthors. Our free will and his grace in cooperation and conflict" (6). But frankly, at this moment I don't feel like an equal partner. After all, He practically put the pencil in my hand, didn't He? Or did I ask for it...? Only God knows. See, He always has the upper hand!!!

Perhaps I should explain, before this gets too confusing. Although I'll warn you that my explanation is only a shot in the dark, literally. You see,

This essay is included courtesy of Prof. Lawrence Cunningham. It was one of the final papers submitted in a theology course at the University of Notre Dame (fall semester 1987–88), in which Prof. Cunningham introduced pertinent literature to have students discover essential characteristics of the Catholic tradition. Nick Rossi notes that Greeley's "message of a caring, gentle God was consistent with the impression I had garnered from the course, and I was easily able to tie *God Game* in with the semester's work."

by 5:00 A.M. today I had reached a definite block in my paper, so I came to
Sacred Heart Church for inspiration. As I knelt before the altar, Greeley's
line about our lives being "stories which God tells, thoughts which God
thinks, dreams which God dreams," ran through my mind (181). At that
same moment I noticed a pencil lying on the altar about a foot in front of
me. Now, chances are that it had been there all along, and I only now
noticed it—but I'm not so sure. After all, "storytelling is a joint venture"
(173). So, we board the 5:05 and leave the blissful land of ignorance. Our
destination: an understanding of the ways of God and man (Shaw, *Man and
Superman*?!?). Oh, by the way, please put on your apostolic eyewear,
compliments of Vatican Vision. We will be taking a distinctly Catholic
viewpoint in our quest. Of course, this assumes that we know something
about what is Catholic about the Catholic tradition (sound familiar?). In
essence, this is a story about a nineteen-year-old's attempt to come to terms
with his faith, and the role of several other stories (literary works) in that
attempt. However, as Andrew Greeley points out in *God Game*, "every
storyteller is a theologian and every story is about God" (16). So, fellow
theologian, here then is my story about God:

> *Note:* Sorry to interrupt so soon. I know this is beginning to
> sound like a commentary on a story which is actually an explana-
> tion of a vague, storylike introduction; *ad nauseam*. But I just
> wanted to quell your initial disfavor with my choice of author. I
> realize that many see Andrew Greeley as a wayward, licentious
> man who profanes the Roman collar. I also know that he doesn't
> win any brownie points in this novel when he directs a summer
> storm toward "Notre Dame, where hopefully it [will] drench the
> Theology Department" (27). Nevertheless, I hope that the appro-
> priate nature of my choice will become clear as my story progresses.
> So please reserve your judgment until the end. Thanks.

Greeley's *God Game* begins with an outlandish premise: with the help of
an electrical storm, a vacationing priest becomes "God" for the inhabitants
of a parallel universe who appear on his television as characters in a
computer fantasy game. However, in the context of this *God Game*, Greeley
discusses several ideas which are key elements in the broader story of God
and man. The bonding agent that links the Creator and the created in both
stories is grace. Greeley defines grace as "God's saving and directing love"
(217). However, as a pseudo-God, Greeley's narrator learns about man's
unwillingness to accept this love. His education in God-hood highlights
"the classic struggle between grace and free will" (6). The narrator/author
must often persuade his people/characters to "stop resisting grace" (217). He
contends that his "grace doesn't have to war with their free will" (305). He
proposes a partnership between grace and free will, in which grace helps
the characters "do what they half wanted but were afraid to do" (207).

However, men are so slow to admit that they need help that "in the grace/free will game, . . . grace [is] always at a disadvantage till the last of the ninth anyway" (125).

Greeley stresses the power of grace, but he also points out that grace does not always involve a dramatic show of supernatural strength. In fact, he explores the idea that even physical beauty reveals "elementary, temporary, ordinary grace. But still grace" (85). This exploration echoes Tom More's realization in *Love in the Ruins* that there is grace "in the beauty of the world and in all the lovely girls and dear good friends" (Percy 104). Throughout the novel, Greeley's characters discover that before they can love others, they must learn to love themselves. This message parallels Bernanos' contention that "the supreme grace would be to love oneself in all simplicity" (296). In the fantasy land of *God Game* the rival principalities have been fighting so long that the hatred has given way to curiosity, which finally gives way to love. "Like an ancient picture the deformity ha[s] faded and left a kind of grace" (Greene 118). In the end, Greeley's characters discover that "moments of grace . . . are worth centuries" (Greeley 263). They stop hoping for cataclysmic acts of divine intervention, because they learn that "grace is everywhere" (Bernanos 298).

If grace is the binding agent between God and humanity, then the love that this grace makes possible is the binding agent between human beings. The power of this love lies not only in the joy it brings but in the sense of mutual obligation which it instills in those whom it touches. Greeley asserts that grace compels love of others, "indeed enormous love, but also such respect that you feel . . . like their father or mother. Or maybe both" (261–62). Similarly, in Graham Greene's *The Power and the Glory*, the whiskey priest becomes "aware of an immense load of responsibility . . . [that] was indistinguishable from love" (66). By loving God men are able to love one another more fully. In *God Game* the hostile Duke and Duchess grow closer to loving each other when they conclude that "there is but one Lord Our God" whom they both love (209). Likewise, in Percy's *Love in the Ruins*, both Victor Charles and Leroy Ledbetter "love the new Christ, so they [can] love each other" (145). Paradoxically, we not only love others through God—we love Him through others. To illustrate this notion, Greeley depicts a woman who sees her lover as a "light in the darkness, Jesus revealing himself in her life" (10). However, perhaps this is not such a paradox if we accept Bernanos' conclusion that "God is love itself" (165).

After we grapple with the concepts of grace and love, the question which arises is "How should these notions affect our daily lives?" Greeley and Percy prove that it is foolhardy to try to control the forces of grace and love through computers or "caliper[s] of the soul" like the "More Qualitative-Quantitative Ontological Lapsometer" (Percy 158). In fact, both Greeley and Percy promote a simple, down-to-earth approach to Christian living. Greeley's advice to his characters is sometimes as simple as "Be nice to each other" (207). He decides that you are doing pretty well if "you do your best . . . and you leave the rest to God" (231). Percy elaborates on this theme in Father Smith's advice to Tom More in the confessional:

> ". . . forgive me, but there are other things we must think about;
> like doing our jobs, you being a better doctor, I being a better
> priest, showing a bit of ordinary kindness to people, particularly
> our own families . . . doing what we can for our poor unhappy
> country—things which, please forgive me, sometimes seem more
> important than dwelling on a few middle-aged daydreams." (376)

The views on Christian life espoused by Greeley and Percy, and also found in the commonsense advice given by Bernanos' nameless Curé and Silone's Pietro Spina, reveal a God who reaches beyond the places and rituals of worship, and into the homes and everyday lives of men and women.

The risks of being such an activist God are manifold (I suppose we are just lucky that He thinks we're worth it). After all, when God opts to make Himself accessible, and even goes so far as to take on a human form, He opens himself to criticism and blame. All of a sudden He is held account-able for every mishap on earth, even those that result from human misuse of free will. By relying on the deeper understanding involved in interper-sonal relationships, God loses some of the authoritarian control found in a subject-master relationship. As Greeley says, "creators always must be prepared to defend themselves" (177). Even Greeley's narrator boasts that "God . . . hadn't done nearly so well" as he could have when it came to creating the archdiocese of Chicago (158). However, as one of the other characters points out, God "has more obstacles" (158). In time the narrator learns that when "you play God . . . you become a scapegoat" (251). But God is not easily discouraged. (You might say He has infinite patience!) "God is nothing if not exuberant" (45). Besides, being God does have its rewards. Often God is "addressed much like a passionately loving and indulgent parent, or even a sexual lover, in terms of endearing intimacy" (34). A boon for any creator/parent/lover. So, although it may be "hell to be God, it's also fun to be God. You are loved by a lot of wonderful people; which is probably why God . . . doesn't quit" (310).

God is obviously very interested in the human condition, and in our potential to become God-like. Herein lies another vital facet of the God/man relationship: the cooperative effort to complete salvation. God asks us to do more than process "through the confessional on the Thursdays before First Fridays" (Greeley 74). In fact, "the world is unredeemed . . . and God is in need of man to be a partner in completing, in aiding, in redeeming. Our lives are a divine need" (227). Just as Dr. More's self-worth is contingent on the fact that "people need him and call him" (Percy 72), so also our self-worth depends on the idea that "God needs people" (Greeley 305). Like Jesus, the whiskey priest, and the Curé, we are servants of God and our fellow human beings.

Especially in the Catholic tradition, the idea of Christian service is heavily associated with the clergy. Nevertheless, in *God Game* Greeley is highly critical of the clergy. He compares the evil clerics of the computer-land to "the sociopaths who currently perform in the Roman Curia" (34). In another instance, he claims to see "some clergy conniving in the darkness" (45). However, closer inspection reveals that Greeley is really only critical of the Church hierarchy. He even refers to stabbing someone in the back as the "stylus curiae" (168). He places the Church leaders in the same ranks as Joyce's misguided priests who are primarily concerned with "the power, the authority to make the great God of Heaven come down upon the altar and take the form of bread and wine. What an awful power" (*Portrait of the Artist* 158). In fact, Greeley's primary antagonist, the officious cardinal who wants to "kill everyone now and begin a new era" (295), resembles Greene's priestlike lieutenant who cares only for the children, and is "quite prepared to make a massacre for their sakes" (58). Greeley advocates the kind of priesthood that works with the laity rather than lording over it. I picture the narrator of *God Game* as one of the free-thinking priests who emerged during the initial post–Vatican II period. He probably played a guitar during mass, asked the children questions during his homily, and wore jeans and sandals under his cassock. Greeley's perfect priest is merely a modern-day version of someone like the Curé, Pietro Spina, or even Father Smith.

So where does this leave me? I am still standing alone in Sacred Heart Church. A dim light is now seeping through the stained glass. The hint of incense conjures images of my Catholic upbringing. How should I take the "insights" of writers like Greeley, Greene, Bernanos, Percy, and Joyce? After all, I was confirmed by the cardinal archbishop of Chicago whom Greeley regards with such disfavor. But, then, I have also read about the possible veracity of the "stylus curiae" in books like Malachi Martin's *The Decline and Fall of the Roman Church* and David Yallop's *In God's Name*. Nevertheless, I still have great respect for (if not unquestioning faith in) the Church and her institutions. I sometimes allow human failings to cloud divine truths, but I remain convinced that the best way to improve the Church is by working within its institutions. I have to admit that for most of my life, I have been much more interested in studying the Church than living its message. So I am trying to change my own heart before I set out to change the Universal Church. Does that make me God-haunted (a term, by the way, used by both Greeley and Percy)? I think that approaching Catholicism through literature has helped me to see a different side of my faith. As the fictional Father Greeley says in his homily: "the end of all our search is to return to where we stand and know it for the first time" (157). Well, I believe this premise, but I don't think I've come to the end of my search yet (just the end of my paper). In many ways this type of self-enlightening search is a never-ending story, "maybe it's the only story, your story, my story, every story" (Greeley 310). Who can be sure? Ask the Coauthor!!!

WORKS CITED

Bernanos, Georges. *The Diary of a Country Priest*. New York: Carroll & Graff, 1983.
Greeley, Andrew M. *God Game*. New York: Warner, 1986.
Greene, Graham. *The Power and the Glory*. New York: Penguin, 1977.
Joyce, James. *Dubliners*. New York: Penguin, 1982.
———. *A Portrait of the Artist as a Young Man*. New York: Penguin, 1977.
Percy, Walker. *Love in the Ruins*. New York: Avon, 1978.
Silone, Ignazio. *Bread and Wine*. New York: Signet, 1986.

VI

A Few Words from the Landlord

30

ANDREW GREELEY

Imagination as a Ragpicker

To begin with, I am grateful to the commentators who have contributed to this volume. They have done me the great honor of addressing themselves to my stories and what the stories try to say. Unlike many other writers, they are not concerned with what I do with my royalties or how I "know about sex" (if indeed I do) or whether I keep my celibate commitment or what other priests think about me or how "the Church" reacts to my fiction or what my Cardinal thinks about me. Such extraneous issues are usually an excuse to ignore what my stories are actually about when they are not exercises in *invidia clericalis*.

When I began to write my stories, I intended to write theological novels, stories of God. It seemed to me self-evident that such was my goal. Yet even the favorable reviewers (and there are more of those than their opposite) seem to miss my theological themes—no matter how much I beat them over the head with two-by-fours to point out the themes.

Readers, if I am to judge by the mail and by the research I have done on them, have no trouble with these themes. I can't quite understand why reviewers seem to miss them. Rather than try to resolve that problem, however, I will be content with thanking the commentators in this book for their reassurance: the theological dimensions of my novels are not as opaque as I might have thought after reading a couple of hundred reviews. It is a blessed relief to converse with such men and women as these commentators instead of having to defend myself and my right to produce fiction.

They have also forced me to consider how my imagination works more self-consciously than I ever have before. They have poked into the secret garden of my *phantasia* as the scholastics called it and tried to discover what goes on there. I confess to watching this exploration with fascination—and I might add general agreement that they are charting the garden with considerable skill and insight.

Moreover, they have approached my luxuriant garden (well, it certainly sounds luxuriant!) with respect, seeking not to judge or condemn but to understand. They are unlike a few writers who stretch my imagination on the procrustean bed of their own ideologies and find, by pulling elements of my stories out of context and distorting them to mean the exact opposite of what I say they mean, that sure enough I am exactly what their ideologies said I had to be before they began their investigations. This is cheap, pseudo-psychoanalysis and indeed a kind of psychological rape—a gratu-itous violation of a person's selfhood. Such behavior tells a good deal more about the ones who engage in it than it does about the author and his stories; since such analysts reduce the author not only to an object but to an inkblot, what they disclose is in fact their own emotional illness.

To be the object of such an assault (copies of which, needless to say, go into the files of my Cardinal and Nuncio against the day of final reckoning) is like having a car pull up to where you are standing on a street corner and the driver lean out the window and vomit all over you.

Not much fun.

But the present commentators, while fascinated about my secret garden, are interested in understanding it and not twisting it to meet their ideologi-cal convictions and their warped emotional needs. Their work is certainly a help to me in the pilgrimage of self-understanding that gives meaning to every human life. Perhaps it will also be a help to others who are interested not only in reading my stories but in studying them (an act which in itself is not necessarily unvirtuous!).

My preliminary reaction to this symposium (for which Professor Shafer would need, I think, a large table and a lot of food and drink) is a certain dubious disbelief. I cannot, in truth, disagree with their map of my *phantasia* but it seems a much wilder and crazier place than I would have thought. What for example are all those angels and saints doing there, crowding around and jostling for position? And why so many boats, most of them named *Brigid*? And why, to anticipate a theme to which I will return, all that fire and all that water?

I would have thought of myself as a much more sober and respectable and cautious a person. So would the men and women with whom I grew up. Whence all the manic romanticism in my garden?

It ought to be sedate and orderly and classical. Instead it sounds like, in these essays, a mixture of rain forest jungle and bizarrely flowering peat bog.

As the real-life counterpart of Father Ace once remarked of someone else, "He's crazier than most people think he is!"

To tell the truth, I think I've kept my imagination under severe constraints in my fiction thus far. What would happen if I took off the wraps?

In any event, I want to reflect for the rest of this essay on the imagination of the author, in the subjective genitive meaning of the phrase—just as I assume that the title of this book refers not to how the author sees the world but what kind of world exists inside his head. How does an author's (well, this author's anyway) *phantasia* relate to his *ratio*, to use the Scholastics' terms?

In brief, I would submit that the relationship is loose, as in a marriage in which two people love one another very much but are coequals living independent lives in addition to the common life they share.

Let me note in passing that I think the *phantasia/ratio* model is far too simple, a product of the Platonic thought which has dominated the Western world for far too long. Moreover the subordinate place of *phantasia* in the Platonic model (which has so influenced Christian spirituality down through the ages) does violence to human nature.

In the Aristotelian framework, *phantasia* is more important because it is charged with "reproduction" both to the intellect and to the outside world through art. Dante, perhaps the greatest of the Aristotelians, was convinced that *phantasia* could do what *ratio* could not—describe the world which is to come.

I prefer to use an "altered states of consciousness" model in which one allows for many different kinds of consciousness, scores, perhaps hundreds, functioning in hierarchies, rhythms, and periodicities that we have only begun to understand.

To use briefly the computer metaphor (with OS/2) many if not all of the various "states of consciousness" (ways of knowing) can be operating in "background mode" while others are operating in "foreground mode."

In truth, I am uneasy with the word "altered" which seems to imply that "ordinary" or "waking" consciousness (*ratio* to the Schoolmen) is the norm and all the other states if not deviant at least unusual.

I would prefer a jazz orchestra metaphor in which the instruments are compared to the multitudinous ways of knowing which work simultaneously, serially, sequentially, dialectically in loose but harmonious (sometimes) relationships with one another as they work through various melodies.

I suppose maturity means that the orchestra is well coordinated in its harmonies.

I suppose creativity means that some of the more expressive instruments are not silenced by the more task-oriented instruments.

The ways of knowing then may not be a marriage so much as a community of affectionate but strong-willed and independent members.

As attractive as I find such imagery (itself a product of my garden—I didn't realize the jazz orchestra was there until I worked my way into this paper. Yet many of my characters, most notably John E. O'Malley in *April and Rosemary*, are jazz enthusiasts) I will limit myself in the present discussion to the *phantasia/ratio* model because we (or at least I) don't know enough yet about the many different states of consciousness which function in the human person (perhaps at the same instant).

My thesis is that *ratio* is often mostly ignorant of what *phantasia* is doing, but not completely ignorant. The husband, a serious and responsible lawyer (if such be *ratio*), has a vague notion of what the wife is up to (if such be *phantasia*) and certainly approves of her and is proud of her accomplishments (even to the extent of living off her salary!), but he is hard put to say what she is doing at any given moment and is astonished often and delighted when he finally learns what she has done.

(*Phantasia* is obviously a muse and muses historically have been feminine. Indeed in Fellini's film *8½* she is the wondrous Claudia Cardinale. But she could just as well be he. The kind of person who writes for the little known Catholic magazine *The Commonweal* would call the above imagery sexist. However, if I reversed the image and said that, as in many real marriages, the husband was the creative outsider and the wife the cautious and responsible homebody, they would also call it sexist. You can't win with such people and probably shouldn't try. The point of the marriage metaphor in this essay, need I add, is not the role of differentiation of the spouses, but the nature of their relationship.)

Let me illustrate: Jim Harkin, having read the first draft of *St. Valentine's Night*, calls me on the phone and observes that once again I have used my fire/water symbolism: Neil saves Megan from the fire (the male element) and she saves him from the water (the female element).

Ah, yes indeed, I say as smoothly as I can in the tone of voice one uses when one is delighted that someone has understood one's aim (or alternatively seen through one's tricks—all storytellers are terrible tricksters!).

Even in *The Magic Cup*, he adds, there is fire and water. Cormac is tempted by the heat of Barbados, Brigid by the water at the foot of the cliffs of Clare Island.

Right?

Right!

Harkin continues: And in *Death in April* the theme of the story is contained in the scene when Lynnie saves the young parents and their baby from the blazing boat in the middle of the lake—thus disclosing the androgynous nature of her personality which is such a threat to Jim O'Neill.

Right?

Right!

After the phone conversation ended I pondered Harkin's insights. Surely the fire and water symbols are important to me—fire representing the male, water the female; fire representing Jesus, water representing the Church (in the Easter Vigil liturgy); fire representing God, water representing His creation (Her people). The imagery became part of my conscious repertory some thirty years ago when I read in a book by Mircea Eliade that the plunging of a candle into water was a spring fertility symbol.

I was greatly amused at the thought of how many monsignors (including my own at that time) had committed ritual intercourse on the main altar during solemn high mass with Mother Superior watching!

Later I confirmed this origin of the Easter Vigil ceremony in a conversation with the great Jesuit liturgist at the Gregorian University, Father Herman Schmidt. The fourth-century Roman Christians, he said, expropriated a pagan Roman fertility rite. "We don't know what it means," he said with a typical smile, "but they did. When Jesus rose from the dead he consummated his nuptials with his bride the Church and we are the first fruits of that passionate union."

I accepted Herman's word for it and still do. To anyone who knows much about either the history of religions or psychoanalysis the implications of plunging a lighted candle into water are pretty obvious. Moreover the old Latin liturgy used the "fructifera"—fructify or impregnate. May this candle impregnate these waters.

Yet I have never seen any scholarly discussion of the liturgy of Easter which considers this symbolism. Indeed the new English rite bowdlerizes the ceremony. Now the priest is told that he "may" dip the candle in the water. And he prays that the Holy Spirit may "visit" these waters.

Not much hint of divine passion left is there?

I think the aim is not so much to eliminate all hint of sexuality from the ceremony as to eliminate all hint of womanliness. I speculate that the liturgists who did the rewrite didn't like women very much.

All right then, the fire and water categories, which probably float around most if not all human imaginations, in my imagination took on connotations both sexual and liturgical. They became the guiding symbols of my story *Lord of the Dance*. Noele Marie Brigid Farrell, conceived at Easter, born at Christmas, child of a fiery father and fertile mother, has flame-red hair and sea-green eyes and, as she brings salvation to her family, stands for the Church product of fire and water which brings salvation to all of us.

The images Jim Harkin saw were surely in the three books. Moreover they were true to the intent and the themes of the books. I must have done them deliberately.

But still . . .

Was I consciously aware of the symbols that Jim saw me using?

The only answer that is honest is that I can't remember but I don't think so. Just as characters can take charge of an author (as I tried to portray in *God Game*) so images can take over and force their way into his work without him realizing it.

Yet when I reflected on my conversation with Jim, it occurred to me that I could agree so easily with his interpretation because there was a vague little recollection in the back of my brain that said in effect, well, yeah, you did know you were doing that.

Kind of.

The husband knows at the fringe of his consciousness that his wife has entered an art competition; he may even have glanced at her painting. He is delighted that she wins, proud of her, loves her all the more. Yet, if he were honest, he really can't recall ever being told about the competition.

Friends who have read some of these essays ask me if I was aware of the themes the authors find. They get the same reply:

Kind of.

I knew I was writing about angels and saints, but hardly realized that in my garden there are not only vast and pushy crowds of such creatures but that I had imposed on them an ordering theology.

But when someone analyzes that theology I must say as I did to Jim Harkin, "Of course" as though I had realized it all along.

I hadn't. Then again I had.

Like I say, kind of.

The point of all this is that in the passion of creating a story, *phantasia* takes command and rushes ahead without consulting or informing *ratio*. The latter comes to know his wife and her behavior more fully only when others tell him about her.

What does he do?

If he has any sense he marvels!

Because this is pretty much the way the creative process works (for me anyway), it's hard to answer the questions which many people want to ask: *Do you write from your own experience?*

Sure. Where else does one get materials. But the experiences are modified and transformed as *phantasia* rushes along, madly splicing together bits and pieces for her story with little or no attention to the sources for her bits and pieces.

For example, in *St. Valentine's Night* Neil Connor and Father Ace meet outside a hospital in Vietnam. They discover they are from the same neighborhood in Chicago and fall to talking about the neighborhood as Neil waits for a verdict on his Vietnamese cameraman who has been wounded in action. For a few moments they are both back in their neighborhood.

In fact the incident is based on a story the real Father Ace told me about a meeting on a plane flying out of Vietnam. My *phantasia* needed a neighborhood story (since the book is about the neighborhood) about people from the neighborhood encountering one another somewhere else. It took Father Ace's story (the *real* Father Ace's story) and revised it, adjusted it, and fit it into the plot.

Moreover it did so with little conscious attention being given to the transformation which was taking place. My *phantasia* took the story and ran with it, jamming it into the continuity of the plot as it ran.

So it was a real experience, Father Ace's and mine when I heard it from him. But it was adapted on the run to fit my fictional story. Moreover bits and pieces of other stories I had heard about heroic Vietnamese cameramen were adjusted to fit the story.

The art, or maybe only the craft, is not remembering many, many stories. Rather it is putting them together, transforming them, and fashioning a new story. Usually the new tale emerges instantly with very little conscious effort or reflection.

Do you write about real people?

Usually, no. Only a few characters, like Monsignor Mugsy Branigan and Father Ace McNamara, are drawn from real life, but even they are changed somewhat in the telling. Noele is a conscious composite of five or six TCPs (Teenage Celtic Princesses) I have known in my years as a teenage priest.

Again, however, my characters are necessarily bits and pieces of people I know or know about, rearranged to produce the character I need for my story. I recognize some of the bits and pieces (when I recognize them at all) only after the character has been created and often only after someone tells me that they think I have based so-and-so on what's-her-name.

Phantasia is a garbage-picker, a scavenger, a scourer of the dump heaps of memory (and of dreams). She takes what she can and does with it what she wants and, as I have said, always on the run. If I (*ratio*) tried to stop her in flight to analyze what she was doing and what garbage heaps she was picking, the stories would never be told.

The imagination is an elegant ragpicker, Ms. Cardinale dancing among the garbage cans as she does on the beach at the end of Fellini's film. She spins and whirls, dances and jumps, leaps and sprints—all the time playing with her prizes from the scrap heap and leaving poor *ratio* at the starting gate.

(She also raids garbage cans and trash heaps when I do sociological analysis, usually limiting herself to the cans and heaps in my garden—filled with debris and rubble be it noted—plainly labeled "social science." However when she's on a roll she does not respect such role definitions: she's perfectly capable of grabbing a tattered bit of sociology and integrating it into a novel.)

I don't want to imply that *phantasia* is unlogical or irrational. Rather she pursues the creative goal with rigorous logic and grim if breakneck rationality— which often means brushing aside the plodding and pedestrian *ratio* which wants to consider every step carefully and to provide a detailed explanation for everything that happens.

Buzz off, says *phantasia* (as Nora Maeve says to Sebi in one of my children's stories). I have important work to do.

I catch up with her, if at all, only when I read a book like this.

Are any of your characters based on you?

All of them are based on me in some fashion because I have created all of them. They reflect me the way we reflect God (as I try to say in the basic metaphor of *God Game*). But none of them are me. Often now when I go to dinner at a house for the first time, a bottle of Jameson's is produced for my enjoyment. I tell the host/hostess that I don't drink hard liquor. "But Blackie does!"

But I (Blackie-like sigh) am not Blackie! I am older than he, taller, thinner, and not nearly so nice. Moreover my eyes are better than his and I am an outcast while he is part of the ecclesiastical establishment. He is a monsignor and I will never be. He is a philosopher (albeit with empirical leanings) and I'm a sociologist. He is based on Chesterton's Father Brown and I'm based on . . . well, you'll have to ask God about that.

Sometimes he speaks for me? Sure. More often he speaks for himself, a character which *phantasia* has created *de novo* out of the bits and pieces that my lifetime has prepared for her garbage picking. Sometimes he says exactly what I would say in the same circumstances, more often not. He's himself and I'm me and please don't confuse us.

He wouldn't like it.

Incidentally, I must say a mild word of defense here about the little monsignor's priestly zeal. Admittedly he doesn't hear confessions much, but no one goes to confession much any more. He preaches, he says mass, he prays, he stands in back of church after mass, he hangs around with teenagers, he helps young lovers, he stays out of the way of his hard-working associates . . . all the things a virtuous and exemplary pastor does these days.

Moreover, he is absolutely obedient to his Cardinal, the mark of true priest virtue we were taught in the seminary. "Blackwood, see to it!" orders Sean Cardinal Cronin and Blackie dutifully sees to it.

I suspect Cardinal Bernardin wishes that Blackie's creator was more like his creature.

But then there wouldn't be any novels, much to the delight of those who don't read them but are shocked that I wrote them (the Cardinal's big worry).

More seriously, I guess, is the frequent charge that *The Cardinal Sins* (especially among clergy who haven't read the book) is a "scarcely veiled autobiography" of my conflicts with Cardinal Cody. It simply isn't true—Patrick Donahue is not in the least like the late Cardinal; and, as my sister puts it, I'm Kevin Brennan only twenty percent of the time though I'd like to have been him maybe forty percent of the time.

Phantasia put him together from a wide variety of sources, some of which were experiences of my own—but even them she changed in the process of her headlong dash for closure. So even the twenty percent of him that might be me has been transformed so that it's him and not really me any more.

(I should be so lucky as to have had an Ellen Foley!)

More to the point if I had written a slightly fiction account of the relationship between me and Cardinal Cody, it would have been dullsville—

like the autobiographical stories that creative-writing graduate students produce these days to get even with their parents.

The two great autobiographical novelists of the century, Proust and Joyce, rewrote their lives to fit the stories they wanted to tell.

Rather their own resident *phantasiae* rewrote the lives of the authors, on the run I presume (she must have had to run pretty fast to pour out all those pages of *A la Recherche*).

It will be said that I distance *phantasia* too much from *ego*. After all it's MY fantasy, isn't it?

Sure. But the point of this line of argumentation is that those states of consciousness (ways of knowing) which can be subsumed under the general title of creativity function on a very loose leash and with only the most minimal supervision of *ego* or *ratio*. It's part of my (the total self's) personality but it operates often (usually) with little attention being paid by me (*ego*).

To return to the marriage metaphor, the wife does pretty much what she wants and is at times impatient with her husband's supervision, even such as it is. But she's still his wife—and he is her husband. The husband doesn't mind her independent ways and is proud to take credit for them. Moreover, he knows that he couldn't stop her even if he wanted to—which he doesn't. My *phantasia* of course is Irish. What else? In fact she sounds like one of my women characters. So *maybe* she's the one that's doing the self-portraits. One thing for sure, she simply won't let me clean up the mess in my secret garden—and certainly not remove the garbage pails.

That paragraph has the makings of a good story—fire and water symbolism and all.

Only I think I may have written it already.

CONTRIBUTORS

DAVID D. ANDERSON is Professor of American Thought and Language at Michigan State University. His major scholarly interest is Midwestern literature with particular focus on the life and works of Sherwood Anderson. He has written or edited five books on Anderson as well as thirty other books and nearly three hundred scholarly papers, essays, short stories, and poems. He edits *MidAmerica, Midwestern Miscellany*, and the *SSML Newsletter*, and is on the board of numerous other journals and organizations. He chaired the Modern American Literature Section of the Modern Language Association, and is currently an American delegate to the International Federation for Modern Languages and Literatures. He has lectured throughout Europe, Asia, and Australia, and has presented more than a hundred papers to scholarly organizations. Currently, *Makers of a Midwestern Dream*, a cultural history, is in press at Wayne State University Press, and he is at work on *The Four Stages of a Man's Life: A Photo Biography of Sherwood Anderson* and *Saul Bellow and the Midwestern Tradition*. He founded the Society for the Study of Midwestern Literature in 1971 and is currently Executive Director. Professor Anderson's most recent honors include the Doctor of Letters, *honoris causa*, from Wittenberg University (1986), the MSU College of Arts and Letters Distinguished Research Professor Award (February 1988), and the Michigan Association of Governing Boards Distinguished Faculty Award (April 1988).

351

ALLIENNE R. BECKER holds the Ph.D. from Pennsylvania State University and is Associate Professor of German at Lock Haven University where she has taught since 1970. She has chaired panels and presented papers at numerous national and regional professional meetings, and her articles have appeared in such journals as *Comparative Literature Studies* and *The Journal of Popular Literature*. Forthcoming is *The Lost Worlds Romance: The Evolution of a Literary Form* (Greenwood Press).

ROGER J. BRESNAHAN holds the Ph.D. in English from the University of Massachusetts, where he worked with Sidney Kaplan. A professor of American Thought and Language at Michigan State University, Bresnahan has received six major fellowships and grants, and is the author of *In Time of Hesitation: Anti-Imperialists and the Philippine-American War* and *Literature and Society: Cross-Cultural Perspectives*. He has presented over forty conference papers and written numerous articles and reviews on American and Southeast Asian literature. His work appeared in such journals as *Philipinas: A Journal of Philippine Studies*, *Midwestern Miscellany*, *Massachusetts Studies in English*, *Studies in Romanticism*, *Minnesota Review*, and *Asiaweek*. The first two volumes of his interviews with Filipino writers are forthcoming. Bresnahan's academic honors include honorary membership in the Manila Critics Circle and MSU's Distinguished Faculty and Teacher-Scholar awards.

RAY B. BROWNE holds the Ph.D. from UCLA and is chair of the department of popular culture at Bowling Green State University. He is founder and director of the Center for the Study of Popular Culture and director of the Popular Press as well as founder and editor of the *Journal of Popular Culture*, *Journal of Regional Culture*, and *Journal of American Culture*. He also founded the Popular Literature Section of the Midwest Modern Language Association. In addition to approximately eighty articles which have appeared in such journals as *Southern Folklore Quarterly*, *Western Folklore*, *Shakespeare Quarterly*, and *Social Education*, Professor Browne has written or edited close to forty books, the latest of which are *Heroes and Humanities: Detective Fiction and Culture* (1986), *The Spirit of Australia: The Crime Fiction of Arthur W. Upfield* (1988), *The Gothic World of Stephen King: Landscape of Nightmares* (1988), *Against Academia: The History of the Popular Culture Movement* (1988), and *Dominant Symbols and Symbolism in Popular Culture* (1989).

MIRIAM ESPINOSA received her Ph.D. in Humanities from the University of Texas after doing graduate work in philosophy and English. She is Associate Professor of English at Texas Wesleyan College. The recipient of several grants and fellowships, she did research on General Education Requirements as well as Recruitment and Retention in Texas colleges. She has presented papers on topics such as the Teaching of Composition, Problems of Non-Traditional Women Students, the Introductory Literature Course, and Women's Roles in Literature.

BERNARD J. GALLAGHER received the Ph.D. from SUNY Binghamton and is Assistant Professor of English at Central Methodist College, Fayette, Missouri. His teaching and research interests include British Romanticism, Victorian Literature, Post-Structuralist Criticism, and Popular Literature. In addition to reading papers at a number of national conferences, he contributed to *The Gothic World of Stephen King: Landscape of Nightmares* and has published in such periodicals as *Athenaeum Society Review* and the *Journal of American Culture.*

JAMES M. HARKIN is a self-employed personal and business financial planner associated with IDS Financial Services, an American Express company. He earned his Ph.D. at the Maxwell School of Syracuse University in 1978. He has done university work, served in West Africa as a Peace Corps volunteer, and is program manager with Catholic Relief Services. He has written for academic and popular publications, including twice on the op-ed page of *The New York Times*, and has spoken at professional conferences on subjects of African development, public finance, and the rise and fall of Tombstone, Arizona.

PATRICIA W. JULIUS is Associate Professor of American Thought and Language at Michigan State University where she has taught since 1969 and currently serves as Director of the Academic Orientation Program for incoming freshmen. Her research interests range from Chaucer and eighteenth-century periodicals to Native American literature, science fiction, and women mystery writers. She co-edited *A New Voice for a New People* (1985), and her reviews and articles have appeared in such periodicals as *Choice, University Quarterly,* and *Midwestern Miscellany.* In progress is a book of Chaucer criticism.

ANNE K. KALER received the Ph.D. in English Literature from Temple University and is Professor of English at Gwynedd Mercy College, Gwynedd Valley, Pennsylvania. She has presented a number of scholarly papers on topics from Shakespeare and Graham Greene to John D. MacDonald. Her essays and poems have appeared in the *Saul Bellow Journal, The English Journal, Clues, The Journal of Popular Literature,* and *Gwynedd Journal.* Her article on Marion Zimmer Bradley's use of the Beguinal communities was included in *Heroines of Popular Culture.* In progress are three historical novels dealing with the Beguines.

PHILIP H. KELLY has a Doctor of Arts degree from Carnegie-Mellon University and is Associate Professor of English at Gannon University in Erie, Pennsylvania, where he lives with his wife and two children. He has presented papers and published essays on humanities education, business and technical writing, administration in higher education, and modern literature.

JUDITH J. KOLLMANN holds the Ph.D. from the University of Colorado and is Professor of English at the University of Michigan-Flint, where she teaches courses in medieval literature, the Bible, fantasy, and murder mystery. Her research interests include Charles Williams and John Varley. She has presented approximately twenty-five scholarly papers since 1980. She has contributed to the *Dictionary of Literary Biography* and has written numerous book chapters, as well as articles which have appeared in such periodicals as *Mythlore*, the *Kansas Quarterly*, *Studies in Medievalism*, and *Extrapolation*. She served as co-editor of *Chaucerian Shakespeare: Transformation and Adaptation* (with E. Tabolt Donaldson).

MARY ANN LOWRY is Associate Professor of English and past president of the faculty at Kent State University in Warren, Ohio, where she coordinates the English program. Her poetry has appeared in *English Journal, California State Poetry Quarterly, Publications of the Arkansas Philological Association*, and others; her prose in such journals as *Poetry Today, English Journal, Crosscut, Western American Literature*, and *Teaching English in the Two-Year College*. She has completed a book chronicling the history of her campus, *Past Dream, Present Reality*, and is working on the novels of heroic fantasy author David C. Smith.

MICHAEL T. MARSDEN is Professor of Popular Culture and Associate Dean of the College of Arts and Sciences at Bowling Green State University. In addition to authoring numerous articles and co-editing several volumes dealing with various aspects of popular culture studies, he also co-edits the quarterly *Journal of Popular Film and Television*. His teaching and research interests include popular literature, popular entertainment forms, film and television studies, and culture theory.

ROLAND E. MURPHY, O. Carm., is George Washington Ivey Emeritus Professor of Biblical Studies at Duke, where he joined the Divinity School faculty in 1971 after twenty-two years at Catholic University. In addition to degrees in Semitic languages and in philosophy, and a doctorate in theology from Catholic University, Father Murphy holds the Licentiate in Scripture from the Pontifical Biblical Institute in Rome. He has been Visiting Professor at Pittsburgh Theological Seminary, Yale University Divinity School, Princeton Theological Seminary, and Notre Dame. He has served as editor-in-chief of the *Catholic Biblical Quarterly* and as member of editorial boards of a number of journals such as *Concilium, Vetus Testamentum, Interpretation, Theological Studies, Old Testament Abstracts*, and the *Hermeneia* Biblical Commentary series. The author of many scholarly articles, he was one of the co-editors and contributors to *The Jerome Biblical Commentary*, cooperated in the translation known as the *New American Bible*, and is currently a member of the board for the revision of the Revised Standard Version. Among his recent publications are *Psalms, Job* (1977), *Wisdom*

Literature (1981), and *Wisdom Literature and Psalms* (1983). He has been president of the Catholic Biblical Association and the Society of Biblical Literature. He has been actively engaged in ecumenical dialogue.

JACOB NEUSNER is University Professor and Ungerleider Distinguished Scholar of Judaic Studies at Brown University. He was educated at Harvard College (A.B. Magna Cum Laude), Oxford, the Jewish Theological Seminary of America (M.H.L.), Hebrew University, and Columbia (Ph.D.) and taught at Columbia, University of Wisconsin-Milwaukee, Brandeis, and Dartmouth before he was called to Brown in 1968. His writings range from specialized scholarly works to books for undergraduate instruction and the public at large (including children). The editor of numerous scholarly journals and several monograph and textbook series, Professor Neusner is the author of over two hundred fifty volumes of translation, analysis, exegesis, history, interpretation, and exposition. Among the more than a dozen books he published in 1987 alone are *What Is Midrash?*; *Vanquished Nation, Broken Spirit, The Virtues of the Heart in Formative Judaism*; *Self-Fulfilling Prophecy: Exile and Return in the History of Judaism*; *The Making of the Mind of Judaism*; *Christian Faith and the Bible of Judaism*. Professor Neusner holds honorary degrees from Brown, the University of Cologne, the University of Chicago, the University of Rochester, and the University of Bologna, and has addressed audiences at major centers of learning on several continents. In 1989 he is scheduled to lecture at three Vatican universities at the invitation of William Cardinal Baum.

NICK ROSSI is a Government-International Studies major at the University of Notre Dame who hopes to attend law school and pursue a career in Public Service or journalism.

KATHLEEN ROUT is Associate Professor of American Thought and Language at Michigan State University, where she has taught since 1967. She holds the Ph.D. from Stanford University. Rout has done research on Flannery O'Connor and is particularly interested in twentieth-century American literature, minority writers, and women's studies. In 1986-87 she was President of the Society for the Study of Midwestern Literature. She has delivered numerous papers, and her articles have appeared in *Beacham's Popular Fiction in America* and *Popular World Fiction*, as well as journals such as *Midwestern Miscellany, Indiana Social Studies Quarterly, Studies in Short Fiction*, and *Intellect*. In 1980 she served as editor of *Good Writing*.

INGRID SHAFER is Professor of Philosophy and Religion at the University of Science and Arts of Oklahoma. A native of Austria, she studied literature (American and German), human relations, and philosophy at the universities of Vienna, Innsbruck, and Oklahoma. As N.E.H. Fellow, she did post-doctoral work at the University of Chicago Divinity School

(Summer 1986). In Spring 1988 she was appointed to a statewide commission to study Humanities Education at Oklahoma colleges and universities. Her articles have appeared in *Chicago Studies, The Journal of Ideology, The Owl of Minerva: Biannual Journal of the Hegel Society of America,* and *The Journal of Evolutionary Psychology.* She is the author of *Eros and the Womanliness of God* (1986) and the editor of *The Incarnate Imagination* (1988) and a special issue of *The Journal of Popular Literature* (Spring/Summer 1988). In progress are a book tentatively entitled *Religious Experience as Focus for an Interdisciplinary World Thought & Culture Program: Theory and Practice* and a translation of Max Stirner's *Kleinere Schriften* (with Lawrence Stepelevich).

DAVID TRACY is Andrew Thomas Greeley and Grace McNichols Greeley Distinguished Service Professor of Modern Catholic Studies at the University of Chicago Divinity School. He holds both the Licentiate and doctorate in Theology from the Gregorian University in Rome and has been at Chicago since 1969. His books include *The Achievement of Bernard Lonergan* (1970), *Blessed Rage for Order: The New Pluralism in Theology* (1975), *The Analogical Imagination: Christian Theology and the Culture of Pluralism* (1981), *Plurality and Ambiguity: Hermeneutics, Religion and Hope* (1987), and *Religion and the Public Realm* (1988). He has served as co-editor of special volumes of *Concilium, Religious Studies Review,* and *The Journal of Religion.* His articles have appeared in *The Journal of Religion, Theological Studies, Theology Today, New Literary History, Critical Inquiry, Daedalus, The Thomist, Thought, Dialogue, Journal of the American Academy of Religion,* and *Concilium.* He has addressed international audiences at Beijing Institute for the Scientific Study of Religion, the World Council of Churches (Geneva), Gregorian University (Rome), Trinity College (Dublin), and Tübingen University, and has lectured in North America at Toronto, Harvard, Yale, Catholic University of America, Vanderbilt, Boston University, Union Theological Seminary, Southern Methodist, and University of the South.

KIRBY WILCOXSON received his Ph.D. from Purdue and is Assistant Professor of Sociology at Sioux Falls College in South Dakota.

I. S.